# The Beat Cop

# The Beat Cop

## CHICAGO'S CHIEF O'NEILL AND THE
## CREATION OF IRISH MUSIC

# Michael O'Malley

The University of Chicago Press   *Chicago and London*

The University of Chicago Press, Chicago 60637
The University of Chicago Press, Ltd., London
© 2022 by The University of Chicago
All rights reserved. No part of this book may be used or reproduced in any
manner whatsoever without written permission, except in the case of brief
quotations in critical articles and reviews. For more information, contact
the University of Chicago Press, 1427 E. 60th St., Chicago, IL 60637.
Published 2022
Printed in the United States of America

31  30  29  28  27  26  25  24  23  22      1  2  3  4  5

ISBN-13: 978-0-226-81870-2 (cloth)
ISBN-13: 978-0-226-81871-9 (e-book)
DOI: https://doi.org/10.7208/chicago/9780226818719.001.0001

Library of Congress Cataloging-in-Publication Data

Names: O'Malley, Michael, author.
Title: The beat cop : Chicago's Chief O'Neill and the creation of Irish music /
  Michael O'Malley.
Description: Chicago : University of Chicago Press, 2022. | Includes index.
Identifiers: LCCN 2021029495 | ISBN 9780226818702 (cloth) | ISBN 9780226818719 (ebook)
Subjects: LCSH: Irish—Illinois—Chicago—Music—History and criticism. | Folk
  music—Illinois—Chicago—History and criticism. | Folk music—Ireland—History
  and criticism. | O'Neill, Francis, 1848–1936. | Police chiefs—Illinois—Chicago—
  Biography. | Irish—Illinois—Chicago—Social life and customs. | National
  characteristics, Irish.
Classification: LCC ML3554 .063 2022 | DDC 781.62/9162077311—dc23
LC record available at https://lccn.loc.gov/2021029495

♾ This paper meets the requirements of ANSI/NISO Z39.48-1992
(Permanence of Paper).

TO KATHLEEN, *grá mo chroí*

# Contents

# Introduction
## The Scholar

Frank O'Neill hated running the Harrison Street station, "in the midst of darkest Chicago" in the notorious "levee" district. "The worst station house in the world" was full of "the most dissolute ruffians of both sexes that can be raked up in the dives of the levee." Prostitution, gambling, illegal drinking, and opium smoking all flourished in the levee. Captain O'Neill, who didn't drink, or smoke, or gamble, made himself unpopular not just by arresting the confidence men and women who robbed people in "panel houses" but by insisting on prosecution. Normally in the levee the arrested person's friends slipped some money into the "receptive palm" of a magistrate, and the charges magically evaporated. "Don't be so rough," a local politician told him, "and you'll be taken care of like the others." O'Neill disliked the vice but even more he disliked the disorder, the corruption, the "friends" doing favors for "friends." Favors and friendship had enabled his rise, and he had done many favors himself, but why should a great city have to run like this? Shouldn't actual merit count? This particular night in the late 1890s he had a dozen or so opium pipes in front of him on a table in his office, recently confiscated from levee district hop dens.[1]

In rare quiet moments at Harrison Street O'Neill liked to work out a few tunes on the flute. O'Neill was "music mad," obsessed with Irish dance music. He had heard it growing up in Ireland, at rural dances; or late at night through stone walls when parties continued after his parents sent him to bed. In Chicago he heard tunes all the time: tunes with no name or many names; tunes that sounded hauntingly familiar; tunes that mixed parts of other tunes, all circulating among the more than 300,000 Irish immigrants who worked, went to church, sinned, and got arrested so their friends could cajole O'Neill into letting them go. The disorder bothered him. He picked up the flute and started to play a phrase. "Captain," someone called, "phone call for you out front." He set his flute down on the table, among the opium pipes, and walked away to take the call.

While he was away at the phone a policeman, or perhaps an alderman or a lawyer or a magistrate or a reporter—some Harrison Street "regular"—walked by and stole some pipes off the table. Opium pipes had lately become a fashionable exotic decoration among the city's elite, a "crazy fad." "Always after a raid we can look for calls from the women who want pipes to decorate the parlor," a police captain told the reporter: "Wives and daughters of millionaires have frequently been here begging for pipes." The thief had promised to get one for a wealthy Michigan Avenue woman: he would do her a favor, and she would surely do one for him. A keyless wooden flute or a tin whistle could look a lot like an opium pipe to a man in a hurry, and when O'Neill returned several pipes and his flute had vanished. The next day the flute magically reappeared, with no explanation.[2]

The story, printed in the *Chicago Inter Ocean*, has so much of Chicago to it that it might even be true. The people doing "favors" for "friends," the sordid vice district, but also the upper-class women's enthusiasm for the exotic artifacts of vice. No matter how much shuddering public distaste people expressed, vice districts went on, generating revenue for the elected alderman who used the revenue to persuade voters or generate extra cash for police and the law.

Calls for reform never ceased, but Chicago reformers often ended up behaving no better than the people they aimed to reform. The journalist Lincoln Steffens praised the Municipal Voters League, a group of reformers trying to "clean up" the city in O'Neill's day, including a young lawyer named Hoyt King. In his zeal, King later hired private detectives to "get something" on O'Neill, telling his agents to spare no effort: "there's unlimited money behind it." A letter to O'Neill warned him that King "would not hesitate to have you assassinated if he could down you by no other means." King represented the *reform* party, the vendors of high-minded rhetoric. No wonder Captain O'Neill turned his mind to the music of his youth.[3]

Francis O'Neill, from Tralibane near Bantry, in County Cork, left Ireland in 1865 at seventeen years old. He spent four years as an itinerant sailor, circling the globe; he was shipwrecked on a barren Pacific island and nearly starved; he herded sheep in the Sierra Nevada foothills, sleeping under the stars for five months. He taught school for a year in rural Missouri and spent a summer working ships on the Great Lakes. Settled in Chicago by 1871, he labored in meat-packing houses, lumber mills, and freight yards. When he found his advancement blocked, he joined the police. A thief shot him in his first month on duty, but he survived and through talent, hard work, patronage connections, and favors from friends he rose to general superintendent of the Chicago police, the "Chief," by 1901. He worked during the Haymarket bombing and the Columbian Exposition; during the Pullman strike he slept at the station house for weeks and daily confronted rioting crowds. The anarchist Emma Goldman praised his courtesy and intelligence. He navigated saloons and back-room politics; he got into a street brawl with a notoriously thuggish alderman that put him on the front pages; and he pulled bodies from the wreckage of the Iroquois theater fire, which killed 600 people. Late in his police career, and in a very comfortable retirement, he published a series of books on Irish music. These books made him a hero in Ireland; he preserved a heritage that might otherwise have vanished, and a memorial statue now stands near his birthplace. A Chief O'Neill's pub graces Chicago, and for decades Irish immigrant flute player Kevin Henry played an annual concert in the doorway of O'Neill's tomb, to honor "the man that saved our heritage."[4]

This story tells about adventure, intrigue, and momentous events, but also about colonialism and what it does to people. Born an Irish colonial subject of Queen Victoria, O'Neill learned in the "National Schools" to see himself as a "happy English child." The smart, bookish boy fled that colonial status for the sea and later escaped it altogether when he took the oath of citizenship to the US in 1873. But then a different kind of colonization took place, colonization by industrial life and the multitude of new ideas and technologies it offered. O'Neill patrolled Chicago as an agent of the state, part of the apparatus that organized and administered the city. He allied himself with the city's business class, not the Irishmen and -women on strike. From his office in city hall he then used techniques of the modern police force to map and colonize Irish music.[5]

The two things—police work and music collection—might seem at first to have nothing in common. In uniform he battled with criminals and broke up crowds of strikers; as a music collector he met ordinary people in homes, theaters, and on the streets and memorized their folk music. But as he rose in police ranks he also tracked suspects and sorted their identities; he photographed them, measured them, and filed cross-referenced records. As chief of police in a city of 2 million people he testified at hearings, managed personnel, oversaw budgets, and wrangled statistics into annual reports. As a music collector he tracked down fugitive tunes and assessed their identity, compared them to thousands of other tunes, established their backstories, sorted the impostor from the genuine, and then formally organized them by type. His police work and his musical work were flip sides of the same coin, part of new ways of thinking about community, part of the administrative and management techniques of modern industrial society.

O'Neill's story also shows how immigrants made sense of their displacement from the old world, and his life matters partly because he shows us an example of how new cultural meanings evolved in confrontation with industrial technology. O'Neill did well in the US, which afforded him opportunities he would not have found in Ireland. But prosperity was not enough: he wanted to make sense of himself as both Irish and American; he wanted to find the meaning of his own journey from Tralibane to Chicago. Irish Americans formed social clubs and political associations that rang false to O'Neill. "Our leaders dope us," he complained, "with vainglorious praise and holiday oratory." Irish Americans rarely met without affirming the ancient dream of freeing Ireland from English rule, but bitter divisions about how to accomplish the dream could go beyond holiday oratory and get people killed. O'Neill rejected both the vainglorious oratory and the violent nationalist politics, in favor of an idealized community of music.[6]

O'Neill's books established the transatlantic relationship of Irish music and Irish people, affirming a sense of Irishness without overt politics. *O'Neill's Music of Ireland*, a massive collection of nearly 2,000 tunes, appeared in 1903. Four years later he refined that collection down to strictly dance tunes and published it as *The Dance Music of Ireland*. Irish musicians sometimes treat the latter collection as the bible of Irish folk music. Both books standardized and codified what had been a casual, informal circulation of tunes from person to person, village to village. He then published a series of books on Irish music and musicians: *Irish Folk Music: A Fascinating Hobby* in 1910, and three years later *Irish Minstrels and Musicians*. He published several smaller collections of tunes, some arranged for piano, and ended with two editions of *Waifs and Strays of Gaelic Melody* in 1922 and 1924. He managed to be both eminently Irish and eminently American.[7]

He ended up offering Irish music and dance as a form of practice, sort of as we might today imagine yoga. Irish music was imbued with romantic ideas about the peasants and the ancient Celtic race, with their knotwork borders and stone circles, and as music it had mystical emotional properties that stirred the soul. From the "grey dawn of legendary history," O'Neill wrote, "the romantic scenery of Ireland echoed" to the "soul possessing and unaffected melodies of the minstrels of ancient days." As a physical, mental, and perhaps spiritual practice, Irish music promised more than just dressing up on St. Patrick's day while avoiding most of the bitter and often dangerous infighting that Irish nationalist politics inspired. It offered immigrants an apolitical way to retain or recover Irishness without hindering one's American prosperity. [8]

Yoga, of course, is a spiritual practice or is invested in Indian spiritual, physical, and mental practice, and in weekly yoga classes we can see the legacy of colonialism and the global circulation of products and meanings. Irish music came to Chicago because Ireland was a colony of England, kept in poverty and political subordination. Yoga came to the US because England colonized India. To say this is not to condemn yoga classes or Irish dance classes, but simply to point out that they represent a kind of displacement, a new way of thinking and engaging with community and tradition. Before O'Neill's day you could learn a tune like "Out on the Ocean" only in person, from a person. Today face-to-face Irish music "sessions" persist, but you can go to YouTube and find yoga instruction, and you can go to YouTube and find out how to play "Out on the Ocean." This is neither wholly bad nor wholly good, but it is clearly *different*: to an extent, technology replaces community. Recalling the Irish American community of the 1890s, and perhaps unaware of his word choice, O'Neill wrote that thanks to his work "their delightful tunes are embalmed for such use as posterity may make of them." O'Neill's collections were a kind of intellectual technology that made face-to-face community unnecessary.[9]

One of O'Neill's biggest problems, when he started collecting tunes, came from his community's unwillingness to share them. He would hear someone play a new tune and ask to hear it again so he could memorize it, and the musician would refuse. He complained often about the "secretiveness, or rather selfishness," of musicians "who treat rare tunes as personal property, to be guarded with as much care as trade secrets." To collect tunes he cajoled, bribed, and intimidated; if necessary he spied on people or tricked them. He got musicians jobs on the police force, he offered them "gratuities" or promotions, or in multiple ways made their lives easier so they would cooperate in his project.

Like a colonial administrator O'Neill operated with a different sense of property, possession, and value. Tunes belonged to individuals or local communities, but O'Neill had a larger vision of Irish music and what he called "a soulful desire to possess, for personal use, but more often for the purpose of preserving and disseminating the remnants which have survived of our musical heritage." From his experience in the police, he had an administrator's demand for overview and systematic organization; he wanted to take those tunes out of their local communities and reframe them, "embalm" them, not as personal tunes but as "Irish music." Irish people had played all sorts of music for centuries; O'Neill invented a specific way to see it and understand it.[10]

He staked out a claim to the "authenticity" of a certain kind of Irish music: instrumental dance music, "tunes" not songs. He held these as genuine and authentic because they came from peasants, not fancy people, and because they had no known authors, no commercial motives, and no political agendas. No one had composed these tunes, he imagined: indeed they "can hardly be said to have been composed at all." The music he collected "has been preserved from generation to generation among the peasantry" by "minstrels whose wandering mode of life was well calculated to effect that purpose." O'Neill arrested that wandering and pinned the tunes in place.

Irish music emerged from the mists of time, he claimed, and in that sense tunes amounted almost to a natural resource that he would map and extract. He referred often to "the wealth of music" possessed by various Irish Chicagoans, which in turn he described himself as capturing or "mining." To meet O'Neill's criteria a tune needed an Irish genealogy and freedom from the taint of Tin Pan Alley, vaudeville, minstrel shows, and the multiple glittering seductions of US commercial culture. Constructing this idea of peasant music also required him to ignore the complex social relations and trauma of the Ireland he grew up in. He used his authority as chief to support his claim of authenticity. But "authenticity," like a mirage, constantly recedes as one approaches it.[11]

He had set out as a young man in search of adventure and experience. As he rose in the US and grew more successful and more deeply enmeshed in the complications of Chicago politics, he worked to define a pure, authentic, and exclusively Irish music. By the end of his life, he had begun to embrace a wider and more cosmopolitan notion of music as a living thing, not a once-lively community "embalmed" for posterity.

O'Neill wrote a great deal. Intelligent and thoughtful, he had a dry wit and sense of irony that endeared him to the press despite his abstemious habits. Although he could brawl with street gangs and lead a charge against a mob, he had a scholar's capacity for detail and order. He appears almost daily in Chicago newspapers during his terms as general superintendent from April 1901 through July 1905. He included details about his own life in two of his published books and wrote a private memoir, discovered by his descendants and published in 2008.

This book follows the chronology of O'Neill's life for the most part, adding historical context to fill in the many gaps this very private man left in his account. He withheld things from the public, he passed over major controversies, and in memory he concealed many things from himself. Historical context fills in those omissions. Chapters 4 and 5 depart from straight chronology to discuss first his rise in the police department from 1870 to 1900, and then the nature of the larger Irish American community during that same period. Chapters 6 and 7 return to a more strictly chronological account of his years as chief of police and in retirement, when he did most of his music collecting. A supplemental website, *thebeatcop.com*, includes musical examples and additional images.

O'Neill was a precise and methodical man. He owned a copy of the 1905 *Centennial History of the City of Chicago*, which included his biography, but penciled extensive corrections into the margins. At the same time he kept scrapbooks and along with stories about Ireland he clipped sentimental images of young lovers or boys catching crayfish, sexist observations about the tyranny of womankind, or poems about rural life in days gone by. The *Chicago Tribune* described O'Neill in the office as "aggressive, short, quick, with a policeman's bluntness," but at home finding refuge from the "cold, garish, workaday world" in his private library, where he "loses the quickness and abruptness that characterizes him at City Hall." The sentimental scrapbooks, his library of Hibernica, and his writing compensated for what his professional life demanded. To navigate a cold and garish and violent world, he constructed the past as warm, idyllic, and graceful.[12]

In all his writing and in interviews he took pains to present himself as an honest man in dishonest times. No decent historian would accept that self-description at face value. He was adept at managing Chicago politics and enjoyed the praise of the city's wealthy businessmen, which he earned by siding with management over labor. O'Neill the nostalgic scholar also endorsed forms of police brutality or torture; he strongly defended "sweating" suspects and the use of what he termed "the stomach pump" to extract confessions. His daughters destroyed his letters after he died, possibly to preserve his reputation or possibly out of commitment to privacy: O'Neill had a very nineteenth-century tendency to conceal private feelings and private life. You would hardly know, from his published writings, that he and his wife watched six of their ten children die. You would never know that his family may have evicted tenants to gain access to their land. The two dozen or so of his letters that survive often tartly criticize Irish Americans, the Catholic Church, and the Irish themselves. More letters may exist: the Irish music community holds information closely, and his books paint a happier picture of his fellow musicians than emerges in the letters. His work demands respect and skepticism in equal measure.

Aside from its anecdotes of adventure and tribulation, its revelations about life in the Gilded Age and Progressive Era, O'Neill's life shows us how displaced people make culture from their displacement. All immigrants to the US engage in a dialogue between their new home and their old, and so the Irish case is both particular and generic. Somewhere in the US, someone like Francis O'Neill uses modern technologies to collect and record the practices and folkways of Somali, Indian, Ethiopian, Salvadoran, Mexican, Vietnamese, and Korean immigrants; someone like Francis O'Neill works to balance personal ambitions and the demands of success against his or her family's heritage. In the process they reinvent that very heritage.

# 1
# Tralibane Bridge
## Childhood and Memory

### Fire and Ice in Chicago

In late afternoon on December 30, 1903, Chicago's lavish Iroquois theater caught fire. During a sold-out performance of *Mr. Bluebeard*, a lighting fixture set the curtain blazing: smoke billowed into the theater, and terrified people rushed for the exits. When they wrenched the outer doors open the dry winter air ignited a firestorm. People struggled desperately to escape, trampling each other; they leaped from the balcony and crushed those beneath them; they died at the exits, overcome by smoke and heat and flame.

That very moment General Superintendent of Police Francis O'Neill sat a block away, in City Council Chambers, at a hearing into charges of graft; one of his lieutenants, a man he'd known for years, was accused of coercing protection money. Show hearings like this happened regularly in Chicago, and O'Neill knew how this would play out. Outraged citizens demanded reform. Public hearings gave the appearance of action; officials testified, reporters reported, stories migrated from the front pages to the back, and then things returned to normal.[1]

As he sat there looking dutifully solemn, O'Neill probably had an old Irish tune running through his head: he nearly always did. He was "music mad" in those days, he told a friend. Part of it seemed familiar—what other tune did it remind him of? He couldn't quite place it, and it nagged at him. Then an officer appeared and spoke news of the fire in his ear. O'Neill excused himself and rushed to the scene.

He arrived as the fire still burned. He and his officers made their way against panicked crowds in and up to the second balcony, where few had escaped. Working by lantern light they found the material of nightmares: the dead, hundreds of them, tangled in a mass, "piled eight or ten high," many burned beyond recognition. Worse, they could hear sounds of people alive within the piles of bodies, and they worked in feverish despair to get them out.[2]

About 600 people died in the fire; O'Neill supervised the removal of nearly all of them, and as the crisis eased, reporters turned to the chief for an official account of the scene. Exhausted and horrified, he told them: "If you ever saw a field of Timothy grass blown flat by the wind and rain of a summer storm, that was the position of the dead at the exits of the second balcony."[3]

From the cold and the dark, the char and the stench of the ruined theater he reached back to a memory of his childhood in Ireland: windblown grass and summer storms; rain and sun, not fire and ice; the season of growth, not of death. Against a trauma particular to the industrial city he called up an image of rural life; asked to make a record for history, he offered a memory of a different place and time.

## Tralibane, Bantry, and the Famine

O'Neill was born into a traumatized land, but he only partly acknowledged and partly buried the memory. "My birth on August 28, 1848, a famine year, could hardly have been a joyous occasion in the already large family of my parents," he wrote. Between 1845 and 1851 a mold, *Phytophthora infestans*, wiped out the Irish potato crop, and as a result, about a million people died, mostly small tenants and laborers. The blight attacked with supernatural, unnerving speed. A healthy field could turn black in a matter of hours, suddenly giving off a "fearful stench," soon "recognized as the death sign." "He went out to the garden for potatoes" went one account: "he stuck his spade in the pit, and the spade was swallowed. The potatoes turned to mud inside. He shrieked and shrieked. The whole town came out. All the potatoes were in the same way."[4]

The Irish grew potatoes because landlords reserved the best lands for cattle and export crops that brought cash, while potatoes thrived in the rockiest and most unpromising soils from which the Irish poor fed themselves. By the 1840s, the majority of Irish people ate almost nothing but potatoes. Diet might also include milk from a single cow, typically the buttermilk left after churning; oats in some regions; seaweed and fish near the coasts. A typical farm might additionally keep a pig, not to feed the family but to sell to pay the rent.[5]

If people ate the pig because their potatoes failed, they had no way to pay the rent. Landlords, who had long wanted to "clear the land" of poor tenants and expand the opportunities for more profitable crops, eagerly sent men with crowbars to pull down houses and evict tenants. Sick, hungry, homeless people sheltered where they could or headed into the workhouses, grim Dickensian institutions quickly overwhelmed by the scale of the calamity. People died on the road to lie unburied. Starvation killed hundreds of thousands of people directly, but it also made survivors weak and vulnerable to disease, unable to earn a living. It is impossible to know exactly how many died—be it from starvation, disease, displacement, or other related factors—but in some regions half the population vanished in about five years.[6]

The O'Neills live in the townland of Tralibane, County Cork, locally pronounced and sometimes spelled more like "Trawlybawn." West Cork, where the O'Neills lived, suffered as badly or worse than any county in Ireland, and the famine circled Tralibane like a garrote. The deaths in Ballydehob, ten miles from O'Neill's home, "average forty to fifty daily; twenty were buried this morning," wrote one witness in 1847: the people huddle in their mud cabins "so that they may die together with their children and not be seen by passers-by." Between 1841 and 1851 more than half the people in Ballydehob died or emigrated. Because illustrated newspapers in England, Ireland, and the US reported it widely, the "famished and ghastly skeletons" of the town of Skibbereen, also about ten miles from O'Neill's home, came to symbolize the famine internationally.[7]

Roughly five mile's walk from the O'Neills, in Drimoleague, "they died so rapidly and in such numbers that the bodies could not be buried in the ordinary way, but were thrown in mass into pits," with hundreds "found dead in their own cabins and in the roads and fields." A police sergeant at Drimoleague reported that the parish "had sunk from nearly 6000 to about 3000 in the course of two years, and this chiefly from death and not emigration."[8]

In the winter of 1846–47, more than 1,000 rural people, facing starvation and evicted from their homes, "thronged into Bantry," a port town of roughly 4,000 three miles from the O'Neill house. The town had a few prominent buildings but also many one-room "mud cabins" made of compacted soil. "In the churchyard there yawned three monster graves; in one of which, up to the 1st of April, had been laid 232, in the second, 215, and in the third, 75 bodies; all from the workhouse." "The mortality rate in the new work-house was appallingly high. Between 1845 and 1851, some 2,896 deaths were recorded there": that is, more than one a day. By 1851 the country population around Bantry "had declined by 3,937 or 34.2 per cent."[9]

Yet closer to home, Francis O'Neill's nephew grew up believing that a mass grave of famine victims lay on his grandfather's land: a hole 100 feet deep, he said, filled with the bodies of "several hundred people including three priests." Irish folklore includes stories of *féar gorta*, patches of "hungry grass" or "famine grass" that, when stepped on, cause famishing hunger and weakness. Stories connect hungry grass to the unmarked graves of famine victims. If he was too young to remember bodies stacked in pits, Francis surely would have heard the tales. That windblown Timothy grass O'Neill remembered might have covered graves, as its memory covered the dead in Chicago.[10]

Nature, in the form of the potato blight, had caused the famine, but everything else about the famine and its catastrophic effects stemmed from English colonial rule. Land in Ireland belonged almost without exception to the English, to distant landlords who ruled tens of thousands of acres and might never bother to visit the lands that produced the rents supporting them in idleness. England deliberately kept Ireland isolated from industrialization so that it might serve as "England's pantry," a source of food and wealth, poor but productive. Well into the nineteenth century, Catholics in Ireland faced legal restrictions that kept them from full participation in the life of their own country; restrictions on voting, on participation

**Figure 1** *Illustrated London News*, December 16, 1848, 380. Copy in author's possession. Published the year Francis O'Neill was born, this illustration depicts an "ejectment" from a one-room mud cabin made of compacted dirt, probably in County Tipperary. English officials called this a fourth-class cabin. The article accompanying it quotes a Tipperary newspaper describing the suffering and calls it "absolutely appalling." But it refers to the evicted as "redundant population" and their eviction as a "necessary social revolution." The inconvenient poor had to go.

in government, and regulations requiring tithes to the Protestant Church of Ireland. England controlled the law and administered justice as a colonial power does, so as best to serve herself. During the course of the famine, while hundreds of thousands starved, Ireland continued to export meat and grain to England. England combined a commitment to aristocracy with a bright new enthusiasm for laissez-faire economics. Doing something to help the starving damaged their moral character; doing as little as possible produced a self-reliant corpse. Hundreds of years before the English had seized land and driven the occupants to the west, they had worked to suppress the Irish language and to demand servility. Irish peasants doffed the cap or curtsied when the lord rode by; they suffered, but the *Illustrated London News* called the sufferers "redundant population," brushed away by a "necessary social revolution."[11]

Although the famine horrified many people in England and they looked for ways to mitigate the suffering, just as many saw the famine as God's punishment of the lazy papists. Charles Trevelyan, the widely hated assistant secretary of Her Majesty's Treasury, insisted that "the great evil with which we have to contend is not the physical evil of famine, but the moral evil of the selfish, perverse and turbulent character of the [Irish] people," while the London *Times* dreamed of a day when "in a few more years, thanks to the Famine, a Celtic Irishman will be as rare in Connemara as the Red Indian on the shores of Manhattan." With impressive restraint Christine Kinealy concludes that British officials regretted the famine but viewed it as "an opportunity to facilitate various long-desired changes within Ireland."[12]

These changes included depopulation: Ireland had too many people wringing subsistence from land that could feed cattle. If they had the resources, or sometimes if landlords subsidized them, displaced tenants emigrated to England, Australia, Canada, and especially the US. Irish people had started leaving Ireland in large numbers decades earlier, but the famine dramatically accelerated the process. Famine survivors often spoke of the "awful, unwonted silence" that settled on the land after so many died or left; it "struck fearfully on the imagination" and gave the Irish "a deeper feeling of desolation." "The rhetoric of fatalism," Cormac Ó Gráda concludes, "is silence." Daniel Francis O'Neill, called Francis or Frank, grew up the youngest of seven in a depopulated land, but in memory he filled that silence with music.[13]

O'Neill was as honest as men generally get, but the only accounts of his childhood come from his own pen, and they don't match the historical record very well. In childhood he would walk past the crumbling ruins of cabins or *clachans*, clusters of houses where people once lived, now abandoned to death or emigration. But he rarely spoke directly about that: instead, O'Neill remembered the sound of flutes across the hills at evening, mothers lilting at their spinning wheels, fathers singing by the fireside, shepherds and blacksmiths whistling, young people dancing at the crossroads. Music "mingled in every feature of Irish life, from the cabin to the castle," he wrote. "The appearance of a piper, fiddler or fluter, or even a man with a jews-harp, was sufficient to draw a crowd of the youth of both sexes to enjoy a dance or listen to the music; and night after night the same youthful hearts would gather around some blazing turf fire, and if there happened to be no musician to stir the dancing spirit, some sweet peasant voice would make up for the loss by singing."[14]

People sang to mark the loss of their loved ones to death or emigration, or they sang about martyred Irish rebels or relatives sentenced to "transportation." But Francis chose not to remember those songs or make the memory of them public. The nostalgic glow he cast over Tralibane obscured the colonial power structures that let people die, drove them off the land, or forced them to emigrate; it especially obscured his own family's complicity in those structures of power. Indeed, Francis O'Neill was unable, fifty years later, to give a clear and sensible account of why he left Ireland, perhaps because a clear-eyed look would have cut through the nostalgic haze he wrapped around his memories.

The O'Neill family, or at least some of them, benefited from the "necessary social revolution" the famine had initiated. In the 1850s the O'Neills held, meaning "leased," almost 100 acres of land in the townlands of Tralibane and nearby Cullomane West. This made them in Irish parlance "strong farmers," families enjoying more than a subsistence living with surplus crops for sale. Although they had little hope of buying land themselves, a strong farmer family like the O'Neills could sublet their holdings to tenants. Their holdings included "offices" as well as a house and land, suggesting perhaps they collected their own rents. The O'Neills lived in a two-story stone house at a time when many neighbors lived in one-room cabins made of compacted mud. Strong farmers were colonialism's middlemen. They contracted their poorer neighbors as labor in a system that directed profit and value toward England.[15]

The strong farmers benefited from the famine: they could turn marginal potato fields to cattle pasture, and "every good tenant soon found out that a broken tenant being put out might mean a substantial gain to himself." After the famine, tiny one-family potato plots merged into fewer but larger farms. "Large farmers holding more than thirty acres," like the O'Neills, "not only escaped almost unscathed but in fact strengthened their position during the Famine

**Figure 2** O'Neill's birthplace in Tralibane. Photo courtesy of Robert Harris, https://roaringwaterjournal.com/. The O'Neills were a relatively prosperous family, and as O'Neill described, the house had room for wedding parties, for neighbors to gather to hear news from Crimea, and for guests like blind widow Mary Ward and her two daughters, who often stayed for weeks at a time.

years." "When the Famine abated in Ireland, middling and strong farmers . . . found themselves less accursed by God than singularly blessed by the decimation of the less fortunate and the consequent restructuring of Irish agriculture." Not only did strong farmers gain more land: "farmers with thirty or more acres increased their share of farm animals by 17 percent," and the number of sheep and cattle in Ireland increased by between 69 and 86 percent. Those sheep and cattle grazed placidly on land that once fed the people in the one-room mud cabins.[16]

In the 1890s Francis told an American biographer how his older brother John had embarked on "investment in stock and cattle dealing" in the 1850–1860s, "a course later well justified since he made a rapid fortune." John put young Francis to work for wages on the family holdings when school let out. As a boy he resented working "in the tillage fields in summer when others of my class were enjoying their vacations," and even more he resented, when he got older, "his

elder brother's persistence in appropriating his salary" to support
the thriving cattle business. The profits went to John and not to the
other siblings since at least three of the six O'Neill children left for
a better chance in America.[17]

But if O'Neill's ambitious brother exploited his labor, the family
took care to give Francis a good education in the new English
system of National Schools. Before the 1840s, "nonconforming"
Irish families—Catholics, Presbyterians, or members of faiths
other than the Anglican Church of Ireland—sent their children to
"hedge schools," semiformal, technically illegal schools that might
meet under cover of a dense hedge but more often met in barns,
storehouses, or wherever they could find room. In a hedge school
students who could afford to pay the schoolmaster received basic
literacy in Irish or English, and in some cases extensive education
in Latin and Greek.

England established the National Schools starting in 1831, after
multiple foreign and domestic accounts had called out the ignorance
and poverty of Her Majesty's Irish subjects. The National Schools
aimed "to unite the children of the poor in Ireland for combined
moral and literary instruction with separate doctrinal instruction."[18]
A governing board composed of two Catholics, two members of
the Church of Ireland, and two Presbyterians oversaw the schools,
which strictly prohibited religious instruction except in specific
classrooms, when signs would appear on the doors warning of sec-
tarian religious instruction within. Catholics went to the Catholic
class, Presbyterians to the Presbyterian class, and Church of Ireland
members to the Church of Ireland class.

The schools offered a free education but in return colonized the
student's mind. They promoted a thoroughly Anglicized curriculum
and "almost ignored the Irish child's own culture and environment."
"They never sing an Irish song," Douglas Hyde wrote, "or repeat an
Irish poem." Children "forget all about their own country that their
parents told them." Hyde, one of the founders of the Gaelic League,
would have an enormous influence on the adult O'Neill. He continued: "the schoolmaster is not allowed to teach Irish history; they
translate their names into English—probably the schoolmaster has

done the same; and what is the use of having an Irish name now that they are not allowed to speak Irish!" Hyde deplored the fact that Irish children started school by reciting this poem:

I thank the goodness and the grace
Which on my birth have smiled,
And made me in these Christian days
A happy English child!

As intended, National Schools eroded specifically Irish culture. Many people spoke of punishment, either at school or at home, for speaking Irish. One school inspector, in 1850, noted that through the National Schools "we are quietly but certainly destroying the national legend, national music, and national language of the country." In 1850 "around 1,500,000 westerners and south-westerners were to some degree bilingual and around 300,000 spoke only Irish." By the late nineteenth century, only about 75,000 children still spoke Irish at home. Part of the silence attributed to the famine involved the silencing of the ancient Irish language, and with it the literature and legend that had helped define Irish culture.[19]

O'Neill undoubtedly knew some Irish and heard Irish at home, but he spoke mostly English, wrote in English, and as an adult had to rely on others to translate from Irish. He was a bright and precocious learner, curious, a book lover. "I had learned to read," he wrote in his memoir, "long before" being old enough to walk to school. He started at the National School in nearby Dromore but later walked the three miles to the new school in Bantry. "Philosopher O'Neill" his schoolmates called him; he excelled especially in mathematics. In O'Neill's day most Irish students never advanced beyond basic literacy, but students who persisted in the National Schools found a demanding curriculum that taught Latin and English grammar as well as "natural philosophy," which encompassed the sciences. The books O'Neill used reveal an advanced high school or precollege curriculum, preparing him for a place in the English colonial system, a place that Tralibane and Bantry did not actually offer.[20]

Francis thrived in school. He developed excellent penmanship, which served him well in his later career and delighted the historian reading his letters 100 years later. He was one or two years ahead of his classmates, so much so that the school appointed him junior monitor at age twelve and senior monitor at age fourteen. In both cases he and the schoolmaster lied about his age "to the Commissioners of Education at Dublin" because Francis was too young to officially hold the positions. By his early teens he did some of the classroom teaching himself, he recalled. He had become an authority, a precocious agent of the school and its modernizing, Anglicizing project, helping other students prepare for life in English Ireland. [21]

Like most colonized people, O'Neill had a kind of double identity, both Irish and English. The O'Neills had deep roots in an Irish community but also had to navigate a colonial system in which they had clawed out a relatively favorable position. Francis wrote very little about his childhood, devoting only eight brief pages of his memoir to his life from birth to age seventeen. The family home included a "more than five foot shelf of books" that he cherished; these almost certainly would have been books in English. He shares almost nothing else about the house, but we can see this dual identity in a story Francis told about John O'Neill, his father, who read newspaper accounts of the Crimean War out loud to neighbors who gathered at the family's house; John then "interpreted the story to those who spoke only the Irish language."[22]

The neighbors who gathered at the O'Neill house had a personal interest in the Crimean War, which Britain waged from 1853 to 1856. Among its alleged benefits, British colonial rule gave a poor man the chance to fight and die in the service of the empire, and at least 30 percent of the British armed forces in the Crimean War came from hungry Ireland. To give a sense of relative priorities, while Britain spent about £9.5 million on famine relief, "a decade later it spent almost £70 million on the Crimean War." O'Neill's county alone contributed more than 1,300 men and boys to the British Navy in 1852. Little wonder the neighbors gathered around what Francis called the "tallow candles and dogwood splinters" that lit the house as John read them news from the Crimea.[23]

Bitter memories of the Crimean War persisted in Irish and Irish

Figure 3 *The Eviction: A Scene from Life in Ireland* (New York: J. T. Foley, Publisher, 117 Nassau Street, c1871). At Prints and Photographs Division, Library of Congress, https:// lccn.loc.gov/2004669163. The memory of eviction persisted among Irish Americans for generations, and the threat of eviction continued to hang over the heads of their Irish relatives and neighbors in Ireland well into the twentieth century. The figure at center left with raised fist has returned from fighting for the Queen in the Crimean War.

American culture. An 1871 lithograph of Irish eviction, produced in New York, aimed to capture the stunned desperation and hopelessness of the victims of eviction. In center left, the man with the raised fist wears the Crimean War uniform of the British Army: he returns from war to find his family homeless. O'Neill rendered the memory of news from Crimea in firelit nostalgia, as an example of community. But the lithograph reveals the injustice of fighting for an empire that evicts you, an injustice O'Neill could not see or chose not to remember.[24]

"Crowded out from the candles," he wrote, "I contrived to study, or to do my tasks, by the fitful light of the turf fire," while his father translated news into Irish. Near the candles anxious parents listened for news of their children, but by the uncertain light of the turf fire O'Neill continued his education. Young O'Neill had both news from London and the fitful turf fire of Irish legend; study and tasks in English, and Irish speakers eager for news of their family members;

a substantial shelf of books in English, and a sense of obligation to neighbors. Colonialism placed him in two worlds, both English and Irish, and in his own telling he set himself apart from his father and the neighbors, "crowded out," on a different trajectory. He remembered his father's solicitousness toward the local community, not the community's anxiety about the empire's war.

The neighbors who gathered to hear O'Neill's father read the news might have been tenants of the O'Neills. The O'Neill family had probably evicted subtenants from the land they held, given their increased investment in cattle raising, or they probably gained the right to lease land made vacant by death or emigration. "The landlords are often accused, and justly so, for their oppression, cruelty and tyranny," Hugh Dorian argued, "but unfortunately a man's very neighbour is very often just as pitiless a tyrant as any man." He added that "many cruel unmerciful acts have been witnessed, arising from the joint action of the landlord and his favoured tenant." The O'Neills, leasing 100 acres from two men, surely amounted to "favored tenants" and almost as surely either subleased land or hired workers—including Francis—on wages. But Francis never seems to have considered what brought those anxious neighbors to his father's door.[25]

The O'Neill family would have kept an eye out for news about neighbors and chances to acquire more land. Francis remembered that "periodically Mary Ward and her two daughters," a blind widow and her family "driven to mendicancy as a result of the famine, made our farmhouse their headquarters for a week or so at a time." He did not say specifically what drove the Wards to mendicancy, or give the daughters' ages, or explain why they stayed with the O'Neills. They might have once been tenants of the O'Neills. Mr. Ward might have died in the famine. Or possibly the O'Neills themselves displaced the family. But Francis remembered the Wards "were always very welcome, for the old woman had all the news of the country to relate." Indeed, O'Neill wrote, "it was through her and her like that news was disseminated in the absence of newspapers in those times." The O'Neills read newspaper stories about the empire in Crimea, but local news passed from person to person. Francis presented her

**Figure 4** Engraving (1871) of Erskine Nicol's painting *Renewal of the Lease Refused* (1863), in author's possession. Scotsman Nicol often painted Irish genre scenes, and this image captures the ambiguous position of strong farmer families. The O'Neills, with their large holdings and "offices" and their shelf of books, might have been more like the seated man evicting his tenant. In slightly less fortunate circumstances, they might have been the standing man, facing eviction. The figures in the engraving avoid each other's gaze, an analogue to those things Francis O'Neill chose not to see. Irish history has often evaded the complexity of the situation by imagining the seated man as English.

as a quaint gossip, but Captain O'Neill, who wrote those words more than fifty years later, well knew the value of informants—"her and her like"—and how to manage them. Mrs. Ward, a blind, homeless woman with few options for making a living and two children to feed, probably offered the competitive and ambitious O'Neills intelligence about their neighbors in exchange for food and shelter.

Perhaps the O'Neills were simply being kind, and this judges them too harshly. But colonialism complicated all motives and made the O'Neills complicit in whatever events had cast Mary and her daughters onto the road. Their generosity in hosting her acknowledged that complicity, even as their relatively privileged position depended on the "social revolution" the famine had brought about and had rendered Mary and her daughters "redundant population."

"Besides," Francis added, "she could sing a good song, and lilt a good tune in spite of her blindness and poverty." He went on to say that he had learned a lively reel, "Rolling in the Ryegrass," from Mrs. Ward, and then he described all the different names under which Irish musicians knew the tune. O'Neill cared about the music, not the circumstances that had impoverished Mary Ward and her daughters. Here again this may seem too harsh a judgment, but Francis's interest in music let him pass over the tensions in the landscape and reduce Mrs. Ward's plight to a charming memory of rustic community. Music mattered, not the class tensions between landlords, strong farmers, and tenants. O'Neill's focus on music allowed him to imagine a unified Irish culture.[26]

## Irish Music and Irish Nationalism

Ireland, in fact, had many different forms of music. O'Neill knew the songs of Thomas Moore, an educated upper-class Irishman who in the very early nineteenth century modified traditional melodies to conform to standard harmony on the piano and then added his own poetic lyrics, which he eventually published to international acclaim as *Moore's Irish Melodies*. Moore infused his lyrics with a pleasing sense of melancholy and longing: the worldwide influence of *Moores's Irish Melodies* clearly affected American Stephen Foster, whose plaintive melodies and lyrics about old times on the plantation coated inequality and exploitation in a similar wistful nostalgia. By the 1830s, well before O'Neill's birth, the first blackface minstrel shows from the US had appeared, to great popularity, in Dublin, Derry, Belfast, and Cork.[27]

Outside of genteel parlors of the middle class, ordinary Irish people heard songs from England, Europe, and the US in theaters: soldiers and sailors brought music back from service abroad; peddlers hawked song sheets in the markets. Although Ireland was poor, it was an integral part of a global empire and a continuous movement of people and goods.[28]

O'Neill would have heard brass bands organized by Father Theobald Mathew, an Irish Catholic priest who led a famous crusade against drink starting about 1840. By the time of the famine, 3 million people had taken the pledge of his Total Abstinence Society. Novel and different, brass bands kept their members socially active, called attention to the cause, and offered amusement for families. By 1840 the movement supported thirty-three brass bands in Cork City alone: Bantry had one in O'Neill's day, and he would have heard it while attending school. O'Neill, himself a teetotaler, complained that "brass bands, nearly as numerous as the branches of the temperance societies instituted as a result of Father Mathew's crusade," had "driven the piper and fiddler out of fashion." He would have also heard fife and drum bands organized by the British troops; the bands made a lively display of administrative authority and discipline. Fife and drum bands later entered into the popular culture of civilian Ireland.[29]

Those military fife and drum bands marched because the Irish did not take their colonial status lying down: the British had to station troops in Ireland to suppress Irish demands for independence. In 1798, for example, the United Irishmen, hoping to establish an Irish republic, had organized a major rebellion. Its noble failure endured in songs like Thomas Moore's "The Minstrel Boy" and "The Rising of the Moon," also known as "The Wearing of the Green." Songs of rebellion against colonial authority, songs about martyred heroes and the dream of an independent Ireland, anchored political gatherings in Ireland and in the US and associated Irish music with Irish political independence. As O'Neill made his way through the Chicago police ranks, he skirted Irish nationalist political organizations as a soldier would a minefield.

But Irish nationalists claimed Irish musical distinctiveness so they could insist that Ireland had its own culture, its own ancient identity, and so deserved independence. Ireland had a tradition of music on the harp: so much so that the harp served as a symbol of Ireland and Irish nationalism itself. One of Moore's most famous songs, "The Harp That Once through Tara's Halls," lamented the ancient Irish harp music silenced by conquest.

In 1792 members of the United Irishmen organized a Belfast Harp Festival. They charged Edward Bunting, an Irish-born, classically trained organist, with transcribing the tunes he heard from ten harpers. The keen-eared Bunting published this first collection of Irish music in 1797, as the *Ancient Music of Ireland*, with a second volume in 1806 and a third in 1840. Bunting told readers that "Ireland has, from a remote antiquity, been celebrated for its cultivation of Music, and admitted to be one of the parent countries of that delightful art." That is, Ireland had an ancient and distinctive musical tradition. He also identified his target audience as upper-class lovers of liberty and Irish patriots, claiming his collection would "meet the approbation of men of refinement and erudition in every country."[30]

Bunting stressed that "the spirit and character of a people are connected with their national poetry and music." Bunting and his peers established certain forms of Irish music as a part of a claim for independence. As the Irish scholar and musician Fintan Vallely puts it, the very idea of "Irish traditional music" has always been linked to anticolonial rebellion, and "what we know as 'Traditional' music is very practically—just like similar kinds of music are in other countries—historically and ideologically enmeshed with identity-assertion and revolutionary politics." O'Neill did not like direct political agitation, but he seized on music as a sign of Irish national character.[31]

The adult Captain Francis O'Neill had copies of Bunting's books in his library, cited him often, and noted his "undying fame," but the music Bunting collected was not the music O'Neill loved. Bunting collected mostly "airs," slow songs, and concentrated on music performed on the harp that lent itself to more genteel listening: not brass bands, rebel songs, sentimental laments, political ballads, or musical hall tunes. O'Neill rejected those forms of Irish music as well, focusing on raucous and lively instrumental dance music.

## Dance Music and Rural Life

Before the famine, tourists had noted Ireland for poverty, a picturesque landscape, and dance music. "All the poor people, both men and women, learn to dance, and are exceedingly fond of the amusement," wrote the English tourist Arthur Young in the 1770s: "the love of dancing and musick are almost universal amongst them." Ordinary people gathered to make music "according to the cyclical calendar of the agricultural year. Imbolg (the feast of St. Brigit), Bealtaine (May Day), Lughnasa (festival of the god Lugh in late July or early August), and Samhain (Halloween) all marked the main coordinates of this cycle." Seasonal communal tasks like planting, harvesting, or cutting turf called for celebration: neighbors and family gathered in homes and kitchens for music and dancing. "These celebrations often coincided with race meetings, fairs and hurling matches." Dancing even at the local crossroads often took the form of aggressive challenges between men or women who showed off their particular skills on platforms or wooden doors placed across barrels. Large fairs could turn violent with local grudges turning into notorious "faction fights." In English, the word "donnybrook" connotes a brawl: the term comes from Donnybrook Fair, a notoriously riotous annual event at the town of that name.[32]

"In those days," O'Neill insisted, "all the young people had a passion for dancing, an acquirement without which no one's education was complete." Many learned dancing from a "dance master," a sort of traveling one-man finishing school. The dance master typically went seasonally from house to house, boarding with a strong farmer family if they had the means, and gave lessons in dance as well as the forms of deportment. O'Neill suggests itinerant musicians and dancers may have stayed with his family but does not say so specifically.[33]

Professional musicians also traveled from place to place, originally with harps, but by the nineteenth century more commonly with fiddles or Uilleann pipes. The Uilleann pipes, originally called the Union pipes, began as an upper-class gentleman's refinement of the more raucous mouth-inflated bagpipe. Played seated and inflated via a bellows strapped under the elbow, the Uilleann pipes had greater range and a softer, more mellow sound. A full set had extra pipes called regulators that could play simple chords. Itinerant musicians—often blind because music offered the blind a trade— also typically stayed at the home of a strong farmer like John O'Neill. While there ensconced and fed, they would entertain the family and perform publicly at established locations.

Locals called the public performance a "patron." A crossroads typically served as one location; bridges often served as another because their hard surfaces and elevation amplified the sound of dancers' feet. Music might also feature at a saint's day or feast day, more like a fair, with multiple pipers and dancers from rival villages. O'Neill remembered patrons and crossroad dances with special fondness.[34]

"There were two pipers in our parish," he wrote: "Peter Hagerty, locally known as the *Píobaire Ban*," on account of his fair hair, and Charley Murphy, nicknamed "*Cormac na Paidireacha*," "Cormac of the Prayers." Murphy, "a respectable farmer's son," O'Neill continued, "got 'a blast from the faeries' one dark night" and was lamed "as a result of the faeries' displeasure." To make a living, he learned the pipes. "In those days succeeding the famine years, Irish was much spoken, and such children as did not get an education in English were obliged to learn their prayers and catechism from oral instruction in the Irish language." Fluent in both languages, O'Neill wrote, Murphy the piper made some money as a teacher of prayers and the form of the Catholic Mass. Between that and "a prosperous 'Patron' which he established at Tralibane Bridge, and playing at an occasional farmhouse dance, he managed to make a fair living."

The other piper, Peter "Bawn" Hagerty, O'Neill described as "a tall dignified man, blind through smallpox since childhood." "He had a 'Patron' at Colomane Cross," O'Neill continued, and "maintained himself and wife in comparative comfort." "He played every Sunday afternoon in summertime . . . the event of the week to the peasantry for miles around. The 'Píobaire Bawn' was a busy man, for there was no let up to the dancing while daylight lasted." At his sister's wedding young Francis was packed off to bed while the Piper Bawn played in the next room: "half asleep and awake the music hummed in my ears for hours, and the memory of the tunes is still vivid after the lapse of fifty years."[35]

In O'Neill's youth, he claimed, anyone who hoped to make a living with music played the fiddle or the pipes, but Francis started on flute. "No musical instrument was in such common use among the Irish peasantry as the flute," he declared. "From the 'penny whistle' to the keyed instrument in sections it was always deservedly popular" because it cost little and needed no strings or reeds or rosin. "Who that has heard the mellow music of either whistle or flute a mile away on a fine evening, will ever forget the experience?" he asked. No formal schools for Irish music existed, and what training O'Neill got came from a local "gentleman farmer" who taught him to play by ear.[36]

In his memoirs O'Neill said little about his parents, but he praised their musicality. "My mother—God rest her soul—would memorize much of the Folk Music of Munster and naturally transmit it orally by her lilting and singing to her children." She had, he wrote, "a keen ear, a retentive memory, and an intense love of the haunting melodies of [her] race." He went on: "Similarly gifted was our father, who, full of peace, and content, and occupying his accustomed chair beside the spacious fireplace, sung the old songs in English or Irish for his own pleasure, or the entertainment of those who cared to listen, of whom there were many not included in the family." The picture O'Neill gives here—the lilting mother, the father full of peace by his fire—tastes of moldy cliché, but in private letters to folklorists he often named his parents as the source of tunes he republished.[37]

O'Neill associated music not just with his family but with Irish faery lore as well, noting "a halo seems to encircle the head of the piper in the mysticism of the Irish mind." According to common belief, wrote O'Neill, pipers were "not infrequently kidnapped by the faeries, so fascinating was their music, and forced to entertain their captors at their subterranean festivities." Tarlach Mac Suibhne (Turlough McSweeney), "the Donegal Piper," claimed that as a young man "there was no music in me," so he decided "to make an appeal to the faeries on the rath [a ring fort or stone circle] of Gaeth-Doir on the hilltop, half a mile away." One night, he plucked up courage, "and with his pipes buckled on he entered the moonlit circle." According to McSweeney, he asked the king of the faeries for a tune. Suddenly "the grandest music of many pipers . . . playing all together, filled my ears; and . . . what should I see but scores of little faeries or luricauns [leprechauns], wearing red caps, neatly footing it, as if for a wager." Terrified, he ran, dropping pieces of his pipes as he went. The next morning he went back, found the pieces of his pipes near the entrance to the rath, and began to play. "Words can't express my astonishment and delight when I found I could play as well as the best of them. And that, gentlemen, is how I came to be the best Union piper of my day in that part of the country." McSweeney related this and other stories "in all seriousness to men not much his junior in years," O'Neill commented tartly. "For obvious reasons such tales are never debatable, yet those who came in contact with the taciturn minstrel felt that there was something strange, inscrutable, and even uncanny, in his whole demeanor."[38]

Exploring as a boy, Francis discovered standing stones, or "raths," and mysterious cairns in the fields around his home. "Raths and forts, which crown so many hilltops in the Green Isle, are held sacred to the memory of a hoary and mysterious past," O'Neill wrote, "and rash indeed would be the one who would desecrate their enclosed area, or mutilate their circular ramparts. As the reputed abodes of the faeries or 'good people,' they are regarded with awe and even dread by a simple, imaginative peasantry." O'Neill cultivated a degree of distance when he talked about faery beliefs and elevated himself, an educated man, above the "simple, imaginative peasantry."[39]

Colonialism again often demands the kind of dual identity O'Neill shows in these passages, speaking in the voice of the colonizer, feeling himself both native and apart. The men who made war on England in the American Revolution started out as ambitious colonial Englishmen, working within a colonial economic and political system. They had to develop a sense of themselves as "American," distinct from the English. An ambitious person in India in 1858 might have used the same schoolbooks O'Neill read in Bantry and, to thrive under colonial rule, would have trained his tongue to English and adopted the practices and beliefs colonial administrators required. We can see this doubled identity again in O'Neill's account of Tralibane, where people have two names, an English name and an Irish name. A man like *Cormac na Paidireacha* might get "a blast from the faeries" causing lameness, but he could also earn money teaching Catholic doctrine, although the Christian Bible makes no mention of faeries blasting people from underground dwellings. We can see colonialism in how O'Neill speaks of music: "the glad tidings flew far and wide," he remembered, "when a piper or fiddler paid one of his periodical visits to a community, and with what delight did the simple, light-hearted people, young and old, boys and girls, look forward with thrills of anticipation to the evenings when they could call at the 'Big house' and listen to the grand old inspiring music."[40]

The phrase "big house" will remind American readers of slavery: slaves used the term to describe the master's home. In England it also referred to the manorial country home of the local lord, but O'Neill surely did not mean the home of the Earl of Bantry. Did he mean the home of his parents, sheltering Mrs. Ward and her daughters, or an itinerant musician? He used the term to describe simple happy dependents and a social hierarchy where the O'Neills sat comfortably. O'Neill was both Irish and a colonial subject, made distant enough from Irish cultural practices to judge them from an outsider perspective.

## The Catholic Church and the Devotional Revolution

When he turned a critical eye to his memories of music, O'Neill targeted not English authority or landlords but the Catholic Church. In O'Neill's youth the church underwent a "devotional revolution" in which it formalized and standardized practice. Before the devotional revolution, "popular Irish religion was tribal, traditional, and permeated with magic." Wakes and weddings typically involved remarkably earthy, bawdy rituals invoking fertility and resurrection, and open parodies of the Mass and the clergy. Wakes sometimes combined wailing, keening grief with dancing, manly contests of strength, and openly sexual games involving sowing and planting as metaphors for sexual acts. The church improved the education of priests, increased their numbers, and built more and better churches in which to conduct more strict rituals. It mostly abandoned Irish in favor of English, and encouraged parishioners to name their children after saints of the church, like Michael, Daniel, Thomas, Francis, or Anthony, rather than giving them traditional Irish names perplexing to the English palate. It established a famously squeamish, prudish, and hostile attitude toward human sexuality in all of its forms. Though a practicing Catholic who counted many priests among his friends, O'Neill's two given names bore the marks of the "devotional revolution," and he allowed himself a pointed hostility to the church throughout his life.

Initially tolerant, the church began repressing Irish music in O'Neill's day and into the 1930s. Peter Hagerty the piper, for example, played his regular "patrons" as well as "weddings, christenings and other festivities," until, O'Neill wrote, "a new parish priest, unlike his predecessor . . . forbade 'Patrons' and dances of all kinds in the parish." O'Neill observed that the old priest "wore velvet knee breeches, preached in both Irish and English, lived in peace and harmony with his flock, and died wealthy . . . [H]e encouraged rather than interfered with the time-honored customs of the people." The new priest "was of a different type altogether. Austere and puritanical, his coming was like the blight of a heavy frost on a blooming garden. All forms of popular pastimes were ordered discontinued . . . and the poor, afflicted piper, with his avocation gone, had no alternative but the shelter and starvation of the poorhouse."[41] Histories of Irish music offer many examples of "musical priests," but many more of the censorious local padre flailing at dancers with a blackthorn stick, along with stories of dancers posting a lookout for the grim priest and sounding the alarm when he hove in view.[42]

## The Distinctiveness of Irish Music

Why did the church dislike Irish music? The church had an implicit understanding with England: influence in the National Schools and the right to worship openly in exchange for teaching in English and ignoring Irish history and tradition. The music itself may have offended propriety. The tunes O'Neill loved were lively and meant to get people's feet moving. The dances he recalled typically involved just one instrument, a set of pipes or a fiddle, and depended on the musician's capacity to generate a sense of what O'Neill called "swing." They danced mostly to jigs, usually in 3/4 time, and reels, in 4/4 time, but sometimes added hornpipes or other dances. Dancing involved "battering" the floor with rhythmic steps, often in an athletic way—who could dance the fastest or the longest? The tunes most commonly had an A section, played twice, and a B section, played twice: this pattern might repeat for as long as enthusiasm lasted, or the musicians might introduce a new tune without stopping. Within this pattern both dancers and musicians would improvise, offering a sense of surprise and challenging the dancers to vary their moves. O'Neill also described "cake dances" in which dancers competed for the prize of a cake. Challenge dances could easily devolve into fighting.[43]

Many of the tunes O'Neill heard were "modal": they did not have a distinct key signature. Listeners hear this most commonly as a combination of happiness and sadness in the same tune, like foods simultaneously bitter and sweet. One of O'Neill's friends in the priesthood, James Fielding, could barely restrain himself as he described this combination: the "irresistible vigor and mighty on-rush" of an Irish reel, expressing "the hurry of flight, the majesty of battle strife, the languishment of retreat, the sweep of a rallying charge with a laugh at fate," yet also expressing "the complaining magic of a minor tone like the whisper of a far-away sorrow." Examples of this modal quality appear in the website supplementing this book, *thebeatcop.com.*[44]

Irish dance music also featured ambiguous pitches, partly because of the physics of the pipes and flutes commonly played. Irish musician Tes Slominski refers, for example, to the Irish "C Supernatural," a note somewhere between concert C and concert C#. The note's ambiguous pitch has nothing to do with lack of skill but rather forms part of the general character of Irish music. Indeterminacy with pitch, or a degree of plasticity with pitch, features in many folk music traditions, and like blues musicians in the US, Irish players would often deliberately "slide" up to a given note. The combination of modality and indeterminate, flexible pitch lends the music a quality often described as wild or yearning: not quite fixed in place. A priest trained on the continent in the 1840s, with a formal music background, might love this music or might equally hear it as disturbingly unorthodox, primitive, or uncivilized.[45]

Frederick Douglass, in fact, heard a similarity between Irish music and the music of slaves. Douglass spent six months in Ireland in 1846–47 to escape slave catchers and to encourage Irish support for the abolition of slavery. Both the Irish and the slaves, he said, expressed their anguish in song. Among slaves, Douglass wrote, "in the most boisterous outbursts of rapturous sentiment, there was ever a tinge of deep melancholy." "I have never heard any songs like those anywhere since I left slavery," he continued, "except when in Ireland. There I heard the same wailing notes, and was much affected by them."[46]

In Ireland Douglass saw white people who in many ways lived as badly as slaves, kept in poverty and ignorance, inured to a class system that demanded subordination and enforced it with violence. "I see much here to remind me of my former condition," he wrote, recalling a meeting of more than 5,000 people he had attended, insisting "that these people lacked only a black skin and wooly hair, to complete their likeness to the plantation negro." Douglass returned to the US with a new sense of the relationship between race and oppression. Slaveowners, he wrote, "care no more about Irishmen, or the wrongs of Irishmen, than they care about the whipped, gagged, and thumb-screwed slave. They would as willingly sell on the auction-block an Irishmen, if it were popular to do so, as an African."[47]

But it was not popular to do so; in fact, it was illegal, and the similarity between slaves and the Irish that Douglass saw rapidly vanished as Irish immigrants grasped the advantages of rising by stepping on someone lower. For the most part, Irish Americans, led partly by the Catholic Church, denounced abolition and the very idea of free black people, and if they remembered the famine as a profound injustice committed against them, they rarely transferred that sense of injustice to the plight of others.[48]

But just as Americans often interpreted African American music making as some sort of natural or genetic skill, visitors to Ireland often interpreted Irish music not as a style people grew up learning but as some sort of genetic product of the "Irish race." O'Neill himself often argued that a specifically "Irish soul" made Irish music: "If there ever was a people gifted with a musical soul and sensibility in a higher degree than another," O'Neill asserted, "the Gaedhil of Ancient Erinn were that people." Douglass heard the music of shared abjection; O'Neill imagined the specifically Gaelic soul.[49]

Claims about the natural, authentic, musical nature of Irish people might mark them as a lesser race, and in this context, critics often treated the reputed Irish talent for music as a genetic incapacity for rationality and self-discipline. The English critic Mathew Arnold allowed that "all that emotion alone can do in music the Celt has done; the very soul of emotion breathes in the Scotch and Irish airs"; but with "what has the Celt, so eager for emotion that he has not patience for science," done in music compared with "the less emotional German?" German music had self-discipline and order and rigor. But Arnold characterized "the Celt" as sentimental and volatile, as loving "bright colors, company, and pleasure. . . . Always ready to react against the despotism of fact." Arnold's Celts lacked the capacity for politics, and "if his rebellion against fact has thus lamed the Celt" in music making, Arnold continued, "how much more must it have lamed him in the world of business and politics! The skillful and resolute appliance of means to ends which is needed both to make progress in material civilisation, and also to form

Figure 5  Fair day in Bantry, undated photo (before 1900). Image courtesy of the National Library of Ireland. The docks and bay are out of frame to the left. The school O'Neill attended is the one-story dark stone building near center left, down the hill from the church and to the right of the white two-story building and the smoke from the locomotive. O'Neill told Alfred Graves "No. 2 ['Fare You Well']" was memorized from the singing of a man who kept a stall at the end of our schoolhouse at Bantry. A mission was in progress and he sold wares common to such occasions."

powerful states, is just what the Celt has least turn for." Ironically, at the very moment Arnold described the genetic shortcomings of the authentic Celt, reformers bemoaned the growing dominance of the Irish in American urban politics. O'Neill himself navigated an immensely complex political structure in Chicago *and* systematized Irish dance music.[50]

## Leaving Home

O'Neill in 1865 was a precocious, smart, restless teen at odds with his ambitious but not especially close family. As the youngest child, Francis had no hope of inheriting the family leases and little to look forward to except laboring for one of his brothers. But he played the flute and excelled at school, where he loved art: "drawing and sketching engrossed every available moment." Though no sketches or drawings by O'Neill survive, he believed he had talent. At one point the parish priest of Bantry came across O'Neill sketching the newly built Convent of Mercy in Bantry town. Impressed, Canon Sheehan offered to send Francis to the School of Design in Cork City. If he drew as well as he says, O'Neill would likely have thrived at the Cork School of Design, which aimed specifically to find and educate boys like O'Neill in the fine and industrial arts.[51]

"His proposition," O'Neill wrote with a tinge of bitterness, roughly fifty years later, "met with no favor at home. Crops and cattle, not art, were their perennial problem." When his family rejected the idea of art school, he wrote, "with no other outlet in view for my goading ambition, I decided to challenge the fates in a wider field of endeavor." He "formulated an excuse" to leave home and headed off to find work as a teacher on the "school ships" the British Navy had anchored at Queenstown [now Cobh] on Cork's southeastern coast. "With one pound of my own salary in my pocket," he related, in 1865 "I bravely set out on top of the mail coach." He was seventeen years old.[52]

O'Neill did not speak of fond farewells, or a mother's tears, or a last look at the beloved home. If he experienced any of those things, he kept them to himself. Neither did he comment on whether he promised to write, his sisters packed food for his trip, his father gave him some money, or his schoolmates waved from the road. Throughout his life he guarded his private feelings closely, and his memoirs give little insight into his emotions. He never mentioned his father's death in 1867. O'Neill went back to Ireland briefly, in 1906, but said nothing publicly about seeing family. Still, after 1906 he paid for a memorial to his parents in the local cemetery, placing his own name first, prominently above theirs. The memorial amounted to a jab at his older brother John, who inherited the farm O'Neill had to leave.[53]

On arriving in Cork, O'Neill wrote, he "presented his credentials" as a teacher to a "gold braided" British officer, who responded that he had no authority to hire teachers, who were in any case rarely hired. O'Neill quickly recalibrated his ambitions and asked about shipping as an apprentice seaman; alas, "the maximum age for the enlistment of seamen in peacetime was sixteen years," making O'Neill too old by a few months. "Depressed but not defeated," he made his way to the

Butter Market in Cork, "to which our farm firkens were consigned." The Butter Market was a major international shipping and distribution point for Irish dairy products. Presumably someone there knew his family. But "the trip was fruitless and a waste of time."[54]

His next step, he said, took him to see the bishop of Cork, William Delany, at his residence, five miles out of town. It seems odd that a young farm boy unable to find a job at the Butter Market could simply walk to the bishop's door and gain entry, but "after looking over my credentials, the kindly prelate offered me a position as a teacher with the Christian Brothers, at whose school I was to meet him later that day." The Christian Brothers, a religious community within the Catholic Church, by then operated an alternative set of explicitly Catholic schools. Brothers took religious vows but typically did not enter the priesthood. "This was by no means the future I had hoped for," O'Neill continued, "but under the circumstances it was acceptable." "Weary and footsore," he walked back to Cork and then to the Christian Brothers school, only to find that "His Grace had been there but had gone again. And so I missed the vocation of a Christian Brother by fifteen minutes."[55]

Very little about this story makes any sense at all, and he gave multiple differing versions in his books and in interviews. O'Neill's inability to tell it straight speaks to his own unwillingness to confront the darker necessities of Irish life. O'Neill's granddaughter, Mary Wade, likely heard something closer to the truth. "He was all set to go to a seminary," she related, "and become a priest or brother when he came to a fork in the road and took the wrong turn. He was afraid to go back home then and continued on to his life of adventure." The O'Neill family, seeing his academic ability and having no clear economic place for him, arranged to send him to the seminary. Many Catholic families took great pride in having a priest in the family—the author's grandmother never stopped trying to convince one of her nine grandsons to take the vows—and all eyes in the O'Neill house would have turned to the most junior son, bookish and scholarly and not in line to inherit land. Francis most likely simply chose not to go and later told a clumsy story of thwarted ambition and frustrated promise.[56]

We have only O'Neill's word on any of these specific events, written by an elderly, successful, well-esteemed US citizen from a distance of fifty years. It seems safe to conclude his family wanted him to join the clergy; it seems equally clear that he wanted no part of it but, even fifty years later, either did not understand why himself or was unwilling to openly say why. Acknowledging the limited opportunities for a boy like him in Ireland meant condemning colonialism directly: but condemning colonialism meant criticizing himself and the English education he took so much pride in.

O'Neill had an exact contemporary who also wrote a memoir, a schoolmate whose path diverged in enlightening ways. Patrick O'Brien also attended the National School at Dromore and also emigrated at seventeen. He also danced to the music of Peter Hagerty, later writing a nostalgic poem about "Dear Old Collomane" and the crossroads dance. "The boys and girls would often go to hear the Piper Bawn . . . To hear old Peter play the pipes—he gave us many a tune." But while Francis remembered mostly instrumental dance tunes, O'Brien remembered hearing explicitly political songs like "The Rising of the Moon," with multiple lyrics about the United Irishmen rebellion of 1798, and "The Croppy Boy," yet another song about the 1798 rising. And while Francis ignored broadsheets and commercial ballads, O'Brien remembered the lyrics to a song called "The Little Shamrock Green," which circulated as a cheaply printed song sheet with another song called "The Rakish Young Fellow." The song urged:

> Oh Irishmen remember what your father's did of old.
> Oh Irishmen remember talks we often had been told.
> How Danish thieves and English curs.
> Through every rage and spleen.
> Thought to run down old Ireland.
> And the Irish Shamrock green.

So we can assume the crossroads dances included not just ancient folk melodies rooted in "the Irish soul" but also political ballads and commercial songs.[57]

English oppression made O'Brien leave. "When a boy of seventeen I was forced to leave Ireland," he wrote, "owing to the despotic and tyrannical English laws." "England has murdered and plundered the Irish people for the past seven centuries," he thundered:

> She has robbed them of their industries and their language; she has leveled once happy homes to the ground by her merciless crowbar brigades; she has thrown aged fathers and gray-haired, weeping mothers out on the wayside with nothing but the blue sky of heaven to shelter them . . . the Irish people are justified in resorting to every means to overthrow English misrule.

O'Brien, a man of unrestrained enthusiasm for his own exploits, made his way to the US and worked for a time in mining camps in the West, where he gained, or gave himself, the nickname "Rocky Mountain" O'Brien. In 1870 he played a role in the ludicrously heroic, or heroically ludicrous, second Fenian invasion of Canada, where in his telling he almost single handedly captured the tiny hamlet of Pigeon Hill, just over the Vermont line. Readers surprised to learn of a *first* Fenian invasion of Canada will be even more surprised to learn of a third, fourth, and fifth Irish American invasion of Canada in chapter 3.[58]

"Rocky Mountain" saw Irish independence as part of an international rebellion against English tyranny. "England . . . blew the Sepoys from the mouths of cannon in India. She destroyed the homes of the gallant Boers who fought for the same God-given rights that George Washington and his countrymen fought for almost two centuries ago. . . . She dynamited the poor Zulus in South Africa when they sought refuge in their caves." Many Irish immigrants served in the US Civil War; O'Brien similarly praised his Fenian compatriots "who fought beneath the Stars and Stripes, the colored folk to free." If O'Neill imagined Irish music as an exclusive possession of Irish people, the "Irish soul," O'Brien situated the Irish struggle in a global movement and demanded that Irish Americans invest themselves in it.[59]

O'Brien further scorned "the St. Patrick's Day Irishman," who loves to parade and "wears a green sash over his shoulders at the head of the procession, and looks at each corner of the street as the procession passes to see who is admiring him. Then he is never heard of for twelve months more." He deplored "the gentleman farmer, who, I am sorry to state, the more he prospers the more loyal he becomes to the British Constitution." The Irish might have called such a man a *shoneen*, or perhaps or a *gombeen* man: someone whose interests focus too closely on the bottom line and the English avenues of power and commerce and not enough on the welfare of his own people. O'Brien denounced them as well.

Those words and spirit might apply to Francis O'Neill's family, but on a trip back to his birthplace O'Brien took care to praise O'Neill as a paragon of Irish success in America. He told his Irish audience about "Frank O'Neill, Chief of Police in Chicago, who in that little schoolhouse learned his A, B, C's side by side with himself. He holds one of the loftiest positions that Irishmen in America might claim," and "burglars and desperados have a 'holy horror' of Frank O'Neill, of Tralybawn." O'Brien shifted easily from champion of the oppressed to enthusiast of law and order.[60]

Both men's stories show us the central problem of Ireland after the famine: as much as O'Neill coated it in nostalgia and as much as he adapted himself to the regime of English colonial rule, Ireland offered few opportunities for an ambitious young person like himself. Wage work on the farm or the Christian Brothers—O'Neill could find nothing else. Indeed, despite their prosperity, at least half of the O'Neill children moved to the US; O'Brien's father and two sisters also emigrated. Irishmen and -women steadily left the island during the next one hundred years, heading mostly to America. In Cormac Ó Gráda's opinion, the famine's greatest injury to Ireland came less from the horrible death toll than from the way it accelerated emigration. In a cascading effect, every relative or neighbor who settled in the US made it easier for someone else to leave.[61]

"When Ireland was a land of music and song, and fireside story," O'Neill wrote, "life, seasoned with national and rational pastimes and pleasures, was more enjoyable and conducive to contented nationhood than in the first decade of the twentieth century, although the savings banks tell a tale of enhanced prosperity." O'Neill's accounts of the "land of music and song" refer, we should remember, to a time a decade after the famine had wiped out close to half his county's population, when the English compelled deference, and religious bigotry kept Catholics out of many jobs and professions. The "land of music and song" was also the land of poverty and unmarked mass famine graves, covered with Timothy grass.[62]

The political and economic system he recalled, in which musicians had to go from house to house seeking patrons, was a specific artifact of both British colonial rule and the poverty and colonial status of Irish people. The US, for example, had no tradition of itinerant fiddlers boarding with patrons, except in the African American community. O'Neill soaked his recollections in a nostalgia that reduced the famine's devastation, and the effects of colonial occupation, to pleasant melancholy. "Who will say that life was less worth living then?" O'Neill asked. The tens of thousands of people who left Ireland between 1848 and 1920 might have said exactly that: life in Ireland was less worth living, and so off they sailed.[63]

Failing to find a job, O'Neill said he "resolved a determination to get away from Ireland, anywhere, by any means, and as soon as possible." "Friendless, penniless," he wandered to the docks and met Captain Watson, of the English barque *Anne*, headed for Sunderland in England. The "humane Captain" took O'Neill on as a cabin boy for wages of three shillings for the entire voyage (that is, for about a week's worth of labor). Except in memory, he would not return to Ireland for forty years.[64]

# 2

# Out on the Ocean
## O'Neill's Life at Sea, in Port, and in the Sierra

The lure of the sea! O'Neill chose the job of cabin boy, for three shillings pay per voyage, over taking religious orders or becoming a teacher. Where did he get his desire to go to sea? "His love of the ocean waves, of which he knew only the beautiful bay of his native place, could not be denied," claimed the *Irish Independent* on little or no evidence. Bantry, where he went to school, has an excellent small harbor at the end of a long narrow bay, but the open sea lies about 10 miles away. From the dock in Bantry, nearby Whiddy Island blocks most of the view to the ocean waves. If you climbed the highest hill to the west of the O'Neill home, you might see the ocean on a clear day, but you would be in Ireland, and clear days would be scarce. O'Neill never mentions looking longingly out to sea, but he must have felt these things because he sometimes mentions having a sense of adventure and from what he wrote, he sailed away in haste, apparently without a word to his family, making an abrupt and decisive break. Why did he choose a sailor's life instead of the more common path of emigration to England or America?[1]

By 1865, when O'Neill turned seventeen and boarded the barque *Anne*, books about life at sea were common. O'Neill described himself as a book lover. In 1916 he sent a nephew in Ireland a book called *Science for All*, a general encyclopedia, telling the boy "what a joy it would have been to me in earlier years, a treasure house of general knowledge." Accounts of O'Neill in Chicago invariably call him a well-educated and scholarly man and praise his large library, which he later donated to Notre Dame. He was a reader: as a child subject of the queen, a precocious student at the National School in Bantry, O'Neill very likely read Robert Southey's widely popular *Life of Nelson*, about the naval hero who defeated the French at the Battle of Trafalgar in 1805. Southey's hagiography treated the battle as a triumph of English nationalism, with the aim of presenting brave, bold Horatio Nelson as "a model for future seamen." If he read Southey, we have no way of knowing whether young O'Neill cheered the English hero or lamented the French defeat, but he would have thrilled to the gallant tales of adventure on the water.

He would also have encountered Daniel Defoe's *Robinson Crusoe*, with its story of escape from civilization. Maria Edgeworth, in her *Essays on Professional Education*, advised parents that *Robinson Crusoe* "has sent many a youth to sea" and suggested parents who plan a naval career for their children should have a copy on hand. O'Neill would recall his time shipwrecked in the South Pacific as a "Robinson Crusoe life."[2]

## The Literature of the Sailor's Life

By the time O'Neill entered school, a new genre of sea tale had appeared in Anglo-American literature, focusing on the ordinary sailor. Richard Henry Dana's memoir *Two Years before the Mast*, published in London and the US in 1840, described a young man from an affluent Boston family who left Harvard College, and the comforts of home and society, to ship as a common seaman. A sailor's life offered dreary and dangerous physical work, harsh weather, cramped conditions, poor food, and strict discipline, but it also offered exotic travel, adventure, and most of all exposure to very different kinds of people.[3]

Did O'Neill read *Two Years before the Mast*? We have no evidence, but three British publishers brought out editions in 1841: Liverpool sailors reportedly bought 2,000 copies in one day. "Dana was showered with letters of praise from English authors," including Charles Dickens, who sought to meet Dana when he visited America. The book remained popular for generations in both Britain and the US. Recall that 1852, the year before the Crimean War, more than 1,300 men and boys from Cork had joined the British Navy. In O'Neill's youth some of them would have returned with tales of exotic ports. O'Neill had set out from home, he wrote, to become a teacher on British Navy ships. We can assume that between education in the National School, an appetite for books, and the experiences of Cork neighbors who joined the navy, he had acquired a romantic notion of the life of a sailor and a set of ways to understand it because his sparse narrative of his time at sea returns to some of the same themes he would have found in books.[4]

Sea tales usually included an element of "passing down," temporarily abandoning the upper class for the lower. Dana had gone to Harvard; Herman Melville, whose tales of adventure at sea made him an international celebrity in the 1840s, came from a distinguished family but boasted "a whale ship was my Yale college and my Harvard." "We must come down from our heights," Dana insisted, "and leave our straight paths for the by-ways and low places of life, if we would learn truths by strong contrasts; and in hovels, in forecastles, and among our own outcasts in foreign lands, see what has been wrought among our fellow-creatures by accident, hardship, or vice." O'Neill, born to relative privilege in a strong farmer family, educated beyond the norm, did exactly that: he left the "straight path" to the priesthood for a life of hard use and hard work as a common sailor.[5]

Through the story of the young man "passing down," the sea literature of O'Neill's day explored two main themes: the multiculturalism of life on ship and the captain's boundless and possibly dangerous authority. At sea a crew drawn from many nations sailed, self-contained, from place to place under one man's rule. The ship itself presented a microcosm of nation or empire. At one point, on the California coast, Dana saw among his fellow sailors

> two Englishmen, three Yankees, two Scotchmen, two Welshmen, one Irishman, three Frenchmen . . . one Dutchman, one Austrian, two or three Spaniards . . . half a dozen Spanish–Americans and half-breeds, two native Indians from Chili and the Island of Chile, one negro, one mulatto, about twenty Italians . . . Sandwich–

Islanders, one Tahitian, and one Kanaka from the Marquesas Islands.

But Dana also described how the captain of his ship brutally flogged a sailor "because I like to do it!—It suits me!" "Don't call on Jesus Christ," shouts the enraged captain; "he can't help you. Call on Frank Thompson! He's the man! He can help you! Jesus Christ can't help you now!" The democracy of the forecastle, where common sailors of all nations mingled, contrasted with the captain's cruel, profane, and unchecked power.[6]

O'Neill referred to his days as a sailor frequently. He lived on the California coast and visited Egypt, Russia, Japan, Mexico, and Hawaii among other places. He experienced arbitrary and cruel authority. His life as a sailor matters not just because he understood it through things he read as a literate subject of the queen, and not just because the ship offered a microcosm of the nation or empire: Captain O'Neill himself would later command men drawn from Chicago's multiethnic, multiracial population and would have to consider how to balance ethnic diversity against the necessity of discipline and order.

O'Neill, cabin boy, left Ireland on *Anne* and sailed to Sunderland, securing a bed in a sailor's lodging house. He quickly found his three shillings gone. "I was obliged to sell, for sixpence, my cherished flute, and later, one by one, my precious books, in order to live."

O'Neill did not tell us that when he left his home in Tralibane, on top of the mail coach, he carried a stack of books and a flute. The books were precious, but not so precious that he bothered to give their titles. He describes himself surrendering cherished and precious things from his old life, but in terse prose he nearly always holds his inner life apart. He had a dry and ironic sense of humor in his memoirs, bordering on cynical, but presented himself as an observer of experience, not a "joiner." This sense of "apartness" appears throughout his published writing. It might have come from his childhood, the youngest son of a prosperous family who could never inherit that family's farm, or it might have come from being both Irish and educated by the English. Or it might have come from the experiences of a policeman, always reporting and observing, or as chief: the man in charge cannot be the thing he is in charge of; he must stand apart from it.

But we might today classify O'Neill as "on the spectrum" of autism, gifted in an eccentric way but hindered in social and emotional life. He had an obsessive and even uncanny memory for music, but his pleasure came less from playing music than from collecting, ordering, and classifying it. He was emotionally obtuse: he never tells us whether he wrote to his family, whether he left them a letter before he sailed from Ireland, or whether he sent them letters from distant ports; he offers no sense that their feelings, or his, mattered at all. He never writes about loneliness or missing home. At the same time, he rarely boasts or promotes his own abilities or accomplishments in more than the slightest degree, and when he does it generally concerns his education.

We can only imagine the combination of anxiety and exhilaration a seventeen-year-old must have felt because his terse style sheds little light. He recognized and valued acts of kindness, but he saw them more as transactional, the exchange of favors, rather than as expressions of a generous heart. He had an unnecessarily keen eye for "ingratitude" in others. Sailors loved their grog; O'Neill did not drink. Sailors loved a pipe of tobacco; O'Neill did not smoke or play cards or throw dice; if he did any womanizing in port, he says nothing about it. He had trouble "connecting."

But soon he signed as an apprentice seaman on a brig, *Jane Duncan*, headed for Alexandria, Egypt. He would stay with *Jane Duncan* for a year. He remembered seeing Portugal and the rock of Gibraltar and observing seabirds stopping on the ship to rest. But he described little of the work at sea. When the ship, loaded with coal, reached Alexandria in January 1866, O'Neill rowed the captain back and forth to shore and watched the "Mohammedans" unload the ship's cargo and stop at intervals to face Mecca and pray. As ballast, *Jane Duncan* used rubble from what O'Neill described as "an ancient necropolis" west of the city. On leaving port the ship's ballast contained "sand, gravel, fragments of pottery, human bones, skulls, even jaws with teeth still in their sockets." The necropolis "had been commercialized," O'Neill recalled, and when the ship continued her voyage to Odessa on the Black Sea, the sailors simply dumped the ballast to make room for their new cargo of flaxseed. "What Egyptian mother," he pondered, "crooning her babies to sleep, could have imagined that a thousand or more years later their bones would find a final resting place at the bottom of the Black Sea?" He expressed empathy for those long dead mothers but, remarkably, none at all for his own.[7]

*Jane Duncan*, with its cargo of flaxseed and one overeducated young Irishman, sailed back to England, docking at Hull where they paid off all the crew but the first mate and O'Neill, still legally bound to the ship. Here O'Neill had a bad accident when the captain, distracted, steered the ship into a stone wharf, pitching O'Neill headfirst over the side. He woke up in a marine hospital with a fractured skull, "the scars of which are still quite distinct on my forehead to this day." Although still weak from his injury, he signed on for a second voyage to the Black Sea in *Jane Duncan*, "with the assurance that I would not be required to do any work until fully recovered. I soon found out that the ship owner's promise meant nothing to the new crew."

Life at sea had many dangers, and crew safety ranked low in the captain's list of concerns. Climbing the rigging in a cold gale, a sailor could count only on the strength of his own grip. Dana argues that sailors cultivated a cavalier attitude about injuries and brushes with death, shrugging them off and paying little attention, not out of indifference to suffering but out of an awareness of danger's immanence. O'Neill's relative silence about his feelings might reflect the sailor's culture or the emotional hardening demanded of the police. Or perhaps his relatively privileged upbringing set him apart. But again we get a sense of apartness. The crew resented his idleness and forgot all about him during the gale. He "would have fared badly indeed" had not one sailor shared some food with him.[8]

Upon the return to England, docking at Bowling Green in Scotland, the owners paid off all the crew except the first mate, O'Neill, and another apprentice, a Belgian named Fred. When they learned that the ship had been sold, they elected to abscond. Bound by the terms of the contract to *Jane Duncan*, they had to sneak away under cover of darkness, wearing or carrying all the clothes they owned. Fugitives from the law, they made their way via a river steamer to Glasgow and then to Liverpool.[9]

Liverpool had grown rich first on the slave trade and then the international cotton trade. The Irish famine sent emigrants to Liverpool by the hundreds of thousands, and by 1851 about one-quarter of the city's population had been born in Ireland. Irish emigrants to America typically traveled first to Liverpool and then boarded a larger ship for the transatlantic voyage.[10]

Within a day of their arrival in Liverpool, Fred found a place on a full-rigged China clipper heading to East Asia. "Oh how I envied the Belgian's luck!" O'Neill wrote, in a rare display of emotion: "a voyage to China or the East Indies was an ambition cherished for many a day." Undoubtedly he got that ambition from the literature of the sea. Shortly after Fred left, O'Neill found a position as an assistant steward on a different clipper, *Emerald Isle*, bound for America.[11]

Built in Bath, Maine, *Emerald Isle* was a large and fast ship, 215 feet long, with three decks, "especially constructed for the transatlantic emigrant trade." So many Irish emigrated that entrepreneurs built ships specifically to carry them. *Emerald Isle* launched in 1857, represented the best of the last days of sail power, and in advertising boasted that it had made the trip from New York to Liverpool in "the same time as the steamer *America*." A "sailing card" printed to advertise the ship featured a man in armor standing on an improbably small rock in the sea. He waves the green flag bearing the harp of Erin, holds a sword, and poses at an angle matching the sharply raked masts of the ship behind him. The card makes it clear that *Emerald Isle* sought Irish passengers, and with its tone of nationalist martial defiance, the image offered the emigrant a consoling vision: he or she was not abandoning home or being forced away by older siblings, but rather continuing a people's epic global movement.[12]

Perhaps reflecting similar feelings, O'Neill declared, "I was paid for coming to America, and therefore not an emigrant." He took pains to make this clear: he left Ireland out of a sense of adventure, not necessity; he arrived as a paid worker, not a supplicant for admission. But his pay as a worker was low, even if conditions may

Figure 6 O'Neill came to America as an assistant steward on *Emerald Isle*. Passenger ships issued "sailing cards" to lure passengers and commemorate the voyage. The owners of *Emerald Isle*, in this instance heading from New York to San Francisco, clearly wanted to lure Irish passengers: the card suggested that travelers see themselves as explorers, soldiers, engaged in the historic movement of the Irish people rather than as people fleeing poverty and limited opportunity. *Emerald Isle* (Clipper), Sailing Ship Card Collection, MSS 470, box 3, folder 47. Courtesy of Phillips Library, Peabody Essex Museum, Rowley, MA.

have improved. "My duty was the distribution of provisions to the passengers," assistant steward O'Neill wrote: he was more or less a salt water waiter.

Chief stewards on big American clippers tended to be African American and to have a close relationship with the captain, who would often bring a favored steward with him from ship to ship. The job paid well, and the chief steward enjoyed a much higher status than the common sailor. Young boys, O'Neill's age or younger, more often served as assistant stewards. Though O'Neill does not say, he might have worked with, and for, African Americans for the first time on the *Emerald Isle*. English rule consigned the Catholic Irish to second-class status, but "flying under the American flag" would show him the more complicated place the Irish occupied in America.[13]

During the five-week trip in 1866 he met a young Irishwoman, Anna Rogers, traveling with her mother and father, her sister Julia, and a brother, John. Whether he served them in a cabin or came across them in other moments, the Rogers family seemed to approve of the well-spoken assistant steward. Anna, a year younger than Francis, was impressed enough that she wrote to him after the ship landed in New York. The Rogers family seems to have continued its travels to Bloomington, Illinois, although at least some of the family lived in Brooklyn. In 1870 Francis and Anna would marry. O'Neill says little of the voyage, only that "I formed acquaintances on that trip that I have been matrimonially associated with for more than half a century." O'Neill's arch and oblique style here is fairly typical of his memoirs: when he comes to something personal, he tacks away from it, revealing little.[14]

The Rogers family disembarked on August 6, 1866, part of a massive immigration into New York that year. About 300,000 immigrants had arrived in New York in 1866 alone, estimated the *New York Times* in late December, mostly from Germany and Ireland. "Let them all come," the *Times* wrote. "We have plenty of room for them and millions more. The producing power of this country is largely increased by emigration, and the tax bearing strength of the people considerably advanced." In 1860 one in four residents of Manhattan had been born in Ireland; by 1870 Manhattan and Brooklyn had almost 250,000 Irish-born people. The *Times* urged "this great flood of people" not to stay in New York but to "bend your steps at once to the West." The Rogers family, at least some of them, did exactly that, and so would O'Neill. Irish immigrants in particular did better in western cities, which lacked the long-entrenched elites and more stratified social structures of the East Coast.[15]

But in the meantime—without his coat, O'Neill wrote, because someone had stolen it—a shipmate, John Brennan, directed him to a sailor's boardinghouse on 66 Oliver Street in Manhattan, run by a Dane who "had an Irish wife and who had a good name," which it would later turn out she did not deserve.

The boardinghouse system, O'Neill wrote, exploited seamen. Sailors looking for their next berth stayed in a known sailor's boardinghouse because ships looking for crew went to those places to recruit. O'Neill had already twice found berths simply because a ship's mate walked into the boardinghouse. While the sailor's money lasts, O'Neill wrote, the "boarding boss" pays him no attention, but once his money runs out the boardinghouse advances him credit on the promise of future wages from his next voyage. At that point the house manager exerts him- or herself to find the sailor a ship. The voyage contracted, said O'Neill, the boardinghouse manager then directs the sailor to an outfitter, who supplies the goods needed for the voyage, again using the credit of the boardinghouse. When the sailor leaves port, the boardinghouse manager goes to the shipping office and collects the sailor's advanced wages, in return for having supplied a sailor.

"You are completely plucked before going on ship," O'Neill wrote, "but what is the cure?" The ship needs a ready supply of sailors and does not want them in a position to change their minds if they get a better offer. "And if paid advance money," the sailor "would probably get drunk and leave town." O'Neill went into significant detail about this system, while saying almost nothing about his feelings when he met his future wife of fifty years, with whom he had ten children. He expressed a degree of both sympathy and contempt for his fellow sailors: the system represents "enforced slavery" from which the sailor "seldom escapes," but the solutions then being advanced by sailors—unionization and the regularization of labor markets—never appear to enter into his thinking, even though in that very year a "soldier's and sailor's union" formed in New York, with incorporated status in Washington, DC. Strikes would occupy a great deal of O'Neill's time on the Chicago police force, but here in memory he stresses that the sailor is just likely to get drunk: defects of character, not political economy, explain the exploitation. Aside from this mention of the boardinghouse, O'Neill's memoir pays relatively little attention to either the specific work life or the culture of his fellow sailors, and we have to reconstruct that world from other sources.[16]

For example, though he spent time in many ports, O'Neill almost never described the music of sailors or the waterfront, even though the musical lives of sailors were exceedingly rich. He passed over it for a reason, just as he passed over the class and political tensions of life in Ireland.

## The Creole World of the Sailor

Sailors typically knew a deep and varied combination of work songs, hornpipes for dancing, ballads, jigs, reels, tragic narratives, and songs of triumph. Merchant sailors chanted as they worked: in *Two Years before the Mast*, Dana described how sailors, when heaving at a windlass, "in order that they may heave together, always have one to sing out, which is done in high and long-drawn notes, varying with the motion of the windlass. This requires a clear voice, strong lungs, and much practice, to be done well." Dana remembered one man, a Hawaiian named Mahanna: "this fellow had a very peculiar, wild sort of note, breaking occasionally into a falsetto. The sailors thought that it was too high, and not enough of the boatswain hoarseness about it; but to me it had a great charm." The music of the sea was a hybrid music: Mahanna had adapted the work chant to his own musical styles; the sailors commented on its musicality as they might comment on a theatrical performance.[17]

Singing played a major role in the leisure time of sailors as well. In San Diego harbor Dana visited another boat. "Among her crew were two English man-of-war's-men, so that, of course, we soon had music." They two men sang, and what Dana called a remarkably musical crew joined in.

> They had many of the latest sailor songs, which had not yet got about among our merchantmen, and which they were very choice of. . . . Battle-songs, drinking-songs, boat-songs, love-songs, and everything else . . . and I was glad to find that "All in the Downs," "Poor Tom Bowline," "The Bay of Biscay," "List, ye Landsmen!" and other classical songs of the sea, still held their places. In addition to these, they had picked up at the theatres and other places a few songs of a little more genteel cast, which they were very proud of.

So the sailors sang "classical songs of the sea" but also new songs; novel, but still recognizable as "sea songs." They also had more genteel songs picked up in theaters and shore points: they had songs for every range of human experience. In *White Jacket* Melville recalled the singing of "jolly Africans, thus making gleeful their toil by their . . . remarkable St. Domingo melodies," and also that when freed from strict discipline, the sailors danced "Hornpipes, fandangoes, Donnybrook-jigs, reels, and quadrilles," mixing English, French, Spanish, and Irish styles.[18]

Even on the rustic and then-isolated California coast, a sailor might hear a mix of music. Dana attended a wedding in the Spanish-speaking community, with entertainment composed of singing accompanied with guitars, violins, and handclaps. "The music was lively, and among the tunes we recognized several of our popular airs, which we, without doubt, have taken from the Spanish." Later an Italian boat moored nearby: "the Italians sang a variety of songs— barcarollas, provincial airs, &c.; in several of which I recognized parts of our favorite operas and sentimental songs." In both these cases, songs from Italy and Spain mingled with songs Dana knew from the American theater. Then, as now, music was *portable*: it took up no space in the hold; it traveled well, mixed easily, and largely ignored national boundaries; it cheerfully mixed the "folk" and the commercial, the traditional and the novel, the formal and the casual, which explains why O'Neill never mentioned it.[19]

O'Neill does say that "in my sailing days an acquisitive ear picked up not a few foreign airs and dance tunes," but he omitted these kinds of mixed songs in his memoir, just as he omitted them from accounts of his childhood in Ireland. Irish sailors, both military and commercial, would have brought these songs back home with them: Irish farmers would have heard them in the pubs and wharves of port cities like Cork, where the O'Neills marketed their butter and cattle. He similarly ignored the dance styles of sailors and how they blended traditions he knew from Ireland with the traditions of other nations and peoples.[20]

Sailors danced and sang in styles that reflected their diversity. Dana described a "Cape Cod Boy" who could "dance the true fisherman's jig, barefooted, knocking with his heels, and slapping the decks with his bare feet, in time with the music." But O'Neill would have known this sort of dancing not as a "true fisherman's jig" but rather as from Ireland, where dancers performed on surfaces designed to amplify the sounds their feet made. A good dancer in Ireland, with precise, controlled footwork, could allegedly dance on a dinner plate or "dance on eggs without breaking them and hold a pan of water on his head without spilling a drop." Irish dancers brought this style of dancing with them to the US, where they mingled it with other styles.[21]

### Afro-Irish Music and Dance

Many accounts of New York mention the role of dance on the docks and wharves: ethnomusicologist Christopher Smith argues that in Jacksonian America, a "creole synthesis" developed between African and Irish Americans, especially on the city waterfronts and river camps and taverns. African Americans learned English and Irish music styles and inflected them their own way; white Americans then reproduced these "Africanized" versions, often in blackface.[22]

Antebellum dance styles involved challenges and competitions with an emphasis on "battering" the dance floor with heel and toe: "challenge dances" pitted one man or woman against another. "Part theater, part sport, challenge dances were jigging contests got up among and between white and black men, and sometimes women." They might happen in saloons or halls or simply on wharves and docks. Accounts of challenge dances on the Catherine Street wharf in New York or Callowhill Street in Philadelphia suggest they "drew large raucous crowds and were viewed, judged, and bet on like prize-fights." Onlookers describe a formal prize, a basket of eels or catfish, that dancers competed for, with the real action involving heavy betting from the crowd.[23]

O'Neill described dancing for a prize as common in rural Ireland, "at least as far back as the seventeenth century. . . . The cake or prize was displayed on the top of a distaff or pole, in full view of all competitors." A single piper might play, and prizes might go to the best dancers, or "the cake, decked out in field flowers or else encircled with apples, was awarded to the couple whose endurance outlasted their rivals in the dancing circle." Irish traditions merged easily with African traditions of challenge dancing, which often involved endurance as much as speed or skill.[24]

Regarding famous dancers like Henry "Juba" Lane and his challengers, historian Tyler Anbinder writes that "just as boxing promoters purposely pitted Irish versus American, or in later years, white versus black boxers to increase interest in their bouts, theatrical agents organized dance contests between Juba and his 'greatest white contemporary,' Irish-American John Diamond." Lane and Diamond performed a series of public dance challenges in which they imitated and parodied each other: Juba especially would perform dances in the style of blackface performers.[25]

Afro-Irish dance styles included what we now call tap dancing, which drew on Scottish and English forms of jigging and dancing as well. In the antebellum decade the term "jig" might describe any form of lively dance music, and "jig dancing" applied to any form of dancing that stressed rhythmic footwork. The fact that Irish and African Americans often worked the same jobs and shared some of the same subaltern status made the Irish influence more pronounced.

Irish and African dance traditions shared an emphasis on dance as competition and challenge, on complex rhythm tapped out with the feet, and on real-time improvisation. In Ireland the melody articulated the rhythm, and dancers embroidered the strongly syncopated melodic line: they danced to the melody; in African traditions drums moved to the fore, and dancers responded to drumming. Both improvised in response to the music and to other dancers. In the US "these accompaniments were passed from one group to the other. In the 1830s, a travel writer in Buffalo noted that 'the beaten jig time' of the Irish boys dancing on the wharves 'was a rapid patting on the fore thighs,' while a journalist at a Philadelphia market observed New Jersey slaves dancing 'while some darkies whistle.'"[26]

Christopher Smith concludes that "cross-accenting of pulse, as with the sound of hard shoes on a resonating surface, represented a crucial sonic commonality, a shared sensibility, in which African American and Anglo-Celtic dance and music aesthetics could meet." "Negro jig dancers were blacks who adapted Celtic culture to their own purposes; they were also whites, sometimes called 'nigger dancers,' who wore blackface or adopted the black jigging style." Challenge dancing "conveyed a national identity shared by lower-class whites and blacks that later forms of segregation erased," a shared "creole synthesis."[27]

We should not mistake this creole culture of the waterfront for some kind of racial utopia: O'Neill arrived in New York not long after the brutal 1863 draft riots in which Irish American mobs attacked African American neighborhoods and institutions and murdered at least 120 people. John Diamond performed in blackface; Henry Lane could not perform in whiteface. John Diamond could vote; Henry Lane could not. But although "racial fear and hatred permeated antebellum America," historian April Masten agrees that "it did not wholly define everyday life in mixed communities." Irish Americans practiced forms of culture that borrowed from their neighbors and from which their neighbors borrowed in return.[28]

This mixed working-class culture persisted well after the Civil War. Writing of Cincinnati's waterfront in the 1870s, journalist Lafcadio Hearn described the mixture of African and Irish. "A very ordinary

looking woman is Mary—bright mulatto, with strongly Irish features . . . this blood seems to predominate strongly in the veins of half
the mulattoes of Bucktown." Hearn described "negro singers" with
a special interest in Irish music: "they can mimic the Irish accent to
a degree of perfection which an American, Englishman or German
could not hope to acquire." Hearn interviewed "Limber Jim, a very
dark mulatto, named Jim Delaney," who "sang for us in capital style
that famous Irish ditty known as "The hat me fahther wor-re." We
can assume "Limber Jim," who "ran on the river," also danced, and
Hearn insisted "Jim Delaney would certainly make a reputation for
Irish specialties in a minstrel troupe; his mimicry of Irish character is
absolutely perfect." We see again a working-class, "creolized" culture
of parody and interchange.[29]

Opponents of Irish immigration perceived this mixture of black
and Irish even as they criticized the Irish for engaging in antiblack
violence and political agitation. Thomas Nast often depicted Irish
people as brutish and degraded, with ape-like features. At times,
in the decade after the Civil War, his depiction of the Irish blurred
with his depiction of African Americans. Nast provided the illustrations for *Miss Columbia's Public School*, a fiercely anti-Irish and
anti-Catholic fable published in 1871. His Irishmen, disorderly and
violent, often look African American.[30]

In the illustration, the harp and shamrocks on the desk and the
Catholic book titles betray the figure's Irishness, but Nast drew him
with dark skin, "wooly" hair, and the simian features often assigned
to both black and Irish subjects. In the ladder of racial hierarchy, Irish
people occupied the lowest rung of whiteness.

This may explain why O'Neill, writing from memory, made so
little mention of sailors' music or the mixed music and dance of the
wharves and docks: it had a taint of impurity or low status he wanted
to avoid. The National School in Bantry would have inoculated him
with notions of racial hierarchy and made him leery of associating
Irish with African American or blurring the lines between them.

O'Neill spent extensive time in New York between voyages in
the years from 1866 through 1870. By the time he arrived, the hey-
day of challenge dancing had passed, and the dominant forms of

THE KING OF A-SHANTEE.

THE CHAIRMAN OF THE HANGING COMMITTEE.

**Figure 7** Left, Frederick Opper, *Puck,* February 2, 1882, 378. From Prints and Photographs Division, Library of Congress, https://lccn.loc.gov/97512306. The cartoon compares the Irishman in his shanty, or shack, with the Ashanti, a notable African culture. Right, Charles Henry Pullen, *Miss Columbia's Public School* (New York: Francis B. Felt, 1871), 18. Published first in the late 1860s, the strongly anti-Catholic satirical fable described the various ways thuggish Irish boys subverted the ideals of the republic. Irish Americans occupied a somewhat ambiguous position in the scale of racial ideation: white but perhaps precariously white.

commercial entertainment came to revolve around the minstrel shows and the variety stage, more respectable forms of cultural interchange. We can find an excellent example in the career of Protestant Irish American Ned Harrigan and his Catholic Irish partner Tony Hart, born Anthony Cannon to parents from County Mayo. Harrigan and Hart initially performed a minstrel act in blackface, but their most famous contribution came in comic musicals about the Mulligan Guard.

In mid-nineteenth-century American cities, men would often form "militia," "guard," or "target companies," quasi-military social clubs that paraded through working-class neighborhoods in homemade uniforms. Many started as extensions of fire companies or as ethnic responses to nativist militia groups. Some included clerks or employees of specific firms that used the guard to advertise their presence. One English visitor in 1850 reported that up to 10,000 men belonged to various guards, with names like the Washington Market Chowder Guard, George R. Jackson and Company's Guard, the First Ward Magnetizers, the Tompkins' Butcher Association Guard, or the Mustache Fusileers. Guard companies paraded with a "target" bearing their name: "profusely decorated with flowers . . . carried before the company, borne on the stalwart shoulders of a herculean specimen of the African race, to be shot at for a prize, or for glory." Nativist, Irish, and German immigrants all formed target companies or guards. O'Neill would surely have seen them while he lived in Brooklyn.[31]

Parading around in homemade uniforms, part sailor and part soldier, with brass or fife and drum accompaniment, the militias expressed neighborhood pride and rivalry and made a perfect target for Harrigan's friendly satire:

> We shouldered arms and marched and marched away
> From Jackson Street we marched to Avenue A.
> With fifes and drums, how sweetly they did play;
> As we marched, marched, marched in the Mulligan Guard.

Harrigan and Hart produced an extremely popular series of plays about the rivalries between the Mulligan Guard and the African American Skidmore Guard.[32] The musical team actively celebrated the multiculturalism of urban life, as in their song about "McNally's Row of Flats" from 1882.

> Ireland and Italy,
> Jerusalem and Germany,
> Chinamen and nagurs,
> And a paradise for cats;
> Jumbled up together
> In snow or rainy weather,
> They represent the tenants
> In McNally's row of flats.[33]

Harrigan especially saw Irish and African American characters as linked: "If I have given undue prominence to the Irish and negro," he told an interviewer, "it is because they form about the most salient features of Gotham humanity, and also because they are the two races who care the most for song and dance." Harrigan saw Irish and African American New Yorkers as comparable through their love of music and dance.[34]

The world of commercial entertainment stereotyped Irish characters: sometimes affectionately, sometimes viciously. Stepping off the boat into a dazzling urban world, a thoughtful person like O'Neill would have had to evaluate these images: they offered him ways of seeing himself. Would he adopt this sense of himself and his Irish compatriots? Or look for his own way of understanding? In colonized Ireland "Irish" meant something slightly different than it did in the US. Irish Americans faced discrimination and bigotry: they often had to take the lowest-paying and toughest jobs as domestics and in construction, but they could vote and join the police and fire companies, run for office, and represent themselves on stage. An Irishman like O'Neill could be an exploited worker in common plight with African Americans, but also eventually chief of Chicago police; a black man could not. O'Neill had a complicated status: Irish, but a subject of the queen; Irish Catholic, and a second-class citizen in his native land; Irish and English, but subject to the captain's authority at sea; Irish in America, but white; white, but close to African Americans in the racial hierarchy. He was exploring new ways to be Irish, new ways of understanding what "Irish" meant.[35]

While living in Brooklyn, O'Neill found a berth on *Louisa Anne*, a schooner heading to Brunswick, Georgia. He recalled sailing past the homes of Irish planters, sent to the West Indies as indentured servants by the tyrant invader of Ireland Oliver Cromwell. O'Neill's job in Georgia included loading cut lumber in "well-nigh tropical heat," so intense all but three of the ship's crew collapsed. He remembered "the Negro hired to work with me showed such consideration for my youth—just eighteen—which the memory of it had never failed to react favorably in my dealing with his race ever after." O'Neill here does the same work as the African American but less well; he needs help. The passage reminds us that in going to sea O'Neill had "passed down," given up some of the limited class privilege that adhered to the youngest son of a prosperous farm family, and entered an American political landscape complicated by different understandings of race. The experience led him to respect and value African Americans, but American society offered O'Neill advantages it would never offer to his coworker.[36]

O'Neill often took pains to mention how his adventures had exposed him to the kindness and decency of others, especially his experiences in the community of the less fortunate and the working class. "Sailing under the American flag," as O'Neill put it, he worked as an assistant steward on *Emerald Isle*, likely the assistant to an African American; and in the hot Georgia sun he depended on an African American coworker who, in his telling, took pity on him. He had entered into another social structure in which "Irish" figured differently: it offered forms of commonality but also made the advantages of whiteness plain.

Again the ambiguity of this new world, its novelty, its creolization, its confusion of identity may explain why O'Neill paid no attention to the mixed music of sailors and ports: he wanted to order and sort it. New York musical life offered many dazzlements, and Irish people played a major role as actors, as singers and dancers, and as the object of stereotype and mockery. The New York Irish sang flattering songs of self-congratulation, sorrowful songs of Ireland's woe, and patriotic assertions of their place in the US. It would have seemed confusing, both familiar and strange to the sailor from Tralibane.[37]

## Being Irish in America

The American Irish used music to reconsider the relationship between the old world and the new. For example, in 1869 Patrick Carpenter wrote lyrics to a song called "Skibbereen." In the song a son asks his father why he left Ireland. The father sings about how a blight came over the crops and adds, "Oh, it's well I do remember that bleak December day" when "the landlord and the sheriff came to drive us all away." The father recalls his wife's death and describes time spent in the hills, fighting in rebellion against the English, until finally he wraps his two-year-old son in his coat and they sail away. The son replies:

> Oh father dear, the day will come when in answer to the call
> Each Irishman with feelings stern will answer one and all,
> I'll be the man to lead the van, beneath our flag of green,
> And loud and high we'll raise the cry, 'Revenge for Skibbereen!'

Carpenter wrote the song to match the melody of "The Rising of the Moon," which began as a song about the United Irishmen uprising of 1798. The Irish playwright Dion Boucicault gave it new lyrics in his 1864 play *Arragh Na Pogue* and called it "The Wearing of the Green." Carpenter repurposed the melody again: now it called the American famine Irish to take revenge on the English tyrant.

The lyrics of the song touched O'Neill close to home, literally. O'Neill grew up ten miles from Skibbereen. And he would have known the tune as well: his schoolmate Patrick O'Brien remembered Peter Hagerty, the Piper Bawn, playing the "The Rising of the Moon" at crossroads dances back in County Cork. But Irish listeners, both in Ireland and in England, took the lyrics to "Skibbereen" and set them to a different melody, a more mournful, less martial tune. You can hear the 1869 lyrics sung today as if they came from Ireland in 1798. A product of transatlantic movement of people and ideas, back and forth to and from Ireland, the song written in New York's commercial ferment now seems like a traditional folk tune.[38]

If O'Neill went out for entertainment, he might have seen Kathleen "Kitty" O'Neil dancing and singing. Kitty O'Neil began dancing professionally in the 1860s and was soon billed as "Kitty O'Neil, the champion jig dancer of the world," using language derived from the traditions of challenge dances. During O'Neill's stays in New York, Kitty performed regularly to enthusiastic, mostly working-class crowds. She might appear on bills with "gymnasts, a velocipede demonstration, blackface comedians, a dog act, banjo players," or "political skits based on the contemporary scandals surrounding Tammany leader Boss Tweed"; later she joined Harrigan's troupe of players. Her trademark tune, "Kitty O'Neil's Champion Jig," was a "sand jig," an innovation of uncertain origin in which the performer spread sand on the stage, allowing for a different set of sounds and tricks. African American tap dancers still sometimes use this effect.[39]

Decades later Henry Chapman Mercer, a prominent American antiquarian with a love of Irish music, wrote to Francis O'Neill about "Kitty O'Neil's Jig." O'Neill replied that it was an American composition, was "by no means Irish in tone," and had a "straight" rhythm rather than an Irish jig rhythm. Puzzled, Mercer wrote again asking whether they were talking about the same tune, and O'Neill responded that "Kitty O'Neil's jig is not in my line—modern." The tune with analysis appears in the *thebeatcop.com*, the website supplementing this volume.[40]

We might understand Mercer's puzzlement. The tune appeared to accompany an Irish American woman insisting to the audience that she danced a jig. It seems in one sense "as Irish as Paddy's pig." But in 1920 O'Neill had no time at all for it and quickly dismissed "Kitty O'Neil's Jig" as not really Irish. By then he had developed an alternative understanding.

Clearly the song had too much of the American stage for O'Neill's taste: redolent of city life, invested with show business gimmicks, and contaminated by the minstrel show. But Kitty got her revenge in the sense that despite its possible origin in or influence by blackface minstrelsy and stage Irish, like "Skibbereen" the song has reentered the "canon" of Irish music. "Kitty's tune can now be heard in Irish music sessions from Belfast to Brisbane" but is often renamed as "Kitty O'Shea's" after the mistress of Irish political leader Charles Stewart Parnell. The tune sailed back across the Atlantic and acquired a new title with a strong reference to Irish history.[41]

During the same period another woman, a singer named Kathleen O'Neill, also no relation, appeared on American stages as "the Original Irish Thrush." In 1863 Kathleen published a song called "No Irish Need Apply," lamenting prejudice against the Irish. The sheet music quoted an advertisement in the London *Times* with the phrase "no Irish need apply." It then asked:

**Figure 8** Kitty O'Neil, 1877. The child of Irish immigrants, Kitty thrived in the mixed entertainments of New York. She represented the kind of adaptation to American life and music that Francis O'Neill resisted. He dismissed the tune that bears her name as "too modern." Billy Rose Theatre Division, New York Public Library. "Kitty O'Neil," New York Public Library Digital Collections, https://digitalcollections.nypl.org/items/76147434 -86d3-d20b-e040-e00a18060ea8.

Now what have they against us, sure the world knows Paddy's
   brave,
For he's helped to fight their battles, both on land and on the
   wave.
At the storming of Sebastopol, and beneath an Indian sky,
Pat raised his head, for their General said, "All Irish might
   apply."

The storming of Sebastopol took place during the Crimean War:
O'Neill remembered his father relating news about the Crimean
War to neighbors back home. Kathleen's song ended praising the
US as a place where the Irish might thrive, with the singer boasting that now she is in the glorious land of the free, where "all Irish
may apply." If Francis did not hear her sing in New York, he might
have heard her sing on the Midway at the 1893 Columbian Exposition in Chicago, held a few blocks from his house. Kathleen's
song acknowledged colonialism in Ireland while praising independence in America: she juggled aggressive Irishness, Anglophobia,
and flag-waving American patriotism, recasting Irish culture for the
New World.[42]

   All three examples touch directly on O'Neill's experience, but
they also show music moving internationally and how different versions of Irish and Irish American identity emerged from a complicated relationship between history and commerce. O'Neill, whether
he heard these tunes or not, sat square in that international movement of music and meaning. As he traveled, he tried to make sense
of his own place as an Irishman, as a product of English schooling,
and soon as an American.

## Off to the Pacific

O'Neill's next berth took him to Japan on the clipper *Minnehaha*, out
of Boston, the longest and most eventful voyage of his career at sea.
Built in 1856, the "medium clipper" had three decks and was rated
at more than 1,600 tons. The ship's elaborately carved figurehead

depicted the female heroine of Longfellow's poem *Hiawatha*, then only recently published but already immensely popular.[43]

O'Neill described Captain Bursley, from Cape Cod, as "a bully and a tyrant" who regularly assaulted the helmsmen: during the voyage "never once did I relieve a helmsman without finding traces of blood on the wheel." O'Neill mostly escaped his wrath, but at one point he mildly and politely corrected the captain's observations on a trivial point: Bursley "seized me by the throat and bent me backwards," shouting "don't talk back to me!" Later events revealed Bursley as an inept coward. In the straits of Sunda in the Java Sea, O'Neill wrote, Bursley ran *Minnehaha* onto a reef, damaging the keel considerably. Rigging snapped from the shock, and Bursley's voice "changed from harsh to pleading" in "the excitement that followed." The ship sent to nearby Batavia, now Jakarta, for divers to inspect the keel. "The bullying captain, whose spirit was crushed, went ashore with the divers for hospital treatment, and first mate Hickman took command."[44]

O'Neill later commanded men himself: groups of men in moments of high stress, tension, and imminent violence. He wrote of these events in a restrained, cool tone that suggests he had learned a lesson about the hollowness of boasting and the degree to which bullying masks weakness. Later in the voyage he described grabbing the drunken third mate returning to the ship from shore and saving him from falling into the sea. "What I experienced later at his hand was brutality rather than gratitude, and the worst of it was that to resent brutality and injustice is to invite a diet of bread and water in irons." The passage is typically opaque, shifting tense from past to present midsentence, making it hard to know whether O'Neill spent time in irons himself or simply described the general rule of authority at sea. But he told the story as an example of authority and its abuse.

"A supply of back number periodicals and old books constituted a portion of my 'tonnage' on every voyage," he remembered, and his bookishness got him into trouble with authority when the ship docked in Yokohama. When two ships met, he wrote, the more literate sailors invariably traded books. "One quiet Sunday morning," O'Neill recalled, he slipped over the side of the ship with a parcel of books tied to his head, to keep them dry, and "swam to a vessel several hundred yards away" to do some trading. While O'Neill swapped books in the forecastle of the other ship, a dinghy arrived from *Minnehaha*, demanding his return. By Captain Hickman's orders, O'Neill had to swim back, while the dinghy rowed slowly behind him. And Hickman further punished him with a week of rising at dawn to climb the rigging and scrape the masts and pulley blocks. "Discipline on shipboard in foreign ports must be maintained," O'Neill wrote.

O'Neill resented the bullying and the cruelty he experienced at sea and treasured moments of kindness, but he endorsed the necessity of discipline and order. He learned how to lead, but he was himself more than capable of bullying and later defended the use of harsh interrogation measures by Chicago's police. He remained especially sensitive to *gratitude*, the bonds of reciprocity and mutuality. Again and again he refers to good deeds done to him in the past, as in the example of the kind African American who helped him load lumber in the Georgia heat, and the ways the impact of those good deeds reverberated over time. In Chicago, where the exchange of favors lubricated the political machine, O'Neill kept a mental ledger of favors done and favors received. His letters show he regarded ingratitude as a terrible offense: it broke the cycle of mutuality and reciprocity. Overdeveloped expectations of gratitude can sour the milk of kindness, and O'Neill in later life seems to have had a marked capacity for falling out with friends. But he also saw relations as human and personal rather than contractual and strictly legal.

*Minnehaha* remained in Yokohama for ten weeks. He noted that while "the social customs of the Japanese may seem amazing to a caucasian," yet "in politeness and fair dealing they compare favorably with the businesspeople of other lands." O'Neill especially admired "inimitable" Japanese craftsmanship and acquired a small cabinet of inlaid wood and, perhaps with Anna Rogers in mind, a lady's workbox.

Yokohama exposed him to at least one vice: "Portuguese sailors who had abandoned a seafaring life," O'Neill wrote, "may be found at all ports in the Pacific." One of them kept a lunch house in the harbor and there O'Neill got drunk for the first and possibly the last time in his life, on a glass of *sake* proffered by the host. "Soon my brain was in a whirl, and I was obliged to rest in a bunk for an hour or two before recovering from its effects." The adult O'Neill did not drink, which must have handicapped him in the Chicago favor market, and his work collecting folk music regularly brought him into saloons and homes where custom demanded sharing a round or treating. He may have disliked alcohol, or possibly his wife asked him to take a temperance pledge. In a letter to an Irish friend in 1912 he wrote that he had very limited "forms of dissipation (can't drink or smoke)," saying he *can't* rather than he *does not*. It set him apart, and a sense of apartness never leaves O'Neill's writing: apart from his family, apart from the "simple peasants" in Ireland, somewhat apart from his fellow sailors, somewhat apart from those who failed to return favors appropriately.[45]

"In ballast, but with a cargo of gorgeous Asiatic pheasants and other Asiatic birds, in the care of Japanese attendants," *Minnehaha* sailed for Honolulu, arriving October 25, 1867. The pheasants, he recalled, were "consigned to Queen Emma, then ruler of the kingdom of the Kamehamehas." Emma, called also Kaleleonalani, had married Alexander Liholiho, King Kamehameha IV, in 1857. A colonized person, like O'Neill, Emma had converted to Christianity under the foster care of her maternal aunt and her husband, an English physician named John Rooke. A converted Christian, comfortable in high Victorian dress, and fluent in English, Emma balanced native Hawaiian cultural practice with Western expectations.[46]

O'Neill remembered the pheasants as gifts for the queen, but newspapers described them as part of a deliberate attempt by an American-born merchant Eugene Van Reed, consul general of the Kingdom of Hawaii to Japan, to develop the Hawaiian economy and foster trade with Japan. The Kingdom of Hawaii depended on the forbearance of heavily armed and supplied *haole*, the foreigners, who wanted to exploit the island's agricultural potential. The Pacific Commercial Advertiser wrote that the cargo of the "fine ship *Minnehaha*" included tea seed and plants, orange trees, 1,000 pine seedlings, and a variety of mulberry seeds and plants, so that Hawaii might enter the silk trade. The *Advertiser* mentioned the pheasants and other birds but said nothing about Queen Emma; and although O'Neill had described Captain Bursley, bully and tyrant, as unmanned by disaster and last heading to a hospital in Java, the *Advertiser* thanked Captain Bursley for bringing the cargo in safely.[47]

After dropping its cargo of birds and plants, *Minnehaha* sailed southwest to Baker Island, between Hawaii and Australia. Seabirds had nested on the treeless atoll for centuries and covered the island, a rough circle slightly more than a mile across at its widest, in guano to a depth of several feet. The guano made an excellent fertilizer, much in demand, so despite the entire lack of freshwater, "four white men and about 150 Kanakas [native Hawaiians]" lived on the island to support the mining operation. In a typical year three ships a month might arrive and carry off over a thousand tons each of what O'Neill called "the nauseous mass," shoveled into sacks. A Captain Johnson, of Wisconsin, governed the operation; "an Irishman named McSweeney" served as gang boss of the shovel crews while an Englishman supervised the loading of ships. "A German chef" cooked for the white men, O'Neill wrote, and the infrastructure included movable rails along which an old white horse pulled a flatcar, loaded with guano sacks. *Minnehaha* had on board "fifty Kanakas" intended to replace or augment workers on the island. "During the voyage those passengers amused themselves in daily contests of strength and agility, outrivaling the best of our crew."[48]

Ships visiting this treeless, sun-blasted island, which had no harbor, moored to buoys fixed just offshore. Ten days after arrival, on November 30, a sudden swell broke *Minnehaha* loose of her mooring and pitched the ship onto the coral reefs that ringed the island. All hands escaped, O'Neill himself swimming to shore with the ship's pet monkey, Jocko, on his head. But the gale that followed over the next days dashed *Minnehaha* and two other ships to pieces, leaving the crews stranded and the island grossly undersupplied with food, water, and shelter. Miraculously, the elaborately carved figurehead of *Minnehaha* appears to have survived and may be seen on exhibit at Colonial Williamsburg in Virginia.[49]

## Colonial Island People: The Irish and the Hawaiians

"Governor Johnson received the Captain and officers as guests while he supplied the crew with limited rations of hardtack and drinking water," O'Neill wrote. The common sailors built rude shelters out of driftwood and pieces of wreckage, and eagerly walked the shore looking for anything to eat. They tried to eat the seabirds, but though "sailors are never fastidious in their choice of food," the seabirds "were so fishy and rank" that "none of us could stomach them." Between *Minnehaha*'s crew of twenty-eight, the fifty Hawaiians brought as supplemental or replacement labor, and two other ships wrecked at the same time, the tiny island would have been desperately short of food and water.

O'Neill spent eleven days in these grim conditions, which he termed a "Robinson Crusoe life," until "the brig *Zoe*" appeared on the horizon. O'Neill misremembered this name. A brig named *Kamehameha V* traveled continually between Baker Island and Honolulu, resupplying the island with food and water five times a year: Hawaiian newspapers reported sailors wrecked at Baker Island returned on *Kamehameha V*. The rescuing ship, captained by a white man but crewed entirely by Kanakas, had already rescued crews wrecked by the same swell on Howland Island roughly 100 miles to the north; it now turned back to Honolulu, under rations "necessarily limited almost to starvation": one and a half biscuits of hardtack a day and a small amount of salt meat twice a week. It would take more than a month to reach Honolulu. All but three of *Minnehaha*'s crew arrived so weakened that they went immediately to the local hospital, but O'Neill arrived in decent shape thanks to extra rations of food he earned with music.[50]

In outline his story seems straightforward. One of the Kanaka sailors had a flute and played a single tune each night. O'Neill borrowed the flute and played several tunes, and as a result the Kanaka sailor gave him extra food. The incident marked the only time he spoke of music at sea; he told the story multiple times, offering the most detail in his 1910 book *Irish Folk Music: A Fascinating Hobby*, and then in his private memoir, written in 1931 when he was eighty-three. It meant something important to him, but his telling suggests he didn't fully understand what.

On the rescuing ship, wrote O'Neill in 1910, "one of the Kanakas had a fine flute, on which he played a simple one-strain hymn with conscious pride almost every evening." Twenty years later he wrote: "one of the Kanaka sailors, who had a flute and was apparently proud of his musical accomplishments, regaled us nightly with a hymn tune which he repeated without change while his wind lasted." In the time between the two tellings, O'Neill eliminated the fineness of the flute and much of the Kanaka sailor's dignity. "A fine flute" suggests a degree of musical seriousness and capacity that O'Neill minimized in his later account. And what he saw as "conscious pride" in 1910 became "while his wind lasted" in 1931.[51]

Hawaiian natives, converted to Christianity like Queen Emma, adapted their own versions of the *himeni* Protestant missionaries brought to the island. By 1867 "Hawaiians had been appropriating and repurposing musical ideas and lyrical themes from other people for decades." While they preserved songs that predated the arrival of Europeans, they had also developed a musical tradition termed *hapa haole*, meaning roughly a mix of European and native Hawaiian. In the 1860s "it was not uncommon to see bamboo flutes of native manufacture in the hands of Hawaiian musicians of the younger generation" wrote one American observer, "avowedly imitations of the D-flute imported from abroad." So O'Neill's sailor played a flute that combined Hawaiian with European musical traditions. If he played a Protestant hymn every evening, the Kanaka sailor expressed longing for home and devotional piety but showed how he had adapted to colonization.[52]

O'Neill implied the sailor knew only one tune, but we could also see playing the same "hymn tune" every evening as a consciously devotional or meditative act, a deliberate choice. O'Neill never tells what hymn the sailor played; and indeed, while the sailor might have played a Christian hymn, perhaps what O'Neill calls a "hymn tune" was not a hymn at all but a Hawaiian melody played as ritual observance. In his retellings O'Neill not only forgot the ship's name—*Kamehameha V*, the name of Hawaii's king at the time—he entirely forgot the rest of *Kamehameha V*'s Hawaiian crew, who would have heard the tune every night. Was it played for them as an observance of day's end? A prayer for safe sailing ahead or to return home? We cannot know, but there is every reason for skepticism about how O'Neill framed the story.

We can see these Hawaiian sailors not simply as displaced victims of imperialism but also as explorers, moving into the larger world, bringing new information and new ideas back to Hawaiian culture. The *Emerald Isle* had wooed Irish emigrants by depicting their journey, driven by necessity, as an epic movement of the Irish into the larger world. Especially in the nineteenth century, we might view Hawaiian sailors in this same way—compelled by economic drives, but also possessed of curiosity and eagerness to see more. "By 1845, one in five Hawaiian men between the ages of fifteen and thirty were wandering the oceans or in foreign lands." We might see the Hawaiian sailors, in other words, as more like O'Neill, a colonial subject who left home seeking adventure at sea.[53]

O'Neill says he borrowed the man's flute and played some tunes. In 1910 O'Neill wrote "of course, this chance to show what could be done on the instrument was not to be overlooked. The result was most gratifying. As in the case of the Arkansas traveler of song, there was nothing too good for me." In 1931 he wrote "being something of a performer on that instrument, I picked it up one evening and rattled off 'the Soldier's Joy,' 'Yankee Doodle' and 'The Girl I left Behind Me.'"

"Whatever may have been thought of my performance by others," he continued in 1931, "I won the Kanaka fluter's friendship, for thereafter he shared his daily ration of poi and canned salmon with me." In his 1910 telling, O'Neill called the Kanaka sailor "my dusky brother musician," but if he learned the man's name he quickly forgot it. In all his tellings, O'Neill arrived in port well fed and ready to move on: "I have no doubt this incident profoundly influenced my future, for while others were left behind, I was on my way to San Francisco and a new life."[54]

In his 1910 account O'Neill compared himself to the protagonist in "The Arkansas Traveler," a story and song widely performed and celebrated over and over on stages across the US. "The people loved it and kept time to it," wrote Henry Mercer, "tramps and sailors carried it across seas to vie merrily in Irish cabins," and "showmen caught it from Western adventurers"; it "gained vogue in the hands of negro minstrels" and drew crowds to the wagons of patent medicine hucksters. Here again O'Neill viewed the tune through the lens of colonialism.[55]

In the stage version of the tune, a city man, traveling on horseback through the Arkansas hills, comes across a farmer's rundown cabin. The farmer lazily scrapes away at a fiddle, repeating the same eight-bar phrase while ignoring the tired traveler's questions about where he might find a bed for the night or giving cryptic, comically unhelpful answers. Frustrated, the traveler pulls out a fiddle of his own and plays the *second half of the tune*. The farmer, delighted, springs to life; his wife and child begin to dance, and they offer the traveler the hospitality of their home. This moment, known as "the turn of the tune," appeared in lithographs and Currier and Ives prints and marked the tale's climax on stage.

"The Arkansas Traveler" let sophisticated urban audiences laugh at rural folk. The city man brings knowledge that completes the tune and breaks the spell of lassitude hanging over the Arkansas farm. In his story about the Hawaiian sailor, O'Neill compared himself to the traveler, who enlightens the rural primitive, but on board *Kamehameha V* both men were travelers, and rather than completing a tune, O'Neill wrote in 1931 that he played multiple new tunes.

Interestingly, none of the songs he says he played would be considered Irish. Besides "Yankee Doodle," a song the English sang to mock American colonists and that the colonists later reclaimed with pride, O'Neill played "Soldier's Joy," which dates back hundreds of years; some versions have lyrics, and today fiddlers associate it with the American Civil War. "The Girl I Left Behind Me," also an ancient tune, appears with many different lyrics as well. O'Neill might have

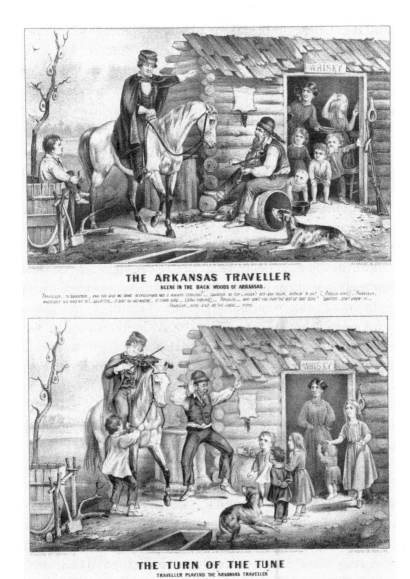

**Figure 9** Currier & Ives, "Arkansas Traveller: Scene in the Back Woods of Arkansas" and "The Turn of the Tune," 1870. One of the most popular tunes in America, it often came with a skit in which the rural man is eventually awakened from the spell of lassitude when the city man plays the second half of the tune. O'Neill mentioned it often and eventually decided it was an Irish tune. [New York: Currier & Ives]. Photograph. At Prints and Photographs Division, Library of Congress, https://www.loc.gov/item/90708789/ and https://www.loc.gov/item/2002697430/.

heard it in Ireland, or the US, or anywhere Europeans and Americans sailed: sailors and soldiers often sang it as they left home. Perhaps he simply forgot what he played at the time and added some tunes readers of his memoirs would know. But in memory, at least, he played songs associated with other homelands and nations, with colonization and military service, with leaving home, and with the political authority of nations. He played not the Irish dance tunes he remembered from Tralibane but songs of the English and American colonizers of Ireland and Hawaii.[56]

At that moment or in memory, O'Neill might have seen Ireland and Hawaii as more alike than different: both colonized island nations, their natives shunted to marginal land and poverty, finding work on the colonizer's ships, required to speak English, and conduct their traditions under pressure from foreigners; entering the wider world and adapting to and modifying the world they found. Indeed, at that moment both O'Neill and his "dusky brother musician" were common sailors, away from home, part of the deeply unpleasant task of packing guano into sacks for international trade. On board *Kamehameha V*, a ship named for the king of Hawaii, O'Neill's health depended on the generosity and empathy of a Hawaiian stranger. In memory he reversed things and cast the Hawaiian sailor as the beneficiary of O'Neill's musical superiority.[57]

When O'Neill thought back about Honolulu, he talked about the Hawaiians as doomed: "Civilization has not been an unmixed blessing for Hawaiians," he mused, "for along with the Bible and the white man's religion came the white man's diseases." O'Neill argued that "they die rapidly when brought into contact with Caucasians, degenerate morally, and eventually lose possession of their lands." He called the native Hawaiians a "hopeless minority without property or influence."[58]

O'Neill is sorry about this, but he writes about it as if it "just happened": as if "civilization" did it accidentally, as if natives "lost" their land the way someone misplaces their cell phone, as if Hawaiians had some genetic deficiency. Richard Henry Dana had praised the intelligence and kindness of the Hawaiians, calling Kanakas "the most interesting, intelligent, and kind-hearted people that I ever fell in with," but O'Neill's description recalls the way English and American critics talked about the Irish, as doomed primitives.

In 1840, for example, the British philosopher Thomas Carlyle had complained that "crowds of miserable Irish darken all our towns." He loathed their "wild Milesian features" and the fact that their "restlessness, unreason, misery and mockery, salute you on all highways and byways." Sunk in "squalid apehood," the Irishman "is the sorest evil this country has to strive with." O'Neill talked about the impact of the white man's diseases on native Hawaiians, while Carlyle compared the Irishman, "his squalor and unreason, in his falsity and drunken violence," to disease: "we have quarantines against pestilence; but there is no pestilence like that; and against it what quarantine is possible?" He insisted that "the time has come when the Irish population must either be improved a little, or else exterminated." Depictions of Irish people as ape-like, dark, and savage appeared regularly in magazines and newspapers in England and the US. O'Neill, product of the National Schools, adopted the colonizer's point of view. By casting himself as the Arkansas traveler and the Kanaka as the rustic primitive who knew only one tune, O'Neill imagined himself as the bearer of knowledge and sophistication.[59]

Hawaii resembled Ireland not just as a colonized island but in the outsized influence its music had on the rest of the world. Music from Ireland, and music performed by the children of Irish émigrés, strongly influenced American popular culture. We might compare songs like "Kitty O'Neil's Champion Jig" or "No Irish Need Apply" to the *hapa haole* songs Hawaiian musicians played: a living mix of traditions engaged in commerce with other traditions, waving an ethnic or national flag while speaking to and with other cultures. The central stringed instruments of Hawaii, the ukulele and the lap steel guitar, would dramatically revise playing styles in both blues and country music. Every time a country band uses a pedal steel guitar or a blues musician runs a bottleneck slide along the guitar neck, we hear the creolized influence of Hawaiian musical voyagers.[60]

One might reasonably argue this is not "real" Hawaiian music but some sort of dilution of the authentic original, in much the same way Francis regarded "Kitty O'Neil's Jig" or brass bands as not authentically Irish. But the very idea of authentic folk culture only arises in commerce and exchange: as Masten writes, "peasant traditions were being produced around the globe by intercultural mixing and a diaspora that sent millions of Irish immigrants and African slaves to America." We might tend to think of "peasant traditions" as things that grew from the cultured soil of a specific land, but, in fact, the whole idea of a specific traditional music arises from contact with the larger world: from the arrival of foreign invader or from the hybridized, creolized world of commerce. Native traditions only look "native" in contrast with something else. The idea of real Irish music, like the idea of real Hawaiian music, arises not from tradition but from innovation, not from isolation but from its opposite.[61]

O'Neill would find his inspiration for the idea of authentic Irish folk music while policing Chicago's skyscraper blocks, and just as he edited his memories of the crossroads dances in Tralibane to eliminate commercial songs and political ballads, he mostly paid no attention to the mixed music of the seas or the streets. O'Neill had curiosity, courage, and a taste for adventure; he had the self-reliance and fortitude to wander alone as a common sailor, taking hard work as it came. He found things to admire and respect in the people he encountered. But very few people manage to think their way out of the box their upbringing builds, and in his memories of "the kanaka fluter" he reproduced the very assumptions of Euro-American colonialism that had been applied to the Irish.

While his former shipmates recovered in Honolulu, O'Neill traveled to San Francisco and back several times on the barque *Comet*, carrying cargo and passengers. In April 1868, when he saw a handbill calling for harvesters to work in Tuolumne County, near what is now Turlock State Park, he decided he needed to see more of California. Past Modesto, when the stagecoach stopped for lunch, he met and accepted a job as shepherd from rancher Calvin Salter.[62]

Salter hired O'Neill and another man, Bill "Scotty" Anderson, to tend one of two flocks of sheep heading for summer grazing in the Sierra foothills, "mutton sheep" intended for food. The two men slept outside with nothing but blankets: O'Neill recalled it as five months without a roof over his head, sleeping on the ground, in semi-arid conditions. Rattlesnakes particularly worried a man raised in snake-free Ireland. Salter had a second herd in the same region, shepherded by two other men. A somewhat unreliable guide appeared at intervals to supply them with food and direct their movements. At one point one of the other shepherds, "Watkins, an irascible Kentuckian," got drunk and came at "the Irishman [O'Neill]" with a knife; in his telling, O'Neill grabbed a shotgun leaning nearby and Watkins backed down. He encountered Native Americans and Chinese immigrants while in the Sierra foothills: "concerning our relations with the Chinese on the plains and the Indians in the uplands," he wrote, "it is but justice to them to say that we found them not less kindly and appreciative of fair dealing than the white race." Again we get some sense of how "Irish" signified differently in America. He was nearly the victim of Watkins's hostility to the Irish. And he expressed admiration toward the Chinese and the Native Americans while placing himself squarely in the white race.[63]

O'Neill learned at least one tune, which he named "Far from Home," "from the whistling of a companion while herding a flock of 3,000 sheep on the plains at the foot of the Sierra Nevada range." The tune appears at the *thebeatcop.com*, the website supplemental to this volume. Presumably he learned the tune from "Scotty" Anderson. The tune may have originated in the Shetland Islands; like many folk tunes, its origins defy precision. People today play "Far from Home" as either a dancing reel or slowly and more plaintively as a song about longing for home. Associated in his mind with rural isolation, unlike "Kitty O'Neil's Champion Jig," "Far from Home" passed O'Neill's test of Irishness and made it into his collections. He attributed a similar tune, a hornpipe he called "Off to California," to his time in the Sierra foothills but said nothing about where he learned it.[64]

"Favored with health, experience, and money," he wrote, "I returned to San Francisco and shipped on the barque *Hannah*, bound for Culiacán, Mexico." *Hannah* picked up logs in Mexico and then headed to New York. In a relatively uneventful journey, it rounded

Cape Horn, so that when it anchored in New York in March 1869 O'Neill could fairly claim to have circumnavigated the globe by his twentieth year.[65]

O'Neill had "come down from his heights," as Dana put it: he had left "straight paths for the by-ways and low places of life." He had learned "truths by strong contrasts," "in hovels, in forecastles . . . among outcasts in foreign lands." By the time he arrived in New York again, he had "determined to bid farewell to Neptune's domain" and seek his fate on land in America.

# 3
# Rolling on the Ryegrass
## A Year on the Missouri Prairie

### Back in New York

O'Neill stepped off the boat with nearly three years' wages in his pocket, almost $200, which he "entrusted . . . to Mrs. Reid, my former host at 66 Oliver Street, for safekeeping." She kept it—literally! He asked for his money, and she kept saying she had used it to pay a pressing bill, but that he would have it soon. Day after day this went on, he wrote, until finally, his patience exhausted, O'Neill went to Erie, Pennsylvania, where his eldest brother, Philip, led a stevedore gang loading coal. It was rough work, often from sunrise to sunset, but O'Neill "endured the strain." He made one more trip back to New York to try and get his money, and then gave up: "I was 'stung,'" he admitted.[1]

We have to wonder why he entrusted all the money he made since coming to America on *Emerald Isle* to the owner of the boarding-house and not to a bank. Immigrants to New York, especially Irish immigrants, took advantage of the Emigrant Savings Bank, founded in 1850 specifically to give Irish immigrants a safe place to keep their money. The bank's records show Irish immigrants used the bank extensively and reveal "a significant stratum of New York's Irish, who although poor, had accumulated significant sums even before becoming account holders, and who were quite willing to deposit it in a financial institution, the likes of which would have been unknown to most of them in Ireland." The quote makes a key point: Irish emigrants had entered into a new world, with institutions like banks able to track them, keep their money, apply interest, and assess their creditworthiness, all of which require the kind of systemic large-scale recordkeeping absent back in Tralibane. The bank's records also show an 1863 account in the name of "Philip Neill," laborer, born in 1839 in County Cork, with parents "John + Cath. Mahony," O'Neill's parents. So it seems eldest brother Philip had an account at the Emigrant Savings Bank six years earlier at least, and the bank records further note that Philip had "a sister in New York, Mary." So Francis would have known what the bank offered.[2]

Why, when Mrs. Reid stole his money, did he not simply go to the police? Possibly O'Neill felt he had no standing, as an immigrant, to address the legal system. But in 1869 no visa requirements or regulations limited his stay in America. There simply was no such thing as an illegal immigrant: newcomers walked onto the dock and got straight to the business of living. A new immigrant had to wait five years before applying for citizenship and had to make a formal declaration of desire for citizenship three years before applying. But US laws applied to noncitizens, who were in no way illegal, and O'Neill had every right to file a criminal complaint. As noted earlier, about one in four New Yorkers had been born in Ireland. Irish brogues resounded from every doorway, belonging to, by 1869, ordinary people but also lawyers, politicians, ward bosses, and policemen. The church stood ready to welcome and assist Catholic immigrants. In addition, though still a very young man, O'Neill had spent four years adventuring at sea; he was no doe-eyed bumpkin and more likely strong, confident, well traveled, and experienced. The story seems odd.

If O'Neill omitted a great deal of information in this account or re-membered details incorrectly, we learn some important things from the way he framed the story. Three years earlier, he wrote that John Brennan, a shipmate, had directed him to the boardinghouse, owned by a Scandinavian "with an Irish wife, who had a good name." Here O'Neill relies on other Irish people for help—shipmate Brennan and the Irish wife of the boardinghouse owner. But Irish community, rather than warming and welcoming, instead robs him. Philip, the eldest brother, had lived in New York in 1863 and had a bank account. He must have had some contact with Philip—how else could he know Philip was in Pennsylvania? But instead of a warm familial embrace in Erie, O'Neill tells us he found only very hard work for very poor wages. This is the first and the last we hear of Philip, but not the last we hear of hard work and low wages. Philip used the Emigrant Savings Bank: O'Neill, to his regret, did not. It would be the last such mistake he would make.

Irish Americans had started coming to the US well before the famine, and the huge Irish community O'Neill joined presented a very mixed picture. Modern readers tend to think of "Irish" as "Catholic," an idea the church energetically advanced, but tens of thousands of Protestant Irish had come over earlier. Ned Harrigan, described in chapter 2, offers one example; Stephen Foster, the composer, or Dan Emmett, the minstrel performer and the man credited with writing "Dixie," offer others. Catholic Irish immigration steadily increased before the famine and accelerated dramatically after. The "famine Irish" who came in much greater numbers after 1847 tended to be poor, Catholic, and to come from western Ireland, and to speak Irish. "It was these immigrants, many of them Gaelic speakers steeped in a traditional peasant culture, who were uprooted by the famine, demoralized by its devastation, and launched on a tide of emigration that deposited them in a booming industrial city that had no use for their meager skills."[3]

The New York editor E. L. Godkin wrote about the contrast between "jolly, reckless, good-natured, passionate, priest-ridden, whiskey loving, thriftless Paddy, and the cold, shrewd, frugal, correct, meeting-going Yankee." Godkin insisted that "the prodigious influx of Irish during the last twenty years has created a large Irish class, apart from the rest of the people, poor, ignorant, helpless, and degraded, contemned by the Americans, used as tools by politicians of all parties, doing all the hard work and menial duties of the country, and filling the jails and almshouses, almost to the exclusion of everybody else." "Concentrated in crowded and dank dwellings," Irish immigrants suffered disproportionately from disease. They accounted for 70 percent of the recipients of public charity. Kevin Kenny reports that while Irish made up 54 percent of the city's immigrants in 1855, they were 85 percent of foreign-born admissions to

Bellevue, the city's public hospital. Irish people made up 55 percent of those arrested, as opposed to 10 percent German immigrants and 7 percent English.[4]

Catholic Irish immigrants faced intense hostility from laboring men who feared competition and from Protestants who feared and detested the Roman church. In Philadelphia rioting between Irish and nativist groups occurred almost monthly in the 1840s. An entire political party, the American Party, nicknamed the Know Nothings, formed to resist the Irish influx. The Irish appeared unassimilable: barbaric, ape-like, prone to violence and drink, poverty stricken, captive to papish superstition; they sent their children to Catholic schools and clustered in dense neighborhoods. Samuel Morse, inventor of the telegraph, called the Irish citizen "a naturalized foreigner, not a naturalized citizen," a man who though "sworn to be a citizen, talks . . . of Ireland as 'his home,' as 'his beloved country,' . . . glories in being Irish, forms and cherishes an Irish interest, brings hither Irish local feuds, and forgets, in short, all his new obligations as an American." Morse regarded the Irish as "at war with propriety, with decency, with gratitude, and with true patriotism." Morse's bigotry toward the Irish appears laughable today, but in 1854 the Irish seemed hopelessly foreign, clannish, and fundamentally "un-American," and moreover they consistently "gloried in being Irish" and worked politically for Ireland's interests.[5]

Francis confronted many different ways of being Irish. He could remember the Irish peasants back home. He had his family as a model; he had the schooling he got as a subject of the queen. Now in America he could find yet more ways of understanding his own identity: as something new, an "Irish American." What did that mean?

## Ireland and the American Irish

Irish emigrants to the US, Kerby Miller concluded, believed England had driven them into exile. Other immigrants recalled leaving as a choice, often forced by necessity, but Irish people understood themselves as exiled by tyranny, whether facts warranted the belief or not. "Throughout the nineteenth and early twentieth century, Irish and Irish American newspapers and orators characterized those who left Ireland as 'exiles,' compelled to emigrate" by "English tyranny." "Emigrant songs and ballads sung by Irishmen on both sides of the ocean usually expressed a pervasive note of sadness," and this sense of sadness at exile appears consistently in the letters they wrote back and forth.[6]

England, in fact, did regularly exile Irish political leaders, sentencing them to "transportation" to Australia or driving them from their homeland to find refuge in Europe, North America, and the New World more generally. John Boyle O'Reilly, poet and editor of the *Boston Pilot*; Thomas Meagher, Union general and Civil War hero; and John Mitchel, firebrand Irish rebel and Confederacy supporter, most had played leading roles in the "Young Ireland" movement of the 1840s, another political attempt to unite Protestant and Catholic Irish in rebellion against the crown. All three men had escaped from imprisonment in Australia and landed in New York to a hero's welcome. Literal exiles, their lives symbolized a broader sense of exile that ordinary immigrants found consoling and perhaps self-flattering. "In their understanding," writes Timothy Meagher, "it was English oppression that had forced them to leave their real home," not simply a desire for gain. The sense of exile, of culture and community lost or vanishing, appeared in Irish music, often said to express this melancholy sense even in its liveliest moments.[7]

But while he heard that melancholy note in music, O'Neill differed from most Irish immigrants in that he had a better education—not that it had done him much good yet—and that he insisted he had left Ireland by choice, neither a political exile nor a victim of economic necessity. But later in his life, he used the language of exile many times. Within Chicago's city limits, he would write, "exiles from all of Ireland's thirty-two counties can be found." And he also claimed a combination of happiness and sadness characterized Irish music. "How often do we hear of Erin's exiles . . . melted to tears or roused to unexampled valor, on hearing the strains of a cherished melody that recalled the sounds and scenes of their youth."[8]

Who exiled O'Neill? English colonialism, but also in truth his family: only one person could inherit that farm, and at least two other siblings left before him. The history of Irish immigration to America is largely the history of the surplus children packing their bags so the eldest could remain to prosper. In a mildly barbed comment at Cork City Hall in 1963, John F. Kennedy reminded his Irish audience that "most countries send out oil, iron, steel or gold, some others crops, but Ireland has only one export and that is people." Kerby Miller cited a story about an Irish father whose son sent him pictures of the family prospering in America; the father dismissed the pictures as useless: "we know what they look like. The pictures I would like to see are a few of Abraham Lincoln's," that is, American cash. If the English bore the blame in a larger sense, Irish Americans might easily imagine themselves as the castoff, daughters and sons unwanted and exiled by their own families. Blaming England defused that volatile mix, and when they didn't focus their anger on the English, Irish Americans often sugared the bitter pill in a cloying sentimentality.[9]

"To the exile of Irish birth," O'Neill wrote in 1913, "the melodies of the old land will bring back memories of the fireside, the lakes, the moors, and clear flowing rivers." He described "many a homesick exile weary of the meaningless music which his American daughter had acquired at the academy." Native-born Americans would accuse successive immigrant groups of being unassimilable, of being too foreign, or of clinging to their own ways of life. Irish immigrants very publicly declared their political and emotional allegiance to their lost homeland, in both loudly sentimental and dangerously violent ways, which only increased nativist suspicion.[10]

As their numbers grew, they found a foothold in politics as well as in public and private construction, digging aqueducts, building bridges, laying streetcar tracks and gas lines. They got jobs in the newly formed police and fire departments, especially in New York, Philadelphia, and Boston. As the right to vote expanded in the 1830s to include all adult white men, Irish Americans restructured the political life of American cities, forging ethnic voting blocks that made overt discrimination harder to practice. That motif of sadness and exile became a commercial property, nostalgia marketed as a set of predictable feelings that could give a common language to

both the committed political rebel and the immigrant merely looking to get ahead.

In 1871 Irish Americans organized a "grand procession" in honor of
the "Cuba five," Irish political activists exiled to America on the ship
*Cuba*. Their ranks included Jeremiah O'Donovan Rossa and John
Devoy, two leading exponents of "physical force" nationalism and
members of the Fenian Brotherhood, an organization dedicated to
freeing Ireland from English rule. The parade involved up to 300,000
spectators. On February 10, 1871, the *New York Times* wrote "the
entire City was surrendered to the reception of the Fenian exiles."
"It was a sort of overture to St. Patrick's Day," the *Times* continued,
noting "the hedge-rows of green ribbons and neckties which lined
Broadway." The *Times* resented that politicians could "impose on the
public by a demonstration of strength in one especial nationality."
"Thousands of men left their employers short of help, without the
slightest consideration, to take part in this demonstration, and many

Figure 10 The grand procession in honor of the Fenian exiles, in New York City, February 9, 1871. At Prints and Photos Division, Library of Congress, https://lccn.loc.gov/
2013645242. Irish Americans here celebrate the arrival of "the Cuba Five," five Irish nationalists exiled to America on board the *Cuba*. Irish Americans followed events in Ireland
closely. O'Neill had left New York by then, but he read Irish American newspapers like the
*Boston Pilot* regularly and would have known of the Cuba Five and their reception.

a mistress, under compulsion, had to allow her servant an entire holiday to witness the spectacle." Irish workers demonstrated their economic necessity and their political muscle.[11]

As the Irish gained political power, they also gained some sympathy. The US formed in rebellion against English colonial rule: it took little effort to sympathize with Irish desires for a republic. Countering the heinous acts of Irish draft rioters, seven Irish-born generals and 150,000 Irish soldiers had fought in the Civil War under the Union flag. By 1868 contributions from Irish Americans funded the first steps in the construction of St. Patrick's Cathedral, the tallest building in New York City when it opened in 1878 and an inescapable symbol of the political and economic power of both the city's and the nation's Irish Catholics.

But O'Neill had left well before to join his brother's stevedore gang in Erie. While in Erie, loading coal on the lakefront, O'Neill certainly heard tales of the Fenians and their multiple bold, ill-fated attempts to invade Canada. Just a few years earlier, the docks of Erie had swarmed with erstwhile Fenian reinforcements hoping to join an advance into Canada. The heavily armed iron gunboat USS *Michigan*, still stationed in Erie, prevented their departure. Mass-produced lithographs celebrated the Battle of Ridgeway, in which Irish Americans under the Fenian flag had briefly routed the queen's troops on Canadian soil.

## The Fenians, Citizenship, and the Invasions of Canada

John O'Mahony, another Young Ireland rebel forced into exile, founded the Fenian Brotherhood in New York in 1858, as the US-based sister organization of the Irish Republican Brotherhood, themselves dedicated to liberating Ireland from English rule. By 1863 they had organized their first convention, and in 1864 they sponsored a "Great Irish National Fair" in Chicago. "Chicago's Fenian Fair illustrates a critical dimension of the organization in the United States," wrote a historian of Irish nationalism: "its largely working-class membership and its deep connections with the Civil War–era labor movement." Multiple unions proudly endorsed the Fenian Fair. In the US, Fenianism's political radicalism included demands for an eight-hour workday.[12]

By 1865 the Fenian Brotherhood could count perhaps as many as 250,000 members from their elegant headquarters on Union Square. They had also established a Fenian sisterhood, with up to 300 "circles" or local branches. The sisterhood primarily raised money for the cause; Fenian women sheltered illegal activities, "nerved their men to action," and made banners, flags, uniforms, and other badges of Fenianism. The founder of the Fenian sisterhood, Ellen O'Mahony, declared "we are an organised body of ladies, whose object is the attainment of an Irish government for Ireland," adding "they call us rebels, and we glory in the name."[13]

Fenian leadership counted many Civil War veterans, including O'Mahony and General Thomas Sweeney, the Cork-born, one-armed veteran of the Mexican American and Civil Wars. But faction plagued the Fenians: some wanted only to work toward fostering and funding rebellion in Ireland, while others convinced themselves their best hope to free Ireland lay with a military invasion of Canada.

Readers may find this astonishing or even incomprehensible but in 1866, the idea made considerably more sense and might even have succeeded. For decades Americans had eyed Canada and wondered whether "manifest destiny" meant the US controlling the entire continent. England had flirted with the Confederacy during the Civil War, and Canada was England: "Union voices accused the British government of turning a blind eye to the construction of Confederate ships in British ports and of tolerating Confederate subversives on Canadian soil," including a notorious raid on St. Alban's, Vermont, by Confederate soldiers.[14]

The nation of Canada as known today did not yet exist, and the colony included many loyal subjects as well as many restive Irish, French, and Native Americans who had no particular love for the queen of England and might well have preferred the Stars and Stripes. About 600,000 Irish emigrated to Canada between 1830 and 1850. Surely they would join their fellow Hibernians?

The first Fenian invasion aimed to capture Campobello Island in

Canada, just off the coast of Maine; it failed miserably. The second, by far the most successful, involved about 1,000 Fenians, many veterans of the Civil War, marching to Fort Erie just across the river from Buffalo. Their leader, John C. O'Neill, no relation to Francis, had served in the cavalry in the Civil War, been wounded in the leg, and ended his army career as a captain. John C. pronounced himself "a firm believer in steel as the cure of Irish grievances" and quickly found a leading role. He wrote, "Canada is a province of Great Britain; the English flag floats over it and English soldiers protect it." "Wherever the English flag and English soldiers are found," he insisted, "Irishmen have a right to attack."[15]

In the Battle of Ridgeway, General O'Neill's Fenians captured the Union Jack. But US warships, including the *Michigan*, still moored at Erie when Francis worked there, prevented reinforcements from joining the advance, and O'Neill's men had to retreat. Two later raids from St. Albans in 1866 and 1870 involved roughly five hundred Fenian soldiers, and captured the hamlet of Pigeon Hill. Both ended in failure without the expected additions of men and materials. General O'Neill then moved his operations to the west: Fenians founded the town of O'Neill, Nebraska, in his honor. He led one more raid into Manitoba, this time with only small force of thirtysome men. Expectations that the Metis would join the Fenians proved ill founded, and American authorities arrested General O'Neill before he entered Canada. The US government would sell guns to the Union veterans in the Fenian leadership, offering tacit approval, and turn a blind eye to both planning and the initial forays. But then federal forces would move in swiftly to stop reinforcements and prevent the raids from from being carried out as planned.[16]

Francis O'Neill did not participate in Fenian raids, unlike his schoolmate Patrick O'Brien, but Fenian activities demonstrate one of the ways Irish Americans tried to make sense of their place in America and of their relationship to the country they had left. Francis could not have missed the Fenians: in each of these episodes, they operated more or less openly, with newspapers reporting on gatherings of men with Irish accents in cities like Erie. Irishwomen sewed green Fenian flags, with either the harp of Erin or a golden sunrise, and Fenians often sported green insignia or homemade uniforms. Newspapers regularly speculated about the Fenians, their constant infighting, and their multiple plans. Mark Twain mocked the strange combination of secrecy and publicity that accompanied Fenian actions: "First, we have the portentous mystery that precedes it for six months, when all the air is filled with stage whisperings; when "Councils" meet every night with awful secrecy, and the membership try to see who can get up first in the morning and tell the proceedings," Twain wrote. "In solemn whisperings at dead of night they secretly plan a Canadian raid, and publish it in the *World* next morning." "No news travels so freely or so fast as the secret doings of the Fenian Brotherhood."[17]

The Fenian raids, as Twain observed, took up space in public imagination far beyond the actual number of participants. While the press and Twain offered ridicule, the press also hyperventilated at length about dangerous Fenian terrorists. And indeed England had thoroughly infiltrated the organization. One of General John O'Neill's closest advisers, "Henri Le Caron," later revealed himself a spy for the queen. "Well before the standardization of the mug shot, the photographing of Fenians and circulation of their images among authorities became part of a mid- nineteenth century consolidation and expansion of state power through the suspension of rights." The word "terrorism" first appeared in relation to Fenian attacks in England. Their activities were at once extremely public, top secret, and known in great detail by English and American authorities. They were at once the objects of scorn and deeply feared as a threat to government authority.[18]

"The Fenian is not that reasoning creature which his critics in England have called him, a swindler, a plunderer, a filibuster," wrote an English visitor: "He is that much more unreasonable animal, a dreamer, an enthusiast, a poet." Francis O'Neill's schoolmate Patrick O'Brien was a Fenian, and a dreamer, and a bad poet, and a very different version of Irish than Francis—although Francis wrote occasional poetry, he liked practical results more than dreamy talk. The "incurably verbal" Fenians were a story Irish immigrants told themselves about themselves, a story about exile and rebellion and ethnic distinctiveness. It was a story O'Neill deliberately chose to hear from a distance.[19]

Figure 11 Advertisement for Fenian Collars, 1866. In Prints and Photos Division, Library of Congress, https://lccn.loc.gov/96512049. Fenianism was both a deeply felt grievance at political injustice and a sentimental form of connection to the Old Country.

In a characteristically American twist, the story included lithographs, prints, and consumer goods like "Fenian's Comfort Tobacco" and Fenian collars for men's shirts. For many, Irish membership in the Fenians probably had as much sentimental as tactical meaning.[20]

Part of that story involved raising money through the sale of "Fenian Bonds." These bonds, purchased each for as little as $5 or as much as $500, earned interest payable six months from the recognition of the establishment of the Irish republic. The bonds bore representations of Irish patriots and a goddess figure with a harp directing a Union soldier's attention to Ireland. Fenian bonds offered a contract with ideals, a tangible symbol of faith in the dream of an Irish republic, an emotional as well as fiscal bond. Purchasers in the

US knew they would never see their homeland again; the bonds represented an investment in both past and future.

But newspapers mocked the Fenian bonds as a foolish project, a confidence game designed to steal "the greenbacks of Paddy and Bridget." "It is quite useless," wrote the *New York Times*, "trying to arrest the fatal alacrity with which the common class of Irish men rush to the snare of every sharper, who would lure them to their ruin." Ellen O'Mahony issued an appeal to "the intelligent women of Ireland" to buy Fenian bonds. We all know what that means, the *Times* wrote: "it means Bridget . . . Poor, honest, hard-working, affectionate Bridget." "We have much faith in Bridget," the *Times* condescended, and we trust that if "any of these mousing bond agents, comes fumbling round her strong-box, or sniffing at her savings-bank book, she will rise in the majesty of her wrath, and turn the trollop out of the kitchen." But the bonds raised as much as $100,000 for the cause of Irish independence. When the Irish republic was finally established in the 1930s, Éamon DeValera's government paid more than $2.5 million to the holders of Fenian bonds.[21]

The Fenians also helped remake the idea of citizenship itself. Lucy Sayler, in *Under the Starry Flag*, tells the story of the Fenians who bought an old ship, renamed it *Erin's Hope*, and sailed from New York to Sligo in 1867. *Erin's Hope* had a cargo of rifles and other weapons to support an Irish rebellion—which English spies had already quashed by the time the ship arrived. The men sailed around the coast to near Clonakilty, in County Cork, where the English authorities arrested them when they came ashore. The English charged the four leaders with "treason-felony" and threw them into Dublin's Kilmainham jail. But these men, born in Ireland, were all now American citizens. They protested their arrest, insisting they had committed no actual crime—they had no idea those weapons were in the hold! And they wrote to the US embassy and American newspapers demanding the rights of Americans.

English law insisted that anyone born a subject of the queen remained a subject of the queen forever. The queen's subjects could no more change that status than they could change the color of their eyes. The claim underlay the War of 1812, which had failed to resolve the question. The most prominent prisoner, Charles Warren, had come to the US in 1853 after the famine devastated his native County Cork. Warren fought with Thomas Meagher's "Irish Brigade" in the Civil War, then became a citizen in 1866. Taking that oath required only being "a free white person" and five years' residence, but new citizens had to specifically renounce the authority of the queen. Salyer captures the ambivalent feeling the oath of citizenship might evoke:

> For Irish nationalists . . . it spoke, on the one hand, of their sense of loss—of being involuntarily thrust from their homeland by the cruel English . . . [but for those] fighting to free Ireland from Britain, it could be a thrilling individual declaration of independence to be able to renounce allegiance to the Queen of England and say "I am an American citizen."

US citizenship freed an Irish immigrant from "the shackles of British slavery" and let an American citizen like Warren demand and receive the protection of the US government. The Warren case—driven partly by the power of Irish votes—led Congress to pass the 1868 Expatriation Act, which insisted that every man had the right to determine "where his citizenship shall be, what country he shall give his allegiance to." It declared citizenship something portable, something one could *choose*. In Dublin, newspapers hailed the act for placing "Irish citizens on a footing of equality with the native-born": an Irish-born citizen was no less an American than the native-born Yankee. If "no less American," were they then less Irish?[22]

## Bound for Missouri

Not yet a citizen, barely an adult, Francis O'Neill labored for his brother in Erie. If tales of the Fenians stirred his blood, he made no mention of it. Instead his blood was stirred by a series of letters in the *Boston Pilot*, then the nation's leading Catholic newspaper. From the town of Edina, Knox County, in the northeast of Missouri, the letters told of the "splendid opportunities for procuring eligible farms at very cheap rates," adding "it is painful to the Catholic pastor, to see fine places which are needed and would be purchased by members of his own religion . . . gobbled up by persons who are opposed to us and to our Church." The author, pastor Bernard P. McMenomy, added that Edina had a fine Catholic church and excellent healthful land going for as little as $5 an acre. A month later the pastor added that "it is the best location, take it all in all, for Catholic emigrants in the West. . . . Will our Catholic people take a hint from the above, and lead the advance before the New England puritans fill up the country?"[23]

In 1869 a letter from William Clancy, an Edina lawyer, sought "an industrious class of farmers and mechanics, who are sober and upright in their ways," insisting "to such a class, a promising future is treasured up in Knox County." Clancy wrote to the *Pilot* and to the *Irish World, Cincinnati Telegraph, Irish American,* and other eastern Catholic journals, translating them into German for German Catholic newspapers. A year later Clancy described the land "rising and failing . . . wave-like, quite unlike the low, flat prairies of southern and central Illinois, and far more beautiful to the eye of the passing traveller," adding implausibly "it is said by Germans that this country will excel the hills and valleys of the Rhine in the products of the vine." Clancy noted the addition of a second Catholic church and a Catholic school, run by the "Sisters of Loretto," and insisted that the growing town needed carpenters, a tailor, and a first-class hotel. In Erie, O'Neill wrote, these "alluring letters" "attracted considerable attention, and so the present writer, the only unmarried member of the [work] gang, agreed to go west to investigate."[24]

The *Pilot* letters give a sense of the degree to which Catholics, mostly Irish and German, felt both apart and entitled, eager to get to Missouri before New England Puritans "gobbled up the land" and closed them out; full of individual ambition, possibly equal citizens, but also aware of themselves as a different, self-segregating community. The letters framed settlement in Missouri not just as a chance to prosper but as a chance to seed Catholicism on the prairie, exactly the sort of thing men like Samuel Morse worried about. O'Neill tells us he went on behalf of members of Philip's work crew, to investigate and presumably write back: he went as a representative of Irish community.

"I found that the beauties of the available land . . . had not been exaggerated," O'Neill wrote, "so while not neglecting the object of my mission," he went to work on a gang cutting a railroad right of way, for $1.75 a day, from 6:00 a.m. to 6:00 p.m., in "well nigh unendurable" heat. One Sunday O'Neill, then boarding in a log cabin, got a visit from Thomas Broderick, a native of Galway. Broderick asked him to take the examination for schoolteacher. "Having had four years' experience as a monitor in the Bantry National School," O'Neill boasted, "I passed without flaw." Broderick, the director of schools, hired O'Neill as a teacher specializing in mathematics. Eventually, he boarded with Broderick's family and tutored Broderick himself, "a fine performer on the flute" whose "knowledge of figures was very weak."[25]

### Irish and American Music on the Prairie

Edina at that point had a population of roughly 1,000 people, but O'Neill described a very lively social life and, in particular, a rich musical world. He remembered it as very Irish and also as very "multicultural." "Not a week passed during the winter months without a dance or two being held among the farmers," he wrote, "one third of whom were Irish." But he also recalled "such a motley crowd—fiddlers galore, and each with his instrument. Irish, Germans, French—types of their respective races—and the gigantic Kentuckians, whose heads were endangered by the low ceilings, crowded in, and never a misunderstanding or display of ill-nature marred those gatherings." The Irish, German, and French could very well have been Catholics, drawn by newspaper promotions, but the gigantic Kentuckians probably were not.[26]

O'Neill described solo playing, with fiddlers taking turns: "As a matter of sociability and helpfulness, those who could fiddle brought their instruments and relieved one another." He remembered as many as nine fiddlers at one dance. "Fiddlers in Missouri and other middle and western states were as numerous as harpers in Ireland in the eighteenth century." O'Neill as a child rarely traveled more than a day's walk from his home. Now, in Edina, he would have a chance to learn lots of new tunes, as each fiddler took a turn.[27]

As in Ireland, dance music in Missouri was a solo art, not an ensemble performance. The dance music O'Neill described in Edina, as in Ireland, involved no harmony. A fiddle might play two notes on occasion: a second instrument might play a harmonized variation while the first played the melody, but as in Ireland this seems to have been almost purely melodic music, with rhythmic melodies calculated to set a dancer's feet to work. Playing for dancers demanded good steady time, endurance, repetition, and a driving rhythm a dancer could neither miss nor lose. All the fiddlers in Edina could deliver these qualities, regardless of nationality.[28]

Many of the tunes O'Neill heard in Edina had no consistent names. People learned them by ear and named them as they pleased: they acquired multiple names in different communities. A musician heard a tune in the moment and committed it to memory, playing variations as he or she saw fit. O'Neill wrote that "seated behind the fiddler, intent on picking up the tunes, was my accustomed post, but how much was memorized on those occasions cannot now be definitely stated." Presumably O'Neill had a flute or a tin whistle. O'Neill "attended every dance among the farmers . . . mainly for the purpose of learning the tunes which attracted my fancy." His description of Edina shows us just how much the dance music of French, German, Irish, and American people had in common.

"Three tunes, however, distinctly obtrude on my memory," O'Neil later wrote: "a reel played by Ike Forrester, the 'Village Blacksmith,' which was named after him; 'My Love is Fair and Handsome,' Mr. Broderick's favorite reel; and a quickstep, which I named 'Nolan, the Soldier.'" Nolan, O'Neill explained, "had been a fifer in the Confederate army during the Civil War. His son was an excellent drummer, and both gave free exhibitions of their skill on the public square at Edina to enliven the evenings while the weather was fine."

Folklorist and Missouri fiddler Howard Wight Marshall has explored O'Neill's time in Edina in depth, focusing specifically on where the tunes came from because, as he notes, "[American] old-time fiddlers and Irish fiddlers share many tunes (albeit with different titles), and they share a love of dance music." O'Neill called Nolan's tune a "quickstep," which Marshall argues would mean a "fife-and-drum marching tune in 6/8 time." Although Noland and son might have learned the tune in the Confederate Army, O'Neill included it in his first published collection of music, *O'Neill's Music of Ireland*, 1903. He omitted it from his second collection, *Dance Music of Ireland*, partly because of criticism that he had included too many non-Irish tunes in his first book.

The idea of national music, of folk music, arises again not from isolation but from its opposite, from contact with the larger world. Watching French, German, American, and Irish settlers dancing in the barns on Saturday nights led O'Neill to think about the differences between the tunes and to sort out what was Irish and what was not. As Marshall notes, many Irish scholars work hard to ascertain the authenticity of Irish tunes. "Tunes from preindustrial times, which many consider valuable, almost sacred, are their icons of cultural heritage that require protection and preservation." Irish music had a long-standing connection to Irish national identity. "Nolan the Soldier" bears a close resemblance to multiple tunes regarded as more "authentically Irish," including jigs called "Paddy O'Flynn," "the Lass o' Gowrie," and "the Wicklow March." O'Neill's friend, the vaudeville piper and comedian Patsy Touhey, recorded a version he called "The Miners of Wicklow," under which name the tune appears in a collection of Scottish and Irish tunes dating to 1782. O'Neill, on the Missouri plains, started drawing up the tune's family tree.

O'Neill's tune "The Village Blacksmith" had an equally complicated genealogy. He named it after Aescelis (Ike) Forrester, a fiddling blacksmith then living in Edina; the tune appears in the same 1782 collection referenced above as "The Merry Blacksmith." It appeared in a 1875 Scottish tune book as "Paddy on the Railroad." O'Neill accidentally listed it twice in his 1907 collection, once as "The Village Blacksmith" and once as "The Corkonian." Marshall reports old-time fiddlers today often call it "Eminence Breakdown." The first recording of the tune came in 1915 from John Kimmel, a German American accordionist from Brooklyn who made a series of Irish music recordings.[29]

Music traveled and moved like a living thing, crossing cultural boundaries, changed by experience. O'Neill's project traced the movement and tried to fix the tune's citizenship. Irish and American fiddlers play a reel called, in Ireland, "Miss McCleod's." Americans interested in Appalachian, "old-time," or bluegrass music know it as "Uncle Joe." Under both titles the song marks a specific kind of national identity or "authentic" feeling: it can be authentically Irish or authentically American. A hornpipe, "The Red Haired Boy," similarly appears in Ireland and North America under different names. Different regions inflect it differently and impart a different "feel"; individual musicians improvise variations or substitute different notes; eventually it might become a new tune altogether. O'Neill would have heard songs that seemed both familiar and unfamiliar. He wanted to sort those differences out, just as he wanted to sort out what of his own person was Irish, what was English, and what was becoming American.

There is, of course, no single way to enjoy or appreciate music. We might imagine a tune as something we "just like" or respond to with "Who cares? Just enjoy the music!" But all music, then and now, arrives to us "coded" in various ways: as "Celtic" or "old-time" or folk or EDM or "Latin" or death metal. The music sounds "like" something, and that something marks a lifestyle, an ethnicity, a nationality, or a way of being. We enjoy or dislike it with those frames in place. The Edina fiddlers must have played tunes from their respective homelands as well as tunes they heard in army camps, work gangs, theaters, saloons, and minstrel shows. Marshall notes the extensive influence Africans Americans exerted on Missouri fiddling styles. The music O'Neill heard in Edina would surely have included minstrel show tunes as well as forms of playing inflected by the African Americans living in Missouri: by 1870, minstrel show music had been the most popular form of music in the US for nearly forty years. O'Neill would later spend considerable time trying to decide whether American fiddle tunes like "The Arkansas Traveler" or "Turkey in the Straw," known in minstrel shows as "Old Zip Coon," were actually Irish.

O'Neill started to police the music, to organize and sort it, precisely because of the blurring of lines and the merger of traditions, the portability of citizenship and identity. Edina neighbors got together to have a dance, and the various amateur musicians played music they and their neighbors could all dance to. Some of it probably came from the old country, some probably from the new. German, French, and Irish settlers likely shared a Catholic identity but also shared a common rural farming culture with Kentuckians and Missouri natives, and they could speak to each other musically with no trouble at all. Here O'Neill found another way of being Irish: not fiery nationalism but polyglot prairie Catholicism and the life of farming.

He clearly enjoyed the culture of Edina, and to a child of farmers like O'Neill, much of it would have seemed familiar. No matter their backgrounds, farmers in Edina talked about weather, crops, livestock: the culture of farming. "Between barn dances, well supplied with fiddlers, and hunting, life in Knox County was never monotonous in winter," he wrote. The German, Irish, and French dancers and fiddlers shared a way of life and a set of ambitions. O'Neill might have made a life in Edina, bought property, possibly ended up directing the public schools; he would have helped create an American culture in Edina out of its settlers' shared experiences. But again we get a sense of O'Neill as "apart." While others dance and flirt or play the fiddle, O'Neill sits behind the soloist memorizing tunes, policing the difference between them.

## A Sudden Change of Plan: Marriage and Chicago

When the school term ended, taking his salary with it, O'Neill decided to head to Chicago for summer work, "with many pleasant memories and a choice of schools awaiting my return next fall." He didn't say why Chicago and not somewhere much closer, for example, St. Louis. He wrote that he sailed on the Great Lakes on the barque *Pensaukee* under Captain Patrick Myers. O'Neill noted only that "every member of the crew could converse in Irish," so perhaps the Irish community attracted him. Chicago indeed had one of the largest Irish-born populations in the US, but O'Neill left after the summer shipping season and headed back to Edina to resume teaching.[30]

Here his recollections grow more oblique, and his language stumbles. "I took a stopover in Normal, Illinois to visit the Rogers family, whose acquaintance I had made on the packet ship *Emerald Isle*, and renewed my friendship with the Rogers family in Brooklyn, New York after each voyage." This odd sentence tells us he visited the family at least twice while living in New York, though he made no mention of it while he described his time with the felonious Mrs. Reid. "The family was preparing to leave, some going south for the winter, others returning to Brooklyn, while the one who had bought a home remained," O'Neill continued. "The outcome of this unexpected turn of affairs was that instead of proceeding to Edina, Missouri to teach school, I married the handsome Anna Rogers on November 30, 1870 and returned to Chicago, while all the rest of the family plan was carried out as intended."[31]

What a strange or even ridiculous way to talk about a marriage that would last longer than sixty years and include the birth of ten children. Readers might like to know more about Anna Rogers, but almost no evidence exists. We know that *Emerald Isle* deposited Mary, the mother, and Anna, Julia, and a son John Rogers in New York in 1866. The 1870 census, recorded in Normal, Illinois, in July of that year, shows an Anna Rogers, age twenty-two and born in Ireland, working as a servant in a German American household. It also shows a Julia Rogers working as a servant in a different home. A Mary Rogers, age fifty-five, appears as a "keeping house" with an Anthony Rogers, twenty-six. Mary lived in Normal, presumably as "the one who had bought a home," but Mary's daughters Anna and Julia worked as domestics.

### Irishwomen and Domestic Work

Irishwomen went into domestic service in very large numbers. "In Boston in 1850, almost 72 percent of domestic servants were natives of Ireland," while in Kingston, New York, in 1860, 94.5 percent of the Irishwomen whose occupations were identified worked in domestic service. In 1880, "44 percent of New York City's domestic servants were Irish natives." In the same year, more than 40 percent of the

OUR SELF-MADE "COOKS."—FROM PAUPERS TO POTENTATES.

Figure 12 The satirical magazine *Puck* especially loved to attack "Bridget," the stereotypical female Irish servant. *Puck*, January 30, 1884, 352. Copy in author's possession.

servants in "Boston, Cambridge, Fall River, Hartford, Jersey City, New Haven, Providence and Troy" were natives of Ireland.[32]

Newspapers and magazines often referred to the domestic help generically as "Bridget," as in the example above describing Fenian bonds. In a cartoon from *Puck*, 1883, "The Irish Declaration of Independence That We Are All Familiar With," oversized, brutish "Bridget" ignores her employer's pleas.[33]

Less than a year later, *Puck* returned to the theme: in this case, the cartoon's left side shows a ragged, barefoot Irishwoman surrounded by her starving family, captioned "They are evicted in the Old Country." On the right side, the same woman, with typically simian and coarse features, wears loudly fashionable clothes and with imperious gesture evicts her employer from the kitchen, while her husband or boyfriend—a policeman, of course—drinks tea. "But in America they do all the evicting themselves," reads the caption. O'Neill would become a policeman and grow an impressive mustache, after marrying an Irish servant woman: the cartoon must have struck close to home.

While the cartoon insults "Bridget," it also points out that in Ireland the starving woman pleads to avoid eviction, while in the US she reads a fashion magazine, wears heels, has a husband or suitor, can express her religious identity freely (the image of St. Patrick on the wall), and enjoys some degree of autonomy and authority over the kitchen.[34]

O'Neill never describes Anna working after their marriage, or before their marriage for that matter. But his tune titles give some sense that he might have objected to depictions of Irishwomen as domestics. One of the most famous Irish jigs, instantly familiar today and almost as much a cliché as "Danny Boy," is usually called "The Irish Washerwoman." In his 1907 collection, *The Dance Music of Ireland*, O'Neill renamed it simply "The Irishwoman," a deliberate choice noted by other scholars at the time.[35]

O'Neill never says what the "rest of the family plan" amounted to or explained the suddenness of the marriage. Why Anna and Francis moved to Chicago goes unexplained. They might have made a life in Edina. Rural life appealed to them: the O'Neills later bought an 80 acre farm and orchard in rural Illinois. In 1901 the *Chicago Tribune* reported that Francis had written to Anna through his time at sea, and in the course of these letters, "O'Neill concluded to give up the life on the sea for a home on the land." This seems likely enough: O'Neill's silence on the subject seems less so, except that his silence on personal matters never changes at any point in his memoir.[36]

## Hard Work and Poor Chances in Chicago

The young couple moved to Chicago "without relatives or friends" in November 1870, and Francis trudged through the snow to find work. He went to a meatpacking house, where he found "scores of eager men" waiting to be "picked for work in the cellar." Told that the "German cellar boss" needed five men one morning, O'Neill saw the foreman eyeing a group of five Germans. He says he ducked under one of the men's arms just as the foreman was making his pick and so snuck into the job of "trucking dressed hogs and pounding ice for $1.75 a day." He earned $50 for his first winter in the dirty, booming city.[37]

In Chicago "Irish" signified differently than it did at sea or in Edina. O'Neill's next job came at the Palmer and Fuller planing mill. He had a discussion with another man about wages and was told to expect less than he hoped. "Then I noticed I was the only man of my race on the job," O'Neill wrote, "so when Mr Shepherd, the foreman, came around, I asked him." The foreman told O'Neill he was a good hand on the planing machine and offered him $1.25 a day, higher wages than the others were making. O'Neill called this "complementary, but by no means satisfactory," and looked for other work. By "the only man of my race," he might have meant the only white man, which could explain his sense of entitlement to higher wages. But he might have meant the only Irishman. In 1870 only about 4,000 African Americans lived in Chicago, out of more than 298,000 people. O'Neill had certainly been in the US long enough to understand how white privilege operated, but he also told a story of how Germans got preference for work in the packinghouse, and he often used the word "race" when describing the Irish people. Earlier we saw him describing Irish, German, and French fiddlers in Edina as "types of their race." Immigrants to Chicago preferred to hire their own, but other kinds of alliance could transcend ethnicity.

He saw this favoritism on his next job, in May 1871, which took him to the Chicago and Alton railroad freight yards. With his education, he ended up doing a clerk's work, he wrote, for a laborer's pay. "Desirable positions and even sinecures were invariably given to the relatives of the railroad officials." He made only $1.50 a day, but supplemented his wages with night work in the yard. "The head checker, Mike Ryan," picked O'Neill for this work: "it was by favor of Ryan that I got this chance." So here favoritism works both for and against him: Irishman Ryan gives him a chance to make extra money, presumably at the expense of someone not born Irish, but good jobs go to the owner's family and friends. O'Neill's "race" gains him slightly higher wages in the planing mill. Favors lubricated Chicago's employment market: favors exchanged through ethnic and personal connections.

"Through an acquaintance made in tracing misdirected freight," O'Neill landed a job with the shipping department of a large dry goods retailer, John V. Farwell. The job paid $2 a day, with some possibilities for advancement. One employee noticed O'Neill's head for mathematics; "confidentially, he suggested a society of which he was a member that could advance my interests." Probably it was the Young Men's Christian Association: Farwell was a leader in the YMCA. A Catholic youth in 1870 would surely hesitate to join. O'Neill's optimism about a future in retail faded as he came to believe that "membership in favored organizations . . . exercised a controlling influence in all departments." He could not advance without joining those organizations.[38]

In all these stories he tells of his early employment, personal, ethnic, and religious ties prevail, not any motion of "merit." At Farwell's, "O'Neill had found himself blocked from promotion by his lack of connections and probably his Irish roots, despite a classical education in Ireland." O'Neill would eventually seek a job on the police force because it offered "one of the few avenues of advancement open to ambitious Irish immigrants who lacked even the small amounts of capital needed to open a saloon or boardinghouse and who faced considerable difficulties securing promotion within established firms."[39]

In October 1871 most of central Chicago burned down, killing roughly 300 people and leaving possibly 100,000 people homeless. O'Neill did not say where he and Anna lived at the time of the fire, but city directories place a Francis O'Neill, laborer, at 461 S. Jefferson Street in 1871. The fire would have come very close to that address, possibly destroying houses there. O'Neill's descendants have a set of dishes scorched in the fire. He said almost nothing about the fire, only that it increased rents and made them start to look for a house to buy.[40]

Roughly a month after the fire, on November 2, Anna and Francis had their first child, a son, baptized John Francis O'Neill. Initiating a grim pattern the O'Neills would come to know horribly well, the boy died ten days later. A year later they had a second son, also baptized John Francis O'Neill, and a year later a daughter, Mary Catherine: both children died on the same day in 1876. A third son, baptized Francis, died in 1879; a fourth son, Phillip, died in 1885 at age two. Characteristically, O'Neill said little about this crushing round of regular grief. He later wrote in a letter that "all died not from an inherent constitutional weakness but from germ or microbe ailment such as scarlet fever, diphtheria, or spinal meningitis." Child mortality was much higher in the 1870s, and Chicago had a notoriously unhealthy drinking water supply, contaminated by human waste and the offal of the stockyards, so the O'Neills would hardly have mourned alone. But he tells us so little that we can only imagine how this affected his life and especially the life of Anna, who bore and nursed the children. Four daughters survived into adulthood, but "the crowning sorrow" came with the death of their last son, Rogers, in 1905, at age eighteen. O'Neill says at multiple times that grief silenced music in his home, that Anna could not bear to hear it, especially after the death of Rogers, who played the fiddle and shared his father's knowledge of Irish tunes. Francis had his work and career: Anna had no such consolations and left no direct personal accounts of her feelings. "I would not sound even a flageolet [a tin whistle] in his mother's hearing," he told an Irish correspondent after Rogers died. O'Neill's granddaughter recalled him fondly, but she recalled her grandmother "as dour and crabby" and "not loving toward her grand daughters." Her life seems to have been circumscribed by home: she does not appear even in the records of the churches to which they belonged.[41]

## Bridgeport and Its Community

While his wife grieved at home, Francis immersed himself in his work and the work of getting ahead. "Frank" O'Neill took the oath of citizenship on May 23, 1873. Timothy Sullivan, presumably a neighbor, attested to Francis's necessary term in residence in the US and his having "behaved himself as a man of good moral character." Francis swore that he was "an alien, a free white person," and that he had

Figure 13 Anna Rogers O'Neill. The hand-colored original of this image comes from the private collection of Mary Mooney Lesch.

arrived as a minor. He additionally twice swore to "renounce forever all allegiance and fidelity to every Foreign Prince, Potentate, State or Sovereignty, whatever, and particularly that allegiance and fidelity which he in any wise owes to . . ." and here Francis in the space provided added, in his own hand: "the Queen of Great Britain and Ireland." As described above, we can only imagine the emotional force of this declaration, which freed the Irish from the queen's authority at the cost of legal and political ties to their homeland and offered a stinging reminder of the queen's claim to dominion over Ireland.[42]

No longer a legal subject of the queen, he still had to work through the mental legacy of colonialism and figure out how to be Irish in America. By 1873 the O'Neills had moved to Bridgeport, probably the city's best-known Irish enclave and the neighborhood with the largest concentrations of Irish poor. Compared to East Coast cities, Chicago had less densely monolithic ethnic neighborhoods. Bridgeport also included Germans, Poles, and "Bohemians" in large numbers. In 1875 a reporter wrote that "there is probably as much real poverty in Bridgeport as anywhere in the town. It is also the haunt of the roughest characters." One resident claimed "every kid knee high carries a pistol and it's quite the thing to let it off every now and then." In 1882 the *Chicago Tribune* observed that Bridgeport had "in Chicago become a generic term for smells, for riots, bad whiskey and poor cigars." Bridgeport was also notorious for labor radicalism.[43]

For example, in 1877 the Great Railway Strike, starting in West Virginia, paralyzed rail traffic across the country. Strikers' demands included an eight-hour workday and nationalization of rail lines. In Chicago "Bridgeporters played a prominent role in the crowd actions and especially the violent confrontations with police. On the third day of the 1877 strike a contingent of Irish stockyard workers led by a butcher behind a Fenian banner sought to join the Bohemians along Halstead Street and fought a ferocious battle with the police." Richard Schneirov notes that police "arrested Mollie Cook and her two sons for firing at police from their home," while in Bridgeport proper "a local grocer, Miles Clynch, led a crowd of several hundred workers against the police."[44]

Newspaper accounts of the Chicago strike called it a Red War and routinely dismissed strikers as lazy toughs or mocked their relative poverty. The *Tribune* described "an old Hibernian with a shovel which he carried like a bayonet. He was dressed in dilapidated trousers that looked like a half-tanned hide, and ragged gray shirt. . . . Tied round his left arm was a red rug that once had done duty as a handkerchief and with this he seemed to waive the rabble on." A crowd of striking lumbermen were described as "mostly of Hibernian extraction." Police arrested another group at the Fuller and Palmer planing mill, where O'Neill had once worked: "the prisoners are mostly Irish and Bohemians." Strike leaders "openly identified the union with Irish nationalism," and police in Bridgeport, themselves mostly Irish, often sympathized openly with strikers. In 1882 police in Bridgeport "took a hands-off approach as committees of strikers beat scabs and visited boardinghouses to remonstrate with the families of strikebreakers." An article in the *Tribune* that same year complained that "the police stood quietly about and begged a few small boys to disperse now and then, but did absolutely nothing to scatter the turbulent strikers." Bridgeport police "were known to and were relatives of the strikers. The representatives of the company saw that it was not at all natural that a brother would be inclined to arrest a brother, or a cousin a cousin." They asked to have North Side police transferred to Bridgeport.[45]

O'Neill had lived as an unskilled worker and had worked in packing houses, in freight yards, and on boats. But he came from the strong farmer class and had an education that set him apart from his Irish American fellows. Chicago offered ethnic solidarity and alliances based on country of origin, but it also offered other forms of alliance or organization that transcended ethnic loyalty.

By 1877 new American Francis O'Neill had joined the police force, having decided in 1873 that "a position on the police force with its salary of one thousand dollars per year appealed to me." The salary would amount to more than twice what he had ever made to date. "But how to obtain it was a problem." Here again Francis noted that in Chicago favors greased all wheels. Though he had on his side "a formal application signed by five citizens and testimonials from a member of Congress, the superintendent of the Chicago and Alton Railroad, and others equally prominent," all these "were ignored by the Board of Police and Fire Commissioners," who did the actual hiring. How he got congressional endorsement is unclear, but it mattered not because "all appointments in those days were charged to the political account of aldermen and others in high favor with the existing administration."[46]

## The Alderman's Favor and a Job on the Force

Chicago, like most cities at the time, had a government in which local aldermen or "ward bosses" held most of the power. Aldermen offered access to municipal jobs: police, fire companies, construction crews.

City workers of all sorts owed the alderman their jobs. Alderman often owned saloons or gambling houses and used the revenue to fund their largess; they helped their constituents if they got into legal trouble. "The alderman gives presents at weddings and christenings. He seizes these days of family festivities for making friends. . . . The alderman procures passes from the railroads when his constituents wish to visit friends or attend the funerals of distant relatives; he buys tickets galore for benefit entertainments." Jane Addams wrote that an alderman like Johnny Powers, born in Kilkenny a few years after O'Neill, could openly boast of providing municipal jobs to one-third of his district's voting population, all in exchange for votes.

Reformers wanted to break this cycle of "boss" politics and install a neutral government of trained professionals. They adopted civil service examinations as their weapon. People should have formal qualifications for the jobs they hold, reformers argued: basic education, but also a level of credentialed expertise equal to the jobs they aimed to fill. An engineer should have an education in engineering; a policeman should have at least literacy and a basic understanding of the law. If only personal favors governed hiring, Chicago would forever have contaminated drinking water, streets paved with randomly compacted garbage, and taxpayer dollars endlessly squandered on employees whose only skills lay in pleasing the alderman. Civil service tests would play a role throughout O'Neill's career. He invariably passed them with near-perfect scores. But the alderman had social charm, money, and the ability to get immediate, tangible results. Addams wrote, "what headway can the notion of civic purity, of honesty of administration, make against this big manifestation of human friendliness, this stalking survival of village kindness?"[47]

Francis experienced exactly this "stalking survival of village kindness" when, having applied for a job on the police force and "lacking any such influence, discouraged by failure, I was leaning against a lamppost, out on a street corner, not knowing what to do, when along came Alderman [William] Tracey, master mechanic for the Union Stock Yards and Transit Company." Tracey, born in New York State to an Irish Catholic family, had come to Chicago in the 1850s and worked as a blacksmith in the stockyards. Six years later he was elected alderman of the Sixth Ward, which included Bridgeport. He served on the Streets and Alleys Committee and on the Harbor and Bridges Committee, which gave him oversight of construction and hiring. Tracey told Francis, "come with me." Francis recollected that an alderman "was entitled to name two of the one hundred new men provided for the annual appropriation." Tracey told the Board of Police and Fire Commissioners that O'Neill was his second man, and presto, Francis now had a provisional job with the police and a long-term debt to Tracey, who had just demonstrated again how things worked in Chicago.

Addams wrote, "A young man may enter a saloon long after midnight, the legal closing hour, and seat himself at a gambling table, perfectly secure from interruption or arrest, because the place belongs to an alderman; but in order to secure this immunity the policeman on the beat must pretend not to see into the windows each time that he passes." The alderman got Francis a job, and Francis would never forget "the memory of this kindly act" and, presumably, though he does not say so, would return the favor by voting for Tracey at every opportunity, as well as by applying the law but lightly to any enterprises Tracey favored: that was how the system worked. Tracey lost his bid for reelection after 1874, but O'Neill would run into exactly this kind of quid pro quo many times. He would agree with Addams that "a certain contempt for the whole machinery of law and order is thus easily fostered." But he had no better options: the police offered Irish immigrants decent pay and avenues for advancement.[48]

## On the Job

O'Neill joined an organization people regarded with mixed feelings. "Between the 1840s and the end of the 1880s, every major northern city built a substantial police force. These new police departments were disciplined, bureaucratic, organized on military lines, and capable of patrolling entire cities." Facing rapid population growth and an often restive workforce, "Businessmen created . . . powerful armed forces that could protect the constituted order." Police departments veered between rational, systematic administration and patronage favoritism: reformers wanted "bureaucratic, efficient forces that could implement unpopular regulations, like temperance," but consistently "clashed with more pluralistic patronage bosses," who saw the police force as a nearly bottomless well of reward for constituents. Most of Chicago's police force in 1870 came from Germany or Ireland: the Irish were more likely to both make arrests and be arrested. At the time of O'Neill's hire, "the Irish never accounted for more than 20 percent of the city's population, but they accounted for as many as two-thirds of all arrests." In 1877 police in Bridgeport sympathized with strikers—their relatives, in many cases—but in the long run, a job on the police force placed the Irish immigrant on the side of "order" and discouraged political radicalism. In Bridgeport people jeered and hooted the new recruit who had left their ranks.[49]

"A new officer wasn't put into uniform directly then," probationary patrolman O'Neill remembered. "He was given a belt, a club, a revolver, and a star, and set loose in whatever assorted garb his wardrobe could provide." Chicagoans recognized him as a novice, "and the chaffing and hooting he had to stand was nearly unbearable. Often he would have missiles and decayed fruit thrown at him." The probationary period typically lasted several months, O'Neill told reporters, and "during that time he had to make good, and there was only one way to do that. This was to lick somebody." A policeman had to gain reputation by "winning at least one hard battle," after which he won the respect of the community and his peers. "If a policeman couldn't fight he had no business in Bridgeport. In those days the coppers did more fighting than anything else."[50]

Although the Irish cop became a stereotype, being both Irish *and* a cop presented complications. That striker, that fiery speaker arrested at a nationalist meeting or a union rally, might be your wife's cousin. But "in fact, integration into the ranks of the police department through patronage politics was probably one of the most important ways that Irish immigrants were turned away from radical politics." They joined the side of authority, and the job itself Americanized them, allied them with an idea of civic authority rather than simple ethnic tribalism. Yet another way of being Irish had presented itself: agent of state authority.[51]

"I wasn't given many instructions when I started out the first night from the Harrison street station in '73." O'Neill remembered: "they handed me a book of rules, I believe, to read at my leisure." The "principal article" O'Neill got "was a hickory night stick." With that "clutched in my hand, I was told to get on the job." One month into the job, on patrol near Clark and Monroe Streets, O'Neill heard a gunshot. Racing around the corner, he "faced a young man with a gun in hand, pursued by a Pinkerton watchman." He jumped to one side as the man fired, but too late. O'Neill had been shot.[52]

A Pinkerton watchman spotted the thief, John Bridges, climbing out the window of a store. He yelled "stop!" but Bridges shot at him instead and took off running. O'Neill came around the corner and confronted Bridges, who aimed his revolver and fired: the bullet took O'Neill in the shoulder. Bridges raised his gun to fire again, just as the Pinkerton arrived with his own revolver drawn. O'Neill brought his nightstick down on the thief's gun arm, then collapsed. Another patrolman, Herman Meyer, came running, and O'Neill went to the hospital for what turned out to be a nonfatal wound. "I am carrying that bullet with me to the grave," he wrote in his memoir, along with what he called a "rigid finger" due to nerve damage. "Next day I was a hero and a cripple and promoted for conspicuous bravery by the Board of Police and Fire Commissioners from probationer to regular patrolman."[53]

A job on the police force had many significant dangers. In 1877, newspapers reported "Officer Frank O'Neill, while attempting to arrest several disorderly men at the corner of Clark and Twelfth streets, was assaulted and handled roughly by seven ruffians. To defend himself he drew his revolver and fired three shots into the crowd. He thinks only one took effect, and that in the hand of the leader of the attack." A fellow officer recalled "many's the time O'Neill came in with the clothes torn off of [him]" from brawling with Bridgeport gangs. But most industrial work at the time had similar or worse dangers. The police force offered O'Neill good wages and prospects for advancement, advancement into a managerial bureaucracy. It would also offer him new ways of understanding himself and his society.[54]

# 4

# The New Policeman
## O'Neill's Rise through the Ranks

Some time around 1874 O'Neill stood a night watch with another young patrolman, Michael Raverty, whose parents had brought him from County Tyrone as a toddler. Raverty started quietly whistling a tune. O'Neill asked him the name: "The Mountaineer's March," Raverty replied. O'Neill, with a keen and acquisitive head for music, quickly memorized the melody. At the end of their shift, O'Neill thanked him for "shortening the night" with a tune.[1]

Not long after, in 1875, the city fired Raverty "for willful maltreatment of a citizen," without specifying the nature of the maltreatment. City Marshal George Dunlap had recently gotten oversight of the police, and the *Chicago Inter Ocean* happily declared Dunlap's reforms "are really being put into execution, and it now looks as if the unserviceable men on the force are to be got rid of as soon as possible." But instead, reformer Dunlap resigned three months later, and Raverty returned to the force. Chicago wore police reformers out: they made a big stir, fired a few people, and then politics cut the ground out from under them and the fired policemen crept back onto the force. By 1895 Raverty had made it to patrol sergeant while O'Neill had made captain.[2]

A few years before Raverty retired, in 1908, General Superintendent of Police Francis O'Neill published "The Mountaineer's March" in *O'Neill's Music of Ireland*, number 1030 in his lavish, carefully curated and organized collection of nearly 2,000 Irish tunes he had heard throughout his career. "I never forgot anything," he told a friend who asked where he got the tunes. Those traits, memory and organization, helped him as a cop and helped him as a music collector: his two careers advanced in parallel. He remembered favors and personal face-to-face contacts, but his professional career also engaged him in statistical communities, aggregations of people who could never possibly all know each other or even meet. The English had colonized his mind in Ireland, but here in Chicago a new kind of intellectual colonization, the mindset of industrial society, modified his earlier ways of thinking. As he placed "The Mountaineer's March" into a systematic collection of Irish music, he also placed Chicago citizens into systematic records. His police career pitted political cronyism and factional intrigue against new and powerful methods of rational administration.[3]

Chicago offered basically three main roles for Irish Americans of O'Neill's generation and talents: labor leader, alderman, or police captain. A labor leader built a community out of a relatively small subset of working-class people, not exclusively Irish. The alderman built a community that spanned more widely across class lines, again heavily but not exclusively Irish. The police captain similarly dealt with all classes and ethnicities. In many ways the police and a large national union, like the American Railway Union O'Neill confronted in the Pullman strike, had a great deal in common: they were both novel administrative bureaucracies with a strong interest in rationality and order. The alderman, as Jane Addams noted, was much more of a survival of the premodern village, and the alderman was the figure O'Neill constantly complained about and worked to escape, even as his career depended on political pull.

Daily life in Chicago turned on close personal connections and alliances, but Chicago was also at the cutting edge of changes in how Americans understood and managed individualism. The concrete, direct personal relations that fostered Chicago's corruption, and let O'Neill hear Raverty's tune, increasingly coexisted with a sense of belonging to a larger network of people united by technological systems, new "systems of order." O'Neill lived through this transition from a society of "village friendliness," personal favors, and ethnic partisanship to something closer to a modern society, in

**Figure 14** *Scientific American,* April 23, 1881, 255. A policeman could telephone to the nearest station and the station dispatch more men or an ambulance. The call box included a dial and pointer device that transmitted the nature of the crime and the location automatically. The police were connected in new ways: their lines of communication spanned multiple neighborhoods and gave the station house captain a wider field of vision.

which systemic administration and recordkeeping made it possible to reorganize society on a larger scale. Sailor O'Neill, just off the boat from California, had rejected the Emigrant Savings Bank, with its ledgers, its records of identity, and its systematic accounting, and trusted his earnings to a boardinghouse keeper. Later in Chicago he embraced the "information revolution" of the Gilded Age and then applied those techniques to music. Police work put him in the heart of this transformation and in turn played a central role in the way he thought about music and culture.

Police functioned as middlemen between government and the people. They had to have personal knowledge of the communities they policed, but as they moved up they had to develop a broader sense of the larger community they worked in, more of a bird's-eye view. O'Neill's scholarly inclinations eventually brought him to city hall as assistant clerk of the department and then later as chief clerk, positions that demanded careful records and an overview of the entire force. A patrolman surveilled his beat, but a captain or the chief clerk had to both manage the patrolmen and make connections between individual neighborhoods and the larger city. In O'Neill's case, this meant initially not just living in the Irish American ghetto but working with Chicago's many other immigrants; forging personal, local relations but also strategic alliances with different political factions. In the struggle for promotion, an Irishman was as likely to be his enemy as his friend.[4]

### Bridgeport Neighbors and the Web of Friendship

"Hard on the heels of the Great Fire," O'Neill remembered, "came the housing problem and the inevitable increase in rents." He looked in Bridgeport, the most Irish of Chicago neighborhoods, and "bought a lot on a side street for $550, paying $50 down and assuming a mortgage for the balance at 8 percent interest." As an unskilled laborer in Chicago, O'Neill made between $1.25 and $2 a day, making $550 slightly more than a year's wages. "On the remainder of our capital, exactly $100, the erection of a home was undertaken," he continued. Here again personal favors and connections ruled the day. "The lumber firm of Gardner and Spry, in whose ships I had sailed the previous year, furnished the material, accepting $50 cash and giving credit as required to be paid in installments of $10 every two weeks." He hired carpenters and commenced building. "The lumber, I regret to relate, being left unguarded at night, came in handy to those living in the vicinity," but when the carpenters finished, "I had a wooden box, twenty by sixteen feet, resting on cedar posts four feet from the ground." The O'Neills stepped up to their front door on a packing box; they had no money for additional lumber to divide the box into rooms, "but we made a home of it and got away from exorbitant rents for the rest of our lives."[5]

He depended on neighbors. "As a special favor a bricklayer

acquaintance was induced to build a chimney for me on Sunday." O'Neill continued: "I got a wagonload of bricks gratis from the ruins of the Chicago, Alton, and St. Louis Railroad freight house, being an employee; bought a barrel of mortar mixed and ready for use; and carried the hod myself." He especially remembered the "Swede who cut out the stringers of the front steps to oblige me after working hours. This gigantic young man was an expert in his trade. When I asked him his price after finishing, he replied; 'Oh, nothing! You are a poor man like myself trying to get along.'"

Earlier we saw Bridgeport residents supporting strikers and jeering the police: here we see O'Neill in community, benefiting from relationships formed at work and from the kindness of people who shared the same plight. The chimney built, O'Neill continued, "in a spirit of liberality," his friend the bricklayer announced that "I'm not going to charge you anything for my work, but I want you to buy my wife, Maggie, a shawl." "This and similar gracious acts by men of other races have never been forgotten," he wrote, "and it affords me pleasure to say that they have been paid with interest in later days when opportunities never anticipated came my way." He mixed kindness and rational calculation, the favors repaid "with interest."[6]

The young O'Neill sat between the cash economy, with interest charged at 8 percent, and a cashless economy of shared exchange and favors, of social reciprocity. In his memoirs O'Neill returns again and again to the cycle of social indebtedness and mutual obligation, seeing in it both the sweet milk of human kindness and the curdled milk of bribery and graft.

## The Progressive Critique

"A very little familiarity with the poor districts of any city," wrote Jane Addams of Chicago, "is sufficient to show how primitive and genuine are the neighborly relations." "There is the greatest willingness to lend or borrow anything," she continued, "and all the residents of the given tenement know the most intimate family affairs of all the others." Shared circumstances make "the ready outflow of sympathy and material assistance the most natural thing in the world." Addams recognized what O'Neill described, the reciprocity of community.

A sainted national figure before World War I and the symbol of Progressive Era reform in Chicago, Addams explained the "difference between the emotional kindness with which relief is given by one poor neighbor to another poor neighbor, and the guarded care with which relief is given by a charity visitor to a charity recipient." What she called "the neighborhood mind" is at once "confronted not only by the difference of method, but by an absolute clashing of two ethical standards," personal generosity and empathy versus systematic aid.[7]

Born to wealth, Addams spent her adult life working to overcome the perceptual blinders privilege imposed. She lived at Hull House, which she founded in 1889 as part of the settlement house movement, an international movement of middle- and upper-class reformers aiming to address the wrenching problems industrialization had brought about. A settlement house, located in "the slums," offered an "outpost in 'uncivilized' territory whose mission was conversion of the 'natives,' not to Christianity, but to culture." Hull House, one working-class visitor poignantly observed, "was the first house I had ever been in where books and magazines just lay around as if there were plenty of them in the world." Hull House offered classes and lectures for neighbors and served as a think tank for reform: in time Addams lost the sense of class superiority and became one of the country's most profound thinkers on the ethics of citizenship.[8]

When she grasped the mutuality of the poor, Addams came to understand that formal aid from institutions broke "the natural rule of giving, which, in a primitive society, is bounded only by the need of the recipient and the resources of the giver." That is, the poor gave to each other from sympathy and immediate need, as O'Neill described. The reformer gave as a result of systematic study and objective, efficient administration.[9]

Addams betrayed her upper-class origins when she called those relations "primitive." There is, of course, nothing at all primitive about social mutuality. Each person keeps in mind a complicated web in which X owes Y who owes Z: O'Neill's bricklayer friend turns down cash payment and instead asks O'Neill to get his wife a shawl. His Swedish neighbor, the carpenter, knew he could count on O'Neill to do him a good turn in the future. Not primitive but different, the working-class immigrant communities Addams and O'Neill described thrived on these complex personal relations.[10]

But the "primitive and genuine" neighborly relations O'Neill experienced in the 1870s were the very problem Addams aimed to solve in the 1890s. Addams recognized and valued the generosity and compassion she saw among working-class immigrant neighbors, but she wanted to find a larger idea of "citizenship" based on something besides tribalism or friendship, a notion of American citizenship that could cross class lines and serve all interests fairly and equally. She worked against the systems of patronage and favoritism that enabled O'Neill's rise and that he himself approached with profoundly mixed feelings. Police work put him directly between these conflicting ideals: on the one hand, in daily contact with the ordinary people he met as he walked his beat, beholden to politicians; on the other, an agent of rational state authority, charged with administering laws that came not from local custom or ethnic tradition but from the city's overall needs.

Proud of his new property, O'Neill worked by lamplight into the night, eventually turning the wooden box into "a nice five-room cottage with porches, and later a two-flat building by which we emerged into the landlord class on an initial capital of $150."[11]

O'Neill tells a story of neighborly generosity *and* a story of rational calculation. Entering "the landlord class" took him out of one community and replaced reciprocity with rent. Later his grandchildren would recall arguing over who got to collect the fifty cents a week O'Neill charged his tenants. Chicago contrasted community—which O'Neill deeply valued—against individual advancement, pitting personal relationships against rational, objective calculation, which he valued equally if not more. The point here is not faulting O'Neill for acting to his own advantage, but rather demonstrating the intellectual, social, and economic transitions immigrants like O'Neill confronted as they entered urban life.[12]

**Figure 15** Deering Street Station in Bridgeport in 1872, the year before O'Neill joined the force. Pictures of nineteenth-century policemen make it seem as though robust facial hair was the foremost qualification for the job. Chicago History Museum, ICHi-025743.

O'Neill grew very prosperous, apparently on real estate investments, but the political machine, based on "village friendliness," resisted all the reformer's efforts to break it. The Chicago alderman, Addams concluded, is not elected "because he is dishonest but because he is . . . a friend of everybody[;] he takes the liveliest interest in their personal affairs." The problem for O'Neill was the alderman's tendency to take a lively interest in *someone else's* personal affairs and promote that person over O'Neill.[13]

### The Favor Bank

Patrolman O'Neill walked a beat in the Bridgeport neighborhood for five years, until in 1878 the transfer of another, more senior officer opened up the position of desk sergeant at the Deering Street station. O'Neill filled the job provisionally, but when he asked about promotion his lieutenant told him to "see my friends, if I had any." The lieutenant had advanced his own favored candidate while he kept O'Neill at the station, on provisional duty, away from contacts who could advance his case. O'Neill wrote: "I went to City Hall and appealed to alderman [James H.] Gilbert, then acting mayor, who promised to see what could be done about it." It tells us a great deal that in a city of nearly half a million people, O'Neill—a common patrolman—could expect to see the acting mayor and further expect the acting mayor to intervene on his behalf. And indeed, while at city hall O'Neill ran into police magistrate John Summerfield. The police magistrate, somewhat like a justice of the peace, handled offenses involving less than $100. Summerfield also knew O'Neill and told Francis to follow him to the office of Valorius A. Seavey, then chief of police. "Chief Seavey, who had been my patrol sergeant in years gone by, was kindly disposed"; sadly other men stood ahead of him in the promotion line. But Judge Summerfield "would brook no refusal," and so "I returned to the Deering Street station a regularly appointed desk sergeant."[14]

At no point does an idea of either "merit" or "qualification" appear to enter this story. O'Neill gets promoted thanks to the chance intervention of a judge disposed on his behalf; appointment seems to depend entirely on whoever has the most pull at the moment. Neither Seavey nor Summerfield nor Gilbert were Irish: alliances in Chicago transcended ethnicity. "The police department," wrote the *Chicago Evening Post*, "is full of unrest, intrigue and self-seeking. Merit has never counted in promotions. No reward is offered for courage or fidelity. The principal officers have never been beyond suspicion." Every promotion involved some sort of elaborate political struggle or appeal to personal favor, with little or no concern for the applicant's fitness for the job. O'Neill's account of Chicago makes it hard to understand how the city managed to function at all.[15]

The Chicago police had formal standards they only casually observed. In 1889 Sergeant O'Neill refused appointment to a man too short to meet the legal requirements for a patrolman. The man went and got his alderman, James McAbee, who told O'Neill the mayor wanted the man sworn on the force. O'Neill measured the man again and found him miraculously taller. "Good for you!" said McAbee, shaking O'Neill's hand.

McAbee then returned the favor, gathering "a delegation of aldermen" to demand O'Neill's promotion to lieutenant. Chief of Police Frederick Marsh replied that he wanted to promote O'Neill but could not because of "pressure and insistence on behalf of others." Marsh told the aldermen to simply add an additional lieutenant to the annual appropriation bill, and then "your friend and mine will get that place." "This was done," O'Neill continued, "and when the appropriation ordinance was signed by the mayor, the order for my promotion was issued without delay, lest other complications arise."[16]

Alderman McAbee would wind up indicted for buying votes and using up to 300 "repeaters" to secure his reelection. McAbee and his co-conspirator, saloonkeeper Mike Corcoran, "furnish to the people of this city a useful lesson of the beauties of Irish rule," wrote a reform journal bitterly. The *Tribune* reported a near riot in the courthouse when McAbee and Corcoran were found not guilty, the judge banging his gavel and shouting "this is not a barroom!" as supporters crowded to congratulate McAbee. He died in office at age thirty-eight, and aldermen of varying ethnicities rose to praise him, all agreeing with Alderman Austin Sexton that

> as a friend he was ever faithful and true. There is not a man in the City of Chicago today who could outdo our departed brother in acts of kindness and friendship to his friends. He would go a long distance out of his way, and would sacrifice his own convenience to do a kind act for his friends.

There we see expressed the alpha and omega of the Chicago alderman's philosophic code.[17]

O'Neill had objective qualifications—he had shown personal courage and restraint; he could also write with clarity, intelligence, and concision. He had excellent penmanship, no trivial accomplishment in the days before typewriters; and he kept careful records. In one anecdote, O'Neill related how as assistant clerk in 1887 he routinely made copies of orders from above. Mayor Carter H. Harrison, the elder, had issued a proclamation regarding the fourth of

**Figure 16** From *America, A Journal for Americans*, December 12, 1889. As depicted in this anti-Catholic reform journal, immigrant laborer Patrick Malloy can take the path of politics or the path of respectable labor. He does well if he "marries an honest girl" and rejects Catholic schooling. On the right, he also seems to do well but in a different way. Though he reclines on sacks of cash, the unconvincing caption tells us, contrary to available historical evidence, that the alderman will die friendless and/or in jail.

July. While watching fireworks that day near the mayor's house, an exploding shell injured a bystander, who then sued the mayor personally. The case turned on the exact language of the mayor's proclamation: were Harrison the mayor and Harrison the citizen the same person, in a legal sense? The anecdote is worth relating in detail:

> It had been my practice to preserve communications from the mayor and heads of departments in labeled pigeonholes entirely apart from ordinary correspondence in the vault. At the end of each year the contents . . . were tied in parcels, dated, and flung high up on the top shelf. Procuring a ladder, I dug out of the dusty mess the proper parcel and in it found the precious penciled original proclamation. When I handed it to Levy Mayer, attorney for [Mayor Harrison], in the courtroom, he exclaimed, "You're the savior of our case!"[18]

## The Information Revolution and Civil Service Reform

The story demonstrates that O'Neill worked at the edge of a coming revolution in information management. Keeping copies of mayoral proclamations, something any mayor's office would now do automatically, was not routine in 1887. Paper clips and rubber bands did not yet exist; staplers were a novelty. No one had yet invented the vertical file cabinet, that powerful symbol of twentieth-century recordkeeping: clerks tied documents in bundles with string and tucked them into pigeon holes or stuffed them onto the top of shelves. Information storage and retrieval had not been systematized or bureaucratic procedures standardized. O'Neill could brawl in the streets with Bridgeport gangs and take a bullet apprehending a thief, but he also habitually copied things that came his way, stored them, and kept the location in his memory. O'Neill had anticipated the importance of recordkeeping in a modern society.

The lack of system or standards, the ad hoc quality, partly explains the tenacity of the alderman system and its accompanying cronyism. Absent formal records, candidates got promoted because they had friends like Alderman McAbee, who kept a detailed mental account of who owed what to whom. But running a police department required systematic recordkeeping and ordered files; developing a standard for promotion required systems of measuring and comparing the performance of individuals over time against a set of objective criteria.

The Civil Service Act of 1883, also called the Pendleton Act, had established that some federal jobs depended on the applicant's scores on a civil service examination, and further, that employees could not be fired merely to make room for a new administration's favored pets. Chicago reformers eagerly seized on the precedent to professionalize the city's hiring and employment practices and undermine the power of aldermen. In 1895 they passed a law establishing a Chicago Civil Service Commission and introduced civil service exams of their own. Hired before the law passed, O'Neill enjoyed an exemption, but "appointment or promotion under that law afforded protection against arbitrary reduction or dismissal," so he took the test in 1894 and scored 99.80, "a record never since equaled at a promotion examination." He took great pride in his test score: it showed his merit, not just his capacity to make friends.[19]

To work well, civil service reform required drawing up a set of standards for each job and then a way of measuring how to meet the standards; needed was an examining board; a means of storing, tabulating, and comparing scores; and an archive of scores for comparison. All those systems of order had to operate away from the clammy hands of aldermen and party bosses. And of course the civil service exam itself professed a set of political goals and objectives, and imagined an ideal person: a person more like O'Neill than not. Ideally a civil service employee would undergo regular evaluations to ensure citizens got what they paid for. If the system worked well, the public got a qualified staff of public servants who knew what they were doing and who could resist political pressure because their jobs survived changes in administration. Or they got an ossified bureaucracy of lazy public employees who resisted firing with the tenacity of barnacles.[20]

The journalist and humorist Finley Peter Dunne, himself born to Irish immigrant parents, would grow famous in the 1890s for his newspaper columns about life in Bridgeport, narrated in thick dialect by "Mr Dooley," from Roscommon, a bartender on Archer Avenue. Regarding the civil service exam, Mr. Dooley observed that

> at prisint whin a man is needed f'r a govermint office, he is called on to set down with a sheet of pa-aper an' a pot iv ink an' say how manny times eight-an'-a-half will go into a line dhrawn fr'm th' base iv th' hypothenoose, an' if he makes th' answer bright an' readable, they give him a place administherin' th' affairs iv a proud people that cudden't tell a hypothenoose fr'm a sea-lion.

Civil service reform even reached Bridgeport, Dooley continued: "Darcey, th' new polisman on th' bate, comes in here ivry night f'r to study spellin' an' figgers. I think they'll throw him down, whin he goes to be examined. Wan iv th' wild la-ads down be th' slough hit him with a brick wanst, an' he ain't been able to do fractions since." Civil service exams amounted to an entirely new way of thinking about the job and about public service.[21]

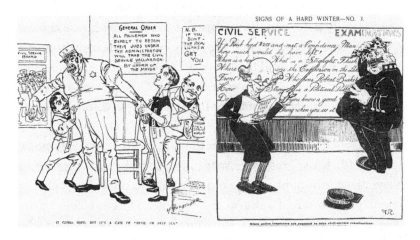

Figure 17 On left, "Taking the Civil Service Treatment," *Chicago Daily News,* December 10, 1897. Civil service commissioners prepare to inoculate an oafish and reluctant policeman with "the civil service virus." On right, "Signs of a Hard Winter #3," *Chicago Daily News,* November 19, 1901. The writing on the blackboard involves questions about Robert Burke, "boss" of the Illinois Democratic Party, and asks the befuddled policeman "what is a straight flush" and "how do you know a good thing when you see it?"

O'Neill valued both merit and competence, but in Chicago, despite efforts at reform, merit still made up only a small part of an officer's case for promotion. As assistant chief clerk at police headquarters, O'Neill ended up doing the work of the actual chief clerk when the superintendent of police, George Washington Hubbard (who "though a native of New England," O'Neill wrote, was "more a pagan than a puritan") delayed in filling the position. Eventually the job went to "a bank clerk, Warden S. Minkler," who served as deacon in the church attended by one of the police commissioners. "But such was his ignorance of the complex duties of his position," O'Neill wrote sarcastically, "that Chief Hubbard diplomatically relieved him of all responsibility except to stand around and talk to people of interest to the Party." O'Neill did all the real work but wisely treated Minkler "with all due respect and consideration." Later Minkler returned the favor: in a moment of pretense at reform, when Mayor Swift threatened to reduce the police rolls, "corporations upheld my record, and it developed that Warden S. Minkler . . . now Mayor Swift's private secretary, was a loyal friend. He had not forgotten the kindly consideration shown him in the days gone by." The event took place after the Pullman strike, during which O'Neill energetically defended the interests of the packing house and rail corporations. And so O'Neill kept his job. In an ideal government, Warden S. Minkler would not have occupied an office for which he had no experience whatsoever, and Francis O'Neill would not have needed the favor of corporations to avoid random dismissal from a position he filled with experience and skill.[22]

Chicago was hardly unique in the Gilded Age. At the national level, Gilded Age presidents spent most of their time appointing allegedly worthy applicants to offices great and small. Every change in party rule brought a swarm of job seekers. Friends, cousins, in-laws, donors, speech makers, stove minders and chair warmers who had supported the new administration formed a line that stretched for blocks around the White House. At O'Neill's level occurred a "biennial struggle for retention and promotion." And Chicago seemed to have a special enthusiasm for graft and for electing men of dubious character, men who had not yet abandoned brawling for bookkeeping.

## A Brawl with an Alderman

By the 1890s, now Captain O'Neill had moved to his final home in Hyde Park. He enjoyed some public reputation, a reputation enhanced by his public brawl with two aldermen in 1896. On the early evening of February 14, two probably drunken fifteenth-ward aldermen, Joseph Lammers and Joseph Haas, encountered O'Neill and his daughter Julia waiting for a streetcar. Lammers, talking to his colleague while "denouncing, cursing, and waving his arms," shoved O'Neill out of the way, knocking him down. They tussled, and with the help of a patrolman who happened by, O'Neill loaded both men into a police wagon and escorted them to the Harrison Street jail. The *Chicago Inter Ocean* reported that the crowd of onlookers cheered as the wagon drove away, and multiple people came forward to testify on behalf of O'Neill, face covered in blood and with a bad cut on his forehead. Other officers escorted Julia, then sixteen, to headquarters to await her father's return.[23]

"This was one of the momentous incidents of my police career," O'Neill wrote. "Here were two Republican aldermen, both prominent leaders, arrested and taken in a patrol wagon to a police station by a Democratic captain of police. Nothing short of decapitation could atone for such indignity." Newspapers put the story on the front page. Aldermen held enormous power and commanded fierce loyalty. But O'Neill had witnesses on his side, and Lammers had something of a bad reputation—a few months earlier he had gotten into a vicious brawl with another alderman, "Buck" McCarthy of the stockyards district. McCarthy had tried to gouge out Lammers's eye in a hotel lobby and, in some accounts, bitten off part of Lammers's ear. Newspapers denounced the earlier brawl as a disgrace and argued that civil service reform would help elect a better class of man to office. "The disgraceful scene between McCarthy and Lammers . . . tells forcibly the need for civil service reform among the folks who are paid to render service to the City of Chicago and its taxpayers."[24]

Men like McCarthy made reform easier to sell. Andrew White, the president of Cornell University, complained in 1890 that in American cities, "a crowd of illiterate peasants, freshly raked in from Irish bogs, or Bohemian mines, or Italian robber nests, may exercise virtual control." Snobbery and ethnic prejudice guided many reformers, and a Dutch immigrant saloonkeeper like Lammers made an easy target as well. But while bogs surrounded O'Neill's childhood home, he was far from illiterate and had a reputation for sobriety and coolness. He had only acted to subdue someone who assaulted him. Snobbery aside, it hardly seems unreasonable to ask that elected officials not brawl in hotels or shove pedestrians into the gutter, that they should respect the law and offer something of a better example to children and dray animals.[25]

The mayor, O'Neill learned, wanted the case dropped. O'Neill agreed not to press personal assault charges and "abide by any disposition the judge at the Harrison Street Court may make of it." Other aldermen condemned Lammers and praised O'Neill for doing his duty: "professors of the Chicago University, Judges of the courts, bankers and packers have written him commending him for his action, and wishing him good luck at the trial." Lammers eventually pleaded guilty and was fined $10 for disorderly conduct. O'Neill rightly pointed out that "the police magistrate, holding an appointive office, was enmeshed in a predicament no less serious than mine. Had not the press and public supported my action, there would have been another vacancy for ravenous politicians to scramble over." The outcome, taking place well after O'Neill's service to the "packers" in the Pullman strike, shows that O'Neill had found a way to escape both ethnic tribalism and the political power of aldermen: his reputation with city elites saved his skin.[26]

## Harrison Street Station and the Levee District

In 1899 the chief of police assigned Captain O'Neill to the notorious Harrison Street station, where "political influence had so undermined police discipline that the authority of the chief was openly flouted by commanders strongly entrenched in political backing." Harrison Street serviced the "levee district," internationally famous for vice. In the levee district two aldermen, John Coughlin, nicknamed "Bathhouse John," and Michael Kenna, uniformly called

"Hinky Dink" in the press, had established a sheltering framework for the usual vices: gambling, prostitution, opium, and after-hours drinking. "We found block after block of low dives in the heart of the city," wrote Franklin Mathews, a New York reporter, "where thieves and thugs and persons of revolting character passed in and out." Accounts of the levee stressed "wide open" vice and also the predations of confidence men and "panel houses," brothels or gambling dens equipped with secret panels. In the panel house, while the unsuspecting patrons enjoyed the multiple diversions so provided, hidden doors would slide open so a thief could lift their wallets and valuables.[27]

Mathews wrote: "If any one would wish to know partly what 'wide-open' Chicago means, he should spend an evening in the Harrison Street station-house." Chicago journalists called Harrison Street the worst station house in the world, "meaning by that the place where more arrests for grave and shocking crimes are chronicled than in any other police station in the country." "It is a busy place," Mathews continued: "as many as 300 arrests have been chronicled there in one night. It is a dull evening when fifty arrests are not made." The frequency of arrests came not from zeal for law and order but from the fact that police magistrates received a fee of one dollar "for every bail bond issued, and also a fee of one dollar for the continuance of any case," according to Mathews. "This makes the office of police magistrate immensely profitable, especially to the two justices who sit in the Harrison Street police courts." The more people arrested, the more money the magistrate made.

Along with illegal gambling and drinking, and "splendidly equipped liquor-saloons, right in the heart of the city, with Hungarian bands in them, all contrary to law," playing on Sunday, Mathews also detailed extensive, regularized instances of "police blackmail," in which businesses paid to keep the police off their backs. He brought the results of his investigations to then police chief Kipley, telling him that "in all my experience of nearly fifteen years as a newspaper man in the four largest cities of the United States I have never seen evidence of so corrupt a condition of affairs as exists nightly in the Harrison Street police station." Kipley brushed the concerns off, insisting New York was much worse. "Of course little games may be running here and there," Kipley admitted, but "you can't expect me to know about them. The fact is we want to make everybody happy, to make them like to live here, you know." He told Mathews the demands of the job kept him tied to his office, not the streets.

Mathews went to the mayor, who denounced "police blackmail" in vehement terms, but also added that he had no desire to enforce unpopular laws, like the law mandating that saloons close on Sunday. "Then you don't believe in enforcing laws not approved by public opinion?" Mathews asked, and Mayor Carter Harrison replied, "No, I don't, and I don't intend to try to do so." He told Mathews that the police required saloons to use discretion and draw curtains over their windows on Sunday, but otherwise they could carry on as normal. The mayor tolerated crime in the levee, which meant the protection rackets and revenue-generating arrests could continue.[28]

"Harrison Street Police Station," wrote English journalist W. T. Stead, "is one of the nerve centers of criminal Chicago." Stead called it "the central cesspool whither drain the poisonous drippings of the city which has become the cloaca maxima of the world." "Behind the iron bars of its underground cages are penned up night after night scores and hundreds of the most dissolute ruffians of both sexes." O'Neill did not disagree:

> This district, in which I found myself ostracized, was a maelstrom of iniquity. Crime was organized, syndicated, and protected. Panel houses, hopjoints, and confidence games flourished . . . all beneficiaries of the system, politicians, police courts, and police, were equally involved, and it was confidently believed that my stay would be brief.

Shortly after O'Neill arrived at the Harrison Street station, a well-known local politician told him that "if I wouldn't be so rough, I would be taken care of like the others." In his telling O'Neill responded, "Do you think I can dawdle around this station and allow panel-house women and confidence men to carry on their operations unmolested?" The politician told him "make all the pinches you want to. We will take care of them in police court." "I found there was no chance of obtaining justice in the police courts," O'Neill wrote: "All that was necessary was to casually meet the magistrate on his way to the police station from the street car and salute him with a handshake and leave a nicely folded five, ten, or twenty-dollar bill in his receptive palm." The crime went away, the magistrate received his fee, the bail bondsman took his pay, and the victim left town "wised up."[29]

O'Neill told the story of George Edwards, sent to the stockyards to buy mules for the British government, who entered a panel house with $14,000 in his possession. A police patrolman made $1,000 a year at the time, so $14,000 amounted to a great deal of money. Newspapers reported Edwards was lured to the panel house by Annie Carroll, twenty-two years old, "a new character in the levee district," selected "on account of her beauty and unsophisticated manner." According to O'Neill, an accomplice "sneaked the wallet through a secret panel of the room in which the victim was being entertained" and made off with $7,000. Edwards went to the police, who learned the details quickly from an informant, and "before an hour had passed the police knew that Annie Carroll was a confederate of Jennie Brew, who is an old offender. A search was instituted for the women and they were traced to the dressmaking establishment of Mrs. L. C. Porter, 307 State street." This fascinating story of three women cooperating in crime ended when O'Neill broke the cycle of "protection" that shielded criminality in the levee.[30]

"I quietly instructed two plainclothesmen to bring me the madam" (presumably Brew). "Anticipating interference, when I heard pounding on the office door for admittance, I stood the madam in a corner, fully hidden, when I swung the door wide open to admit my impatient callers, the inspector and a police court attorney." The two Harrison Street regulars saw no one but O'Neill: surprised, they uttered a few insincere pleasantries and left. "Their motives were well understood," O'Neill wrote: they had come to take custody of Brew, so they could release her and pocket their share of the loot. O'Neill then went with Brew to recover the money "keeping in actual touch with her all the time," and then "with the madam and the money I proceeded to Chief Kipley's office." The chief was "much elated," reported the *Tribune*. Newspapers covered the case closely and credit rebounded to O'Neill, except among those who had hoped to get a share of the stolen money. But although both Carroll and Brew pleaded guilty, neither was ever sentenced. O'Neill bypassed the Harrison Street Court and took the guilty party directly to the chief, but even then, the criminals escaped justice, and according to O'Neill he was still being "hounded and almost persecuted" four years later by the men who had hoped to get their hands on the stolen money.[31]

The lurid accounts of Chicago corruption by journalists and reformers invite skepticism. Sensational accounts sell papers, and much of their tremulous disdain for vice has to do with class dislike of "low persons." But O'Neill's tales confirm the sense of Chicago as deeply corrupt, with a political system built on cronyism, "friendship," and open tolerance of graft, extortion, and theft. Chicago politics made "vice" legal in a de facto way, and police served less as the enemy of vice than as regulators of the system. Gambling, drinking, and prostitution funded the alderman's campaign and his ability to spread largess. Police looked the other way or accepted contributions designed to encourage their inability to see.

Here again O'Neill had to find new ways of understanding "Irish." The main protectors of the levee, his aldermen-antagonists Kenna, Coughlin, and Johnny Powers, all had parents from Ireland or hailed from the auld sod themselves. O'Neill posed himself as a principled man taking a stand against corruption, but it seems reasonable to point out that he owed his appointment on the force to an alderman and his promotion to exactly the type of police magistrate happily pocketing fees in police court. The police chief and the mayor openly admitted to averting their gaze when it came to vice, and O'Neill could go only so far in his opposition to the "lords of the levee." O'Neill writes about these things in a tone of resignation and jaundiced bemusement: he liked order and had a notion of justice. He disliked the way politics interfered in police work and undermined the objective rule of law. He called Harrison Street station "Hell with the lid off." But he lived in the community of favors on which his own advancement depended. And that community involved not just the Irish but other immigrants and Chicago's capitalist class.[32]

**Figure 18** Undated cartoon by John McCutcheon, "When Harrison Was Mayor," probably referring to Carter Harrison Sr., mayor for most of the 1880s. Along with drinking, gambling, and same-sex sociability, the cartoon shows a policeman on the middle left, literally wearing blinders and accepting a bribe while another greets a woman, possibly of ill fame, he knows well. Also worth noting: the same-sex pairings. Chicago History Museum, ICHi-062276; John T. McCutcheon, artist.

From the distance of time, the vice districts have a certain raff-ish charm, but they shielded child trafficking, prostitution, opium addiction, alcoholism, and a creative array of stratagems for sepa-rating hard-working people from their money, often by violent means. "During the late nineteenth century, Chicago was the most violent, turbulent city in the country," "the city in which the crises accompanying industrialization and the development of a wage la-bor economy reached their most threatening peak." Lincoln Stef-fens in 1903—while O'Neill served as chief—called the city "first in violence, deepest in dirt." Not just violent crime: O'Neill's career involved him directly and indirectly in two of the most violent events in US labor history, the Haymarket riot and the Pullman strike. [33]

## Anarchy and the Great Labor Crises

Chicago had a very strong labor movement, and part of that labor or-ganizing effort drew on the philosophy of anarchism, which argued that people, left alone, naturally cooperated as needed and governed themselves amicably. The law, and its vaunted order, mostly served to enforce and shelter inequality: laws, in fact, created the antagonisms they claimed to protect against. Anarchists saw labor unions as a first step in which people joined together to restore self-government to workplaces where law served only employers. Samuel Fielden, a Chicago teamster born in England, declared: "a million men hold all the property in this country. The law has no use for the other fifty-four millions. You have nothing more to do with the law except to lay hands on it and throttle it until it makes its last kick." He told workers to "keep your eye upon it, throttle it, kill it, stab it, do everything you can to wound it—to impede its progress."[34]

On May 4, 1886, a squadron of police led by Captain John Bonfield marched into Haymarket Square, where about 2,000 workers had rallied to demand the eight-hour day. As Bonfield ordered the crowd to disperse, someone—no one has ever found out who—lobbed a bomb at the police. The bomb killed one policeman instantly and left six others mortally wounded: Bonfield's men opened fire on the crowd. The resulting carnage left an additional thirty or more policemen wounded, with at least four members of the crowd killed and possibly many more. An anonymous police official told the *Chicago Tribune*, "A very large number of the police were wounded by each other's revolvers. . . . It was every man for himself." O'Neill does not mention being at Haymarket, and a list of police officers present that night, compiled twelve years later, does not include O'Neill. But the battle against "anarchism" dramatically shaped both the police force and O'Neill's career.[35]

Anarchism, like Fenianism, enjoyed a public reputation far in excess of either its accomplishments or its actions. You could blame all sorts of things on "anarchists." Anarchists used actual dynamite rarely, but as a symbol of how the powerless might level the playing field against the mighty, dynamite had extraordinary theatrical significance. The police actively engaged in their own vigorous public relations about Haymarket and anarchy, most notably Captain Michael Schaack, who wrote a book about the Haymarket riot defending the police and dramatizing the anarchist menace.[36]

O'Neill detested anarchism, but in a thoughtful way. In 1902 he spoke to the International Association of Chiefs of Police at their annual meeting. He gave a detailed and scholarly history of anarchism, praising the educational level and mental force of anarchists he had met. "They are, as a rule, well read in history and matters of general information," men of "considerable mental power and educational attainment." They do not, he said, conform to the newspaper cartoon stereotype of a dirty, bearded, unkempt wild man in a basement saloon. O'Neill understood anarchism as a set of plausible ideas he opposed: he stood squarely on the side of order and state authority. Regarding Haymarket, he told them "the Chicago Police showed of what stuff they were made," and depicted the police as outnumbered and bravely defending themselves, an account not borne out by other historical evidence.[37]

## The Pullman Strike

Less than a decade after Haymarket, the largest strike in US history began in Chicago when workers at the Pullman Car Company walked off the job. George Pullman had made a fortune building luxury rail cars for middle- and upper-class travelers. As the size of his operation grew, Pullman recognized how industrialization had changed society, and he worried about working-class slums, the moral effects of drink, and the concentration of workers in neighborhoods where they might fall into vice or organize into unions—in Pullman's mind, basically the same thing. Remarkably, he built his own town, Pullman, Illinois, for workers at his factories. He imagined it as a utopia and hired an architect to design housing, a market, stores, wide paved streets, an artificial lake, a church, park, and schools all owned by George Pullman. Workers would live in healthy surroundings with modern conveniences and avoid the dirt, disease, and crowding of Chicago. But Pullman expected the town to turn a profit. The 8,000 residents of Pullman lived in Pullman housing, bought food and clothing only at Pullman-owned stores, and enjoyed no drinking in Pullman saloons since Pullman prohibited alcohol. Pullman donated books for a library but charged workers a monthly fee to use it. They banked at the Pullman bank, which issued their pay after deducting the costs of rent and food and other amenities. Rents began at $4.50 a month for two rooms (recall O'Neill's daughters remembered collecting fifty cents a week, or less than half); one-quarter of the residents earned $1.30 a day. Pullman believed he had provided a better alternative to the housing in the city proper, but workers noticed that by necessity they kicked back a large part of their wages into Pullman's pockets.[38]

Economist Richard Ely toured Pullman in 1885 and found it deeply troubling. "All the property in Pullman is owned by the Pullman associations, and every tenant holds his house on a lease which may be terminated on ten days' notice," Ely pointed out. A worker fired from Pullman lost both job and home. Pullman managed the town, and criticism of the company or the town led to dismissal. Ely praised the fact that "not a dilapidated door-step nor a broken window ... is to be found in the city" and that "the streets of Pullman, always kept in perfect condition, are wide and finely macadamized, and young shade trees on each side now ornament the town." But he ended up appalled at the very idea, calling it "benevolent, well-wishing feudalism, which desires the happiness of the people, but in such way as shall please the authorities." If Pullman's experiment became a model for American industrial society, Ely asserted, it would mean "the establishment of the most absolute power of capital, and the repression of all freedom." Pullman had built a rational and systematically organized community, but governed it like a feudal baron.[39]

Pullman responded to the depression of the early 1890s by cutting wages, while keeping rents and food prices in his town unchanged. The newly formed American Railway Union asked Pullman to negotiate; he refused and fired the workers who made the request. The American Railway Union announced a boycott: their members would not handle any train that included Pullman cars.[40]

The strike soon paralyzed freight traffic in Chicago and nationally, as other unions joined the ARU in sympathy. Railroad companies responded by attaching Pullman cars to essential mail trains, but workers then decoupled the cars, blocked the rails, or sabotaged the tracks. At the urging of US Attorney General Richard Olney, a former railroad lawyer then enjoying a retainer from railroad companies larger than his annual salary, President Grover Cleveland authorized the use of federal troops and haphazardly organized "deputy US marshals" to move trains. Rioting broke out in July, and with police and the army ending the boycott of trains, the strike was broken. The leaders of the ARU were arrested for violating the Sherman Antitrust Act.

Jane Addams compared Pullman to mad King Lear, blindly bitter at his children's ingratitude and unwilling to listen. He had tried to order his community around his own theories, but workers had built a union, an organization that combined men of different nationalities and skills so they could act as one. The ARU had officers and a hierarchy and a commitment to discipline: it held regular meetings, tracked membership, collected dues, and issued reports on its budget. It was not unlike the police force, an example of systematic and rational organization. Organizations were the future; men like Pullman represented a vanishing era.[41]

Newly promoted Captain O'Neill was put in charge of the stockyards district during the strike. At the height of the crisis, he slept on a mattress in the attic of the station, and "all pretense of doing regular patrol duty was abandoned now and our energies directed toward the preservation of peace and the protection of property along the different railway lines." But the police did more than simply "protect property." They openly assisted in moving trains through crowds of strikers determined to stop them.

On July 2 Swift and company tried to take a train of "dressed beef" out of the yard. "Coupling pins were repeatedly pulled and the engineer and trainmen were mercilessly jeered and stoned. The police were well nigh powerless in such a mob and even while Lieutenant Fitzpatrick was on the steps of the cab to protect Fogarty, the engineer, stones crashed through the windows." O'Neill called for reinforcements, and they managed to drive the crowd back away from the tracks. But Fogarty, the engineer, "leisurely stepped out of the cab and stood beside his engine. He refused to pull his train out and neither request nor entreaty from Mr. Louis Swift or the railway officials could induce him to change his mind." Swift was one of the richest men in Chicago and had the police there to help him, but Fogarty openly refused to move the train. "The engine was then detached and Mr. Fogarty climbed aboard and started away amid the exultant shouts from the multitude," leaving the train of cars unmoved.

It's worth noting that the union engineer driving the locomotive and the policeman assigned to protect it both had Irish names, but worked for opposite sides. O'Neill planted himself firmly on the side of the packing house owners and acted to assist them in getting trains moving, putting any solidarity with his Irish brethren aside. But he tried to maintain a stance of objectivity by complaining about the bosses and the militia as well as the crowd.

On July 3, he wrote, he heard that the general manager of the Lake Shore and Michigan Southern Railroad planned to move a different train of cars from the yard. O'Neill says he tried to learn when this would happen, but the general manager "seemed determined to keep the secret to himself." He spotted a locomotive steaming at high speed into the yard, and "I entered the Stockyards gate with the patrol wagon" aiming to protect Newell, the general manager, and his team. A crowd assembled and began taunting them. Newell ordered his son to read an injunction against the strikers, "which the latter pompously drew from his pocket." The crowd responded by taunting him and "telling him to stick the paper in his___ pipe, for all they cared." Newell gave up, but meanwhile "some cunning hand placed a coupling pin in such a position that the first revolution of the driving wheels drove it through the cylinder head and disabled one side of the locomotive." The rash Newell had no one to blame but himself, O'Neill insisted.

On July 4 "the United States Regulars arrived in the Yards and camped at Dexter Park." These were the federal troops authorized by President Cleveland, and media accounts depicted them as heroes. About 5:00 a.m. that day O'Neill assembled twenty-five policemen and escorted out "the beef train which engineer Fogarty had refused to pull out on the evening of July 2nd." At that hour the police faced little opposition. As the train moved out, O'Neill continued, "the United States Regulars came out of camp and marched beside it as far as Clark Street. There being no necessity for their escort they returned. This is the train for which the Regulars received so much undeserved praise. No appreciable opposition was encountered and the danger, if any, had passed before they appeared on the ground."[42]

In a later attempt to take a cattle train out, O'Neill described standing on the roof of a caboose while "soldiers with fixed bayonets marched on either side of the train and guarded every coupling." Hundreds of people watched the spectacle: "howls and jeers rent the air." "Beneath me in the caboose were a score of deputy United States Marshals, who discreetly kept themselves out of sight." Near the yard exit "the mob had overturned cars in every conceivable direction along the tracks for blocks in advance and effectively barred further progress." O'Neill observed tartly that "the United States Regulars, Infantry and Cavalry were unequal to the task of taking a train of cattle more than half a mile from the yards."

O'Neill described the police as serving order and property but also mediating between unreasonable forces: unruly mobs, rash capitalists, unnecessary federal troops, and cowardly, duplicitous "deputy marshals." His men at one point came across a group of deputy marshals setting train cars on fire, as instructed, so they could blame the fire on strikers. Indeed, he says, it became impossible to tell strikers, looters, and deputy marshals apart.

During these nights and days, O'Neill wrote, "the clubs played a lively tattoo on the anatomies of those not too young or too old to bear such heroic treatment . . . while the snap and bark of the revolvers of both contending parties sounded like a small boy's celebration of the 4th of July." O'Neill at one point "noticed that a saloon run by an anarchist at the corner of 49th and Bishop Streets was full of men who were shouting defiance and denunciation of us. Acting on a sudden impulse I decided to clear out the saloon. We rushed in impetuously and administered a salutary drubbing to all found within except the proprietor, who stood behind the bar in mute terror." These men had committed no crime: saying mean things about the police violated neither statutes nor ordinances. We can understand the men's desire to jeer: the police worked closely with employers to help bring in "scabs" to take their jobs. Terming the saloon owner an anarchist allowed O'Neill to do as he pleased; he offered no apology for his police clubbing and terrorizing a roomful of innocent men.

A Federal Strike Commission, organized to investigate, concluded "that policemen sympathized with strikers rather than with the corporations can not be doubted" since the police "are largely recruited from the laboring classes." The commissioners saw this as a major problem: police, they thought, would always side with union workers. This is not what O'Neill describes: rather, he represents a model in which police, a third party, serve the specific desires of capitalists under the pretext of "order."

O'Neill did admit that "reports of intimidation, pin pulling, switch throwing, and assaults" were exaggerated, and also that "new employees who succeeded the strikers charged every mishap resulting from their own inexperience to the strikers," which he regarded as unfair. But he was now very far away from the young sailor who resented the tyrannical captain's bullying or the newlywed laborer who built a house with help donated by his neighbors and praised their mutuality. "Complementary and appreciative letters coming from the corporations interested, and various other sources, were most gratifying." No doubt: O'Neill would henceforth butter his bread with the oleaginous enthusiasms of Chicago's business class.

At the same time, his report displeased someone at headquarters because when he went to retrieve it, at the request of the Strike Commission, he found all the relevant pages cut out of his report book. He never found out who, but someone—worker, capitalist, policeman, a deputy US marshal?—found his report objectionable and tried to make it vanish. He re-created it from memory, and the Strike Commission called it "the only one worthy of the name produced by the Police Department of Chicago." The commission liked the way O'Neill had described the role of the police in keeping "order."[43]

But it's vital to note the American Railway Union wanted "order" as well: it detested looters and mobs as much as the police did and tried to suppress them. The newly formed ARU claimed up to 150,000 members nationwide in more than 400 local organizations. The union kept membership records, elected officers, issued reports, and assessed the fitness of locals. Both the police force and the ARU represented modern forms of order and organization, with alliances based not on tribe, ethnicity, or local community but on participation in citywide and national business.

## New Systems of Order and Administration

New systems of order were transforming Chicago in uncounted ways. For example, in 1883 Chicago adopted central standard time, one of the four standard time zones introduced by the American Railway Association on November 18 of that year. At noon that day, all clocks in Chicago stopped for approximately nine minutes and then restarted in synchronization with a telegraph signal transmitted from the Dearborn observatory. Chicago newspapers compared the change to Joshua commanding the sun to stand still. A reporter visited railroad offices and wrote that railroad officials "all looked unusually solemn, and their faces showed that something of an extraordinary nature was about to happen."

In the past, time of day came from the local sun: noon happened when the sun passed overhead, and every town, village, and farm had its own noon. After 1883, all towns in the central zone kept the same time, regardless of the sun. It had already peeked over the horizon in Atlanta while residents of Austin would have to wait nearly an hour for sunrise. But in 1883 the central zone covered a wide swath of North America including Atlanta, Austin, Chicago, Detroit, Cincinnati, and Bismarck: their clocks now all said 7:00 a.m. regardless of the sun. Everyone's morning activities, from farm to factory, now took place under the authority of a national system of standardized time, referenced to the master clock in the US Naval Observatory in Washington, DC.[44]

Standard time announced a change in thinking about the authority that governed daily life. Standard time zones put Americans in a new form of abstracted community, one bound less by geography and local place and more by the imperatives of commerce. What linked individuals was not their place on the earth so much as their place in an interstate rail and communications network.

In his history of Chicago, William Cronon points to a similar change, both subtle and radical in its implications, in the grain industry. Traditionally a farmer grew grain and loaded it into sacks for transportation to a merchant. Individual sacks, and the quality of the grain within, marked an individual farmer's labor and skill. "As the sack of grain moved away from the farm—whether pulled in wagons, floated on flatboats, or lofted on stevedore's backs—its contents remained intact," unmixed with grain from other farms, "marked as the product of a particular tract of land and a particular farmer's labor." Before 1870 "a farm family sending a load of wheat from Illinois to New York could still have recovered that same wheat . . . inside its original sacks, in a Manhattan warehouse several weeks later."

Chicago grain merchants worked with the railroads to sell grain not by the sack, but by the rail car load. To do this they devised standards for assessing the color and size of a representative sample of the crop and assigning it a grade. If a shipment represented a particular grade of grain, rather than an individual farmer's work, "then there was no harm in mixing it with other grain of the same grade."

By 1888 each family's crop went into rail cars with other grain of the same standard grade and then, in Chicago, into enormous grain elevators, capable of storing up to 3 million bushels, that moved the grain from rail cars up into separate bins for each grade. From there gravity could send the sorted grain down another chute and into boats or rail cars bound east or overseas. A New York grain merchant no longer bought a specific farmer's wheat: he bought X bushels of a specific grade. "A has bought 50,000 bushels of B. A gives B a check, and B gives A a little piece of paper a receipt from some elevator for the 50,000 bushels. There can be no need of sampling, no question about quality. The State inspection," sorting the grain into grades, "has settled all that," *Harper's Weekly* observed. "It dawns on the observer's mind that one man's property is by no means kept separate from another man's." Cronon wrote:

> The linkage between a farm's products and its property rights came to seem worse than useless to the grain traders of Chicago. Moving and trading grain in individual lots was slow, labor-intensive, and costly. By severing physical grain from its ownership rights, one could make it abstract, homogeneous, liquid. If the chief symbol of the earlier marketing system was the sack whose enclosure drew boundaries around crop and property alike, then the symbol of Chicago's abandonment of those boundaries was the golden torrent of the elevator chute.

You can see an example of wheat grades in statistical formulation in Department of Agriculture reports to Congress by 1884. The US has specific grades for each kind of grain, and aggregate output of each is quantified, cross tabulated, and embedded in national policy debate. No individual farmer's name appears: none *could* appear, which is exactly the point. New systems of order and organization, of standardization, had replaced the old.[45]

Jane Addams had described the reciprocal generosity of the poor as "natural": the "ready outflow of sympathy and material assistance" was "the most natural thing in the world." Just as the systematic grading of wheat, and the ability to treat wheat as a homogenous product independent of any single farmer's labor, seemed "unnatural," so too did the systematic rationalization of charity: "their ideas of right and wrong are quite honestly outraged by the methods of these agencies." Addams wrote: "They feel, remotely, that the charity visitor is moved by motives that are alien and unreal. They may be superior motives, but they are different, and they are 'agin nature.'" They represented the imposition of standards on custom.[46]

But Chicago, especially in hard times, had unemployment, homelessness, crime, and sanitation problems on an unprecedented scale: neighborhood generosity could not cope with tens of thousands of homeless strangers; neighborly favors could not provide safe drinking water or sewer service to millions of people. Francis O'Neill thrived in the favor market, but he lost six children to disease, diseases spread partly by poor sanitation. The police department stood at the boundary between the personal and the systematic, between face-to-face knowledge and institutional bureaucracy.

The Harrison Street station, for example, served not only as the marketplace of graft but also as a shelter for the city's homeless and mentally ill. Before 1900, much of Chicago police work consisted of "activities that social service organizations would later assume. The police lodged 'tramps' in station houses, returned lost children to their parents, captured stray dogs, enforced health and building codes, picked up dead horses, and even provided first aid to injured people." There were no trained EMTs: police provided ambulances. As chief, O'Neill wrote annual reports to the mayor detailing the department's activities. In 1903 he reported "two thousand seven hundred and thirty-four lost children were picked up, temporarily cared for and eventually restored to their anxious parents. 10,381 sick and injured persons were cared for in various ways by the signal service and ambulance corps of this department." The city dog pound reported to the chief of police: in 1904 the agency impounded more than 11,000 dogs.[47]

Chicago's homeless problem attracted national attention, and in 1901 the city established a Municipal Lodging House under the authority of the police. In 1903 Chief O'Neill reported the lodging house had accommodated 9,315 people and served more than 15,000 meals. "The work accomplished by the Municipal Lodging House during the past year," O'Neill wrote in his 1903 report, "has demonstrated the wisdom of those who originated and established the institution":

> It has served a double purpose: First, by relieving the Police Department of the necessity of annually caring for the flotsam and jetsam of humanity at the different police stations; and, second, by aiding the needy without pauperizing and robbing them of their self-respect. A gratifying diminution in the number of tramps who infest our city every winter is plainly evident under the new conditions. Employers of labor have also come to recognize the fact that the people accommodated at the Municipal Lodging House are not entirely of the "hobo" element, but that many of them are laborers and artisans in temporary difficulties and are worthy of consideration. As a result 2,264 persons were sent to places of paid employment.

O'Neill's language here combines contempt for the tramp, who "infests" the city, with a desire to preserve the humanity and dignity of "laborers or artisans" who find themselves in trouble. The lodging house administration, in O'Neill's view, could sort this mass of humanity into the deserving and the undeserving, grade them by quality, and connect them with employers. "The central purpose of the administration of the municipal lodging house," he wrote, "has been to provide a clearing house for all the homeless men and boys stranded in Chicago. Each morning for the past year, the lodgers for the previous night have been distributed in accordance with their capacity and need." It would send "the worthy displaced laborer and willing but ignorant and discouraged country boy to paid employment, the sick and disabled to dispensaries, hospitals and homes, and the criminal to the House of Correction."

Government by personal favor begins to give way to a notion of standardized practice and rational administration. The lodging house had to keep records—O'Neill had the statistics at hand—and it had to make qualitative judgments about the persons within: sort and grade them, and determine the correct course of action. The director of the Municipal Lodging House reported to O'Neill that they had established an employment bureau, "which in the past year has sent 2,366 lodgers to paid employment," and called this aspect "one of the most satisfactory features of the work." The Municipal Lodging House also had a medical director from the board of health, who vaccinated 1,352 people and sent contagious persons to isolation.[48]

The Chicago police engaged in new ways of tracking people and organizing information. O'Neill's annual reports listed more than twenty distinct nationalities among the arrested, and categorized and tabulated the types of crimes that brought them to the station house. He could also report that "ninety-four persons were arrested on the charge of murder, of whom eighteen were convicted. . . . The murderers who escaped by leaving the city are being constantly and persistently traced with the assistance and ready cooperation of police officials in other cities." He added that "seventy-one persons who committed crimes in Chicago and fled to other cities were arrested by the police officials of such cities and returned to Chicago for trial; while 211 fugitives . . . were arrested by members of this department and turned over to the authorities from whom they escaped." He not only tracked Chicago crime but took part in a national reformation of record keeping and identity tracking.[49]

Chicago police had started taking "mug shots" in the 1880s and then, late in that decade, enthusiastically adopted the Bertillon system. Alphonse Bertillon, a French criminologist, noted that photographs often failed as a marker of identification. People's faces changed as they aged. Facial hair could obscure features. Bertillon reasoned that some aspects of the body never changed. Eye color, the shape of the ears, the length of the arm from the elbow to the tips of the longest finger, the width of the head: Bertillon compiled a long list of measurements that stayed consistent throughout an adult lifespan. Ideally, he insisted, if done well, the Bertillon system would allow police in one city to telegraph Bertillon measurements to New York and re-create the person's face and body from the Bertillon numbers.

Illinois officials had begun using the Bertillon system on prisoners in Joliet in the late 1880s. Bertillon exhibited his methods in Chicago at the 1893 Columbian Exposition, where he re-created both the measurement stations and the elaborate file system necessary

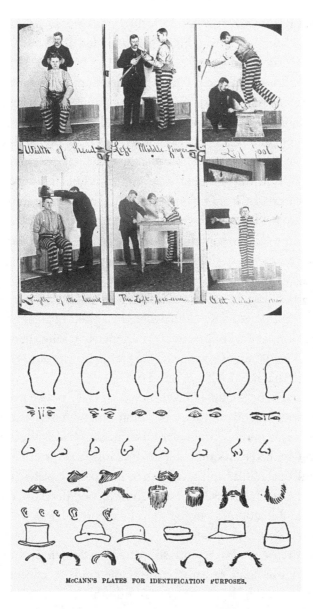

McCANN'S PLATES FOR IDENTIFICATION PURPOSES.

**Figure 19** Top: Bertillon measurement of prisoners, from Chicago History Museum, ICHi-061789; S. W. Wetmore, photographer. See also *Chicago Tribune*, February 28, 1888, 10. These are one part of a much larger series of measurements Bertillon trained police to take. The Bertillon system was an archive that indexed and organized people by physical features, easily retrieved that information, and made cross-comparisons. Bottom: *Chicago Tribune*, February 13, 1893, 1. Officer McCann's scheme for recreating faces. There's no evidence this system was ever adopted, but it reflects the widespread interest in reconsidering how identity was understood, mapped, and tracked. Each man would be considered as an assemblage of standardized types of parts.

to make the records usable. O'Neill would surely have seen the exhibit, a few blocks from his home in Hyde Park, which Chicago newspapers covered widely.

Indeed, an enthusiastic Chicago policeman, W. B. McCann, offered his own system in which each station house would have a large blank panel with head shapes in outline. Officers would select from a collection of different eyes, noses, hats, and facial hair and re-create the face of the suspect. McCann claimed, "I believe the Bertillon system to be the best system for identifying criminals after they have once been caught, but I believe mine is the best for catching them." There is no evidence of the police adopting McCann's scheme, but along with Bertillon measurements McCann's project showed the multiple new ways of thinking about, tracking, and managing people. O'Neill was an early enthusiast of these new technologies of identity tracking. When the Chicago police started their "Rogues Gallery" in the 1880s, O'Neill assisted Captain Evans in his work "and got a great deal of practical experience in taking snap-shots of thugs." O'Neill said of his time taking pictures of crooks, "that is one of my sins that has not been found out."[50]

In Chicago, by the time O'Neill served as chief, police would measure an arrestee and compile a Bertillon card with numerical scores for each measurement, then place the cards in an alphabetical index cross-referenced by a simplified set of scores. The system required a room full of card files and careful attention to filing systems. O'Neill reported in 1903 that "we have now some 43,000 Bertillon cards and records and 10,000 old photographs taken previous to the installation of the Bertillon system."[51]

Measurement errors and subjective judgments about how to classify eye color or ear or nose shape made it inaccurate, and fingerprints, offering a simpler method of identification, soon replaced it. But we can see here again new ways of imagining individuals and their relations to each other, reformations in the nature of community. The aldermanic favor bank depended on personal knowledge and face-to-face contact. Bertillon indexing promised to give police a record of any person independent of his or her community and situate that person in a national and international web of

LET NO GUILTY MAN ESCAPE.

**Figure 20** This cartoon from the *Chicago Daily News*, August 27, 1901, 1, references Chief O'Neill's enthusiasm for forensic technologies of identity tracking as he tries to wrestle "the grafter" into place for a mug shot.

records and surveillance, rather than in a local network of "friends" or ethnic compadres. It replaced community with a new form of *manageable* individualism.[52]

In 1904 O'Neill gave an address to the International Association of Chiefs of Police in St. Louis, praising both the Bertillon system and the network of electric call boxes the police had installed across the city, which let an individual officer send a signal to the local station house naming the type of crime and location. He told the assembled chiefs that "if anyone had been so bold as to affirm only a few years ago" the one individual could "be positively identified among thousands, if not millions, his statement would have been met with ridicule." Thanks to the Bertillon system, he continued, "we are able to give such detailed descriptions of any individual that his identification becomes a matter of absolute certainty." Police, now connected to each other by a web of telegraphic signals, could count on a system of positive identification so that no individual could hide, even in a city of millions.[53]

In multiple ways life in Chicago transformed individuals and communities. Civil service exams, charitable agencies, railway unions, Bertillon cards, lodging houses, standard time, and grain elevators are not the same things, but they all involve a similar mentality: replacing custom with standardization and face-to-face improvisation with administrative rules and procedures. This new form of statistical identity supplanted older forms, like "Irish" or "Bohemian" or "German." These identities still existed, but they meant something different now.

Sometime in the 1890s, Captain O'Neill began intensively collecting Irish folk music, formalizing his habit of memorization and putting the tunes on paper in an organized way. Maybe in suffering the heat and danger of the stockyards, clubbing the crowd, or compiling statistics, he dreamed of the rural crossroads and the gentle community he described there. Or perhaps as he became more American, forming alliances with non-Irish and with the city business owners, he sought a way to redefine what "Irish" meant. O'Neill would apply systems and standards to the folk music of his past, sorting the music of different Irish counties into one stream of Irish folk music, and he would discover new ways of understanding himself and his relation to his community.

# 5

# Rakish Paddy
## The Chicago Irish
## and Their World

O'Neill's rise in the police department depended less on being Irish than on being liked by aldermen and politicians, who might be German or Swedish or English or any number of dozens of ethnicities. Irish names accounted for a high percentage of the police force, and Irish names featured prominently on the aldermanic rolls, but at most only 20 percent of Chicago's population came from Ireland. By the 1890s, Italians, Jews, and Poles had joined Germans, Bohemians, Luxembourgers, Swedes, Slavs, and native-born white Americans seeking work in the city. By 1900 African Americans had started boarding trains from Mississippi to Chicago. To get ahead, O'Neill had to cooperate with the full range of Chicago's population and develop the new skills of modern administration, forms of administration that transcended ethnic community. Socially diverse, table-flat, sprawling, rapidly growing, laid out in a grid; a technological and economic marvel of department stores, skyscrapers, slaughterhouses, granaries and factories, O'Neill's Chicago bore scarce resemblance to Ireland.

But Irish immigrants marked Chicago in vivid greens. They held picnics and fairs and rallies. They met in social clubs and dance halls. They had their own newspapers. They built churches and schools. And they subscribed to the cause of Ireland with varying degrees of ferocity. Some of the nationalist organizations harbored a great deal of danger for an ambitious man; political infighting over Irish nationalism led to at least one murder that tarnished the police shield

itself. As O'Neill moved through Chicago, he met Irish people holding the full spectrum of jobs the city demanded, and as he moved
up the police ranks he began making a new meaning for "Irish" out
of the music he heard.

"In a large cosmopolitan city like Chicago," O'Neill wrote, "exiles from all of Ireland's thirty-two counties can be found." This crucial fact, the way immigration formed a new sense of nationality,
marked nearly all immigrant groups to the US. A man from Sicily
might regard himself as a Siciliano; a woman from Calabria called
herself a Calabrese. In the US they both became "Italian," and while
regional differences persisted, immigrants found political, social,
and economic advantages joining in a common American ethnic
identity. Assuming the larger identity of "Irish" or "German" or
"Italian" often required embracing cultural practices or styles un-
heard of back in the immigrant's village or county, but here they became markers of ethnic and national solidarity. Patrick Ford, editor
of the *Irish World*, wrote that life in the US changed "the littleness
of 'countyism' into the broad feeling of nationalism." In O'Neill's
childhood he probably never traveled farther than 50 miles to
Cork, where his family marketed produce. But within a few blocks
of his Chicago home, he could hear tunes from the entire island
of Ireland.[1]

"During the winter of 1875," O'Neill recalled, "James Moore, a
young Limerick man, was in the habit of spending his evenings at
my home . . . [on] a cosy seat on the woodbox back of our kitchen
stove." Moore had no flute of his own, O'Neill remembered, but
"he enjoyed playing on mine, and, being an expert on the instrument, it can well be imagined how welcome he was." O'Neill had
only recently joined the police, but in 1875 he had steady, decent
pay and two young children, with a third on the way. He must have
been proud to invite Moore to sit by the stove, and Moore must have
enjoyed the sense of family.[2]

"While he had a wonderful assortment of good tunes," O'Neill
continued, "he seemed to regard names for them as of little consequence—a very common failing." Common indeed: as mentioned
earlier, people learned Irish folk tunes by ear, and they gave them

names, or not, as they pleased. Tunes represented a specific community or the memory of face-to-face transmission of knowledge. O'Neill remembered learning the tunes from a specific person in his cozy kitchen. He continued: "of the reels memorized from his playing, the 'Flower of the Flock,' 'Jim Moore's Fancy,' and the 'New Policeman' were unpublished and unknown." O'Neill would memorize these tunes, and later discover variants, and name one after Moore himself, and then publish them in his collection. "The 'Greencastle Hornpipe,' one of the best traditional tunes in our collections, also came from Moore, as well as many others too numerous to mention." Moore "went to New York in the spring" O'Neill noted, "and was never heard from after."[3]

Irish music came to O'Neill in this unorganized way, in face-to-face contact or heard while on duty. He would begin to organize it as a policeman tracked information about his beat. Tunes circulated under multiple aliases, but he had identified and named two previously "unknown" tunes: he had tied them to a specific Irishman to certify their authenticity, named them, and eventually published them, so even when Moore moved away and was never heard from again, the tune had taken its place in a formal record of Irish music. The Bertillon system let police see through anonymous circulation of identities and pin them down; O'Neill's collecting impulse arose from the same modern mentality.

In the Gilded Age, Americans *standardized* nearly everything, reformulating local customs and traditions into sets of general rules and practices. Instead of local time, O'Neill would soon set his watch to central standard time. Instead of watching individual sacks from individual farms go into warehouses, he could watch millions of bushels of Grade A wheat stream into elevators. Jim Moore's tunes lived in Jim Moore's head unless he chose to share them, face to face, with his neighbor. But O'Neill would take the tunes out of this world of personal circulation and local community; he would present the song in fixed form, as part of a stream of culture any owner of the book might dip into at any time. He was standardizing Irish music and redefining Irish culture.

Joining the police "broadened the field of opportunity" for hearing new music, he wrote. Transfer "to the Deering Street station was particularly fortunate. It was largely an Irish community, and of course traditional musicians and singers were delightfully numerous." A policeman walked a beat: patrolling the streets, making it his business to know what went on. He moved across a wide geographical space, mapping it in his head, and then reported back on what he had seen and heard. This surveillance gave him a broader sense of Irish music and culture than O'Neill could have ever gotten in Tralibane. But it also led him toward an administrative rather than a personal video of the Irish and Irish music.

O'Neill wrote about his early days on the force in his 1910 book *Irish Folk Music: A Fascinating Hobby*. Many policemen played music: he remembered Patrick O'Mahony, "Big Pat," "a magnificent specimen of Irish manhood and a charming fluter." "His repertory of rare tunes was astonishing, the 'swing' of his execution was perfect." He named other patrolmen and recalled how "many an impromptu concert in which the writer took part enlivened the old Deering Street Police Station about this time." Policemen played music in the station house, then located at the corner of Loomis and Archer, and "within a few squares of the police station lived the Maloneys, a noted family of musicians," all "good performers on the German flute." The father loved to dance, and when "Jimmy O'Brien, a Mayo piper who spent a few months among us in the early seventies," played a jig Maloney liked, O'Neill named it "The Jolly Old Man" in Maloney's honor. O'Neill often named the tunes he learned in the station house, on the streets, and in the air.[4]

"While traveling on post, one summer evening in 1875," "the strains of a fiddle coming through the shutters of an old dilapidated house on Cologne street attracted my attention." The musician was an old man named Dillon," and "his only solace in his solitary life besides his 'dhudeen' [clay pipe] was 'Jenny,' as he affectionately called his fiddle. A most captivating jig memorized from his playing I named 'Old Man Dillon' in his honor." "Inferior versions of it have since been found," he continued, "entitled 'A Mug of Brown Ale,' and I am satisfied this is the original and correct name." O'Neill sorted and organized the music police work brought to his ears and tried

Figure 21 Bridgeport's Main Street: Archer Avenue, 2800 block, 1885. The road would not be paved with asphalt until 1901. Chicago History Museum, ICHi-032342.

to find or supply correct names. While on duty as a desk sergeant at the Deering Street station, he heard "the strains of a slashing but unfamiliar reel floating out on the night air from the lowered windows of Finucane's Hall," across the street from the station. "I had little difficulty in memorizing the tune." Republican Alderman Michael Finucane ran the social hall, and Finucane's Hall featured regularly in Finley Peter Dunne's account of the community of Bridgeport, and particularly in accounts of music.[5]

For example, in one of Dunne's later columns the Donahues, a Bridgeport Irish family aspiring to gentility, have installed a piano in their parlor for their daughter, Molly. Mr. Donahue asks her to play an imaginary but plausible-sounding tune, "The Wicklow Mountaineer."

"She'll play no 'Wicklow Mountaineer,'" says Mrs. Donahue. "If ye want to hear that kind iv chune, ye can go down to Finucane's Hall," she says, "an' call in Crowley, th' blind piper," she says.

"Molly," she says, "give us wan iv thim Choochooski things," she said. "They're so genteel."

"D'ye know 'Down be th' Tan-yard Side'?" asks their neighbor, Mr. Slavin.

"It goes like this," says Slavin. "A-ah, din yadden, yooden a-yadden, arrah yadden ay-a." "I dinnaw it," says th' girl. "'Tis a low chune, anyhow," says Mrs. Donahue. "Misther Slavin ividintly thinks he's at a polis picnic," she says. "I'll have no come-all-ye's in this house," she says.

Dunne nicely lays out the social hierarchy of Irish music. "Come all ye's" refers to political ballads and songs of love gone bad: "Come all ye young rebels (or workers, lovers, miners, or sailors), and list while I sing . . ." The police had a reputation for playing "low chunes" like the imaginary "Wicklow Mountaineer" or "Down by the Tanyard Side." "Irish music" in the US included the jigs, reels, and hornpipes O'Neill described policemen and laborers playing. But it also included more "genteel" songs, like the songs of Thomas Moore, or commercial dance tunes like "Kitty O'Neil's Jig" or angry laments like "Revenge for Skibbereen." The aspiring Mrs. Donahue wants no low tunes in her parlor, such as played by O'Neill and his police cronies; she had her own idea of what "Irish" meant.

Dunne described music in Bridgeport in another column, in which Felix, a local man smitten by Molly Donahue, tries to serenade her with "The Vale of Avoca," a Thomas Moore song also known as "The Meeting of the Waters."

He used to sit in his window in his shirt-sleeves, blowin' "Th' Vale iv Avoca" on a cornet. He was wan whole month before he cud get th' "shall fade fr'm me heart" right. Half th' neighborhood 'd be out on th' sidewalk yellin' "Lift it, Felix,—lift an' scatther it. Shall fade fr'm me ha-a-rt,—lift it, ye clumsy piper."

In Bridgeport everyone in earshot knows what he has planned, and when the day comes a boisterous neighborhood crowd both supports and taunts the young suitor.

Las' week he pulled himself together, an' wint up th' r-road again. He took his cornet with him in a green bag; an', whin he got in front iv Donahue's house, he outs with th' horn, an' begins to play. Well, sir, at th' first note half th' block was in th' sthreet. Women come fr'm their houses, with their shawls on their heads . . . Befure Felix had got fairly started f'r to serrynade Molly Donahue, th' crowd was big an' boisterous. He started on th'ol' favor-ite, "Th' Vale iv Avoca"; an' near ivry man in th' crowd had heerd him practisin' it. He wint along splendid till he come to "shall fade fr'm me heart," an' thin he broke. "Thry again," says th' crowd; an' he stharted over. He done no betther on th' second whirl. "Niver say die, Felix," says th' crowd. "Go afther it. We're all with ye." At that th' poor, deluded loon tackled it again; an' th' crowd yells: "Hist it up. There ye go. No, be hivins he fell at th' last jump." An', by dad, though he thried f'r half an hour, he cud not land th' "shall fade fr'm me heart." At th' last break th' light in Molly Donahue's window wint out, an' th' crowd dispersed. Felix was discons'late.[6]

Dunne's accounts show us how little privacy people had; it shows us how "low" tunes, "Come all ye's," mingled with more genteel songs; and it shows us how the community asserts ownership of Moore's song. Young Felix picks a classic sentimental song, and the neighbors treat his serenade like a hurling match, cheering him on: "we're all with ye!" With affection, he shows music in community—if you want to hear "The Wicklow Mountaineer," go to a "polis picnic," says Mrs. Donahue, or down to Finucane's Hall to hear "Crowley, the blind piper."

Blind pipers figure in Irish music much as blind guitarists figure in the history of the blues, and O'Neill drew on the mythic status of the blind piper in an appalling anecdote that shows the darker side of both O'Neill and the police, and undermines any temptation to romanticize the Bridgeport community.

A "character" named Murphy, O'Neill wrote, lived "alone in a shanty on city land at the approach to Archer Avenue bridge." Nearly blind, Murphy ran a modest store. "There was but little demand for his tobacco and candies, but a black bottle or two carefully placed

out of sight in a dark cupboard had many patrons." The "mentally
irresponsible" Murphy "pretended to play the pipes," O'Neill continued, "and never was there so dignified and self-conscious a 'performer' as he." "His so-called music was simply atrocious," tells us,
and "he was complacently regarded as a 'joke.'" Murphy had committed one of the cardinal sins of Irish and Irish American culture:
having "notions" or putting on airs. "His seriousness and egotism
were irresistible," O'Neill declared.

At one point "Michael Houlihan, a recently appointed policeman,
gave a neat exhibition of jig and reel dancing on the smooth station
house floor one day while on reserve duty." An onlooker told him
he should go and dance for Murphy, the famous blind piper. Houlihan understood the legends about blind pipers and eagerly agreed.
O'Neill, the desk sergeant, relieved Houlihan of duty, and he and
two other officers trooped over to Murphy's shanty, followed shortly
after by O'Neill.

> The scene at Murphy's when I arrived was ludicrous beyond de-
> scription. Houlihan, already alive to the joke, good humoredly
> pranced about the floor, while [Murphy] . . . figured a chanter
> that emitted spasmodic squeals, which by no stretch of the imagi-
> nation could be identified as tunes. "Big Pat," who enjoyed the
> rare faculty of voiceless laughter, was apparently in convulsions.
> Patrolman Fitzmaurice, who was on duty, sat in a dark corner, but
> betrayed his presence by explosions of hilarity which he did his
> best to control. This jerky jocularity of Fitzmaurice was evidently
> disconcerting to the piper, for after a few interrogative glances
> towards the former he reverently put away his "little instrument,"
> as he fondly called it, heedless of Houlihan's compliment, "Begor,
> Mr. Murphy, you can almost make 'em spake."

Murphy, in his "shanty," entirely at the mercy of the police sergeant
and his cronies, tries and fails to maintain his dignity. O'Neill describes two other times police or aldermen mocked Murphy, a legally blind, "mentally irresponsible," poverty stricken, and lonely
Irish immigrant with few resources. He added patronizingly that

Murphy did not live in vain, for "he served his adopted country faithfully as a soldier during the Civil War, and furnished much pleasant entertainment for his fellow man for many years thereafter."

The casual cruelty and bullying contempt shown here, the willingness to abuse authority for a joke at the expense of a blind, mentally challenged veteran, reflect badly on O'Neill. He was a thoughtful man, capable of kindness and generosity, but the anecdote about Murphy—and the fact that he celebrated it in his book and related the multiple times the police practiced similar jokes at Murphy's expense—suggests a glaring lack of empathy or compassion, and paints O'Neill again as emotionally obtuse. It also shows that despite his nostalgia for the musical Deering Street station house, he and the police stood outside the community they served. He blinds himself to the power relations his anecdote reveals, just as in the case of blind Mrs. Ward and her daughters, where he chose not to see or remember class conflicts back in Tralibane. [7]

O'Neill described other musical gatherings with great warmth. He especially praised "sergeant Jim Kerwin" "as a host at his magnificent private residence on Wabash Avenue." "A select company . . . met monthly on Sunday afternoons at his house for years." He remembered "pipers, fiddlers and fluters galore, with a galaxy of nimble dancers and an abundance of sweet-voiced singers, furnished diversified entertainment the like of which was never known on the shores of Lake Michigan before nor, unfortunately, since." He remembered gatherings at the home of Johnny Doyle, a city fireman, and his wife, "for every one felt that the kindly welcome and hospitality of Mr. and Mrs. Doyle were genuine." He notes instances where musicians gathered at his home before death silenced it. One of his friends complimented Anna, saying "Mrs. O'Neill, you always had such a fine ear for music."[8]

O'Neill formed a community of particularly good musicians and eventually an Irish Music Club. Newspapers often suggested that O'Neill, as he moved up the police ranks, hired men simply because they played music well. As we have seen, joining the police force required the enthusiasm of an alderman or judge, but O'Neill had influence, and he used it to hire at least three people and likely many more. Sometime in the 1880s he added a particularly good piper, Barney Delaney, to the police rolls. One afternoon, Sergeant James Cahill told O'Neill "about a good Irish piper just arrived in town, who was playing in a saloon on Van Buren Street." O'Neill went to hear the man and "found Bernard Delaney, a comparatively young man, rolling out the grandest jigs, reels and hornpipes I ever heard." With the help of O'Neill and Alderman Michael McNurney, Delaney "became and still is a member of the Chicago police force."

In 1886 Delaney married O'Neill's sister-in-law, Julia Rogers, last seen in domestic service in Normal, Illinois. O'Neill praised Delaney as a musician many times but privately groused continually about Delaney's "ingratitude." Delaney retired a wealthy man, but he eventually stopped cooperating with Francis altogether: "I found [Delaney] playing in a cheap public house," O'Neill told an Irish friend in a 1911 letter: "He is now a man of property" with a good salary. O'Neill wanted to record his playing, but "he doesn't have to make records and he won't either, not even for me!" The relationship soured because, O'Neill claimed, "he lacked even a germ of gratitude or appreciation of picking him up off the street or tavern and making him what he is."[9]

Similarly, in the early 1890s Francis helped hire James O'Neill, no relation, onto the force because James played the fiddle beautifully and could read music well. James would play a crucial role in O'Neill's published collections, but eventually they too had a falling out. James was "a coal heaver when I discovered him," O'Neill wrote privately, "quite expert in fiddling from the printed score. He could not be utilized for that purpose now." He speaks of him in this brusque way, yet Francis O'Neill had spent many hours playing music at the younger man's house, calling it "mecca." James O'Neill owed his position to Francis, who greatly outranked him on the police force. What the much wealthier Francis saw as friendly hospitality, James and his wife may have seen as something they could not easily refuse.[10]

One of the few glimpses of O'Neill's private life comes from letters he wrote in retirement to his nephew in Ireland. One of his sisters, nicknamed Nancy, lived in Chicago. "For gossip and conviviality, my sister Nancy's house was the favorite meeting place for the boys and girls from home," he remembered. "Eating, drinking, gossiping and of course courting was the order of the day, and you may imagine the 'teasing' or 'dressing' people got from the bunch (to use an American slang word)." O'Neill's sister had married a man named Jerry Daly, whom Francis had known in his childhood back in Cork: "Old man Jerry Daly was a great funmaker for an antediluvian in his own peculiar way, and his son young Joe Daly, the only member of the family born in America, was quite a fiddler so that dancing added zest to the 'gathering of the clans.'" O'Neill recalled this warmly and happily, but he added that the Dalys, a more casual and friendly family, "were under some restraint at our house and then we were always beastly sober, and so where was the fun in visiting us unless you wanted a job?" He added tartly, "unless at a funeral I never see any of my Chicago nephews. They are all occupying positions fully commensurate with their somewhat limited abilities . . . they may as well be a thousand miles away as far as I am concerned."[11]

The poignant letter, taken with the comments above about Delaney and James O'Neill, conveys a sense of O'Neill as socially awkward and easily offended. He can enjoy young Joe Daly, "quite the fiddler," but Joe never appears in O'Neill's Irish music circle. He feels nostalgia for the liveliness, warmth, and fun of the Daly house, so unlike his own. His daughters played the piano, and "occasionally the girls play a passing modern fancy, which has no charms for me," he wrote. He seems to think the Dalys only ever saw him if they wanted a job. He seems to have gotten a job on the force for one of the Daly family, son Eugene, but they may have wondered why he found a job for his brother-in-law, Barney, or for James O'Neill, no relation, but not all of them.[12]

O'Neill's rise through the police force similarly strained or poisoned his relations with his fellow musicians, because police work could pay well indeed. Newspapers described officers Nicholas Hunt and James Bonfield, both enemies of O'Neill, as worth $1 million and $250,000 respectively. In 1898 Sergeant Jim Kerwin either failed, or failed to take, the civil service exam and was "reduced" to common patrolman, a position at which he retired while O'Neill was chief superintendent of police. When O'Neill made chief, the Kerwins threw a lavish party for him at what the *Chicago Citizen* called their "mansion" on Wabash Avenue. "James Kerwin is reputed, on good authority, to be worth $150,000," a reporter wrote: "Truly, he is a fortunate policeman. How did he manage it?" A good question indeed: when asked, Kerwin attributed his prosperity to sobriety, which seems an insufficient explanation. Attendees at the Kerwins' reception included Sergeant James O'Neill; Sergeant James Early, hired the same year as Francis; and Sergeant Barney Delaney, all musicians. It might have included Sergeant James Cahill or perhaps "patrolmen Timothy Dillon, William Walsh and John P. Ryan," who O'Neill also remembered as musical policemen. It surely included John Ennis, also a patrolman, an opinionated and literate man who often wrote about Irish music for Irish newspapers.[13]

The hierarchy of the police made them all subordinate to O'Neill and dependent on him for promotion. Chicago politics, and the police force, depended on friends doing things for friends. We cannot really know how much of O'Neill's considerable prosperity came from fortuitous real estate investments and how much might have come from Chicago "friendships." O'Neill told Henry Mercer that he owed his musical accomplishments to his "seven years as Captain and at last appointment as Supt.," "of course exercising great opportunities for favors and friendship." While he named a charming jig, "Tobin's Favorite," after Adam Tobin, a piper and collaborator, he did not find Tobin a job. Census reports in 1910 list Tobin as "musician," crossed out and replaced with "Laborer Rail Road." The 1920 census reports list Tobin as simply "Laborer, Meat Co." Clearly O'Neill helped some but not all.[14]

It would be a difficult situation for anyone to manage, and varying notions of property and possession compounded the difficulty. O'Neill complained later in life about "the many gratuities inevitable in my intercourse with the class of people from whom co-operation was to be expected." By that point his old community had become "that class of people" demanding "gratuities." O'Neill helped form a Chicago Irish Music Club and cherished the friendships and music that came out of it, but it fell apart as well. He described a meeting

IRISH MUSIC CLUB, CHICAGO.

Father W. K. Dollard.    Ed. Cronin.   Rogers F O'Neill.   Francis O'Neill    Timothy Dillon.   John McFadden.   Michael Kissane    James Kennedy
John McElligott.    M G Enright.    John Duffy    John Ennis  Chas. O'Gallagher.  Wm. McCormick   Michael Dunlap.   Thos. Dunphy.  Father J. K. Feilding
John Conners    Barney Delaney    John K. Beatty.    Tom Ennis    James Early    James Cahill.    Adam Tobin
Garrett J. Stack    James Kerwin.

Figure 22 The Chicago Irish Music Club, sometime after 1901. O'Neill is in the back row, fourth from left: his son Rogers is next to him. From Francis O'Neill, *Irish Minstrels and Musicians: With Numerous Dissertations on Related Subjects* (Chicago: Regan, 1913), 479. At least eight of these men were policemen, subordinate to O'Neill on the force.

of the music club that blew up in acrimony. "Personally I've been through the mill, and nothing but the prestige of rank and authority enabled me in one instance to prevent a probable tragedy at a special meeting of the officials of the Chicago Irish Music Club." "Having narrowly escaped a serious scandal, I never attended another meeting." Some of the jealousies and rivalries must have stemmed from disagreement about music, but a job in the police meant security and, with the right connections, affluence as well. "I made life more pleasant for most of them—rank, office, money enabled me to do this," O'Neill wrote in another letter. It cannot have made relations easier that some prospered more than others.[15]

## Irish Republicanism and Community

This kind of patron/client relationship never went away, but Irish Americans increasingly organized themselves into larger communities. Irish immigrants always had a cause to rally around—liberating Ireland from English rule—and while getting on with life in Chicago, the Irish immigrant could also subscribe to various societies, leagues, and movements dedicated to Irish freedom. In the 1860s and 1870s the Fenian Brotherhood had dominated nationalist sentiment, but after the embarrassing failure of the Canadian invasions, a new organization, Clan Na Gael, arose to capture republican sentiment. It too quickly fell to internal disagreements.

The goal of an Irish republic offered a great deal to disagree about. Would it be a socialist republic? Or model itself on the US? Would the Irish want a secular, tolerant republic? Or would the republic shun Protestants and form an explicitly Catholic nation? And then the divisions over tactics: "physical force" nationalists wanted armed struggle. Others favored a more gradualist, strictly political approach. Another faction argued for "home rule," so that Ireland might remain under the British flag but gain more and more autonomy.

When the Chicago Irish came together, the general ideal of an Irish republic helped unify them regardless of the intensity of their commitment. The Irish, Finley Peter Dunne observed, "give picnics that does bate all. Be hivins, if Ireland cud be freed be a picnic, it'd not on'y be free to-day, but an impire." Dunne's fictional bartender, Mr. Dooley, continued: "Whin we wants to smash th' Sassenach [the English] an' restore th' land iv th' birth iv some iv us to her thrue place among th' nations, we gives a picnic. . . . It costs less; an', whin 'tis done, a man can lep aboord a sthreet ca-ar, an' come to his family an' sleep it off." Visions of Ireland would hover over every gathering—Ireland as lost home; a nostalgic dream, an oppressed people; Ireland as a cultural style and heritage. And each gathering would help the gathered define their sense of what it meant to be Irish in America.[16]

Dunne characteristically made light of the Irish picnic, but Clan Na Gael, deadly serious, funded dynamite attacks on English targets including the House of Parliament, and it continued to fund Irish republicanism up to the 1916 Easter Rising.

Clan na Gael formed in 1867. It had a public face, organizing picnics and social events, but it also carried out "physical force" attacks on the English. John Devoy, exiled from Ireland for revolutionary activities, led Clan Na Gael nationally. In Chicago leadership came under the control of a dodgy character, Alexander Sullivan. Good at giving political speeches and claiming the resultant patronage reward, Sullivan had a hot temper and narrowly avoided conviction for killing a man who insulted his wife; he also twice dodged accusations of embezzlement. Sullivan represented the western branch of Clan Na Gael, increasingly in tension with Devoy's East Coast branch.

In the 1880s Irish and Irish American nationalists embarked on a bombing campaign in England. "Between 1881 and 1885, there were at least forty instances of the use of dynamite or discovery of what the authorities referred to as 'infernal machines' in England and Ireland." In that same time, "twenty-nine Irish nationalists from America were imprisoned in England for their use, or intended use, of dynamite." Clan Na Gael commissioned a working three-man submarine to attack British shipping in Canada, and tried to blow up the Tower of London and the House of Parliament, among other targets. Recall the centrality of dynamite to the language of anarchism, and the general anxiety Clan Na Gael provoked becomes clear.[17]

Many Irish cops belonged to the Clan, and "within the Irish community, Alexander Sullivan was well known as the man to go to for police or public works jobs." Sullivan had served as secretary of the board of public works, a fountainhead of patronage jobs. Gillian O'Brien suggests many of Chicago's Irish "joined the Clan not because they had any overriding interest in Irish nationalism but because they saw membership as a way of securing a good job."[18]

But divisions within Clan Na Gael ran hot and, in 1889, ended in a murder that captured the entire country's attention for months. Dr. Patrick Henry Cronin, a Clan member affiliated with the Devoy wing of the organization, accused Sullivan of, yes, embezzling funds. Shortly after, Cronin disappeared while on an emergency medical call. His body turned up eighteen days later, naked and shoved into a sewer. The murder caused a sensation: Cronin also had many loyal admirers in the Clan Na Gael, and because so many policemen belonged to the Clan, Chief Hubbard ordered Irish American detectives removed from the investigation. "The Irishman's prejudices are very strong," Hubbard said, "and if any one of them sympathized with any of the warring factions he could not do efficient work on the case." The men eventually tried for the crime included a police detective, John Coughlin. Captain Michael Schaack, seen earlier defending police at Haymarket, was removed from the investigation for concealing evidence and replaced with Herman Schuettler, whom Chief O'Neill would later name as his assistant.[19]

Almost 12,000 people had filed past the coffin at Cronin's funeral, representing all classes and all ages, "from the child scarcely able to toddle to the aged man, walking with faltering, uncertain steps. Parents took their children and their grandparents. The day laborer walked beside the well-dressed professional man." The *Tribune* claimed 40,000 people lined the streets to witness the funeral procession. The case, termed "the Crime of the Century," made the front pages nationally and in England and Ireland.[20]

Although a police detective was convicted for helping murder Cronin, a platoon of Chicago police marched in the procession: the department was dangerously divided. O'Neill—at that time acting chief clerk under Hubbard, doing the job of the aforementioned Warden S. Minkler—says nothing at all about Clan Na Gael or the Cronin case in his memoirs. The only possible mention comes a year after the funeral, when O'Neill took charge of the stockyards district. The area "was controlled politically by a limited coterie whose influence may be considered dictatorial," he wrote, meaning Father Maurice Dorney, then "known as 'the king of the yards,' . . . famous for his ability to find employment in the stockyards and packing houses." Dorney belonged to Clan Na Gael, "held an annual celebration of the birth of the Irish republican martyr Robert Emmet, regularly spoke at the Irish republican events, and was a very close friend of Alexander Sullivan." O'Neill's reluctance to speak any names suggests the intensity of Irish nationalist politics, still felt thirty years later.[21]

## Irish Popular Culture

O'Neill steered clear of Clan Na Gael and the more radical nationalists as he moved up in the police ranks. To rise in Chicago, O'Neill had to abandon specifically Irish tribal alliances and make alliances with people from other ethnic groups as well as the city's capitalists. His eventual political patron, Mayor Carter Harrison, had no Irish in his family: Edward Dunne, his successor, was a fierce Irish nationalist educated in Ireland, but he demanded O'Neill's resignation. At many points in O'Neill's career, people with Irish names tried to "do" him. He continued playing music and identifying musicians, but he increasingly saw himself, and his musical allies, through less overtly politicized understandings of Ireland and the Irish.

For example, the young O'Neills would surely have gone to see a Hibernicon. Before the Civil War, Americans had enjoyed watching panoramas, performances that blended painted scenery with live action and stage effects. The owner of the panorama set up a large canvas scroll, eight or more feet high, painted with some moving scene, like a boat trip down the Mississippi River or around Manhattan Island. As the scroll unwound, actors performed while music played and stage hands added sound effects or manipulated lighting to mimic sunrise or sunset. A ticket to the Hibernicon bought a tour of Ireland: scenes like the lakes of Killarney, Blarney Castle, the Cliffs of Moher, the Rock of Cashel scrolled past as actors played in front of them.

"McEvoy's Hibernicon" played in Bloomington, Illinois, in the late 1860s, where Anna Rogers lived. When Anna and Francis moved to Chicago, they would have had multiple chances to see some sort of Hibernicon. Michelle Granshaw found "a selection of companies touring in the late 1860s and 1870s," including

Charles MacEvoy's *Famous Original Hibernicon*; Dare's *Hibernicon*; Blaisdell's *Gigantic Panorama of Ireland known as the Hibernicon*; Dailey's *Hibernicon Minstrels*; John MacEvoy's *New Hibernicon*; Frank McEvoy's *New Hibernicon or Ireland in America*; Sullivan and Emmett's *Panorama of Ireland*; Bordwell's *Mirror of Ireland*; Healey's *Hibernian Minstrels and Mirror of Ireland*; Flaherty's *Mirror of Ireland*; McGill and Strong's *Mirror of Ireland*; Dr. Correy's *Panorama or Ireland in Shade and Sunshine*; Howarth's *Mirror of Ireland*; John MacEvoy's *Erinopticon*; John Burke's *Tableaux of Erin*; and Dr. Barlow's *Mirror of Ireland*.

One Ohio man recalled seeing "Jerry and Helen Cohan, George M. Cohan's father and mother," in

> a program that consisted largely of the Cohans and a panorama background on hand-cranked rollers. A few seconds' earnest twisting of the crank brought about a miraculously quick change of scene from the Giant's Causeway to the Streets of Dublin to Lakes of Killarney and so forth ... and the Cohans did something gloriously exciting in front of each scene: a song and dance, or a jig, or a reel, or a sentimental ballad perhaps.

In the standard family-friendly plot, a well-off American couple hire "a pert young Irishman" to give them a tour of the Emerald Isle. Often named "Barney," the guide narrates the trip and also adds a subplot: he hopes to marry Nora, a young farm woman. The course of love predictably fails to run smoothly when a widow appears with her eye on Barney, and suitors vie for Nora. Eventually all resolves happily, and the tourists embark for home.[22]

In 1872, shortly after the O'Neills arrived, "McEvoy's New Hibernicon" played in Chicago, offering "panoramic views of the principal cities and historic localities of the Emerald Isle, comic and sentimental songs, and witty sayings. The paintings are well mounted, and it is said by those who have travelled in Ireland that they are remarkably true to nature." A year later Francis and Anna could have seen McEvoy's Hibernicon in Chicago with Jerry Cohan featured as "Barney the guide."[23]

Granshaw points out that the Hibernicon made Irish American audiences into tourists. A man or woman from Donegal likely knew nothing at all about the lakes of Killarney: the Hibernicon taught them to understand Killarney's lakes as a heritage they shared. "They will with pleasure recognize the dear old scenes of their youth; and the little ones will feel a renewed pride in being descended from the people of fair Ireland," MacEvoy claimed, but the Hibernicon always concluded with the tourists saying goodbye and heading back to the US. It enacted Irish Americanness, celebrating Ireland and the viewer as an American, experiencing the past as a foreign country. It replaced the Ireland audiences might remember

**Figure 23** Advertising poster for "The scenery, music & antiquities of Ireland illustrated by MacEvoy's original Hibernicon." The Hibernicon helped explain to Irish Americans how they should understand larger ideas of Ireland than their personal experience encompassed. M. Keogh Litho., [1870]. At Prints and Photographs Division, Library of Congress, https://www.loc.gov/pictures/item/2014635899/.

with a stylized version of Ireland the entire audience experienced the same way, creating something like what Alison Landsberg has termed a "prosthetic memory" of Ireland: a common "memory" of things that even the Irish-born never experienced. The Hibernicon moved memory from particular to general, from personal experience to a generalized and abstracted experience. It made Ireland both greater and lesser.[24]

Hibernicon shows did the greatest business in the 1860s and 1870s; by 1884 they had lost their novelty and declined. But other popular entertainments cooled Irish rage at England or glossed the bitter relations of landlord and tenant with sentimental sugar. Rebecca Solnit, speaking of Ireland, described sentimentality as "the enjoyment of emotion for its own sake, a kind of connoisseurship of feelings without the obligation to act on them." Sentimentality might lead to action by creating empathy for the suffering of others, but the sentimentality of Irish American culture often substituted for a more painful confrontation with the meaning of the past.[25]

Vaudeville shows and popular songs treated Irish people not as violent revolutionaries but as alternately boisterously comic or sentimentally longing. On stages across America audiences got to know the ubiquitous "stage Irishman." "The stage Irishman habitually bears the general name of Pat, or Paddy or Teague. He has an atrocious Irish Brogue, perpetual jokes, blunders, and bulls in speaking, and never fails to utter . . . some wild screech or oath of Gaelic origin at every third word." Typically red-haired, "he is rosy-cheeked, massive, and whiskey-loving." He wears "knee breeches, worsted stockings, and cockaded brogue shoes." He invariably carries a shillelagh. Irish characters "performed the parts of bumbling, shuffling, stuttering intermediaries between hero and villain," "woeful creatures, always bumping, dropping or breaking something, getting lost, misunderstanding or mistaking someone."[26]

In theater, "Paddy" played much the same role as "Sambo," the comic African American. "At the center of both stereotypes was the same 'natural,' irresponsible, irrepressible *joi de vivre* that the disciplined and businesslike Anglo-American culture has always held suspect, but longed to possess." "Paddy, like Sambo, was a creature of his superiors," "a classic example of the tendency of all regimes to sentimentalize their victims." Blackface comic J. C. Murphy kept a jokebook "made up of negro spirituals, parodies of hymns, drinking songs, Irish ballads, limericks, riddles, cross-talk parlor poetry, one liners, and even chemical formulae for various kinds of stage fire."

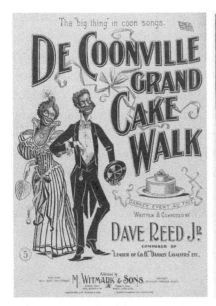 

Figure 24 George M. Cohan began his career in both blackface and "Irishface." Here we see the similarities between the stage Irishman and the stage "coon." The men strike similar poses, with the same raised left leg and bent right arm; both tilt their heads in the same way and both wear watches dangling from a vest. Music Division, New York Public Library. "De Coonville Grand Cake-Walk," 1897, New York Public Library Digital Collections, https://digitalcollections.nypl.org/items/510d47e3-fc3b-a3d9-e040-e00a18064a99. "The Irish Cakewalk," 1898, from American Folklife Center, *Ethnic Recordings in America: A Neglected Heritage* (Washington, DC: Library of Congress, 1982), 88. O'Neill described dancing for the prize of a cake in his youth in Tralibane, but his collections of specifically Irish music segregated Irish music from this kind of commercial hybridity.

His acts "ranged from blackface and rube doubles acts to a traditional minstrel trio" to a skit based on "the Irishmen's first game of baseball." Irish performers like the Cohans slipped easily between "stage Irish" characters and minstrel show characters. Jerry Cohan recalled, "The papers make me sore when they give people the impression that I started out in the variety shows and that the only work I have ever done was the swinging of an Irish shillelagh in a hoe-down. No, sir, I made my start in a minstrel show, and I'm proud of it."[27]

The stage Irishman or Irishwoman could engage in pathos, invariably expressed as longing for the past, and here again the stereotype of Paddy echoed staged performances of blackness: "the same romantic formulas applied to both the Irish and the African-American stereotypes." Sentimental songs about the happy plantation slave, longing for old times at home, "easily slipped into songs about old Erin." William H. Williams concluded that "unable to escape the stereotype that preceded them, the Irish gradually remolded it into something they could live with—and eventually, something they could use to express pride in themselves." Similarly, African Americans began performing in blackface in the 1890s and eventually began mocking and then attacking the stereotypes themselves.[28]

Vaudeville performers gleefully trafficked in ethnic stereotypes of all sorts and forms of racial and ethnic imposture, so the Irish were very far from alone as targets of satire. By the 1890s, however, Irish

CHASE THE BEAST!

**Figure 25** From *Irish World and Industrial Liberator*, February 1907. The heavy-handed stereotyping Cohan had engaged in ten years earlier increasingly came under fire as Irish Americans advanced a version of respectability politics. O'Neill's efforts to police Irish music took place in the context of this effort to change public images of the Irish.

Americans began organizing against "stage Irishman" and stereotypical depictions of Irishmen and -women. "In the 1890s, radical Irish nationalists turned against the 'stage Irish' as a way to rejuvenate Celtic race pride, including the revival of the Gaelic language and the elimination of Anglo influence in American culture." O'Neill witnessed this changing notion of performed Irishness, and a more refined and racially purified version of "Celtic" culture, at the 1893 Columbian Exposition.[29]

## The World's Fair of 1893

The internationally famous Chicago Exposition—which saw more than 26 million visitors—combined a formal, utopian fairground with a carnivalesque Midway. Frederick Law Olmstead designed the formal part, with artificial lakes, canals, and islands. Eminent American architects designed vast gleaming white buildings in which Americans and other nationalities displayed their art, their clever machines, and the dazzling products of industrial abundance. Several forms of phonograph appeared at the fair, including Thomas Edison's foil and wax cylinders; a decade later O'Neill used this device to make some of the earliest recordings of Irish music in existence.

On the Midway, fairgoers could ride the first Ferris wheel, see exotic dancers, watch Wild West shows, or tour villages set up by entrepreneurs from various countries. A Dutch and a German village, a street in Cairo and Algerian and Tunisian villages, a Javanese community, a Hawaiian cyclorama, replicas of Chinese, Dahomey and Austrian villages: all offered a combination of tourism, anthropology, and gift shop.

Two competing Irish villages graced the Midway, both depicting Irish landmarks and Irish handcrafts and rural industries. The Irish village of Alice Rowland Hart boasted a half-size replica of Donegal Castle while the village of Ishbel, Countess of Aberdeen, let visitors into a two-thirds-sized replica of Blarney Castle, allegedly including a piece of the Blarney stone. Both sites employed comely maidens to dance and demonstrate linen weaving and lace making, authentic Irish artisans to carve crosses or other artifacts, pipers to play Irish tunes, and sellers to hawk Irish crafts or other merchandise. Both women worked to get Irish handcrafts added to the stock of large department stores.[30]

Reform-minded women ran both villages, women who favored "home rule" for Ireland, a political scheme in which Ireland would remain a part of Great Britain but gain increased political autonomy. Both wanted to recast Ireland in a more modern but not too modern image. In both villages, visitors could see art described as "Celtic" and framed as a specific racial heritage, and in both villages Irish natives demonstrated cottage industry with an eye for a growing international market. Both villages claimed to have actual Irish soil or sods of turf from the peat bogs, an enticement soon to become general in Irish American fairs. Mrs. Hart called her site the Irish Industrial Village and described "her work in Ireland in the establish- ment of cottage industries and technical schools, by means of which the willing workers of Ireland were taught self-reliance." The colo- nized always enjoy lectures on self-reliance from the colonizer: pre- sumably she did not mean self-reliance in the Clan Na Gael sense.[31]

Lady Aberdeen's village represented the rival Irish Industries As- sociation and similarly demonstrated cottage industries Irish people could pursue while remaining charming. Aberdeen called for Irish immigrants to come "with their children in order to call to mind the stories told by parents of the scenes of their childhood, or muse over bygone days," for "those recollections . . . forge lasting ties between those of the same kindred and the same country." She assured them that the village gives "a faithful and truthful representation of the scenes. . . . Blarney Castle is an exact reproduction (on a scale of two thirds)." As with the Hibernicon, Irish Americans who never saw Blarney Castle in their lives, or even knew it existed, would gain a memory of an Ireland that both was and was not the Ireland of their childhoods: cottages and crafts unencumbered by incessant demands for rent, family homes no one had to leave.

Aberdeen described the furniture as "copied from special designs; the iron pots, the old delft ornaments . . . and the bog-turf! Inhale its fragrance!" Burning turf has a distinctive fragrance, even on a hot summer day in Chicago: Irish immigrants would surely have experienced the shock of abrupt memory at the scent, which would have lent authenticity to the scaled-down castle and reproduction furniture, simultaneously "typical" and "special." "Yes," she continued, "for it is here that Ireland lifts high her green flag from the battlements of Blarney and calls on the sons and daughters of Erin to show proof that a surpassing love for the old country and for all that reminds them of her is a part of their inheritance which they have not yet lost."[32]

But Lady Aberdeen's Blarney Castle saw a small riot when she flew not the green flag but the Union Jack from the castle's battlements. When her husband, Lord Aberdeen, joined her at the village in October 1893, she hoisted the British flag. The sight of the Union Jack flying over an imitation Blarney Castle in Chicago enraged a small group of Chicago Irish, who climbed its interior stairs, pulled down the flag, and hurled it to the streets below. When a replacement flag appeared, they snuck past the guards and for a second time Lord and Lady Aberdeen "saw the emblem of England's pride come fluttering down again and go flying over the castle wall like a bundle of old clothes." "The guards summoned the patrol wagon and tried to arrest the whole number, in the face of threats from a crowd of several thousand sympathizers who quickly gathered around the village." When police arrived "they no sooner had got one or two of their prisoners into the wagon than the men who pressed around it pulled them out." Police managed to get three men to jail, only to release them on insufficient evidence. The *Chicago Citizen*, the Irish American weekly, rejoiced in the fact of Irishmen "who are always the enemies of the British flag wherever it happens to be displayed."[33]

Most Irish immigrants likely had little or no idea of Blarney Castle or of its alleged significance; they came from isolated rural areas, and what education they got was haphazard or strongly Anglo-centric. Now in Chicago they rallied around a novel symbol of what they were told represented Ireland. Both villages combined staged local color and nostalgia with a vision of "modern" that kept the Irish in cottages. Both served as flashpoints for memory, but also for nationalist anger. Ireland was depicted as familiar and alien: Chicago's Irish did not spin flax or cut turf but labored in the factory heart of a vast and innovative industrial machine.[34]

Aberdeen and Hart both located their exhibitions within the "Celtic revival," a literary and artistic movement that sought to invent an idea of the Celtic culture, and a Celtic race, to a wider audience while bypassing overt nationalist politics. The Celtic revival resonated strongly with the educated O'Neill.[35]

## The Celtic Revival

Late nineteenth- and early twentieth-century artists and intellectuals often countered industrialization with a romantic view of the premodern past. Romantic nationalism looked past the complexities of modern life for a racial "soul" and often found it in marginalized people, the folk. In the US, for example, folklorists reframed people formerly scorned as "hillbillies" as the true bearers of Shakespearean English and Anglo-Saxon tradition. In Ireland, England, and the US, a Celtic revival used folklore and archaeology to present a new idea of Celtic culture. Most historians today view this movement as an example of "invented tradition," which based claims of authenticity on often fragmentary evidence of some isolated customs: for example, the idea that the Scots always wore kilts and that each clan had a specific tartan. Isolated evidence was generalized into standard practice. The Celtic revival neatly fit into racial theories in which a largely imaginary Celtic race differed from its equally imaginary neighbor, the Anglo-Saxon race, and so decorative forms found in Ireland and possibly derived from Viking settlements or merchant traders became emblems of Irish "Celticness."[36]

The literary Celtic revival, led by William Butler Yeats and his patron, Lady Gregory, insisted that Ireland had a distinctive culture and folklore worthy of serious study and capable of bearing artistic greatness. Both Protestants, born to relative wealth, they reveled in the language and customs of the rural Irish west. Both collected folklore and local tales, and both worked to make the Irish landscape and language the foundation of serious literature. The Celtic revival tried to specify the characteristics of Celticness, both visually and in language.

As part of the Celtic revival, O'Neill especially admired Douglas Hyde, founder of the Gaelic League. Hyde, a Protestant professor of languages born in Roscommon, dedicated himself to "de-anglicizing" Ireland. In a famous 1892 essay, Hyde lamented how Ireland "continues to apparently hate the English, and at the same time continues to imitate them; how it continues to clamour for recognition as a distinct nationality, and at the same time throws away with both hands what would make it so." In 1892, he charged, "all our Irish names of places and people" have turned into English names; and "our Irish intonation changed, as far as possible by English schoolmasters into something English; our history no longer remembered or taught; the names of our rebels and martyrs blotted out; our battlefields and traditions forgotten." Hyde described the education O'Neill had gotten in the National Schools, devoid of Irish history.

Hyde wanted the revival of the Irish language and literature; secondarily, he urged the practice of specifically Irish sports, music, and dance. Hyde imagined a "Celtic" race with distinct culture traditions and practices, and he insisted that culture transcended politics, and that Ireland politically free, but speaking English, would never be truly Irish or free.[37]

Hyde's Gaelic League argued against political agitation and advanced cultural revival instead: it now seems somewhat fusty and bourgeois. Blood and steel created the Irish republic, one might argue, not jigs and reels, and the Proclamation of the Irish Republic in 1916 stirs the imagination as effectively in English as it does in Irish. But in his day Hyde was powerfully inspirational. Sean O'Casey, the playwright, remembered Hyde as an epic figure "ever shouting out, with his right arm lifted so that its shadow seemed to stretch from one end of the land to the other; shouting in a strange tongue, 'Come and follow me, for behind me marches the only Ireland worth knowing.'" Inspired by the Gaelic League's ideals, O'Casey, a Protestant, wore green kilts, joined a hurling club, and played a set of bagpipes. Hyde offered a vision of unified Celtic Irish culture, not the tribal pettiness of politics or religious sect.

O'Neill found Hyde equally inspiring. By 1901 at least he was organizing music programs at Gaelic League events. He dedicated one of his books to Hyde's Gaelic League and its "patriotic work." And when Hyde came to Chicago, O'Neill threw a private party in his honor. Hyde's apolitical stance offered O'Neill, by then the friend of Chicago capitalists, a way to be Irish without engaging in direct political conflict and violence: Ireland as cultural and not political nationalism, purified of low comic stereotypes and minstrel shenanigans.[38]

The "Celtic race" never existed the way its boosters imagined. At every point in history, "Irish culture" was always under construction: modified and reconsidered in light of changing political circumstances, called into being by the act of describing it. Irish musicians had always borrowed from other cultures: how could it be otherwise? Imagine the absurdity of a culture in which people played the same tunes in the same way on the same instruments for hundreds of unchanging years. The idea of distinctive Irish music arose in the context of nationalism: it anchored a claim of distinctiveness and entitlement to independence. As O'Neill grew more prosperous, he embraced the idea of Celtic culture because it offered a sense of Irishness purged of impurity, rooted in history, and larger than politics.[39]

Multiple versions of Irishness circulated for O'Neill's consideration. Hibernicons and other entertainments presented a nostalgic, staged memory rendered in stereotypes. Nationalist organizations played on a sense of immigrants as political exiles dreaming of Irish independence. The Gaelic League focused on the island of Ireland but stressed culture—language, music, and sports—rather than politics or religion. The Celtic revival imagined a quasi-racial identity expressed most clearly on the island of Ireland. They had respectability on their side: no clowning, no blackface antics, no murdering.

We have already seen O'Neill rejecting things not deemed Irish enough. Although written and played by and for Irish people in the US, "Kitty O'Neil's Champion Jig" did not count. At first, he counted as Irish "Nolan the Soldier," heard on the prairie, but then under criticism removed it from his second collection of tunes. Irish farmers in Edina, Missouri, apparently had no trouble dancing to the

Figure 26 O'Neill's house at 5448 Drexel Ave, from the Chicago *Record Herald*, May 5, 1901, 16. Much better views of both exterior and interior of the house, taken in the 1960s, exist at Hyde Park Historical Society Collections at the University of Chicago Library, and in the collections of the Chicago History Museum, but neither will allow reproduction because of restrictions placed by the photographer, Nancy Campbell Hays, who died in 2007 with no heirs. The house, which extended well to the back, was torn down in the 1970s to make way for the present Ronald McDonald House.

music of German and French and American fiddlers at barn dances, but though Irish people joined in those dances the tunes needed intellectual policing, sorting out. O'Neill had embarked on a project of defining Irishness through a specific kind of music, heard in America from his policeman's point of view.[40]

By 1893 Lieutenant O'Neill lived on Drexel Avenue in Hyde Park, only a few blocks from the Columbian Exposition. The discretely respectable house had ornate interior woodwork and a stained-glass portrait of the guardian angel above the stairs. A faction on the police force, he reported, had wanted to promote him to captain and put him in charge of policing the fair, but another faction thwarted them. "The conditions which developed during the progress of the fair convinced me that in losing the appointment I was favored by the Fates," he wrote later; "many things beside a knowledge of police business had their values in the maelstrom of selfish human interests." "Powerful influences paralyzed the arm of the law," he continued cryptically, "and even the chief of police "was obliged to yield to expediency." What he referred to here remains vague: it was likely the influence of Inspector Nicholas Hunt, an enemy of O'Neill's. As often the case in his private memoir, O'Neill concealed important details.[41]

But he must have known about the flag incident at Blarney Castle. He visited the exposition: at the Donegal Village O'Neill met the mysterious faery-contacting Turlough McSweeney, mentioned in chapter 1, hired from Ireland to pipe outside the Donegal Castle. McSweeney—whose name appears variously as "Charles MacSweeney," "Tourlough MacSwiney," or "Tarlach Mac Suibhne"—"set the feet of visitors to tingling," wrote the *Chicago Tribune*, which noted his "genial but impressive manner" and "comical dignity." "He claims to be the lineal descendant of The McSwine of Donegal," the *Tribune* pointed out. McSweeney described himself, in other words, playing in America before a half-sized replica of the castle his family once controlled. Like the fragrance of burning turf, McSweeney's presence lent authenticity to the temporary village, simultaneously enlarging Ireland and diminishing it: enlarged as part of a presentation to the world at the fair, but diminished as a generalized replica of itself, playing for hire.[42]

O'Neill also met another piper, Patsy Touhey, whom he admired very much and came to regard as a friend; "a gentleman altho a piper," as O'Neill drily put it. Born in Ireland, Touhey came to the US at age three. He made his living on the stage, a professional Irishman. He played in Hibernicons and vaudeville shows—with the Cohan family for long stretches—and like most vaudeville performers, he had an "act." He told jokes and did comic skits, often with a partner; later he and his wife formed a song and dance team. The work involved intensive performing and practicing. In the early days, Jerry Cohan's troupe regularly gave "six performances a day, six days a week with all-day Sunday rehearsals thrown in for good measure." Even late in his life, "Touhey was not afraid of hard work, playing three shows a day," a contemporary remembered. Recordings of Touhey, some made by O'Neill on wax cylinders, show Touhey as a virtuoso piper, exceedingly nimble and inventive. "A truly great player," O'Neill wrote: "captures his audience by storm even mixed nationalities." A vaudevillian, Touhey could mount stages anywhere in the US and quickly capture the motley mix of natives and immigrants in a typical audience.[43]

Touhey played a set of pipes made in Philadelphia by the Taylor brothers, William and Charles, who had emigrated around 1872 and eventually settled in Philadelphia. Skilled artisans and players, they made stunning sets of Uilleann pipes that combined a high level of craft artistry with extremely robust and practical construction. According to O'Neill, "a short experience of the changed conditions prevailing in the United States convinced them that the mild tones of the ordinary Irish pipes were too puny to meet the requirements of the American stage or dance hall." O'Neil continued, "genius that he was, 'Billy' Taylor experimented, remodeled and developed a compact, substantial instrument of powerful tone, which blends agreeably with violin and piano." Taylor pipes have "superseded the old mellow-toned parlor instrument almost altogether." O'Neill saw Taylor pipes as unique to America: "the soft, plaintive tones of the pipes manufactured [in Ireland] so delightful in the parlor, proved too weak to produce the desired effect in concert halls and theatres of modern times." Taylor pipes, he claimed, served a performer in a crowded saloon or concert hall, in a loud industrial city.[44]

The two pipers, McSweeney and Touhey, offered O'Neill a provocative contrast and yet another version being Irish. McSweeney "may have fittingly represented an antiquated and oppressed Ireland, playing his ancient instrument outside the entrance to Mrs. Hart's Donegal Castle," O'Neill wrote, "but the hopes and aspirations of a regenerated nation were pleasingly typified in 'Patsy' Touhey, the spruce young man in corduroy breeches and ribbed stockings, whose expert manipulation of a great set of Taylor pipes made him the centre of attraction within."[45]

McSweeney represented an "ancient," "antiquated and oppressed" Ireland, while Touhey represented both Irish tradition and an energetic version of modern Ireland developed in and for the US. Touhey was decolonized. McSweeney, O'Neill tells us, played *outside* a replica of the castle his ancestors once owned while Touhey dazzled audiences *inside*. Touhey authentically represents a "regenerated nation," more authentically Irish *because* he represents Irishness for the American stage. Touhey performed Irishness for Americans: for most of his career McSweeney played in Ireland for Irish people; the music of people who used to own the castle now occupied by someone with an English name. O'Neill argued that Touhey, an American vaudeville performer, represented Ireland more truly than McSweeney, whose pipes O'Neill described as "puny," "weak," "plaintive," and "soft." As with the Hibernicon, or replica castles, the representation of Ireland—Touhey's "act," the decolonized performance of Ireland, becomes more real, more authentic, than the past experience of Ireland itself: the performance of Celtic Ireland, rather than simply the playing of local Irish music. Touhey, as O'Neill described him, charmed audiences with a style both broadly Irish and energetically American.[46]

The Columbian Exposition gave O'Neill a sense of Ireland at once reduced—in fractional-sized replicas of itself, with "typical" furniture and artifacts, marked by cottage industry and rural simplicity—and enlarged, taking its place in the world, "regenerated" by exiles and emigrants in new contexts, exhibited and reframed as part of a Celtic revival, enlarged from particular local music to a generalized "Irish music" performed by a virtuoso showman. This was an Ireland invented for American needs.

In 1897 the Ancient Order of Hibernians organized an Irish fair in Chicago, which Captain O'Neill visited. Intended to raise money for the construction of a "Robert Emmet Memorial Hall," the fair included a panorama show of "A Day in Ireland," wandering musicians, displays of craft organized by county, and Irish-themed souvenirs, all in a vast armory building on the lakefront. O'Neill did not write about the 1897 fair, but he held on to a souvenir medal from the County Cork booth.[47]

As its main attraction the fair offered a giant "sod map" of Ireland, 40 by 60 feet, laid out on the floor "with county lines marked out by three-inch strips of hickory laths." Fairgoers could stand on their home county—newspapers described County Cork as 4 feet long and 2 1/2 feet wide—and dance a jig or shed a tear or jostle people standing on neighboring counties. Starting in 1897, first in New York and then in Chicago, "within the space of just a few years, such maps would become the standard feature at any Irish Exhibition around the world through at least the 1960s." In 1897 Chicago newspapers followed the progress of the several tons of soil: once it arrived in Irish barrels and was settled on the map, "the man who sold tickets to the inside of the inclosure made money faster than the United States mint" as Irish Americans crowded onto their home counties.

Irish Americans who could not have owned land when they lived in Ireland delighted in owning a piece of Ireland in America. "In both of the 1893 Chicago villages, often to the amazement of the organizers, bricks of turf" had become "some of the most popular souvenirs." "There was a portion of Irish soil that the queen did not reign over last night," wrote the *Tribune* in 1897. "It came in barrels . . . and was sprinkled over the map of Ireland in the middle of the floor and men from Cork and boys from Galway jumped up and down on the Old Sod." Speeches given "on Irish soil" recalled Irish heroes and told 1897 fairgoers: "all of you have relatives, fathers, mothers, sisters and brothers, buried in this soil. Every spot of it is dear to you," and predicted that "the smiling valleys and rushing rivers of Ireland will yet be presided over by the Goddess of Liberty to the end of time." The *Inter Ocean* claimed "a great many patriotic exiles insist upon taking off their shoes before treading on the soil of the Emerald Isle," but it noted the soil had "peculiar reddish color," suggesting perhaps a suspect provenance. The soil allegedly came from each county in

Ireland, an unlikely prospect indeed, and at the fair's end, exhibitors attempted to auction it off at twenty-five cents an ounce. "I now know what is meant by 'dear old Ireland,'" said a fairgoer quoted in the *Inter Ocean*: "at this rate a few acres of the Green Isle are more valuable than all the real estate in Chicago!"[48]

The sod map might seem equal parts profound, venal, and silly. A piece of one's homeland had powerful meaning in an age of more limited travel, but the nakedly commercial aspect of the attraction tarnished the sentimental appeal. Like pipers at the Columbian Exposition or the Hibernicon show, the sod map simultaneously enlarged and diminished Ireland for Americans. They could see the entire island and its actual soil at a glance. Available as a tourist experience for a few cents, it put the Irish American in the position of consumer of Ireland, carried off as a souvenir. But the other product it offered, nostalgia, enlarged the idea of Ireland in the consumer's mind, offering an emotional connection to a larger Ireland than they remembered.

Life in Chicago, life on the police force, challenged O'Neill's thinking. He experienced forms of standardization and administrative control, the aggregation of face-to-face communities into "statistical communities," but also forms of commercial spectacle in which one's own memories of a townland in Cork might give way to generalized memories of a stylized and generic Ireland.

O'Neill evolved a way of understanding Ireland and America that increasingly put him at some tension with both his friends and the larger Irish community. He sided with capitalists in the Pullman strike, not the Irish immigrants in the American Railway Union, and his relations with relatives and with Irish musicians seemed to often end in recrimination. O'Neill longed for and delighted in community, but in multiple ways his life eroded the communities he valued. The "village friendliness" of the working-class young man gave way to the complications of systemic authority. Under the influence of the Celtic revival, he was coming to see Irish music not as something people played together but as an aspect of a generalized Celtic culture that he needed to disaggregate, collect, catalog, and preserve.

**Figure 27** O'Neill pasted this John McCutcheon cartoon, from the *Chicago Tribune,* January 25, 1913, 1, in his scrapbook. The sod map he saw at the 1897 fair had allowed each Chicago Irish immigrant to stand on his or her own native county. O'Neill kept a souvenir medal from the County Cork booth at the fair. "Home rule" represented probably the most conservative Irish nationalist position, offering a degree of autonomy from England but perpetuating colonial status. From the private collection of Mary Mooney Lesch.

He began deliberately collecting tunes for publication and, in the process, exposed complicated problems of ownership. Did a tune belong to the one who memorized it and held it dear, or did it belong to some larger notion of "the Celtic race?" O'Neill would increasingly use the authority of the badge to compel people to "share" their tunes: he would alienate the tunes from individuals and local communities to place them in a generalized, abstracted notion of "Irish." Just as his rise in the police alienated him from his community, his music collecting redefined his relationships with the music he loved and the people who played it. His promotion to general superintendent of police at the end of April 1901 gave him the authority and the financial means to realize his plans.

## Named Chief of Police

Newspapers praised O'Neill lavishly when news of his appointment broke. They published his picture and pictures of his Hyde Park home. According to the *Tribune*, "cheers broke out in the galleries, which were packed with visitors," when Carter Harrison II named O'Neill chief. The *Chicago Eagle* called him "honest and fearless," while the *Inter Ocean* called him "the most scholarly man in the department" and "an efficient policeman in every capacity in which he has served." He is also "an untiring book collector, his library being especially rich in works on Ireland." "Frank O'Neill, a splendid type of Irishman and policeman," headlined the Chicago *Record Herald*, "has gone to the top solely on his merit as an honest, efficient and courteous officer." "He has never been connected with thieves, lewd women, cheap bartenders, money loan sharks or other characters of shady reputations," the reporter gushed. "He is financially worth at least $125,000 if not more. Most of his money has come to him through fortunate investments in property annexed to Chicago since 1888." "He has never been mixed up in an official or personal scandal, never been scathed by a grand jury, never been pilloried by the press, never been accused of taking a bribe." Better yet, it added, "he is cordially disliked in the Harrison Street district by the inmates of that place of wretchedness."[49]

O'Neill reassured readers that although "I've been an Irishman by birth all my life," "I am an American in all my sentiments." He followed "Celtic literature and the history of my native land because I have always been proud of the contributions of my race to the knowledge of the world." "The new Chief is an ardent bibliophile," wrote the *Tribune*, "with a leaning toward history and literature of the Emerald Isle. In his library are 1,500 volumes of rare works, first editions and other curioso." The *Tribune* quoted O'Neill as saying, "I suppose I shall have a lot of friends now. That is customary. I shall not be surprised at their number."[50]

Chicago police chiefs typically served only one term of two years. Pressure from factions and friends inclined mayors to rotate the office frequently. Although some newspapers had mentioned O'Neill as a possible candidate for chief, the appointment of "Frank" O'Neill—"no one calls the little fighter and scholar 'Francis'—" took journalists by surprise. With the exception of the more jaundiced *Inter Ocean*, which denounced O'Neill for describing himself as "the Mayor's hired man," they greeted O'Neill's appointment as a sign of reform.[51]

Mayor Carter Harrison called O'Neill "a No. 1 first-class all around, clean-cut, thorough, practical policeman. He knows the business from the ground up and back again." He is well educated and will make the kind of chief Chicago needs, the mayor continued, adding also "he's modest." He didn't lobby for the job or "run around and get people to write me or come see me. He just went on about his business and not a soul but one spoke to me about him."

That one person, Harrison explained, "is Mrs. John Doyle, who was my brother Preston's old nurse." Mrs. Doyle's husband, a fireman, had just passed away and had named Harrison executor of "his little estate." "She came to my office to see me on business, told me about Frank and sang his praises in all sorts of keys."[52]

Kate Doyle died in 1911, and newspapers retold the story of how she had selected the chief of police. By then reporters had the mayor call her "my second mother" and gave her a stereotypical Irish accent. "Carter," she allegedly said, "I'm going to ask a great favor of you, but gra machree, I know you'll do it for Kate." "Gra Machree," spelled "grá mo chroí" in Irish, means "love of my heart." Mrs. Doyle allegedly continued, "I saw by the papers that a new chief of police is going to be appointed. Now, what brought me here was to ask you if you would appoint my old friend, Frank O'Neill, chief. That's all." The obituary continued: "years ago her house in Dearborn street was a meeting place on Sunday for all the Irish pipers, fluters, and fiddlers in Chicago. Among those who met there to play the tunes of Ireland were Barney Delaney, James Early, John Ennis, James Kerwin, James Cahill, and her choice for chief of police, Francis O'Neill, who played the pipes and flute." The article added attendees at Mrs. Doyle's funeral included "Mayor Elect Harrison, his wife, his brother, Preston, and former Chief of Police O'Neill."

The story deliberately trivialized Kate Doyle, who one newspaper called "Chicago's foremost woman politician through her activities in behalf of the members of the Harrison family." She worked as a nanny for the Harrisons, but also she "became acquainted with many of the Irish voters of the city, assuming a political leadership over them that became an important element in the political affairs of the city," and she worked further as a poll captain, wrangling voters for Harrison. Earlier we saw that O'Neill wrote fondly about his friendship with Johnny Doyle and his wife and the many evenings he spent at their house playing music. In his scrapbooks he pasted a copy of that very story from 1911, which described Kate Doyle not as a formidable "lady politician" but as the Irish equivalent of Mammy. As with his memories of Tralibane, O'Neill let nostalgia soften and blur history's rougher and more complicated surfaces.[53]

# 6
# Chief O'Neill's Favorite
## The Chief in Office

In under thirty years Francis O'Neill went from itinerant unskilled laborer to general superintendent of police, in charge of more than 3,000 men, responsible for order and public safety in a city of almost 2 million people. Once he slept outdoors in the Sierra foothills or swam between boats in Yokohama harbor with books tied to his head to keep them dry. Now he owned rental properties, two homes, and a marvelous private library. Once he pounded a beat in the city's worst neighborhoods. Now he had an office and a staff and met regularly with the mayor. Once he grieved at the loss of less than $300, the fruit of three years' labor at sea. Now he enjoyed a salary of $6,000 a year, six times the salary of a patrolman.

As chief he often borrowed the language of Progressive Era reforms and endorsed civil service examinations. With Mayor Carter Harrison, he warred with the Robert Burke faction of the Democratic Party. But neither he nor Harrison would allow "reform" to extend very far: they needed the support of corporations, and Harrison needed also the alderman's ability to herd and corral votes: Harrison regarded graft and vice as something best dealt with by looking away. But Chief O'Neill turned the authority of office toward his music collecting, using the techniques of modern police work to collect and catalog the music Chicago's Irish immigrants played. He sent men undercover; he tracked down rumors and identified witnesses; he put forensic teams to work reconstructing evidence. The music collecting lifted him up, but the job of chief and personal tragedy

**Figure 28** Chief O'Neill. From the *Annual Report of the Chief Superintendent of Police*, 1903. O'Neill used this image in most of his books: it symbolized his authority as the manager of a large, complex modern administration.

bore him down, and he resigned his last appointment to focus on music. Even in retirement, he drew on his experiences and authority as chief.

In Ireland the police, nicknamed the "Peelers," served the British crown, agents of an occupying oppressor. Peelers battered down doors, pulled people from their houses, burned away roofs, and put evicted tenant families on the road, homeless. "In America," O'Neill wrote, "officers of the law are citizens and voters," not "employees of an unpopular government." As "peace officers of the State and Municipality and therefore men of standing in the commonwealth," they are "rather looked up to than otherwise."[1]

Certainly Chicago police did not serve an occupying foreign power. But they would equally certainly evict someone for nonpayment of rent; and if a union called a strike, O'Neill's police protected "scabs" hired to take strikers' jobs. The men in the "anarchist saloon" to whom O'Neill administered a "salutary drubbing" in chapter 4 probably hated the police. If blind piper Murphy remembered the Peelers as bullies in Ireland, what did he think of the police who tormented him in Bridgeport? If you enjoyed illegal vice while the police pretended not to notice, they might even earn your esteem, depending on how much their averted gaze cost. Then, as now, police might bully and throw their weight around, or they might empathize with the struggling poor.

Walter Wyckoff, the Princeton theology graduate who spent months in Chicago as an itinerant laborer, sleeping at times in the Harrison Street station, found a "quality of natural bonhomie in the relation of the police officers to the vagrant and criminal classes." The police had "sturdy common sense and genuine knowledge and human sympathy," and Wyckoff believed them good judges of character: when looking at a stranger, the officer "is not far misled by either his virtue or his vice. He knows him for a human being, even if he be a vagrant or a criminal." Some of that realism about people and their frailties comes through in O'Neill's memoir. Sam Mitrani, in his history of the Chicago police force, notes that "a pessimistic view of human nature runs through the main police-produced works of the time" and cites O'Neill's memoir as an example, but we might also see O'Neill as resigned and pragmatic. He might have preferred a world where only merit counted, but he did not live in that world.[2]

O'Neill's first test as chief came in a long-promised "crackdown" on the levee district, legendary for gambling, prostitution, opium, and after-hours drinking. Within a few weeks, newspapers that initially praised O'Neill as the champion of reform began wondering what delayed his action.

Figure 29 Images of O'Neill as reformer. On the right, "Chief O'Neill Finds that the Last Tenant has Left the Usual Amount of Rubbish." On the left, "How Chief O'Neill will Handle the Levee Leeches." O'Neill grabs the bulky figure of Alderman "Bathhouse John" Coughlin and prepares to toss him away. *Chicago Record Herald*, May 1, 1901, 1.

Figure 30 O'Neill, reformer, disappointing Chicago newspapers. Left, *Chicago Daily News*, September 28, 1901, 1. O'Neill asks Mayor Harrison to open the door, but Harrison replies that something—Robert Burke—is holding it. Right, *Chicago Daily News*, June 5, 1901, 1. "Papa O'Neill" says "bless you my children, until Aug. 31!"

In June 1901 O'Neill issued an order regulating piano music in the levee: the *Tribune* reported "the keepers of the resorts were told to close their pianos, and, in addition, to keep women away from the doors and windows of their places. As a consequence, the levee was as quiet as a country churchyard last night," and "the entire district that usually shows signs of a strenuous life after dusk, wore a deserted look." O'Neill claimed "the priests connected with the Franciscan Church there complained that the noise from the saloons and rooming houses across the street interfered with their sleep."

He said this with a straight face, in a dry deadpan style as if he actually believed it, but likely no one—not O'Neill, or the reporters, or readers, or the Franciscan priests—believed their sleepless evenings had anything to do with it. O'Neill often adopted this winkingly flat

**Figure 31** "Why Stop at the Levee?" *Chicago Daily News,* June 15, 1901. City dwellers living in "Wagner, Chopin, Opera and Ragtime" buildings ask Mr. O'Neill why he can't "stop piano-playing in our district too?"

tone with reporters: his willingness to play straight man to Chicago's glaring ironies endeared them. The *Daily News* published a cartoon asking O'Neill to suppress piano music more generally.[3]

## A National Audience

In the summer of 1901 O'Neill wrote an article for the *Saturday Evening Post* laying out his ideas about "policing a modern metropolis." "'Place hunters' formed the single largest problem," he wrote. "The official life of the chief police executive of a large city is mainly an unremitting effort to say 'No'—and to say it with the least possible offense to those whose requests and demands are denied," he argued. Without "civil service rule," the demands never stopped. "If the policemen's clubs were made of gold instead of locust wood, competition for them could scarcely be more strenuous." And indeed, a 1904 newspaper described how "stepwarmers assail O'Neill" because "Chief O'Neill soon will appoint forty-five new policemen. Politicians camp continually on his trail. They visit him in his office, follow his rounds through the city, and waylay him at his home."[4]

O'Neill insisted that "civil service, when it is the real thing, shuts the flood-gate on the old channel of entrance into police life." The article allied O'Neill with Progressive reformers. He also explained that "a great city cannot be transformed into a Sunday-school by the application of brute force." He argued police should suppress "public gambling to a point where the police force does not know of its existence," and "vice to a point where it cannot directly affect" those who do not "seek its haunts." Earlier we saw Mayor Harrison insisting that he had little interest in suppressing vices people enjoyed; here we see O'Neill suggesting a pragmatic policy of discretion or, if you like, willfully turning a blind eye to gambling, perfectly tolerable so long as the police "don't know of its existence."[5]

In a further sign of the social distance he had come since 1873, he admitted: "the materials with which a chief of police has to work are not ideal." He termed the policeman's job "hardly attractive to a man of acute moral sensibilities or highly developed intellectuality," meaning a man like himself. He called the work "rough" and "repulsive to the man of refined sensibilities." Constantly seeing the "harsh, the corrupt, the vicious and the sordid sides of life," no wonder so many policemen "yield to the unwholesome influences of such a contact."[6]

## Anarchism, Political Faction, and Police Reform

An example came early in his first year when a scandal broke around Captain Luke Colleran, head of the police detective bureau. Detectives, more so than patrolmen, worked as free agents, investigating largely as they pleased. Colleran, born in Sligo, had joined the force in 1883, enjoying the backing of Robert Burke, "boss" of the Democratic Party in Cook County, and apparently did his bidding in matters relating to the investigation and prosecution of crime.[7]

In 1901 Mayor Carter Harrison entered into a political battle with Burke that began with attacks on his supporters, including Colleran. Colleran and some associates initially stood accused of faking expenses and lining their pockets to the tune of slightly more than $75; eventually the charges escalated to allowing criminals to escape and destroying evidence. O'Neill does not say so in his memoirs, which do not mention Colleran by name, but he clearly seems to have "had it in" for Colleran, as Carter Harrison had it in for Burke. Between August and November 1901, newspapers reported almost daily on the Colleran case, typically on the front page, accusing him of either deliberately failing to arrest known criminals or helping criminals escape justice in return for cash.[8]

The Colleran case gained extra urgency on September 6, 1901, when an anarchist shot President William McKinley in Buffalo. Colleran's detective division, seeking a diversion, arrested Emma Goldman, the notorious feminist and anarchist then visiting Chicago, and began interrogating her harshly. Newspapers favorable to Burke then lavishly praised Colleran for heroically defending Chicago from Goldman.[9]

Emma Goldman was one of the most remarkable women in US

history, a bold and consistently radical thinker, contemptuous of convention, committed to revolution. The *Tribune* called her "the high priestess of anarchy." Born to a Jewish family in Russia, she came to the US at fifteen and quickly embraced anarchism's emphasis on political action and also on "free love," the idea that women should choose to love whomever they pleased rather than enduring marriages arranged by patriarchy and convention. "Free love" added a whiff of the salacious to Goldman's enthusiasm for principled speeches, and her arrest in Chicago pushed Colleran's misconduct off the front pages.[10]

O'Neill detested anarchism, as described in chapter 4. Goldman, he wrote accurately, "consistently denounced the police and volubly expressed her contempt" for the law and its agents. But "Chief of Police O'Neill of Chicago came to my cell," Goldman wrote in her autobiography. "He informed me that he would like to have a quiet talk with me." "I have no wish to bully or coerce you," she remembered him saying, adding "perhaps I can help you." Goldman told him she had no role in the assassination, and O'Neill then concluded that "unless you're a very clever actress, you are certainly innocent. . . . I am going to do my part to help you out."

Goldman wrote, "I was too amazed to thank him; I had never before heard such a tone from a police officer." O'Neill kept his word. Suddenly "my cell door was left unlocked day and night, and I was told by the matron that I could stay in the large room, use the rocking-chair and the table there, order my own food and papers, receive and send out mail. I began at once to lead the life of a society lady," she wrote sarcastically, "receiving callers all day long." O'Neill publicly undermined Colleran's decision to arrest her. "Chief of Police O'Neill is frank in saying it does not look as if the anarchists under arrest were involved in a plot," wrote the *Chicago Journal*, which noted that "Capt. Colleran likes to 'swell things up' more or less." Goldman was soon released.

When she told a friend, a Chicago journalist, about O'Neill's courtesy, he told her about O'Neill's efforts "to put several captains in the penitentiary for perjury and bribery."

Nothing could have come more opportunely for those black-guards than the cry of anarchy," he explained; "they seized upon it as the police did in 1887; it was their chance to pose as saviors of the country and incidentally to whitewash themselves. But it wasn't to O'Neill's interest to let those birds pose as heroes and get back into the department. That's why he worked for you. He's a shrewd Irishman.

By proclaiming Goldman's innocence, O'Neill deprived Colleran of a distraction and refocused attention on Colleran's misdeeds.[11]

O'Neill's enemies fought back by accusing him of slipping his allies the answers to questions on the civil service exam. The charges came to nothing. The somewhat crazed *Chicago Eagle* then attacked the Civil Service Commission itself, claiming anarchists had infiltrated the organization—anarchists on a Civil Service Commission seems a comical proposition—and also accusing it of anti-Irish bigotry, "the most intolerable know-nothingism that ever existed anywhere in the United States," further demanding the Civil Service Commission be "purged of anarchists, bigots, and pay-roll voluptuaries," a delightful phrase. While some accounts of O'Neill's treatment of Goldman see it as a sign of his fundamental decency and courtesy, we might see it equally as an example of his talent for political infighting. It seems plausible that his article in the *Saturday Evening Post*, written shortly after he became chief, itself served to cement his connection to civil service reform in the face of the Burke faction. By interviewing and releasing Goldman, he undermined Burke and Colleran while positioning himself, not inaccurately, as a courteous and reasonable man on the side of modern reform.[12]

In his memoir, O'Neill never mentioned Colleran by name, another example of his many glaring omissions, though he mentioned a need to reorganize the detective bureau because of "sensational charges published in the *Chicago Tribune*." He described how Goldman initially evaded the police detectives by disguising herself as an old market woman, and how she avoided arrest even while living "but a few doors away" from Colleran's home. Eventually O'Neill

THAT ORPHAN DETECTIVE BUREAU.

Mayor Harrison (to Chief O'Neill—"I'm afraid he's too healthy to work."

**Figure 32** In this cartoon from the *Chicago Daily News*, November 23, 1901, 1, Luke Colleran reclines idly while citizen complaints and charges lie discarded. O'Neill, standing next to Harrison, assumes the pose of an Irish dancer about to begin. The caption reads "Mayor Harrison (to Chief O'Neill)—'I'm afraid he's too healthy to work.'"

testified against Colleran before the Civil Service Commission, which found him guilty of dereliction of duty and conduct unbecoming a police officer, whereupon O'Neill fired him ten minutes after the announcement of the verdict.[13]

Why his memoir tells so little about a story that occupied front pages for months remains puzzling. O'Neill, as mentioned earlier, rarely boasted, and he cultivated a reserved and ironically distanced language fitted to the "man of acute moral sensibilities or highly developed intellectuality" he described in his *Saturday Evening Post* article. He and Carter Harrison represented the "reform wing" of the Democratic Party, but both men's interest in reform had sharp limits. Calling attention to his skill at working Chicago politics and shafting his enemies would undermine his position as an objective reformer, interested in replacing factional patronage with an idea of merit drawn from civil service exams.

### Reforms

While chief, O'Neill saw to it patrolman got a salary increase of $100 a year. He called for a redesign of the policeman's star, advancing a new design an officer could not alter or efface. O'Neill also floated the idea of revising police ranks to match the military. Under this new proposal, O'Neill would be "colonel" and his assistant superintendent "lieutenant colonel." O'Neill told reporters "the strict obedience to orders and absolute discipline which prevail in the army are necessary to all large police forces." During the Pullman strike, he had pointedly compared the Chicago police to the US Army and found the army wanting: now he wanted to organize the police on military lines. "I am aware the plan can be made the subject of ridicule easily and laughed out of court," he added.[14]

And indeed the next day the *Chicago Daily News* ran a cartoon mocking O'Neill's plan as pretentious, foppish, and vain. O'Neill did not mention the idea again.

Years after he retired, O'Neill clipped an article from an unidentified Chicago newspaper describing the lives of retired chiefs and glued it into one of his scrapbooks. O'Neill, while chief of police, was given many nicknames by his subordinates, including "Honest Francis," "Blue Pencil Johnny," and "Bagpipes." The first stemmed from the episode, described earlier, where he arrested a thief in the levee district and prevented corrupt local officials from siphoning off the recovered money. "Blue Pencil Johnny" referred to an editor's pencil, used to mark up, correct, and censor manuscripts, and spoke to O'Neill's scholarly inclinations and careful prose. The last needs

WHAT "COLONEL" O'NEILL MAY EXPECT

By the time the military spirit reaches the policeman on the crossing.

**Figure 33** *Chicago Daily News*, November 9, 1901, 1. The caption reads "By the time the military spirit reaches the policeman on the crossing."

no explanation: O'Neill took the other nicknames in stride, "but pity the policeman that was caught referring to the chief as 'Bagpipes.' Not only was he immediately transferred, but it was a case of putting wheels on his trunk to make moving easier."[15]

O'Neill could speak and act clearly for fairness and equitable treatment. In 1905, for example, he promoted an African American officer, William Childs, to desk sergeant: "This is the first such promotion of a colored policeman in the history of Chicago," wrote the *Tribune*, "and is possibly the only one in the history of the country, for as far as the police annals of the large cities show there is no colored man a commanding officer in any city." O'Neill said of Childs and the other sergeants promoted at that moment, "I took them just as they came, regardless of nationality, color, or anything else." This is the sort of language people often use when they in fact do the exact opposite, but O'Neill added that "regarding the appointment of Childs . . . I will say that we have twelve colored policemen on the force at present and they are all efficient." O'Neill had little to gain by promoting Childs, especially since African Americans in 1901 almost invariably voted with the Republican Party. He might just as easily have simply ignored Childs, and while taking a public stance in favor of merit over race might seem trivial today, in 1905 it stood out and earned O'Neill the esteem of the African American press.[16]

A much more complicated instance came in the 1905 teamster's strike, O'Neill's last action as chief. The bitter, long, and violent strike began at one small firm serving Montgomery Ward and soon spread throughout Chicago. Unionized teamsters—the men who operated the teams of horses used to do heavy hauling—refused to haul any goods. Manufacturers responded by forming the Employers Association of Chicago to oppose the union. One of their first acts was bringing in strikebreakers, many of them initially African American. Rioting broke out, and twenty-one people were killed. Under orders from the mayor and at the urging of the Employer's Association, O'Neill announced a call for "special policemen" to protect the drivers, meaning the strikebreakers, and included African Americans among the "special police," which gave African Americans authority to act against white strikers or angry crowds. During the strike, which lasted for more than 100 days, it then became difficult to tell a "scab" from a "special policeman."[17]

O'Neill drew praise in the African American press for his actions during the strike. "Francis O'Neill," wrote the Chicago *Broad Ax*, "was one man who could not be swayed by the tin-horn politicians and their lackeys, and who absolutely refused to bow down in front of the altar of race prejudice." Despite opposition, "he firmly adhered to his first or original idea of selecting colored men to serve as special policemen, and the result is that between five and six hundred colored men are serving as special police officers at the present time, and with few exceptions they are rendering better service than any other class of men sworn in."[18]

African American "scabs" did not simply break a strike, they took jobs prejudice typically blocked them from holding. While the *Broad Ax* objected to using African Americans to break the strike, it praised O'Neill for giving African Americans authority to protect strikebreakers, and also for making African Americans agents of the law in the service of employers. "The sturdy and courageous Chief of Police of Chicago," continued the *Broad Ax*, "boldly declared that as long as colored men were full fledged American citizens, they had the undisputed right like any other class of citizens to serve as extra or permanent policemen." In at least one instance, merchants who wanted the strike broken protested against African Americans as special police. "When the lumber merchants protested to him against sending colored policemen into the lumber district," wrote the *Broad Ax*, "the Chief plainly intimated to them that they had no right to dictate to the city as to the color or the nationality of the men it selected to guard or to protect their property and his plain words cooled them off."

Chapter 2 introduced an eighteen-year-old O'Neill remembering the help he had gotten from an African American laboring next to him in the hot Georgia sun; he claimed that the man's kindness had kindly disposed him toward African Americans for the rest of his life. Or so he wrote: we could dismiss O'Neill's action here as simply part of a "divide and conquer" strategy, common in American labor history, in which racial divisions undermine worker solidarity. Indeed, employers quickly fired African Americans who had served their purposes: by 1910 there were fewer African American teamsters than there had been before the strike.[19]

But at the time, Julius Taylor, editor of the *Broad Ax*, did not see it this way, and he would go on to lavishly praise O'Neill's first book on the history of Irish music on the front page of the Broad Ax, proudly noting that O'Neill, "one of our steadfast friends for a number of years," had gifted him a copy of *Irish Minstrels and Musicians* inscribed "To Julius T. Taylor, Esteemed Editor of The *Broad Ax*, compliments of the author, Captain Francis O'Neill."[20]

By the standards of his times, certainly, O'Neill did not act the bigot; he counted Taylor as a friend, and Taylor responded in kind. In a comment on gambling in Chinatown, O'Neill told reporters, "the Chinese live by themselves and have customs different from ours. They eat differently, they dress differently, and they amuse themselves differently. They don't bother outsiders and outsiders don't bother them. When they gamble, if they do gamble, they gamble quietly, and evidently enjoy it. There seems to be no reason to interfere with them." By the standards of the time, this amounted to a statement of cosmopolitan tolerance.[21]

O'Neill showed less tolerance for the rights of suspects. "Right here I wish to remark," he wrote in one of his annual reports, that some critics claim that "that to 'sweat' or persistently interrogate a prisoner is barbarous and that such a practice should be abolished." Referring to the recent and sensational case of the "Car Barn bandits," in which a gang of thieves had killed eight people including an officer, O'Neill declared "that if the 'the stomach pump,' as it is sometimes called, had not been applied" to one of the suspects he would never have confessed and "neither would he have 'squealed' on his accomplices in that and several other crimes." In the same report, he mentioned a robbery suspect who confessed to murder "after a 'sweat box' investigation." As Elizabeth Dale describes, the "stomach pump" referred to the practice of forcing water into a suspect's stomach via hoses. "Sweating" described isolation in an extremely hot room coupled with other forms of physical abuse. That man "of acute moral sensibilities or highly developed intellectuality" that O'Neill described before might balk at the idea that the rule of law did not apply in police stations. At least on this subject, O'Neill was not that man.[22]

A policeman's rise through the ranks demanded moral compromise. O'Neill remembered that in the 1870s, when he joined the force, a policeman had to prove himself by "licking someone" in a fight. In 1903 he again addressed the International Association of Chiefs of Police at their annual convention in St. Louis. He repeated and expanded on the article he had published in the *Saturday Evening Post*, explaining what forces prevented the effective suppression of crime.

"The causes of crime," O'Neill insisted, "are as complex as are the conditions of our complicated city life," and "there is no one specific to cure it." An outbreak of crime "is a harvest that was seeded down long ago." O'Neill endorsed typical Progressive Era assumptions about the social causes of crime rather than seeing criminals as innately bad. Saying this to his fellow police chiefs put O'Neill in the Progressive camp. At the same time, O'Neill also blamed "lack of proper home training" and inadequate influence of "the moral restraints of religion." But "every city is more or less wicked," he concluded, and the chief "must successfully grapple with what is known as a carnival of crime."

Far and away, O'Neill blamed "the constant and persistent effort of interested persons to interfere with the operation of the law." Everybody the policeman arrests "is the son of someone, a brother-in-law or relative of someone else whose friendship is valuable," or belongs to some organization "desirable to aid or placate." The friends of the arrested first try to convince the arresting officer to drop charges; then witnesses "are importuned and threatened and not infrequently bought off." If that fails, friends of the criminal game the court system, filing endless continuances that wear down the complainant, and the politician's very existence "depends largely on his being useful in getting his acquaintances out of trouble, and in keeping his constituents out of jail. Hence he must come to the aid of criminals who fall into the hands of the police."

O'Neill gave a remarkable example of how his police overcame these tendencies in one case in which the criminals robbed an Englishman on Christmas Eve. The Englishman, "in a state of great excitement," reported the crime and identified the criminals very clearly. Police arrested them, but they "were socially well connected and had successfully run riot in the southwestern part of Chicago."

The friends of the arrested men tried to stall the case, "but our Englishman was a stubborn individual." Finally the friends of the robbers bought him off, reimbursing him for his loss and "promising him $50.00 when the case should be stricken from the docket. He then disappeared from the neighborhood, leaving no address." An officer who knew him "was instructed to look for him in new buildings, as he was a carpenter." O'Neill continued: "on the third day he was discovered on a roof," at which point the police presented the Englishman with a subpoena and took him into custody three blocks from the court building.

Had the Englishman shown his face in court or the vicinity, O'Neill told them, the criminals would have filed for yet another continuance of the case. But the defense team, assuming the case would be dropped in the absence of a victim, went ahead with the court proceeding. At that point an officer "ran to the saloon where the complainant was reluctantly engaged in a game of [cards] with his captor. When brought into court the Englishman testified without hesitation," and the thieves got jail time, "a sentence which I am happy to say caused the reform of both, as they are now leading honest lives."[23]

Although skepticism about the reform of the criminals seems well in order, his fellow chiefs heartily applauded the story. While we might also applaud the sentencing of habitual thieves, the Englishman must have asked himself what sort of justice system required *arresting the victim* and compelling his testimony. And he must have lamented the loss of the $50 he had been promised once the case had been dismissed. And he had now lost wages from the time the police held him in custody, and worse, earned the ire of the friends of the robbers. No wonder he had dodged testifying.[24]

O'Neill realized the absurdity of the entire business but could see no solution. The civil service exam system offered one path forward, but it too could succumb to corruption and political attack, and O'Neill himself worried that it might produce "book smart" officers with no practical experience. O'Neill deplored the political machinery of friendship and patronage, but his own rise depended on it, and he had more than a little skill at working its levers himself.[25]

If the chief "is a sensible man," he continued, "he will have arrived at the conclusion that . . . following his own mature judgment" will serve him better than trying to curry favor. But he noted that "the official life of a Chief of Police is proverbially short," averaging less than two years in Chicago. O'Neill's appointment to three terms had no precedent. "The new man," O'Neill observed, "will always work wonders and reform things until he gets enmeshed in the difficulties of his predecessors," and the cycle of "good intentions, intermittent criticism, and eventual disappointment is repeated with variations."[26]

Indeed, the *Tribune* shortly afterward summarized the trajectory of reform under O'Neill thusly:

*Chronology of a Comedy.*

Here is the chronology of the average police crusade from the day of its inception until the moment of its death, set forth in twenty-one progressive and recessional movements:

(1) A few individual citizens complain of a certain abuse to their nearest police stations.

(2) The police tell the citizens to mind their own business and not be so ready to overburden an already overworked department.

(3) More citizens complain.

(4) Police give them the laugh.

(5) Citizens write to the newspapers.

(6) Newspapers print the letters.

(7) Police begin to sit up and take notice.

(8) Newspapers and numerous aroused citizens resurrect the law and dwell on it.

(9) Police show signs of life.

(10) Mayor Harrison is interviewed.

(11) Chief O'Neill becomes talkative on the subject.

(12) Police show many signs of life.

(13) Inspectors, captains, and lieutenants begin to talk and promise to do things.

(14) One arrest is made.

(15) Police, spurred to activity, make many arrests. Story is printed on first page of the newspapers.

(16) "Something doing every minute" in the screaming farce, "The Great Awakening of the Official Conscience of the City of Chicago."

(17) Police watch the newspapers carefully.

(16) Then some big news event crowds the crusade story off page 1.

(19) Fewer arrests are made.

(20) Crusade retreats to the back part of the paper.

(21) AND FINIS.

The article ended with a drawing of a tombstone engraved "rest in peace" in Latin and offered examples of eight short-lived "crusades" that O'Neill had "become talkative" about, including crusades against poker, numbers running, "evil pictures," "immoral literature," "Sunday openings," and most recently, spitting on sidewalks, which all ended the same way. O'Neill was trapped in a political system that made corruption inevitable and sheltered vice.[27]

But O'Neill's scholarly inclinations and abstemious habits, combined with his willingness to scrap with aldermen and his worldly-wise attitude toward reform, endeared him to the press, and he appeared very often in the newspapers, usually with favorable coverage. In the winter of 1902, his musical hobby became embarrassingly public after he took a break one afternoon and rumors spread that the Chief had been kidnapped or assassinated by anarchists.

### O'Neill's Musical Activities Exposed

As O'Neill told it, he had a rare moment of freedom from work and decided to go for a ride in the city. Noticing his empty office, someone started a rumor that O'Neill had been kidnapped or killed—in one account, "the rumor was spread through a telephone fiend." A caller to the Harrison Street police station "asked if it was true that the chief of police had been assassinated." A second and third call came in with the same question. Soon rumors spread throughout the city. "The first report was that he had been assassinated. This was soon followed by a rumor that the head of the police department was kidnapped by Greek fruit peddlers and was being held for ransom." "A third report insisted he had been held up by robbers near his home." The reason for the alleged animus of Greek fruit peddlers remains obscure, but apparently the entire police force went on high alert looking for Chief O'Neill.[28]

"It was known that the Chief has several quiet haunts to which he is prone to slip away when he wishes relief from the cares of the police department," one account reported, and eventually a police sergeant went to the home of the chief's friend James O'Neill in Brighton Park, where they found the chief and his friend playing the flute and fiddle. "The sergeant informed him that it was currently reported in the city that he had been killed. The Chief laughed. A moment later, when he remembered his family might have heard the report, he became indignant. Then he bustled into his coat and hurried home." He found his family anxious and his friend Father Fielding "waiting to shrive me." The next day he told the *Morning American* "the reports of my death are greatly exaggerated. I emphatically deny that I was assassinated. I make this statement without fear of denial and stand ready to prove what I say at any time."[29]

Someone invented the story to embarrass O'Neill because newspapers had to explain why he vanished from his job and turned up in Brighton Park fluting "The Wind that Shakes the Barley" on the taxpayers' dime. Although a letter to the *Chicago Eagle* complained that the chief of police reappeared "shepherd-like, playing his flute in true pastoral style" while gambling continued openly in Chicago, reporters mostly treated the whole story as amusing and charming. Coming only a few months after the Colleran story, it may have helped immunize O'Neill and the Harrison administration from the charge of anti-Irish prejudice. The *Inter Ocean* explained, "Jim O'Neill, though he is no relative of the chief, has always been a staunch friend. . . . The Chief often takes a run out to Brighton Park and spends hours listening to Jim's fiddle." The chief "has made the study of Irish airs a hobby," the story continued, and "he has never passed an opportunity to have old men who come here from Ireland sing or hum old air for him. In his leisure moments he puts them down on paper." O'Neill had been "outed."[30]

The *Tribune* ran a large illustrated piece on O'Neill's musical activities, with photos of the two men and examples of musical notation.

"It is a difficult task to collect these old pieces." O'Neill told them. "Many of them are hundreds of years old and never were written out. Some of the melodies are handed down from generation to generation by ear, and the only way to preserve them is to write them as someone plays the music on an instrument." The chief plays some Irish melody on a flute," the story continued, "and his subordinate transcribes it." Sergeant O'Neill observed, "the Chief carries more than 500 of those Irish airs in his head"; Francis told the reporter, "I have about 1800 pieces of Irish music, and some day I may be able to give them to the public, but for the present I shall keep my collection for myself."[31]

## Police Work and Music Collection

The *Tribune's* revealing description shows us how music offered Francis O'Neill a respite from the job, from its compromises and pressures, but also how the prerogatives and problems of the job extended into his private life. James O'Neill, an immigrant from Belfast, had worked shoveling coal until Francis heard of his musical talents and brought him onto the force. James played well and could read and write music with far more proficiency, and he became Francis's main collaborator. While the article describes them as friends, it seems reasonable to wonder whether James, "his subordinate," could have turned his boss away when he showed up unannounced at the house on James's day off. We might also note the possessiveness of O'Neill's language here: the chief carries 500 tunes in his head; "I have about 1800 pieces of music," he told them, and added that "some day I may be able to give them to the public, but for the present I shall keep my collection for myself." How did they become his to give? Who did the tunes belong to before O'Neill acquired them? Did they belong to the person playing them? Or to the musician's family or home village? Or to some larger notion of "Ireland"?

O'Neill uses "have" rather than "know": "I have about 1800 pieces of music" rather than "I know about 1800 pieces of music." Irish people, then and now, often use "have" where an American would use "know." Instead of asking "do you *know* 'The Green Mountain,'" they will ask "do you *have* 'The Green Mountain'?" This usage appears consistently in Irish music well into the twentieth century. In oral interviews, Junior Crehan, a legendary fiddler from County Clare, says things like "Paidnin Kelly was his name and he had a lot of old tunes"; "then there was Martin O'Brien. . . . A flute player, he had a lot of tunes." "Maire Criochain . . . Twas all Irish songs she had. Her son, Jamsie Sally, had the world of songs." Henry Glassie quoted Peter Flanagan, a musician, on hearing a new song one night in a pub: "on the way home that night he declared 'I *must* have that song.'" Later at home a guest asks him, speaking of a tune, "Have you that one?" Mike Rafferty, a flute player from Galway who settled in New Jersey, recalled that when he first arrived he played music with another immigrant from Galway, Jack Coen. "We'd have an odd tune together. . . . He had the tunes."[32]

Part of this comes from the ways Irish folk musicians passed music along from person to person, largely by ear. They *internalized* the tune rather than writing it down in an external form; they possessed it internally rather than as an external object, a page of music. The tunes had no copyright and typically no known author, and so they belonged to the person who had memorized them, although that person typically kept a chain of provenance in memory. Possession in such cases can grow complicated; sharing the tune involves sharing a piece of yourself.

Crehan recalled learning a tune called "The Drunken Gauger," which he got from a man named Barron. "God, I'd give anything if I had it," Crehan told a friend. He tracked Barron down at a house dance. "He played it four or five times. He played it around three times and stopped and your man put him on again and he played it maybe four times. By the time he was done I had it. And I was the only one that kept it. . . . I gave it to Bobby Casey and Bobby was delighted with it. All the musicians in London have it now." Crehan described music possessed by individuals, in memory, and passed on in face-to-face contact, but only with individuals willing to share and teach. Barron might easily have refused to share the tune at all, played it once and not again in Crehan's hearing. But he taught it to Crehan, and Crehan taught it to Bobby Casey, and now all the musicians in London have it. Private property became community property, passed from one person to the next.[33]

O'Neill often wrote in this way—recalling Jim Moore, who sat on the wood box in O'Neill's kitchen: "he *had* a wonderful assortment of good tunes." O'Neill told a story of how "one Monday morning I unexpectedly encountered John McFadden in the corridor outside my office door in the City Hall, and wondering what could have happened since we parted the evening before, I asked, 'What brings you here so early, John?'" McFadden asked whether they might meet privately in his office. O'Neill reluctantly agreed, and after passing through three outer offices, they closed the door behind them. McFadden blurted out, "Chief, I lost the third part of 'Paddy in London' which you gave me last night. I had it all when going to bed, but when I got up this morning, all I could remember were the first and second parts, and I want you to whistle the missing part for me again."[34]

The charming anecdote nevertheless further demonstrates some of the ways music circulated as both possession and gift. O'Neill *gave* the tune to McFadden the night before, but McFadden, having "lost" it, went to city hall and asked for a private meeting in the office of the man he addresses as "Chief." In the process of collecting tunes, O'Neill often ended up taking them from people who had little besides their tunes, and who hesitated or outright refused to share them. As among the men who helped young Francis build a house, a tune might circulate as a gift, a sign of community. O'Neill, the chief, acquired possession of the community's music.

O'Neill complained constantly that musicians would not share. "Choice and rare tunes were regarded by not a few pipers and fiddlers as personal property," he wrote, "and zealously guarded accordingly." They never played "their 'pet' tunes in the hearing of any one known to possess the happy faculty of a grasping ear and tenacious memory." O'Neill had "a grasping ear" and a "tenacious memory"; and he repeatedly admitted that only "the authority of the badge" or "the prestige of rank" allowed him to get people to share their tunes. He remembered persuading one person to share tunes by coming to her door "dressed in the full uniform of a Captain of Police."[35]

With the help of several collaborators, he tricked people into playing tunes while someone else wrote them down. He followed people through the streets, memorizing; he bribed them with beer, with money, or a job on the police force. "Happening into a Chicago theatre one evening a pianist was pounding No. 761 for a stage dancer. The tune was mine before I left," he wrote. Three other tunes "were similarly acquired." "I followed a hand organ about for an hour in Chicago in order to pick up the strains of No. 1222." Did he ask the player of the hand organ, before taking the tune and assigning it a number?

He told a story about a neighbor, a piper named Gillan, who on a trip to Ireland had heard a tune he loved from "a Mr. Kennedy of Ballinamore." Kennedy told Gillan he had heard it from a strolling fluter. Gillan tracked the fluter down and paid him to write out a copy. "When he returned to Chicago he was not at all inclined to be liberal, and only as a special favor to his particular friends" would he let his daughter play it for them on the piano. "One day while engaged in a pleasant chat with Mr. Gillan, whose daughter did not share her father's sentiments, she slipped upstairs, copied the tune and quietly gave it to me. When I got home with my precious document I contrived to commit the tune to memory, and whistled and played it for others until the tune is now pretty well known in Chicago."[36]

Gillan brought the tune back as a memory of his trip and tried to keep it in the family. O'Neill contrived to steal it and then teach it to others. He later published it in his first book. In another instance, he described a friend, Conners. At the funeral of Conners's wife, O'Neill and his friends tricked him into giving up a cherished tune, "oblivious of the draped casket and its lamented occupant in the front parlor." More than a few musicians, he wrote, tried "to keep from circulation their best tunes, and which they do not choose to remember except on special occasions." He watched one man reel off a dozen unknown tunes on the pipes. "Very civilly he agreed to give us the tunes whenever Sergeant O'Neill was prepared to note them down." But when they arrived at his home a few days later, "he couldn't remember any of the tunes." We see here two worldviews, two very different notions not just of property but of the nature and function of music. The willfully forgetful piper saw it as personal property, but O'Neill wanted to add the tunes to his systematic archive.[37]

As chief, O'Neill intensified his efforts to collect tunes, and by 1902 he had begun to think of publishing. By then he had the resources and the authority to locate musicians and bring them into cooperation. "Rumors were afloat to the effect that a youthful prodigy on the fiddle lived somewhere in 'Canaryville,'" O'Neill wrote. "When located he proved to be a modest, good-looking young fellow," an orphan of about seventeen named George West. He had no fiddle, but O'Neill bought him one and took him to James O'Neill in Brighton Park: his playing was "a revelation, truly, and it was little wonder that admiration of his gift was succeeded by jealousy occasionally." O'Neill found him a job as a blacksmith's assistant. The *Tribune* described West as a "musical prodigy" O'Neill had discovered; "that discovery has given him more satisfaction than if he had located a score of crooks," claimed the *Tribune*. It ran a picture of West, well dressed with cap in hand, and described how he had never had a formal lesson. "Since O'Neill has discovered West the boy has been under his watchful eye," and the chief had taken him to perform before the American Irish Historical Society, to which O'Neill belonged.[38]

The language here clearly draws on O'Neill's police work. As he might in the case of a criminal, O'Neill hears rumors of a fiddler in a working-class district and tracks him down. He "discovers" West, which makes him happier than locating "a score of crooks." Having bought him a fiddle, O'Neill now has him under watchful surveillance.

Alas, O'Neill wrote of West, work "was not to his taste. Ambition along that line held no lures for him. Three good tunes were taken down from his playing—two double jigs, 'The Boys of Ballinamore' and 'The Miller of Glanmire,' and a hornpipe called 'The Boys of Bluehill.' This latter tune, which West heard from a strolling fiddler named O'Brien, was entirely new to our Chicago musicians." West, he added, "has degenerated to a common barroom or 'shindig' fiddler." He wanted to play American dance music, not tunes from a country he had never known for a bunch of older men who held coercive authority over him and imagined a future he did not want.[39]

This may seem unfair: O'Neill did West a kindness, finding him a job, buying him a fiddle, and presumably showing him an alternative way of living. Or at least he meant it kindly: we can glimpse how West might have felt in the story O'Neill tells about going to visit West's "friend O'Malley, who eked out a living by playing at house dances." According to O'Neill, they passed through "a few dark passageways and up a rickety back stairs" to where O'Malley, no relation to the author, lived. The description recalls Progressive reformers visiting the dwellings of the poor. "There was welcome for West, but his introduction of me as Captain of Police was very coldly received." Reluctantly, "O'Malley produced the fiddle, on West's request, while his wife and children viewed me as an interloper, with unconcealed misgiving." O'Neill said he gave the children some coins, and beer soon appeared on the table, and then O'Malley, "though handicapped with the loss of one finger from his left hand, played 'like a house on fire' as long as we wanted to listen. His rapid yet correct execution was astonishing."

O'Malley has a finger missing yet plays astonishingly well: O'Neill shows no interest in the origins of the missing finger—congenital? industrial accident? He makes no effort to assist O'Malley in "eking out a living" and shows no interest in the "house dances" O'Malley played. If he learned O'Malley's first name, he never bothered to give it. Nor does he show any interest in how West knew O'Malley, an apparently older man who we might assume taught West how to play the fiddle, except to note that West filled in for O'Malley if the latter had too much to drink. "Thus lived the careless, improvident but talented Georgie," O'Neill wrote, "until an incident in his life rendered a trip to the far west advisable."[40]

Here again it may seem unfair to criticize O'Neill. He can hardly be held responsible for the welfare of every fiddling Irishman in Chicago. But recall his nostalgic fondness, in chapter 1, for Peter Hagerty, the "Piper Ban" from the Collomane crossroads: handicapped by blindness, eking out a living, who ended up with "no alternative but the shelter and starvation of the poorhouse." And recall how he relished the memory of village dancers, the Irish culture of the vanished past. Those very dancers and their children now lived in the Chicago neighborhoods O'Neill policed. They enjoyed O'Malley's playing at "house dances." O'Neill mustered compassion for the long dead piper in Ireland, but only a kind of drily amused disdain for nine-fingered O'Malley and his fiery fiddle, and he seems to show no interest in the music played at house dances, the living continuation of the crossroads dances in Ireland O'Neill waxed nostalgic about. But O'Malley is of no use because he has no new tunes to offer. All is not lost: "three good tunes were taken down" from George West before police apparently chased him out of town.[41]

O'Neill the policeman viewed himself as the protector and defender of property, but O'Neill the collector, with what he called a "grasping and tenacious ear," thought of artistic property differently. You might regard tunes learned from your neighbor in the old country as belonging to you, or to your home village, or to your family or your valley. You might play them in a style unique to you or with variations of your own. But then an alarming stranger in a uniform and a badge arrives, claiming they belong in the collections that will bear his name, or to some larger notion of "Irish" not under your control, to appear in a book you cannot afford, with notation you likely can't read. The man with the badge wants your cooperation in this project: give him your tunes. O'Neill imposed a new kind of order on the music of those milkmaids, plowmen, and spinners he praised in memory, now working as laborers and domestics and firemen in Chicago or eking out livings playing house dances. He would save their music by taking it out of their context, the context of living community, and writing it down in his book.

How else would he collect tunes except by getting them from people who played them? We could ask the same question by considering, say, the religious artifacts of Native American societies: how else can "we" learn about them except by taking them from their context and locking them in a collection? The desire of the people in question matters not at all to that impulse: that they had no need for our knowledge of them means nothing to the collector. O'Neill approached George West and his friend O'Malley from on high, an authority figure doing them favors they had not asked for, indifferent to their lived community. O'Neill engaged in a kind of colonial project, extracting resources from the city he administered.

An extremely informative article on O'Neill's music collecting in the *Chicago Tribune* made that comparison explicit. The *Tribune* described the city itself as a "gold mine" of Irish music and named the largely Irish neighborhood of Brighton Park as the "the mine richest in its yieldings." James O'Neill told the reporter how they "just got two tunes out of one man in South Chicago." O'Neill and the writer used colonial metaphors, metaphors of extraction and possession. The nameless South Chicago man, the tunes "gotten out of him" by the police, vanished from history.[42]

The article referenced above—lavishly illustrated with pictures of both O'Neills, drawings of dancers, and images of sheet music—took up a full page of the Sunday edition and supplied an excellent description of O'Neill's musical collaborators in 1902 and how they worked. According to the author, O'Neill had been collecting tunes for the past five years and had compiled seven volumes of eighty pages each.

The article's headline referred to Chicago as a "storehouse" of Irish music, again a commercial metaphor like "mining," but also referred to O'Neill's musical friends as the "Inquest Committee," with O'Neill as "coroner," James O'Neill as "expert witness," and a "jury" composed of people mentioned before—patrolman John Ennis, Sergeant Barney Delaney, Sergeant James Early, and John McFadden, all members of the Chicago Irish Music Club. An "ex officio" committee included many others mentioned earlier.[43]

The language spoofs O'Neill's police work, but in fact the work as described looked very similar to policing. For example "sometimes a whole company of enthusiasts have been enlisted to run down a certain air, jig, reel, or hornpipe which was known to them by name, or perhaps by a single strain. Weeks and months have been spent on the lookout for it and perhaps after many difficulties it would be picked up in the whistle, song, or humming of some unexpected and adopted citizen of Chicago." The author of the article deliberately compared O'Neill's team to detectives fanning out across the city looking for suspects, until, as the reporter phrased it, the "elusive fugitive air" is finally placed in custody. "Whenever he encounters a fugitive air," wrote the *Inter Ocean,* O'Neill "cannot rest . . . he has in this manner caught 1400 different melodies."[44]

O'Neill himself described "Patrolman John Ennis," who, "suspecting that several pet tunes were withheld from us by a couple of good players . . . conceived the scheme of ingratiating himself with the musicians. Affecting unconcern, he contrived to memorize the treasured tunes, and then had them promptly transferred to James O'Neill's notebook." Ennis went "undercover," "ingratiating himself" to acquire the tunes musicians resisted sharing, then brought the information back to headquarters. In his memoir of his police career, O'Neill told a story about how his informants, placed in a brothel, gained early word of a possible anarchist attack. "In fancied secrecy and security, the leaders met nightly in a house on Indiana Avenue near Eighteenth Street. . . . Plans and schemes were discussed in the hearing of the painted ladies and entertainers," who memorized "everything of importance that concerned the police department." It takes little effort to see the similarity between patrolman Ennis ingratiating himself to gain tunes and O'Neill's informants ingratiating themselves with anarchists.[45]

If they found a song or a fragment of a song, they would examine it carefully and make sure of its distinctive identity. According to the article, they would often forensically re-create tunes from partial phrases. "Now and then a bar has been missing. Then the genius of Officer O'Neill has come in and the necessity of the 'Inquest committee' has been emphasized. The Chief had deep knowledge of composing, and "the 'brogue' of Irish music," so "the building in of three or four missing bars is easy to him. On this work the 'inquest' sits in especial judgement and when it has been O.K.'d it is ready for a final transcription into an entirely new set of music books." They re-created tunes forensically.

For example, Chief O'Neill remembered his mother singing a tune of which he could remember only one phrase, "The flourishing state of Killmurry." "Officer O'Neill put these bars on paper, played them to the taste of the Chief, and then set to work to write backward on a strange Irish air to a logical Irish beginning. This he has done and Chief and Inquest committee are satisfied that the world's judges of Irish music will find it so." They named the reverse-engineered tune "The Woods of Kilmurry." The *Tribune* article obviously meant this kind of forensic re-creation to recall police work. It suggests that O'Neill did more than collect: he and his friends modified tunes to suit their sense of what "Irish music" meant.

In their quest for a comprehensive investigation, they used many different sources, as a detective might. Some of the music they collected came from songbooks printed in London and "mutilated" at the disrespectful publisher's whim, and they would again revise those tunes and make them "better Irish and better music than were embodied in the print." Here, as they did using Bertillon measurements, they tried to rebuild a true identity out of misleading appearances.

"As the unquestioned leader in this movement for the recovery of Irish music," the article concludes, "Chief O'Neill is looked to by all the others." Francis himself saw the authority of the badge as central to the enterprise: "under no other conditions would it be possible to induce such musicians as I have had to deal with to give up their cherished tunes," he wrote to Henry Mercer. Of his musical friends, as mentioned in chapter 5, "I made life more pleasant for most of them," he wrote: "rank, office, money enabled me to do this." "From first to last everything connected with it was financed by the writer," he told an Irish collector. Of the twenty-four men listed as collaborators by the *Tribune*, at least half were police subordinates or owed their job to O'Neill.[46]

We should not minimize the effort required here. The work involved a difficult, painstaking process of writing tunes down and then comparing them to hundreds of similar tunes. The magnitude of the work, as Aileen Dillane points out, matches the scale of Chicago itself. It offered an "aerial view" of the music, mapped to a grid and systematized, and reflected what she calls "a modernist urge to colonize Irish music, to write a definitive representation, and to render this version the most real and authentic."[47] The *Tribune* agreed, because "searching Chicago for Irish music, to find within 200 square miles a wider selection than Ireland itself probably contains at this time," a team of experts has vetted each piece of music, modified it as needed, and committed it to one of seven volumes organized by type, with each song numbered. It was less a simple collection than a re-creation or re-imagining.

Comparing the collection of music to policing makes it seem vaguely sinister or authoritarian. Police used Bertillon cards, fingerprints, and filing systems to organize the citizens of Chicago. They recorded physical details and ethnicity; if men entered the jails homeless, they recorded information about them and later used that information to establish a homeless shelter. They systematized recordkeeping and established fixed identities for repeat offenders. O'Neill and his team did something very similar for music and, in fact, could hardly have done otherwise. Their efforts fit in with much larger, more general efforts at reorganization and system building, like the standardization of time or the standardization of grain or lumber: a worldview based on the impulse to rationalize. Although they focused on the anachronistic music of the premodern rural poor, theirs was preeminently a modern project, drawing from and building on the innovations of industrial urban life, no more or less sinister than industrial life itself.

O'Neill had left Ireland more than thirty years before; he had lived in the US roughly twice as long as he had lived in Ireland. Most of his cronies had lived in the US for about the same time, in an era before recorded sound existed in any but a rudimentary way. They had a memory of Irish music in Ireland, but memory plays tricks, and we modify memories as we retell them to ourselves. They assembled a version of Irish music from the many sources Chicago offered, then modified and polished it to suit their preference. That preference, formed in Ireland, had inevitably been shaped by decades of music heard in America, in saloons, music halls, barn dances, parade bands, vaudeville acts, minstrel shows, and ragtime. American popular music—by then in the throes of a "ragtime craze"—seductively mixed genres and traditions in styles designed to leap across ethnic and cultural differences and grab any listener in earshot.

O'Neill's team made their decisions against the background of American popular music. The act of rejecting it, of trying to make tunes more "Irish," shows that influence: their sense of Irish music came partly in defining it against what they felt it was not. If *they* had collectively approved a song, they concluded "it must be Irish." O'Neill published the tunes a year later, in a book titled *O'Neill's Music of Ireland.*

We can see this relationship with American music clearly in the fact that of the more than 1,800 tunes in O'Neill's first book, at least 192 came from an 1883 Boston publication, *William Bradbury Ryan's Mammoth Collection.* Issued by music publisher and entrepreneur Elias Howe, the collection mixed minstrel show tunes, English folk songs, Scottish reels, Irish jigs, American tunes, and political songs. William Ryan, the collector, led his own band and possibly booked other bands. His promiscuous collection gives us a snapshot of what working New England musicians played in the daily life of 1883.[48]

Though it contained clearly Irish tunes, some still played as "Irish traditional music," *Ryan's* showed no interest in Irish nationalism per se. It was "political" in the sense that it included tunes titled after political figures, and "many of the tune titles evoked the nineteenth-century North": examples include "The Boston Reel," "President Grant's Hornpipe," "General Sheridan's Reel," "Belles of South Boston," and the "Cape Cod Reel." Otherwise it represented a "medley of clippings from all Nations dance halls operas etc. old and new American Negro etc.," as Henry Mercer put it. "This single volume," wrote musician and historian Patrick Sky, "is one of the most important repositories of nineteenth century American music created for or by blackface minstrel shows, songwriters, instrumental musicians, singers, and dancers, trained or traditional." The book later reappeared in the twentieth century as *1000 Fiddle Tunes,* commonly known as "Cole's" after the 1940 publisher. In this guise, *Ryan's Mammoth Collection* came to serve as the bible of American old-time fiddlers.[49]

O'Neill had a copy, and his letters show he knew it well: indeed, he not only took 192 tunes from *Ryan's* but he often changed the names to make the tunes sound more Irish. "Belles of Omaha" became "Bells of Omagh"; "Lincoln's Hornpipe" O'Neill changed to "Larry Lynch's Hornpipe"; "Humors of Rockstown" became "Humors of Ballincarrig," which means "Rockstown" in Irish. O'Neill concealed *Ryan's* as a source, preferring to tell the story that all his tunes either came from Irish immigrants in Chicago or from old yellowing manuscripts he tracked down. We might consider this an act of reclaiming, O'Neill restoring Omaha's Belles to their original place in Omagh's belfry, or we might see it as simple plagiarism, or we might see it as an expansionist view of what "Irish music" meant, in which his "inquest committee" modified the tune until it met their standard of Irishness. We might see it as O'Neill attempting to establish himself as the authority on Irish music. All these things seem likely.[50]

But we see here again an act of policing. O'Neill has surveyed the terrain and sent out his lieutenants to gather information from living people and from paper sources, by subterfuge, persuasion, bribery, or tricks if necessary. He has overseen an elaborate forensic examination and restoration of tunes and then declared on the evidence of the result. If tunes once circulated privately between musicians, O'Neill has arrested that circulation and made the tunes public in a standard form.

The point here is not to condemn O'Neill's work: on the contrary, musicians would demonstrate its value repeatedly over the next 100 years. The point is rather that O'Neill's collecting was a product of policing industrial Chicago, of the social, political, and economic context in which he thrived; and the form of the book, its intent, its method, its execution, reflected that world. Raised as a colonial subject of England, he extended the mentality of colonialism using the techniques of industrial society.

As grain merchants made individual farmers irrelevant to the purchasers of grain, O'Neill's book made the face-to-face sharing of tunes irrelevant—he did not have to care at all about nine-fingers O'Malley and his community. As Chicago turned the labor of individual farms into a homogeneous stream of grain, O'Neill's labors turned the music of individual people, individual communities, into a single "thing," *O'Neill's Music of Ireland*. As police work demanded neighborhood surveillance, tracking down tunes required neighborhood and citywide surveillance. If administering a police force required systematic analysis and records, collecting and publishing the tunes required systematic analysis and records, and careful study to sort out the original from duplicates, impostors from the genuine. O'Neill's nostalgia for the past concealed his indifference to the communities of the present.

## Nostalgia in the Context of Trauma

The book's publication deeply gratified O'Neill. But two events in particular, happening shortly after the book appeared, bore down his spirit and might have broken a different man completely. In the Iroquois theater fire, multiple things went wrong; none of the safety measures functioned as imagined. On December 30, 1903, O'Neill and Assistant Superintendent Herman Schuettler arrived as the fire still burned: "Men, women and children were madly struggling to escape from the burning building," he wrote, and "the weakest of them fell and were trampled to death." The scenes that greeted rescuers in the gallery, where the most death occurred, "will haunt them for years to come." Bodies were piled eight or ten deep.

O'Neill and Schuettler took charge of the several hundred policemen who arrived while the firemen battled the fire. In the darkness and smoke, police working by lantern light found people burned beyond recognition. Worse, they could hear sounds of people alive within the piles of bodies. The dead were intertwined and tangled. The *Tribune* quoted a patrolman: "We can't do it, chief! We can't untangle them." O'Neill directed and assisted in removing the dead. "The horrors of that day will never be effaced from the memory of those who took part in the rescues," O'Neill wrote in his official report. The bodies, he told reporters, reminded him of a field of Timothy grass, blown down by a summer storm: they drove a mental retreat back to rural life in Ireland.[51]

Less than two months later came "the crowning sorrow": his son Rogers died of meningitis at age eighteen. The boy "was the favorite of his father," who "had watched constantly besides the boy's bed" for a fortnight, "with its alternating hopes and fears and disastrous ending." His friends feared for his health "as a result of the boy's death." The O'Neills' grief must have seemed unendurable. They had already lost three sons and two daughters: now they lost a promising son on the brink of adulthood. In a letter to his nephew in Ireland years later, O'Neill remembered himself as worn, heartbroken: plagued by the "nerve wracking responsibilities" of the job. Rogers had played the fiddle in the Irish Music Club, but O'Neill took the most pride in his academic accomplishments. Thirteen years later, he could still recite the fact that "his average in original composition prose and poetry was 98, in Greek 97. . . . In addition he was a splendid fiddler, a fine young man of great promise. And now there is no music in my house." Here again comes one of the few glimpses we get of Anna's grief and the silence that fell on their home. Rogers's marker, in Francis O'Neill's tomb, describes him as "a collegian of exemplary life and great promise," and adds "death loves a shining mark."[52]

O'Neill started construction of the tomb where Rogers came to lie shortly after Rogers died, but according to the *Inter Ocean*, he had begun "designing his own tomb" some years before. Though other deceased family members reside within, the large and imposing structure in Chicago's Mount Olivet Cemetery says "Francis O'Neill" above the entrance, not simply "O'Neill": it is *his* tomb. O'Neill's writing contains little boasting or obvious self-glorification. He seems to have saved that for the tomb and for the prominence of his name on his books. The starkly neoclassical design makes no reference whatsoever to Ireland or Irish music. For all his love of Irish culture and nostalgia for Ireland, he made no plans to return his remains to Ireland or be buried next to his parents. He had made his life in Chicago, and there he would lie.[53]

Along with the horrors of the Iroquois fire and the death of Rogers, in early 1904 the City Club of Chicago, an organization of businessmen, reformers, and civic leaders, hired Alexander Piper, formerly deputy commissioner of police in New York, to investigate the Chicago police. With O'Neill's cooperation, Piper and two assistants spent a month and a half interviewing and observing police and citizens. Their damning report called the Chicago police both "inefficient" and "insufficient": "In my opinion the discipline of the police force could hardly be in a worse condition," Piper wrote. Old age and incapacity combined with laziness: "your patrolmen pull the box on the hour or half hour and then lounge in their holes or some saloon." Of O'Neill, Piper expressed sympathy. "He has not the proper assistance; he has not a sufficient number of men by fully two thousand to take care of this great city." Piper called O'Neill "an honest, hard-working, yes, over-worked man."[54]

Asked to comment on the Piper report by reporters, O'Neill replied, "Every man knows how to manage a woman until he gets married . . . every reformer will tell you how he would manage the department, if he were chief. I had some of those ideas myself till I got to be chief, and then, like the man who got married, I found out." It would be easy to credit O'Neill with integrity for cooperating with Piper—Piper does exactly that—but the Piper report entirely served O'Neill's interests in that it vindicated his character while shifting blame elsewhere and calling for the hiring of more and better policemen.[55]

O'Neill remained on the job another year, appointed to an unprecedented third term by the newly elected mayor, Edward Dunne. He stayed on for a few weeks of that term, until the end of the 1905 teamsters strike, but then resigned when Dunne, as O'Neill put it with typical reticence, asked him to do something that would "endanger a reputation acquired during my long service."[56]

Newspapers reported that once the teamsters strike ended, newly elected Mayor Dunne called O'Neill to his office. "Neither he nor the mayor would repeat what was said there. It is known that Mayor Dunne has been in possession of O'Neill's resignation since the day he reappointed him." Dunne, an American-born ardent Irish nationalist, had come into office in April and reappointed O'Neill because, said O'Neill, business interests in Chicago—the Employers Association—wanted him kept on until the teamsters strike ended.

The *Chicago Eagle* saw the reappointment as a defeat for Inspector Nicholas Hunt, part of the "powerful influences [that] paralyzed the arm of the law" back in 1893 and blocked O'Neill's appointment to captain in charge of the Columbian Exposition. Hunt had dodged civil service requirements and represented the Robert Burke faction.

"Chief O'Neill's reappointment constitutes such a slap in the face for Hunt," said the *Eagle*.

O'Neill had only recently denied a permit to an amusement park ride, the "Scenic Railway" at White City Park, which Hunt had declared safe: one person had earlier died and three were injured when a boy threw a brick on the rails. The park had the backing of three aldermen, who enlisted Hunt in their service, but "the chief said he preferred to talk with the building commissioner and did not care particularly what the Inspector had to say." O'Neill had made his disdain for Hunt clear: Dunne may have asked O'Neill to reverse this decision.[57]

O'Neill may also have resigned because of another typically complicated scandal involving party faction and graft. In 1901 Hunt apparently hatched a plan to rob a jewelry store, with the help of a patrolman named Mahoney. Mahoney would direct burglars to the store, he said, and busy his gaze elsewhere while the crime took place. He would in the meantime alert Captain Patrick Lavin to the crime, so that Lavin might swoop in and claim the glory of the arrest and, presumably, both men would get promotions and a share of the $9,000 worth of goods stolen, $2,000 of which mysteriously vanished. The plan went awry, and Mahoney was arrested; he later testified, in 1905, that Lavin had bullied him into the scheme. O'Neill resigned just before the scandal landed on the front pages. When called by the grand jury, O'Neill testified that he had begun the investigation of Mahoney himself, with no pressure from Lavin or anyone else, which appeared to clear Lavin of Mahoney's charge: O'Neill may not have wanted to give that testimony as chief of police.[58]

O'Neill's decision might also have related to the demise of the Policemen's Protective Association, which sounded like a union and performed some possibly union-like functions but seems to have been a money-making scheme and a way for the Burke faction to get control of the police department. O'Neill, under direction from then-mayor Harrison, had announced that officers who joined the Protective Association would be dismissed, although he does not seem to have carried out the order. The Policemen's Protective

Association then reformed as—and yes, this does seem odd—a corporation known as the Mexican Plantation Company, which urged police and firemen to buy shares. Alderman Johnny Powers was treasurer, which fact speaks for itself.[59]

No wonder he sought refuge in an idea of the pure and authentic Irish folk music of the rural peasants or windblown summer grass. In all these instances of graft and intrigue, O'Neill had to navigate between a notion of the public good, his principles, his self-interest, and the hunger of various Chicago political factions for power and cash. He had negotiated the moral ambiguities of Chicago life for more than thirty years. In retirement, he could focus on his musical passions and enter into a different kind of life. At age fifty-seven, his most significant work still lay ahead of him.

# 7
# King of the Pipers
## O'Neill's Work in Retirement

"I have not had a vacation for eleven years," O'Neill told reporters: "I need a rest. I resigned voluntarily. The strike is over, and there is nothing to hold me." He told reporters he would stay in office until the new chief arrived, and "then I go east, and when I come back I intend to go out to my farm in the town of Palos and live according to my own ideals." He wrote in his memoirs that he loved studying plants and the natural world. "I have 60 acres there, part of the farm that Jack Shea's father used to own. It has some water and natural forest on it, and I shall go into the farming business." A rural refuge would surely seem appealing. O'Neill gave at least part of the farm over to an apple orchard. Mary Wade, O'Neill's granddaughter, remembered "a huge farm house on the property—large enough for my mother and her six children to live in during the summer. Grandfather came out two or three times a week and was always laden with goodies for all of us." But "rural life failed to smother his years of activity and he again returned" to 5448 Drexel Boulevard, and by 1912, he could "be seen these spring mornings promenading the boulevard with his pet collie Micky."[1]

Carter Harrison II, his political patron, called O'Neill "a conscientious, industrious, if not brilliant chief." O'Neill had a strong capacity for work, courage, and coolness under pressure. Though he labored at Chicago politics as Chicago politics required, any scandals or charges cooked up against him evaporated quickly. That does not necessarily prove innocence: "innocence" seems a word ill suited to describing Chicago politics. But Harrison had a point: in his address on anarchism, for example, O'Neill offered a scholarly, thorough, and largely unoriginal set of observations. His descriptions of the problem of modern policing stopped well short of offering effective or imaginative solutions. His treatment of other people often seems emotionally unintelligent. Not only his mockery of blind piper Murphy or his indifference to poor nine-fingered O'Malley, but what had son Rogers, who played the fiddle, thought of his father's enthusiasm for George West, the orphan prodigy O'Neill "adopted" and fostered? What did his piano-playing daughters think about his effusive praise for Selena O'Neill, described below?[2]

His musical work showed ambition and intellectual drive. He had a vision of unifying the different individual voices of Chicago's Irish; he had a scholar's patience and a quality of leadership that, along with the advantages of office, persuaded people to join his project. He established a standard set of tunes, a canon, but he missed the role recordings would play in the ways people learned tunes. Though not a braggart and not prone to hyperbole, he had a generously sized and controlling ego nevertheless.

The sort of man who builds himself a large tomb also labels his collection of music *O'Neill's Music of Ireland*. The title itself expressed a confused and ambiguous sense of possession: is this *O'Neill's* music, or Ireland's? The apostrophe attributes possession to O'Neill, but the "of" attributes it to Ireland. If this seems a stretch, consider an alternative title, something like *The Music of Ireland: Collected and Edited by Francis O'Neill*. That eminently plausible title contains no such ambiguity about who "owns" the music. *O'Neill's Music of Ireland* calls attention to the renegotiation of ideas about personal and communal property O'Neill engaged in when he "acquired" other people's tunes.

We might also read the title O'Neill chose as establishing a "brand": "O'Neill's Music of Ireland" like "Kellogg's Cornflakes." Products branded by last name appeared on shelves everywhere, and O'Neill used "O'Neill's" like a brand on several other books. He worked with a team of Irish musicians and modified both tune titles and the actual notes as he or they saw fit, but its publication placed him in a very different community, a community of eminently respectable upper-class scholars and antiquarians, and the book foregrounded O'Neill himself as an authority in multiple ways.

Printed by Lyon and Healy in large format, the book appeared in multiple versions, sometimes bound in a dark reddish brown cloth with heavy cream paper and gilt-edged pages, sometimes with a green cover. The cover, always in gilt ink, shows a harp and a tree with shamrocks. In ornate, Celtic revival script, it reads "Music of Ireland" and then "O'Neill" beneath. An intertwined Celtic border edges the front cover. Aileen Dillane notes that "Celtic graphics were part of a larger branding issue. The particular 'look' that O'Neill's book generated was in part a response to a Celtic iconographic commodity culture already present in the city." Mrs. Donahue, the fictional lover of "Choochoski," could have owned this book without embarrassment: the Celtic revival culture of the cover elevated the "low chunes."[3]

The frontispiece has a photograph of O'Neill in uniform as chief. The title page displays *O'Neill's Music of Ireland* in a very elaborate typeface, with Celtic revival bordering clearly inspired by Irish illuminated manuscripts, while adding "collected from all available sources by Capt. Francis O'Neill" and "arranged by James O'Neill." Francis chose to depict himself in uniform and as captain, not as a private citizen: the choice lends the authority of the police to the collection. He did not list James O'Neill's rank. Francis, of course, was entitled to pride in his accomplishments and his rank, but the book's presentation foregrounds O'Neill the chief as an authority figure.

Irish "natural musicality" could figure as a kind of inferiority, what Mathew Arnold described as the naturally "musical celt" with a childlike love of bright colors, but there was nothing at all natural about police work, and the systematic, scholarly aspect of the project underlined that the book's owner had bought a well-organized collection carried out under modern administrative discipline.

O'Neill's ambitions drove the production, and he financed the printing of the beautiful book himself. He dedicated it to "the multitude of non professional musicians of the Gaelic and English speaking races who enjoy and cherish the melodies of Ireland." He wrote, in the introduction, "there is perhaps nothing of which an Irishman may feel more justly proud than the melodies and music of his native land"; they offer "an unerring index of national character." Not simply a collection of tunes, the book expressed ethnic pride in an orderly and dignified way.

O'Neill further insisted that "true melody, the music of the soul, has no mortal artist for its inventor"; the "origin is with few exceptions, involved in the dim obscurity of the past." Modern music, he argued, simply recycles old melodies. He called Irish music "a magnificent ruin from which every modern builder may filch desirable material to be used in the erection of new structures." He faulted Irish people for neglecting their own heritage, insisting "Irish musicians, until lately, were doing nothing for Irish music, either as archaeologists or artists." "It is to the peasantry we owe whatever is left of our musical heritage," he concluded, "and it is to them those have gone, who are endeavoring to preserve." The peasantry now live in Chicago: "in the metropolis of the west, one thousand miles beyond the broad Atlantic, Ireland's sons and daughters . . . have brought with them treasures of song and dance music, never noted down."[4]

In this telling, the real Ireland has moved to Chicago, where "the peasants" now live. Concentration in the modern city makes their music available to Captain O'Neill; the Irish "national character," "unerringly" expressed in music, now lives in Chicago. O'Neill took pains to point out that his collaborator, James O'Neill, hailed from Belfast, about as far away from Tralibane as one could get and still remain on the island, yet here they worked closely, a few miles from each other's homes: Ireland concentrated.

He organized the tunes—none with lyrics—by type. His categories included "airs," jigs, reels, polkas, and hornpipes, among other types of tunes. Each tune had a name in Irish on the left, in Celtic script, and a name in English. Where known, he gave the name of the person who contributed the melody. Each amounted to a "setting" of a particular tune: O'Neill noted the real tune lived in performance, in the improvisations the performer brought to it. O'Neill had created a standard template for each tune.

O'Neill's book received mostly favorable reviews. The Minneapolis *Irish Standard* praised "the patriotic Corkonian" and called the book "the greatest collection of Irish music in existence." Perhaps without full awareness of what he implied, the editor of the *Chicago Citizen* wrote that O'Neill "has embalmed the musical genius of the Irish people."[5]

In Ireland, W. H. Grattan Flood said of the "sumptuous quarto volume," "nowhere is there procurable such a large collection of folk tunes, many of which are here printed for the first time." He reinforced the connection to the police, pointing out that "Captain O'Neill, the compiler of this collection, has the care of 34,000 [*sic*] police in a city of two million inhabitants, and that it was only in the intervals snatched from his duties that he was able to glean from all available sources—printed, manuscript, and oral—the tunes he liked best." "As a gift-book to music-loving Irishmen and Irishwomen in any part of the globe, we can unhesitatingly recommend *O'Neill's Music of Ireland*." The *Chicago Citizen* published an article from an Irish Australian who had only good things to say about the collection of "the grand old music—the weird, beautiful, wild and mournful reel tunes that entranced me when a child, a youth, and a man, in the street or barn, at the bonfire or on the hill top." In May 1903 the meeting of the Gaelic League surprised O'Neill with a concert of music taken from the book, played by James O'Neill. His friend, Father James Fielding, called the chief "the busiest man in Chicago."[6]

An ardent nationalist, Father Fielding had gone to Ireland in 1903 and given a speech that inadvertently dragged O'Neill into the sort of Irish and Irish American political feuds he avoided. During a music festival in Dublin, to a packed house, Fielding described "How Irish Music was Saved in America." "Father Fielding credits Francis O'Neill, a Cork man, the General Superintendent of Police in Chicago," newspapers reported. When dancers and musicians were driven from the rural crossroads, Fielding told them, they went to America. "When men capable of performing on the Irish pipes arrived in Chicago ... as a rule, Francis O'Neill put them in the police, and the majority of the best pipers in Chicago were to be found in the police force." Multiple accounts of the speech have Fielding saying that O'Neill got musicians jobs on the police force. Fielding then turned to Ireland and noted instances where the police played Irish music and joined the Gaelic League.

At that point the crowd turned on him and began to heckle and taunt, denouncing the police for using their batons on the people and evicting their fathers and mothers onto the road. Fielding told the crowd that the Gaelic League was nonsectarian and nonpolitical, and that Irish people should take police jobs, play Irish sports, and treasure Irish music. The crowd jeered; some were removed. Order restored, the meeting ended with Fielding playing some cylinder recordings of Chicago musicians O'Neill had made. The display of technology, possibly novel to the Dublin audience, calmed the crowd.[7]

O'Neill had earlier pointed out the difference between the police in Ireland and the police in the US: in Ireland the police served an occupying foreign power. The Dublin crowd hated them and rejected the idea that the police could express Irish culture.

Shortly thereafter O'Neill received a strongly negative review from Father Edward Gaynor of Cork, a man deeply engaged in a tedious and pedantic battle with another of O'Neill's friends, Father Richard Henebry. Gaynor attacked O'Neill's book, accusing him of reprinting tunes already known, and the New York Irish magazine the *Gael* quoted Gaynor and added its own attacks on O'Neill: "The book is said to be the result of many years of labor and research on the part of its compiler, yet among the 1,850 airs contained in it there are few that were not accessible in one form or another or that had not been published before." Even worse, the review accused O'Neill of reprinting "many English, Scotch, Welsh and modern Irish-American melodies, ballad-tunes and operatic airs which, speaking correctly, are not Irish tunes at all and should not be included in the collection." It noted the endorsement of "two versatile gentlemen. Dr. Henebry and Father Fielding, who each assisted in his own peculiar way." The article further accused O'Neill of charging Irish people a higher price than the cost of the book plus shipping warranted. It damned with faint praise, noting "apart from the defects which we have pointed out, the volume should have a large sale. It is well printed on good paper and contains some ornamental Celtic borders and ornamentations that are very well done."

In a second article, the *Gael* specifically mentioned Father Fielding's contentious speech in Dublin, noting that Father Fielding

in Ireland last year took frequent occasion, when speaking in public, to say that Francis O'Neill, Chief of the Chicago police, had organized the finest band of Irish pipers in the world composed almost exclusively of policemen, and that an excellent qualification for prospective membership in the Chicago police force was a working knowledge of Irish pipes. [He] did not go as far as to say outright that a blind piper, or one with a single leg, or one lacking brains could get on the Chicago police force, but [he] came very near it.

The *Gael* then referenced the Piper report, described in chapter 6:

in which they say that more than 500 policemen of [Chicago] "are cowards in the face of danger," are "saloon loafers," are "in collusion with thieves and unfortunate women, dividing spoils of vice and crime." The report says further that they "are indifferent to their work," and "are no more fit than old women to be policemen."

O'Neill, the article concluded, "is to be pitied because of his injudicious and indiscreet friends."

Doubtless infuriated by this attack, O'Neill responded diplomatically to the "suggestion of unfriendliness, which, coming from this source was wholly unexpected." Saying he had long subscribed to the magazine, he insisted "there was no occasion to 'pad' *O'Neill's Music of Ireland*, as far more material was on hand than was considered advisable to include." As to profiteering, he insisted that if he will "succeed in disposing of the first edition without financial loss he will feel well satisfied with the result of his labors." He added that he "hopes to be able to issue a second and more comprehensive edition free from serious defects."[8]

In his 1910 book, *Irish Folk Music: A Fascinating Hobby*, O'Neill scorned Gaynor for claiming superior "Irishness."

> His Reverence, of whose existence we were entirely ignorant, lectured on Irish Music in [Cork], warning his audience against the great danger to Irish music by the efforts of those who had not the advantage of being born and bred in the real traditional atmosphere, like himself. Why, bless his simple soul! What could have led him to imagine that Watergrass Hill [near Cork City] had a monopoly of the traditional atmosphere of County Cork, not to mention the rest of Ireland?

This entire testy exchange makes sense only in light of the larger heated debates about the nature of Irish nationalism. In Ireland ideas about managing the relationship with England ranged from "home rule," to dominion status, to "dual monarchies" to a full-fledged republic. And within those options, further debates raged about that character of an Irish state—how Irish would it be, the role of the Catholic Church, how socialist or capitalist—and how to accomplish the goal, by negotiation or by arms. In the US, these fights gained extra passion from the fact that so much of Irish American cultural expression took place in the realm of sentiment and nostalgia, an ocean away from practical effects, so it was safe to talk a much bolder game that you might actually be willing to play. In England Her Majesty's police evicted people. In the US evictions mostly formed a memory of injustice in song and on stage. As O'Neill discovered, disputes over authenticity, and the role of the Gaelic League, dominated discussion of his musical work.[9]

The Gaelic League tried to avoid politics and revive specifically Irish cultural forms, like the Irish language, games like hurling, or Irish dance and music. The league's founder, Douglas Hyde, argued instead for intellectual and cultural independence from England. The Gaelic Athletic Association was probably the most successful outcome: GAA clubhouses and fields dot the outskirts of most Irish towns, and while the Irish follow soccer and rugby, GAA football and hurling outpace both in popularity. A sign of the close interconnection of GAA sports and Irish nationalism comes in the fact that Dublin's Croke Park, where the GAA plays its national championship games, also memorializes the 1920 death of fourteen people killed by British soldiers during a Gaelic football match.[10]

Hyde, a poet and writer, assumed that intellectual, cultural, and eventually political independence would all flow from a revived Irish language. "We stand immovable on the rock of the doctrine of true Irish nationhood," Hyde proclaimed: "an Ireland self-centered, self-sufficing, self-supporting, self-reliant; an Ireland speaking its own language, thinking its own thoughts, writing its own books, singing its own songs, playing its own games, weaving its own coats, wearing its own hats, and going for nothing outside the four shores of Ireland that can possibly be procured inside them." A fine idea, perhaps, but Hyde needed support from the millions of Irish Americans who had money and influence, and in 1905–6 he embarked on an exhausting fundraising tour of America. He met privately with President Theodore Roosevelt, who told Hyde that thanks to Irish nannies, "Cuchulain and Finn MacCool had been familiar and vivid figures to him before he ever saw their names in literature," and that he fully endorsed Hyde's program for a de-anglicized Ireland.[11]

When Hyde came to Chicago in early 1906, 3,000 Irish citizens, including Mayor Dunne and the inevitable "procession of dignitaries," greeted him. In addition to the usual speeches, "an organ recital of ancient Irish airs by Arthur Dunham opened the program," and the Irish Choral society sang "The Harp That Once Through Tara's Halls" and the "Minstrel Boy." Then O'Neill and his friends watched as "a little girl, dressed in green and gold, came out from the wings and covered the speakers' table over with a magnificent design of a harp and a laurel."[12]

O'Neill and his friends found the whole business tacky and inauthentic: "so disappointing—ludicrous, it might be termed." Both the songs mentioned came from Thomas Moore and amounted to clichés. To "take the bad taste out of his mouth" and show him Chicago's musical talent, O'Neill and his cronies invited Hyde to a party at the home of Barney Delaney. Pipers, fiddlers, and dancers entertained Hyde, and according to Irish American newspapers, "on several occasions he was visibly affected. He was moved to ecstasy at the thrill of his own music heard in a foreign land." Chief O'Neill chatted with him at intervals in Irish, and at the end of the night Hyde "expressed himself as delighted with what he had seen and heard." He thanked "Chief O'Neill, whom he complimented on his great efforts in keeping alive in a foreign land the jewels of our fathers."[13]

Hyde wrote about the event in his diary, in Irish, in considerably less fulsome tones:

> I spent the evening with O'Neill, once the chief of Police, who is now on pension. . . . Every single piper, fiddler or musician from Ireland that came to Chicago, O'Neill used to get hold of him, and make him a policeman and after a while he would get their tunes and music from them. . . . Tonight, he had gathered dancers, singers, pipers, and other musicians, and the crowd continued with the dancing and music for two or three hours. The majority of them were Irish-speakers and the dancers were excellent. He presented me with a large book of tunes which he had printed.[14]

Everywhere Hyde went Irish Americans held banquets and demonstrated their Irishness, and even Hyde, who had a strong appetite for sociability, must have grown mightily weary. In the US, the Irish language was far more praised than practiced. Most Irish immigrants to the US came from the west of Ireland, where Irish-speaking endured longest, but American life demanded and rewarded English speaking. O'Neill told Seamus Ó Casaide "while I speak and read Irish I have not attempted Irish manuscript therefore I must rely on the *Bearla*," meaning English. The article quoted above describes him conversing with Hyde. But he probably exaggerated his fluency in Irish, as he needed the help of Father John Carroll in translating song titles. Carroll, O'Neill's parish priest at St. Thomas the Apostle in Hyde Park, owned "what is claimed to be the only Gaelic typewriter in the world," wrote the *Tribune*. A scholar of ancient languages, he wrote learned treatises on the alleged similarity of Irish and ancient Greek and on St. Patrick's day preached his homilies in Irish.[15]

"The real work of the Gaelic League in America," one member concluded, was to "banish such monstrosities as the stage Irishman, to educate our church and Catholic societies up to the standard of the Gaelic League," to introduce Irish history to school curricula, and "promote in every way possible Irish industries, music, dances, and pastimes and in this manner to create a strong, healthy irresistible public opinion in favor of a free Ireland." O'Neill substantially agreed and directed the rest of his public work to exactly this sort of project.[16]

Not long after Hyde's visit, Frances and Anna steamed for Ireland—their first time back in forty-one years. In six weeks abroad, they visited the Cork Piper's Club and Bernie O'Donovan, "the Carbery Piper," "a young musician of fine promise," who shortly after emigrated to Chicago. Hyde gave a banquet in O'Neill's honor at the Rotunda in Dublin. The chief visited his relatives in Tralibane: his nephew Phillip and Phillip's son John, who would later stay with the O'Neill's in Hyde Park while pursuing postdoctoral work at the University of Chicago. If he saw his mother, he says nothing of it in surviving accounts.[17]

O'Neill took copious notes while in Ireland and published his findings later in *Irish Minstrels and Musicians*, a unique account of musical practice in Ireland at the turn of the century. But he noticed a decline, he thought, of music in daily life and in memory. "A generation ago," he wrote, "a wealth of folk music was the common possession of the peasantry, now scarcely a fraction of it is remembered." We are told, he continued "that Irish music will speedily resume its sway when Irishmen govern Ireland. Let us hope so—but how? when? where? Who is to teach?" His six weeks in Ireland "disclosed nothing which afforded much evidence of a musical regeneration. Not a piper nor a fiddler was encountered at the five fairs attended." The players he heard at competitions in Cork and Dublin "were amateurs, except one or two flutes . . . easily outclassed here in Chicago." The axis of Irish culture had shifted, he argued, from Ireland to the US. "More and better Irish music can be heard in dozens of American cities than in Cork or even in Dublin. Why? Because it is encouraged, appreciated and paid for." As he had when he compared pipers

Patsy Touhey and Turlough McSweeney, O'Neill found the Irish in America better and more authentic than the Irish in Ireland.[18]

Sometime around 1912, O'Neill clipped a poem called "Going Back" into his scrapbook. It claimed "Oh, Ireland is the merry place when one is but a boy/But Ireland is a lonesome place, a strange and eerie land/When after years of exile on its shores again you stand." O'Neill had siblings in Ireland and spent time with them, but the piece he pasted in his scrapbook continued "The air has lost its graciousness, the sun its golden light/And where are all the hawthorn blooms that used to be so white?" Considering O'Neill could not leave Ireland fast enough as a seventeen-year-old, it seems easy to dismiss this nostalgia as automatic or rote: a cliché one was expected to express. This kind of nostalgia for the peasant past obscured the degree of cold calculation required to pull off his musical collections.

For example, in the early twenty-first century Thomas Tupper, a musician in Clonakilty, County Cork, related a family story about an ancestor, a flute player, who emigrated to Chicago because in Ireland "the word on the street" "was if you played an instrument you go to Captain O'Neill and you get a job in the police." According to the story, the man got an interview with O'Neill. "Well, he played the flute and he wasn't good enough!" The man had played flute for a living in Ireland, but according to legend, O'Neill turned him down. Tupper concluded O'Neill "wanted a variety of music . . . and he knew all my relation's tunes so he was no good to him. . . . He wanted somebody from Sligo or from Antrim or from somewhere else." He already had songs from Cork: he was building a different Ireland than the Ireland of any one person's memory and experience.[19]

By 1900 just under 79,000 Irish-born people lived in Chicago, the fourth largest city in the US in terms of its Irish population, behind New York, Philadelphia, and Boston. Far more Irish and second-generation Irish lived in the US than lived in Ireland. But did they still count? Or was their music altered by the experience of the US? In his comments on the night he spent at Barney Delaney's house, Hyde said nothing at all about the quality of the music or the players. It may not have sounded quite right to him, perhaps as Irish music in Ireland no longer sounded quite right to O'Neill.

O'Neill, not himself an accomplished performer, enthusiastically embraced the new technology of recording as a way to document and share it. Sergeant James Early, he wrote, learned at least three tunes from Edison cylinders sent to him by a musician in Canada. Unlike the disk players that came to dominate the market later, the early Edison Cylinder machines made recording relatively easy. Patsy Touhey recognized the value early on and advertised his willingness to record Edison cylinders of any Irish song his fans requested. O'Neill began recording Touhey and his Chicago musicians; eventually he made more than sixty recordings, some of which he sent to friends in Ireland and some of which he kept at the home of Sergeant Early. A voice, possibly O'Neill's, typically introduces the song and the player on each cylinder. Despite the poor audio quality, these recordings give us a good sense of what the music sounded like in Chicago in 1905.[20]

O'Neill issued a second book, titled *Dance Music of Ireland*, in 1907. It contained 1,001 tunes, mostly the same as published in his 1903 volume; but as its title suggests, this book focused strictly on dance music. This second book, less lavishly printed, had a much greater influence among musicians, especially in Ireland. "A reawakened interest in our national music, especially the jigs, reels, hornpipes, long dances, etc., of the old days has been happily aroused by the Gaelic revival and its apostle, Dr. Douglas Hyde," O'Neill wrote in the introduction. He listed the people who had contributed tunes and the twenty-two Irish counties they represented. No one would out-Irish him this time.

But his Chicago community started to come undone. O'Neill faced criticism not just for republishing tunes or for including "un-Irish" tunes, but because he got the key signatures wrong. In the simplest sense, Irish jigs and reels often tend to float between a major and minor feel, ambiguously expressing both: they are often not clearly in a key signature but, like much folk music, they are rather in a "mode." For one person playing alone, this poses no difficulty, but not so if someone tries to play one of the tunes in *Dance Music of Ireland* on the piano. The pianist will try to harmonize it, to add chords, and so will want the music squarely in a key signature.

This problem caused O'Neill a great deal of expense and seemingly the friendship of his two closest collaborators, James O'Neill and Edward Cronin.

The chief read music haltingly and had only a rudimentary understanding of music theory. He relied on his more musically educated friends to transcribe tunes and to assign a key signature. "I overestimated the musical learning of Sergt. James O'Neill and others. He deemed himself infallible yet to my sorrow he lacked much in his knowledge of keys and signatures." When O'Neill gave the music to his daughter to play on the piano, "we discovered that all tunes ending in 'A' do not require three sharps." The chief then turned to Cronin, an excellent fiddle player and the source of many tunes. "In all my writings," he told Bernard Bogue, "I never alluded to the fact that one edition, 1000 copies, of *The Dance Music of Ireland* was destroyed on account of the numerous errors in key signatures made by Edward Cronin." "I had to 'eat humble pie,'" O'Neill wrote, and he then went back to James O'Neill. "In his jealousy of Cronin the pendulum swung in the opposite direction" and after being given carte blanche in correcting the errors, "the new edition my daughter and I found had no less than 39 wrong key signatures." "When confronted with the rendering of these disputed tunes on the piano," "amiable yet unyielding," Sergeant O'Neill "reluctantly admitted that 28 tunes [were] incorrectly marked—and away went another edition to the chopping machine." "This little expense," O'Neill added, "cost me $1,200." Recall that O'Neill, in 1904, proudly listed the fact that he raised the patrolman's salary to $1,100 a year. The errors cost him a patrolman's annual salary and, he reported, many hours spent correcting individual books by hand.[21]

The problem the four of them experienced, aside from O'Neill's perfectionism, involved the poor fit between the music theory underpinning Western "art music," which O'Neill's daughter had learned on the piano, and the folk music of "peasants." Cronin and Sergeant O'Neill assumed, reasonably, that because the tune ended on an A, the tune was in the key of A major. But the notes played did not conform to A major. Cronin and O'Neill grew up learning mostly by ear and in a tradition that simply did not bother much about harmony. If the sheet music called for a C# and they disliked the way C# sounded, they just played a C: they typically played alone. We see here again how O'Neill's project necessarily imposed standardization on casual practice.

The particular problem comes from the piano, the instrument on which Mrs. Donahue's daughter Molly used to play "Choochooski" rather than "The Wicklow Mountaineer" (see chapter 5). The piano in the parlor stood for respectability, rootedness, and American success and status. It represented a formal system of harmonic rules developed in the baroque era. James O'Neill and Edward Cronin both played Irish dance music well but usually without accompaniment. James O'Neill played unaccompanied for the Gaelic League event described above. The chief made two cylinder recordings of Cronin, playing solo as they all typically did. But now the chief insisted they had to get the keys right, according to musical standards distant from the lives of rural folk.[22]

The social situation could end only badly: two adult men, one older than the chief, both better musicians than the chief, and both having donated many, many hours of their own time to the chief's project of collecting Irish tunes, learn of their incompetence at a system of musical understanding *totally irrelevant* to their musical practice. "When Edward Cronin, an excellent fiddler of the traditional school, was brought into the limelight from obscurity," O'Neill wrote, "little did we suspect the wealth of rare folk music which lay stored in his retentive memory. Generous as the sunlight, he dictated without hesitation musical treasures known only to himself. In every variety of dance music he was a liberal and prolific contributor." The two men freely shared their knowledge and expertise, or more or less freely, because one of them, James O'Neill, owed his job to the chief and depended on his goodwill for promotion. According to the 1910 federal census, the other, Cronin, at age sixty-eight, still worked as a "grinder" at a "harvester works." The chief lavishly praised both men in his 1910 book, *Irish Folk Music: A Fascinating Hobby*, making it plain that they played a central role in the collecting effort, and his sponsorship helped Cronin make extra money with his fiddle. Both men's reputation in history comes entirely from their work with

O'Neill and from his writing. But now the chief's daughter tells them they don't know what they're doing. Who put the chief's daughter in charge of Irish music?[23]

O'Neill had four daughters, and he says almost nothing about them. One of them, Julia, married James Mooney, a policeman soon to make captain: in 1906 Francis sold them a flat around the corner from his own for the nominal sum of $1. The unnamed daughter of O'Neill's prosperity, "who was a member of our church choir, and who had a fine free rhythmic swing in her Irish dance playing on the piano," outranked the two men in judgments about Irish music.[24]

The two men must have been mightily irritated, and, in fact, collaboration seems to have stopped at that point: as mentioned earlier when writing about James O'Neill's skill at transcribing tunes, the chief wrote "he can no longer be utilized for that purpose." And three years later, by 1913, the chief's tone toward Cronin had changed substantially, and he wrote about Cronin as a colonial administrator might speak of his territory. For two years, twice a week, Francis wrote, he made a 12 mile trip to Cronin's house. "Mr. Cronin's memory proved a rich mine of traditional Irish melody," he reported, "but it took years of cultivation and suggestion to rouse his dormant faculties to their limit." O'Neill compared Cronin to an unexploited mine or a field laboriously worked into cultivation.[25]

Other relationships broke down as well. The Irish Music Club fell apart in near violent acrimony. Collaborators drawn to Francis by the possibility of advancement now balked about being told what to do. "The favorable conditions vanished on my retirement from office, and clearly clinched the end of possibilities in that direction," he wrote. His brother-in-law, Sergeant Barney Delaney, an excellent piper, grew increasingly distant, and eventually Francis would complain about his "ingratitude" repeatedly in letters to multiple people. "When I was in office" as chief, O'Neill told William Halpin in 1911, "I could have [records] made as required by Barney Delaney, a member of the police department." A month later he complained that Delaney, now "a man of property," "doesn't have to make records and he won't either, not even for me!" We see the degree to which O'Neill's authority as a policeman made his collecting possible. Before he could simply order Delaney to make recordings, but Delaney must have wondered at the purpose, and now he balked at being told what to do with his musical talents. O'Neill told everyone he wrote to about Delaney's lack of gratitude, often telling each person more than once.[26]

After 1910 O'Neill began collaborating with a young woman, Selena O'Neill, also no relation, who had a BA in music performance from the Chicago Musical College. Selena played equally well on the piano and the violin, and she performed regularly at Irish-themed events. In 1911 O'Neill helped arrange a concert for her: the *Inter Ocean* mistakenly wrote, "Miss O'Neill has arranged her program from the collection made by her father, former Chief of Police Francis O'Neill." The understandable mistake must have rankled his actual daughters, at least one of whom sometimes played Irish music on the piano with a "fine free rhythmic swing" and had served as arbiter of key signatures. The chief had earlier "adopted" George West, the same age as his son Rogers and a more gifted fiddler; now he sponsored Selena O'Neill, easily mistaken for his daughter. Selena collaborated with O'Neill on four books: *Popular Selections from O'Neill's Dance Music of Ireland* (1910); *O'Neill's Irish Music: 400 Choice Selections Arranged for Piano and Violin* (1915), and two editions of *Waifs and Strays of Gaelic Melody* (1922, 1924).[27]

O'Neill sent her copies of the books with his personal inscriptions, effusive enough that they might raise eyebrows. For example, in 1917 he wrote: "To Selena O'Neill, B.M. Talented Arranger of this Work."

> As a Token of
> A thousand nameless ties
> that link our lives and sympathies
> Of Kindred thoughts and aims and ends
> By fate's decree-Artistic friends

And in 1922 he inscribed a copy of *Waifs and Strays of Gaelic Melody* "To Selena A. O'Neill, 'The Fairy Fiddler,'" and included a poem he seems to have written himself.

Tis not her playing although it be
   the pearl of perfect minstrelsy
That moves us most; it is to feel
   The spirit that her eyes reveal
The kindliness of soul and heart
   That measures greater than all art
She is her music—it is she
   Who masters her own melody
And gives to art the gentle ways
   That make us love her when she plays
     From a loyal friend
     Capt. Francis O'Neill

It takes little effort to imagine O'Neill, in his sixties with his old community fallen away, growing moderately infatuated with the younger woman, especially since Anna had banned Irish music from their home. Selena had the intense focus on Irish music his daughters apparently lacked.[28]

Selena competed in the Gaelic Feis (festival) O'Neill helped organize in 1912 and again in 1913. Irish newspapers reported the Gaelic League in Ireland collaborating to organize the 1912 event and praised "Ex-Chief of Police, Francis O'Neill," as a "prominent worker for the Feis." The Feis combined Irish music and dance with Irish sports. Advertisements showed a determined-looking Celt with sword and shield gesturing decisively. O'Neill saw the event as part of the mission of the Gaelic League and explained to Seamus Ó Casaide in Ireland, "We are ordinary people filling various positions in public or commercial life in no way connected with professionalism in either music or literature. We are just contributing our mite (or might if you will) to a cherished cause."[29]

The *Chicago Citizen* reported more than 15,000 people attended the 1912 Feis, at Gaelic Park just south of Bridgeport, and it featured a large photo of O'Neill in his captain's uniform. Selena O'Neill, whom the *Citizen* called "probably the greatest Irish violinist in Chicago," won first prize in the fiddling contest. Her brother John, who the chief felt could have been better but never practiced, took second place after Francis "coaxed and coerced" him into appearing.[30]

The *Tribune* described how "these festivals have all been organised by Donal O'Connor, a delegate of the Gaelic League of Ireland, who came to this country on behalf of that patriotic organization," a "nonsectarian, nonpolitical society" "whose objects are to revive the Irish language, foster Irish industries and literature, and develop the Irish drama."[31]

As a sign of the policing of Irishness, the *Tribune* detailed how "two young Irishmen, dressed in knee breeches, green stockings, ragged swallow tail coats and wearing dilapidated hats and green neckerchiefs," the dreaded stage Irishmen, "walked up the stairs to the platform where Irish dances were being danced in Gaelic park yesterday." According to the *Tribune*, two officials of the Feis spotted them and "the two young men were firmly but courteously thrust back down the steps." The *Tribune* quoted O'Connor, the Irish representative of the Gaelic League: "We have been fighting this sort of thing for twenty-five years," he said. "This is no place for burlesque stage Irishmen." "The youths retreated abashed," wrote the *Tribune*, "protesting that they were as good Irishmen as any present." Through the Feis and the alliance of Irish and Irish Americans, the Gaelic League and O'Neill tried to offer a different image and framing of Ireland, one rooted in a notion of Celtic authenticity and ancient, allegedly racial, traditions.[32]

The *Tribune* described the 1913 Feis as "an exact reproduction, as far as circumstances will allow, of the modern Irish Feis which is doing so much toward strengthening Irish nationality today." The *Citizen* mentioned smaller attendance at the 1913 Feis but called it a "monster success." "The Feis has come to stay. In a few more years no doubt it will become the greatest Irish institution in this country." The *Citizen* again noted O'Neill's close involvement and added, "Ireland now believes the only way to win her salvation is by going back to the language and customs of her old days. Irish is again becoming the language of the homes and the counting houses. The song, the dance and the music are all getting careful attention, and it looks as

Figure 34 *Chicago Tribune*, July 20, 1913, B6. The 1912 Feis and this one, a year later, both involved direction from and/or cooperation with the Gaelic League in Ireland, which sought to exercise some control over how the Yanks were depicting Irish culture. The Irish representative, Donal O'Connor, booted two Chicago Irishmen offstage for being inauthentic.

if Ireland in the near future will again be an Irish-speaking Ireland." None of this turned out to be true in Chicago: the Feis did not recur after 1913, and in a 1918 letter O'Neill described infighting and rivalry over the Gaelic Park grounds that divided the community.[33]

By then O'Neill had grown increasingly bitter or resigned about the fate of Irish music and culture in the US. When he went to Gaelic Park in 1918, he told a friend, he found "a typical Irish audience to which athletics were far more attractive than music and dancing combined." The aspiring immigrant wanted children to Americanize. "The poor scrub who graduated from the pick and shovel and the mother who for many years toiled in some Yankee kitchen," he wrote, will have nothing less for their children "but the very latest [musical] agony if you please." O'Neill told William Halpin that "time and again I have been disgusted by the tittering and mockery of Irish audiences when a piper strikes up a merry tune, and this disconcerting conduct comes not from the American born but the Irish born mainly." The music O'Neill championed seemed old-fashioned, a residue of poverty, overlaid with memories of a difficult life easily replaced by ragtime, jazz, or the stylized memories of Ireland that Tin Pan Alley offered.[34]

O'Neill repeatedly blamed the Catholic Church, which he claimed cared for little but the extension of its own authority and, as mentioned earlier, sought to make "Irish" synonymous with "Catholic." The church had often suppressed the wholesome music of the people in Ireland, with the blow of the proverbial blackthorn stick, O'Neill wrote, and "in a country like Ireland, where the clergy are not only venerated but almost deified, the frown of the priest was as deadly as a boycott." In a rare statement of political nationalism, he denounced the way the English got the clergy to knuckle under, adding passages to the Catholic catechism like those below:

Question. What are the duties of subjects to the temporal Powers?
Answer. *To be subject to them, and to honour and obey them, not only for wrath, but also for conscience-sake; for it is the will of God.*

Question. Does the Scripture require any other duty of subjects?
Answer. *Yes, to pray for Kings, and for all who are in high station, that we may lead a quiet and peaceable life.*

"It was Sir JC Hippisley who negotiated the deal," O'Neill wrote, whereby the Catholic Church agreed to suppress Irish music, language, and culture and teach servility to the colonizer as catechism. "It would make your blood boil," he wrote, "to read how he suggested the assignment or promotion of the kind of men deemed safe to parishes and Sees, and the free and easy way he refers to the cardinals and ecclesiastics he has on his string." The Roman Church helped Anglicize Ireland, and now it helped Americanize Irish Catholics.[35]

In the US, O'Neill felt, the church continued to suppress Irish culture in return for power and influence. "Religious organizations, propaganda and church extension fostered and forced by the most powerful influence in the world monopolize the energies of our race," he wrote. "Every organized effort not affiliated with the church or encouraged by the clergy seems doomed." He told Father O'Floinn that "the energies of our race and creed have been organized in the interests of church building and the preservation of the faith." In 1921 he told Henry Mercer, "all the power which the Catholic Church wields is being exerted in behalf of the perpetuation of the faith and church membership. Our Catholic clergy are mostly American born[;] to them the music of their ancestors is of but little concern."[36]

His own religious community offered a poignant example. In 1915 Father John Carroll, the man with the only Gaelic typewriter in America, who had regularly preached in Irish on St. Patrick's Day and helped O'Neill translate tune titles to Irish, retired as head of St. Thomas the Apostle Catholic Church, a few blocks from O'Neill's Hyde Park home. To replace Carroll, the diocese chose Thomas V. Shannon, born in Chicago. The new priest later wrote a self-congratulatory account of his efforts to revive the parish and sweep away the past. "The old pastor had let all modern progress go quietly on its way," Shannon wrote, anonymously, and the church was now "very much run down." After "the old pastor conveniently died in the odor of restful sanctity," Shannon began social reforms aimed to rejuvenate membership, including piano lessons and the performance of light operettas. The parish continued to celebrate St. Patrick's Day, but though they had an international expert on Irish music in their membership, O'Neill played no visible role. Eventually Shannon replaced the old red brick gothic church with a stunning new modernist church in the Prairie style. The church, of course, ministered to all Catholics and gained more power and influence in American politics by uniting Irish, Italian, German, Polish, and other ethnicities as monolithically "Catholic." O'Neill's new parish church and community, run by modern, assimilated Irish Americans, made little acknowledgment of Irish culture.[37]

## Irish Music and Commercial Recordings

No one could deny O'Neill's commitment to the music of the ancestors or his desire to see Irish culture as a living practice rather than a one-day-a-year stereotype. O'Neill's books amounted to a truly remarkable accomplishment, especially the first, produced while working full time as chief of police. The collections of Irish music took an extraordinary degree of hard and careful work, and memorialized the musical culture of nineteenth-century Irish immigrants. His 1913 *Irish Minstrels and Musicians* offers almost the only source of information about the lives and work of a wide range of Irish musicians active in the early twentieth century. His *Irish Folk Music* illuminates the lives of Irish Americans in late nineteenth- and early twentieth-century Chicago vividly, with humor and insight.[38]

But he felt very keenly that he and his generation had failed to make the practices of Irish culture part of the daily life of Americans. His musical friend John Ennis lamented that Irish Americans ignored their own music in favor of "the alleged 'negro melodies' that emanate from a few degenerate Irish-Americans and Hebrews in New York." His friend and champion Father Fielding told the Gaelic League that the Irish in America, without their native language, "were like a ship without a rudder at the mercy of every wave of sentimentality and sham." Thus they became, like Mrs. Donahue, "too 'dacent' to sing Irish songs." "We sang the songs of the nigger that were made to order in Chicago and New York for the Irish in America. We sang the vile, vulgar, vaudeville songs of the Sassanach." O'Neill would not have used that sort of language—ethnic or racial slurring was not his style—but he keenly understood the lure of American popular music and "Americanization," and believed he had lost the battle.[39]

By the early 1920s, in his seventies, O'Neill confessed to feeling his age. He believed he was going blind, and the *Tribune* reported that news to the public in 1923, although later photos show him wearing thick glasses and he continued to write, at a much slower pace, for the last ten years of his life. But he demonstrated another kind of blindness in that he failed to see the explosion in Irish music then taking place in New York, Boston, and other cities. Records, rather than print, offered a new form of cultural transmission, and O'Neill would live through "the golden age of ethnic recording." These records mixed "authentic" Irish music with the languages of American commerce.

O'Neill had done pioneering work in recording his friends, but the results disappointed him. Cylinder recordings captured the pipes especially very poorly, the drones barely audible, and the American-style pipes that sounded good in a hall sounded harsh on recordings. O'Neill shipped some two dozen cylinders to Ireland for the benefit of friend Father Richard Henebry, the eccentric scholar of languages and music, but the two men had some sort of a falling out and Henebry never listened to them. O'Neill had an extensive exchange about records and recordings with William Halpin, an amateur archaeologist and historian and "respectable shopkeeper" in County Clare. Halpin sent O'Neill some 78 rpm disks from Ireland, which O'Neill lacked the equipment to play; he had to go down to the offices of Lyon and Healy, his publisher, to hear recordings of an Irish piper he said "couldn't hold a candle to some of the pipers I know."

Halpin seems to have proposed a business selling recordings of Irish music, as he sent O'Neill recordings and O'Neill sent him recordings in return, but O'Neill discouraged him, saying "I see you are an enthusiast and consequently over sanguine in everything related to pipes and pipe music. If the genuine demand for Irish pipe records existed, it would be gladly supplied, but it doesn't. Few of our people care a snap for even Irish music."[40]

O'Neill was simply wrong. Considerable demand for "ethnic" music of all sorts existed in the US. By 1916 Columbia Records offered recordings in twelve different languages, and in the years around WWI, record companies began working urgently to fill that demand, often pushed by immigrant communities themselves. In the 1910s Ellen O'Byrne ran a record store on Third Avenue in New York City. Irish people would often ask not for standard commercial Irish songs like "The Kerry Dances" or "The Vale of Avoca" but instrumental dance tunes of the kind O'Neill collected. Her son recalled "Irish people were always coming in and asking for old favorites like 'The

Stack of Barley.' Well, she'd no records to give them because there weren't any." She sent him to Gaelic Park in the Bronx, and he found two musicians, Eddie Herborn and John Wheeler, playing accordion and banjo. In 1916 she brought the two musicians to Columbia and convinced them to record "The Stack of Barley." "The five hundred records sold out in no time at all."[41]

Francis O'Neill never listed banjo or accordion players in his accounts of Irish musicians. John Kimmel, a German American, had made a series of recordings of Irish music on accordion before WWI. Henry Mercer, who loved Irish music, had bought the entire series: to his knowledge they represented the only recordings of Irish dance music in existence at the time. Banjo, on the other hand, clearly came from the minstrel show. The banjo originated in Africa: the enslaved played it. By the 1850s, minstrel show performers had adopted it, and banjos universally stood for the music of burned cork and greasepaint. Irish Americans who adapted the banjo to Irish music reflected this heritage, described in chapter 2: O'Neill recognized it and wrote about it in a way that aimed to resegregate Irish and African American music. By the 1920s, record companies had established Irish music catalogs, recognizing the vibrant musical life of dance halls that emerged in eastern cities especially.

A very wide range of cultural options appeared to urban Irish Americans. A person living in New York in the week of May 20, 1916, could find page after page of varied amusements advertised in the *Irish Advocate*. The reader could attend "The Munster Boy's Social" at "Gannons Hall," or the "Tyrone Social Set" at "Murphy's Hall," or go dancing at "O'Hara's Hall (Under the Management of the Young Mayo Men)" or "Coffeys Popular Dance Hall under the management of Capt. Pat Casey and featuring Hogan's orchestra," among others. To prepare themselves for the social strain, they could take classes at the "Emerald Isle Dancing Class" or the "Longford and Cork Dancing Class" or the "Tipperary Men's Dancing Class." Women could choose the "Clare Ladies Dancing Class with music by McGrath's band" or the "Roscommon and Galway Dance Class at Fitzpatrick's hall." They could buy tickets for "Ireland Acushla Machree" at the Criterion theater or attend a concert by Irish tenor

John McCormack. If they needed to hire musicians, the *Irish Advocate* advertised more than a dozen different bands led by "Professors" with Irish surnames like Kennan, Kehoe, Lynch, and McQuade. Each issue of the *Advocate* offered the Irish immigrant a dazzling range of Irish-themed music, sports, and dance from the old country.

Irish newspapers, by contrast, showed no such options. The *Cork Examiner* for May 30, 1916, shows a single dance and a single theatrical play between agricultural and livestock shows. The Dublin-based *Irish Independent* on May 19, 1916, advertised five plays and no dances, dancing classes, or musical professors.

The comparison is not entirely fair: as part of the United Kingdom, Ireland was at war in 1916, and further, the Easter Rising had only just occurred. In addition, Dublin and Cork were much smaller cities than New York. With few exceptions, *all* music and dancing in Ireland was Irish music and dancing, so declaring Irishness would make little sense. But the difference gets to the way life in the US changed Irish music. A good musician in New York had literally dozens of opportunities to play for pay but also faced fierce competition. In Ireland a musician might play dances for his or her community, but in American cities they had to *perform*, to "sell it"; and any working musicians had to move easily between Irish tunes and foxtrots, ragtime, and later, jazz numbers. These musicians began recording their playing, and the records made it back to Ireland, where they had a galvanic effect.[42]

Michael Coleman, a fiddler born in 1891 in Ballymote, County Sligo, gives us the best-known example. He grew up playing the fiddle along with his brother at local dances. In 1914 he emigrated to the US. By some accounts, he performed on the boat over, and a passenger who booked acts for the Keith Vaudeville Circuit heard Coleman playing and "lost no time signing him to a long term theatrical contract that was to take him eventually to many cities from Grand Rapids, Michigan to Bangor, Maine." Several accounts suggest he also danced: "Coleman himself was a most artistic dancer.... The 'Stage' hornpipe got its name because of Coleman's having played and danced it simultaneously when he performed in Keiths' theaters." Around 1917 he married, stopped touring, and settled in

New York. There he played often at Irish events. In the 1920s he appeared as part of the Irish Victor Band, and in several "all-star" lineups of musicians.[43]

By 1921 he had begun to make records, typically with piano accompaniment. The musician and historian Fintan Vallelly wrote of Coleman, "Occasionally . . . there occurs an event so stunning in its impact that it rapidly changes the course of evolution. In the recent history of Irish traditional music, such was the experience following the release of the recordings of fiddler Michael Coleman." Jim Donahue, a flute player from County Roscommon, said, "Coleman's records, ah, let me alone! You wouldn't be tired listening to them." John Blessing, another flute player from Leitrim, remembered, "When Coleman's records came here, he put the real touch to it. The old players thought he was a genius because no one could take music out of a fiddle like he could." Another musician recalled, "I heard of Michael Coleman about 1924 and I thought he was wonderful altogether. The first Coleman record I heard was 'The Boys at the Lough.' I was only starting at the fiddle then, and to hear him play wasn't good encouragement because he was far ahead of every other one." "His recordings were among the most enduring cultural remittances sent home to Ireland by emigrants in the New World."[44]

Other New York fiddle players from Sligo, notably Paddy Killoran and James Morrison, and flute player John McKenna, had similar impacts. Tommy Gilmartin recounted that the 78 rpm recordings of McKenna made a tremendous impact when they filtered back home. Around his native area,

> no matter what the cost, if you were to sell the last cow, you'd buy one of his records at the time. If you were to be without a meal a day, you'd have got the record in preference to anything else. . . . That house would be full to capacity that night because John McKenna's record had arrived new that day. And there would be no work done that day in the area till it be heard, or there would get no contentment in it till it would be heard. That was the atmosphere that existed, that's what went on.[45]

Multiple factors explain this influence. If Coleman toured in vaudeville houses, like Patsy Touhey the piper, he had to develop a flashy, impactful style, full of novelty; one that could grab the attention of what O'Neill had called, speaking of Touhey, "even mixed nationalities." A musician like Coleman was *professionalized* in a way simply not available in Ireland at the time. The records of Coleman, Killoran, Morrison, and McKenna often had piano accompaniment, which added—even in the many instances where the piano accompaniment was terrible—a note of novelty and sophistication. "Two things are notable about this vast treasure trove of American 78s: firstly that virtually all of them are accompanied by piano 'vamping,' and secondly, that to fit the tunes on to a recording lasting around three minutes, they seem to define the duration of sets of reels and jigs as played to this day, repetitions of two or three tunes."[46]

Recording itself, the machine process, had a profound effect on music. Not only did it establish a mode of playing two or three tunes in succession, to fill out the available time on a record, but it made listening private instead of social; repeated, instead of evanescent; it froze time and space. A Coleman record literally documented three minutes in an American recording studio, repeatable at whim. Dancers complained about records: "the only fault that was in the gramophone was you see ... the dance! There was nice music alright in it; it was very lively very fast ... [but] it might stop before the figure was finished ... [and the dancers] would have to stand up on the floor. So they preferred the musicians."[47] Records began to sever Irish dance music, experienced in privacy, from dance. Records also might be too good: the polish, execution, and recording quality, the *professionalization*, might have a chilling effect. Fiddler Patrick Kelly recalled:

When Coleman's records came in around here, people left up their fiddles and flutes. . . . [H]e drove a lot of players stone mad. . . . I knew several grand players around here who never again played a note after hearing Coleman and [James] Morrison. We had a lot of great music here around west Clare, you know, some of it going back to the time of the famine and before, but people had no great meas (value) in it after they heard Coleman. It was an awful pity! I would say he did as much harm as good in a lot of places.[48]

The musical environment of the US had musicians playing multiple sets a night, while despite the clichés about Ireland as "the land of music and song," opportunities to play for pay remained rare, the dance music of rural people retained a taint of backwardness, and more than a few Irish people looked down on music as time wasting. Junior Crehan remembered, "Arra, the old people were very hard and very severe; you should always be working!" Micho Russell, from Doolin in County Clare, took care not to practice in earshot of the neighbors. "You wouldn't want to be heard playing in the daytime because . . . the neighbors might think it very strange to be playing music" when you should be working. "Any house where they'd hear a concertina or a tin whistle playing . . . there wouldn't be any great respect for 'em. So, it had to be kept a little bit quieter." Demand for the music O'Neill collected varied in Ireland, Russell insisted. "The poor people played the old type of music. Poor fishermen and the people that was living by the seashore . . . and small farmers. The upper class people . . . they didn't want it anyway." The musical contexts of Ireland and the US varied dramatically at the time Coleman's records began to appear.

But musicians in Ireland and the US increasingly learned from records as much or more than they learned from other musicians or from printed music. Mick Moloney recalled playing in a music session with American players and asking how they learned the tunes. "No fewer than 75 percent of the tunes, it turned out, had been learned from 78 rpm recordings." One of them, born in Ireland and arrived in Chicago at the age of nineteen, "learned to play by listening to the Victor releases of Patsy Touhey. He would shut himself in a room alone for hours trying to figure out exactly what Touhey was doing on the pipes." Junior Crehan recalled, "At night time I'd go in the room and bolt the door and let nobody in and I'd pick up a good few tunes off the gramophone"[49]

The records represented Ireland to itself, in a different frame than

O'Neill's books. The books appeared as part of a Celtic revival, under the chief's authority, expensively respectable. The records appeared as lively modern commercial novelties. As Irish Americans had seen a new presentation of Ireland in fake Blarney Castles and sod maps, so Irish musicians and dancers would hear Ireland reverberating across the ocean, reframed.

Finally, the records came to Ireland at a time when the Union Jack came down everywhere but the six counties of the northeast, replaced by the long dreamed-of flag of Ireland. In 1916 the Easter Rising began in Dublin, with its bold and aspirational declaration of an Irish republic. Put down quickly and initially mocked, it soon gained widespread support when the English summarily executed its leaders. The Irish War of Independence, the "Black and Tan War" of 1919–21, followed. It ended with the negotiation of a treaty with England, which partitioned the Island and formed the Irish Free State, which had its own flag, uniforms, courts, police, and governing bodies but still pledged loyalty to the crown. A large minority refused to accept the treaty, seeing it as a betrayal of the ideals of the republic, and the country plunged into a vicious civil war from 1922 to 1923. The end of that war left the majority of Ireland, excepting six counties in the northeast, increasingly autonomous from England. So the records from America arrived at a time of heightened nationalism and a heightened ability to promote and foster Irish music. The music O'Neill collected, and Michael Coleman played, came to occupy a unique place in the Irish national imagination.

Accounts of Coleman's playing describe it as simultaneously completely unique and virtuosic *and* completely typical of Sligo, a contradictory position. Music historians often group Coleman, Morrison, and Killoran as exemplars of the "Sligo fiddle style," since all three came from Sligo. But all three also spent years playing in theaters and music halls in New York: could they also exemplify "the New York Style"? Some accounts of Coleman assert his essential Irishness, and that "everything that Coleman recorded was played in the same manner in his native district, before he was born." Multiple people in Ireland asserted that Coleman's brother James, who never left Ireland and never recorded, played better. "Michael was good, but he was nothing compared to the brother. The brother was twice as good!" A story in the National Folklore collection in Dublin claims the brothers owed their talents to the faeries.

> The Coleman brothers set off home about midnight and they took a near way across the fields. And somewhere over in them fields there's an old fort supposed to be around two thousand years old . . . an historical place, a strange place. They were supposed to have lost their way and found themselves in a beautiful garden with the loveliest trees they had ever seen, and the fields opened up into a large landscape. Instead of being afraid, it was a joy. They had no fear. Jim was carrying a fiddle under his arm and after a while they sat down and started to play the most beautiful music that was ever heard. All of a sudden the whole thing faded away from them: fear came over them and they went off home. They returned to Hunt's some nights after and their music, well, there was a noticeable improvement in their music

Did Coleman's skills come from faery intervention or three shows a night in dance halls and vaudeville houses? The larger point is not which came first or which is more real or authentic; rather it is that despite O'Neill's efforts to locate it in the rural Irish peasantry, Irish music always existed in transatlantic circulation, in a relationship between its native and emigrant practitioners and between Ireland and other musical countries. That relationship only deepened as records grew more common.[50]

If records introduced an "American" quality, what might it consist of? The US was no paradise, but it had shaken off colonialism 100 years earlier, and records from America expressed a people free of colonization. O'Neill himself said so when he compared Patsy Touhey and Turlough McSweeney: McSweeney, he wrote, represented an "antiquated and oppressed" Ireland. Touhey and Coleman may have been forced to emigrate, but they worked in a context that saw Irish dance music as a product worth celebrating and selling.[51]

In addition, as would be said of American jazz, Irish tunes depended on conveying a sense of "swing" or "lift." This "feel," this quality of "swing," notoriously escapes musical notation: playing the tunes exactly as written in O'Neill's book results in a lifeless and largely uninteresting musical experience. O'Neill used the term "swing" repeatedly, long before it appeared as a description of African American dance music. For example, in his later 1910 book, *Irish Folk Music: A Fascinating Hobby*, he praised patrolman Pat Mahoney and "the 'swing' of his execution"; he similarly commented on the "thrilling" "rhythmic swing" of his friend James McFadden. He recalled a Scottish friend playing a song with "a suspiciously Irish swing to it." He heard another jig and noted "the 'swing' of it ... pointed strongly to an Irish origin." He noted his daughter's "rhythmic swing" playing dance music on the piano. "The swing and spirit of the Gael however was always discernible in their reels," he insisted. "Few musicians of any nationality find difficulty in playing Irish airs," O'Neill noted, "but many appear to have little conception of that peculiar rhythm or swing without which Irish dance tunes lose their charm and spirit." He used the term repeatedly and consistently.[52]

For much of the twentieth century, American popular music had a "swing" beat. We often call the 1930s and 1940s "the swing era." Searching for the phrase "swing music" using Google Ngram Viewer, which measures the frequency of appearance of words in Google's corpus of digitized books, shows a very sharp spike in 1930. Most accounts of "swing" focus on its expression in African American music. O'Neill used the term habitually thirty years earlier. His use of "swing" so early raises the question of where this sense of "swing" came from.[53]

It seems reasonable to suggest a connection between American "swing" and Irish music. As we saw in chapter 2, Irish immigrants and African American shared a great deal of musical and dance culture. Irish surnames appear commonly in the African American community; surely Irish music, heard on streets and wharves, in dance halls and saloons, would have had an influence on people who shared some of the same economic circumstances?[54]

The historic connections between African and Irish Americans hide in plain sight, in names like, say, Shaquille O'Neal: much of the work of racism involves denying or eliding those connections and enforcing a legal or psychological segregation, so that claiming Shaquille O'Neal as Irish seems ridiculous. And this is exactly what Francis O'Neill's work did: he described an Irish music of "peasants" straight from the island: if a connection between African American and Irish swing existed, he did his best to police and segregate the two, at least in his early publications.

Yet it shows up: on one of Michael Coleman's most famous records, "Bonnie Kate/Jennie's Chickens," from 1934, the accompaniment comes not from a piano but a guitar. The guitar shows the unmistakable influence of the guitar/fiddle duo of Eddie Lang and Joe Venuti. You could lay a standard swing beat against the record and both the guitar and Coleman's playing would work perfectly well. Similarly, one of flute player John McKenna's most famous recordings, "Tripping to the Well," would easily fit against a standard swing beat. Paddy Killoran recorded a number of sides with Irish American guitarist Jack McKenna, who also had obviously listened to a lot of Eddie Lang: their records again fit easily with a standard swing beat: listen to, for example, the record of "My Love is Fair and Handsome/ First Month of Spring." The "swing" feel appears in many of fiddler James Morrison's records, including "Farewell to Ireland," backed by banjo. On his recording of "McFadden's/Blackberry Blossom," the guitar plays very much in the manner of the Reinhardt brothers in the Hot Club of France: at about 1:48, the piano player clearly quotes Benny Goodman's "Sing Sing Sing." These records show the influence of American jazz clearly and reflect the variety urban dance hall patrons demanded, but they also display the easy fit between Irish music and "swing." Earlier we saw O'Neill discussing "The Arkansas Traveler" with Henry Chapman Mercer. Mercer wrote a history of the tune describing how it moved from blackface companies to medicine shows to camp meetings to the stage. O'Neill called it a "fairly acceptable reel."[55]

He included "Turkey in the Straw" in his collections and, as noted, the tune had a parallel career under the title "Old Zip Coon." In minstrel shows, the character Zip Coon represented a flashily dressed, slick, urban black character. If Jim Crow dressed in rags and sang about the old plantation, Zip Coon dressed in absurd high style and boasted about his success. Patsy Touhey, O'Neill's favorite piper, reportedly used the tune to close his act. O'Neill corresponded with Mercer about the tune's origins and claimed it as Irish in his 1922 book, *Waifs and Strays of Gaelic Melody*. "As played nowadays [it] may suit the rapid movements of buck-dancers," O'Neill insisted, "but the frenzied rhythm is ruinous to the melody. Rendered after the manner of the famous Dan Emmett of Bryant's Minstrels, in slow reel time, this popular tune acquires a much enhanced appeal." Emmett, he reminded readers, "was the author of the immortal 'Dixie,' and it was his version of 'Turkey in the Straw,' which we obtained from John McFadden of the Chicago Irish Music Club, that is here presented." "The staple repertoire of the minstrel shows was a multicultural mix," Mick Moloney concluded: "the music and dances were taken from Scottish and Irish sources. There were jigs, reels, and songs old and new. There were sentimental ballads, Negro sermons, plantation sketches and steamboat sketches, and parodies and satires. There were thousands of Irish and Irish-American performers." Dan Emmett, who O'Neill praised, kept a "jig notebook" in which he wrote down the tunes he heard African Americans playing in his native Ohio, tunes he could adapt for the minstrel stage.[56]

In the case of "Turkey in the Straw," O'Neill removed the burned cork and the history of Emmett's appropriations from African Americans, and recast the tune as Irish. In referring to "buck dancers," he blamed African Americans for "ruining the melody." But O'Neill cited the fact that Emmett's family came from Ireland, and "the pioneers or early settlers of West Virginia, Kentucky, and Tennessee, were largely of Irish ancestry, and obviously their music or tunes . . . were of Irish origin." He added that "the best in what may be regarded as American folk music is the product of Irish brains."

But he also began to acknowledge the hybridity of American musical forms. In his last book, O'Neill embraced the kind of mixed music that appeared on records or that he had enjoyed in his days on the prairies in Edina, Missouri. He wrote, "In addition to 'Dixie,'" "such classics as 'The Old Folks at Home,' or 'The Suwanee River,' 'My Old Kentucky Home,' 'Old Black Joe,' and dozens of others, were the productions of Stephen Collins Foster." He tried to fix these tunes as "Gaelic" but also acknowledged the complicated, racially entangled history of American music.[57]

Who knows where "Turkey in the Straw" came from originally? O'Neill wanted to find out so he could assert a fundamental Irishness. Some scholars point to origins in England, not Ireland. What matters here is not the tune's origins so much as how it circulated, signifying variously authentic blackness, authentic white rustic charm, or authentic Irishness, all of them mingled. O'Neill's collections of Irish music worked to arrest this circulation of meaning and establish stable origins. But the disorderly borrowing and reappropriation on records would continue despite O'Neill's efforts in print.[58]

For example, in 1936 James Morrison, one of the New York/Sligo fiddlers, made a 78 rpm record backed by a banjo and piano. Morrison paired "The Wreck of the Old 97," from a popular recording often described as the first example of the "country" genre, with "Oh Dem Golden Slippers," written by African American composer James A. Bland for the minstrel stage. The verse of "Golden Slippers" is identical to "Goodbye Mick and Goodbye Pat," also known as "Leaving Tipperary," considered a traditional Irish song. Morrison played "Goodbye Mick" in the verse and "Golden Slippers" in the chorus, blending the American minstrel tune with the Irish emigrant tune.[59]

The lyrics of both songs concern leaving home and friends. In "Golden Slippers," the singer expects to leave this world for heaven and says goodbye to his old friends; in "Goodbye Mick," the singer plans to leave in the morning for Castle Garden in New York Harbor and says goodbye to his old friends. Both songs explore a common experience of displacement and reflect sadness and joy at leaving: the songs borrow from each other both musically and thematically.

"GOODBY MICK AND GOODBYE PAT
(LEAVING TIPPERARY)"

The ships it sails in half an hour
to cross the broad Atlantic
Me friends are standing on the quay
with grief and sorrow frantic

I'm just about to sail away
in good ship Dan O'Leary
The anchors are weighed and the gangway's up
I'm leaving Tipperary

And it's goodbye Mick and goodbye Pat
And goodbye Kate and Mary
The anchors are weighed and the gangway's up
I'm leaving Tipperary

"OH DEM GOLDEN SLIPPERS (VERSE)"

So, it's good-bye, children, I will have to go
Whar de rain don't fall or de wind don't blow,
And yer ulster coats, why, yer will not need,
When yer ride up in de chariot in de morn;

But yer golden slippers must be nice and clean,
And yer age must be just sweet sixteen,
And yer white kid gloves yer will have to wear,
When yer ride up in de chariot in de mornin'.

Bland, born in New York City, wrote "Golden Slippers" while living in London, where he spent most of his adult life writing songs about the country he had left behind. Morrison, living in New York City—where he spent most of his adult life playing songs from the country he had left behind—recognized the easy way that "The Wreck of the Old 97" and "Golden Slippers" blended with Irish or Irish American fiddle styles. It is difficult if not impossible to know which came first or who borrowed what. The similarities document the continual circulation of people and ideas and culture, in North American and back and forth across the Atlantic. By the last years of his life, even O'Neill had to acknowledge it.

Irish music showed the influence of America, and the records that steadily crossed the Atlantic, perhaps mostly clearly in the rise of ceilidhe or céilí bands, "which gained widespread popularity in

Ireland during the 1930s and 1940s." Céilí bands, which typically included piano, drums, accordions, banjos, basses, and sometimes even saxophones, played repertoire that ranged from traditional Irish dance tunes found in O'Neill's collections to pop tunes from the radio and records. "Irish-American dance bands became models for bands in Ireland," and "musicians from ceili bands ... particularly cit[ed] the influence of Paddy Killoran and his Pride of Erin orchestra." New Jersey flute player Mike Rafferty, growing up in Galway, played in céilí bands. He remembered that normally they could play different styles of music, but when they played dances organized by the Gaelic Athletic Association "it was all traditional Irish music at that time. You weren't allowed to play even 'Buttons and Bows.'" "Buttons and Bows" first appeared in a 1947 Hollywood movie, *The Paleface*, starring Bob Hope. Rafferty recalled "we started 'Buttons and Bows' one night and we were told to stop, or we wouldn't get paid! That was a rule of the Gaelic Athletic Association, GAA." Céilí bands played all sorts of music, unless officialdom required authenticity.[60]

This kind of commercial circulation, the disorderly cross-contamination, that mixed Irish, black, American, and "country" is exactly what O'Neill had worked to avoid with his collections of Irish music. He had wanted to police the boundaries of music and culture and maintain order. At the same time, as an intelligent and broad-minded man, he could not ignore the hybridity of musical forms and the ways music escaped confinement. In his last decade, he seemed to develop a broader sense of music and a sharper eye for what folk traditions had in common.

# Epilogue
# Happy to Meet, Sorry to Part
## The Legacy

Henry Chapman Mercer was one of the more significant figures in O'Neill's intellectual life, although only seventeen letters between the two survive. An eccentric man, born to the wealth and status of Philadelphia's upper class, Mercer devoted his adult life to collecting preindustrial artifacts. He built a huge, rambling, reinforced concrete castle to house his vast collection, which ranged from thimbles and buttons to whaleboats and Conestoga wagons, and nearby he built a similarly odd reinforced concrete château for himself, adjacent to—yes—a reinforced concrete tile works. Mercer's decorative "Moravian tiles," based loosely on traditions of Pennsylvania German immigrants, found a ready market among devotees of the arts and crafts movement. His house, stuffed with his own colorful tiles and eccentric bric-a-brac from around the world, had couches and dressers made of reinforced concrete, with plush cushions and wooden drawers. He detested artificial light and designed the house, "Fonthill," so he could work from room to room, following the sun. He made a very large and elaborate tile mosaic of the "Arkansas Traveler" story and placed it above a huge fireplace in one of the many odd rooms of his castle. The Mercer Museum in Doylestown, Pennsylvania, preserves his collection and his remarkable work.[1]

Mercer's interest in preserving preindustrial culture mostly ignored the racism so common in folklore and archaeology. The arts and crafts movement, in the US and England, countered industrialization with a renewed appreciation of the skill, ingenuity, and creativity of ordinary people. Mercer believed the real life of a nation lay in the handcrafts and arts of its ordinary citizens, what he called "the tools of the nation maker." He was interested not in Anglo-Saxon or German or Irish culture per se but in *premodern*, precapitalist culture: a culture shared by all the people who lived in an imprecise period before Mercer thought modernity had intruded. His collecting amounted, he admitted, to "almost a mania."[2]

Mercer wrote to O'Neill in 1920: among his other enthusiasms, Mercer loved Irish music, and he told O'Neill how as a young man, about 1885, he had heard Patsy Touhey when "Harrigan's Double Hibernians" passed through his hometown. Enthralled by the music, he invited Touhey and John Egan, the other piper traveling with the show, to his home. Their music put him in mind of a place "where the steam whistle of modern American life is not heard to drive away the fairies." He marveled at the ingenuity and craft of the pipes they played, made by the Taylor brothers in Philadelphia: Mercer visited the Taylors at their North Philadelphia shop multiple times and eventually acquired a set of Taylor pipes for his museum. He was delighted when he discovered O'Neill's books: no one had ever written about Irish folk music before.

"I feel impelled," Mercer wrote to O'Neill, "to thank you, however inadequately, for the great pleasure which these books are giving me." He praised the contribution O'Neill had made not just to Irish music but to folklore in general, and he told O'Neill about his memory of an Irish tune, played in the evening "until it filled the night air betwixt the katydids and crept deep into my heart where it has remained ever since, getting into the blood and inspiring the heart to conquer fatigue and press onward." Within a short time O'Neill would be addressing Mercer as "Dear Kindred Soul."[3]

The two men combined an enthusiasm for modern innovation—Mercer had built some of the first reinforced concrete structures in the US, and O'Neill had administered a thoroughly modern police department—with nostalgia for a past imagined as better. Mercer told O'Neill "from first to last you have evoked a romantic atmosphere about the subject, taken us as it were into an old garden full of memories." Mercer several times described how Irish music revived his spirits and cured "the blues."

They compared notes on "The Arkansas Traveler" and "Turkey in the Straw." Mercer asked several times about "Kitty O'Neil's Jig," which the chief insisted was "too modern." They discussed sea songs, which Mercer believed had "negroid" origins: Mercer emphasized the mixed character of sailor's music, not the idea of purity. They discussed the utility of recordings as a tool for preserving folk music. Mercer repeatedly urged O'Neill to keep working on folk music, but O'Neill protested that advanced age and failing eyesight would make his forthcoming book, *Waifs and Strays of Gaelic Melody*, his last. Mercer, gentlemanly, ignored instances where O'Neill repeated himself and contributed illustrations and other material to *Waifs and Strays*, so much so that O'Neill acknowledged that "for years the correspondence of Dr. H. C. Mercer of Doylestown, Pa., was an intellectual stimulant." He further noted that Mercer, "an enthusiast on folk music, both Gaelic and American," had contributed illustrations "at his personal expense."[4]

In his flowing hand, O'Neill inscribed copies of his books for people in the US, England, Australia, Canada, and Ireland. A project initiated by Scott Spencer at the University of Southern California has collected images of more than fifty of these dedication pages, which show the range of O'Neill's intellectual community. O'Neill sent a copy of *Irish Minstrels and Musicians* to Henry Ford in 1926, an act that raises troubling questions.[5]

Before WWI Ford appeared in the press as a symbol of up-to-date modernity and creative efficiency. Ford also shared O'Neill's fascination with the preindustrial past and had begun collecting artifacts of American rural life. O'Neill probably sent the book to Ford knowing that Ford's grandfather, like O'Neill himself, hailed from West Cork.

But Ford had a much darker side. After 1920, he became obsessed with anti-Semitic conspiracy theories and bought a newspaper, the Dearborn, Michigan, *Independent*, to spread his virulent message. Adolf Hitler, then on the rise in Germany, kept a picture of Ford in his office and praised Ford's anti-Semitism in his autobiography. In 1926, when O'Neill sent Ford this copy of *Irish Minstrels and Musicians*, objections to Ford's bigotry appeared often in Chicago newspapers.

Did O'Neill share any of Ford's views? Sadly, O'Neill's daughters destroyed his letters after he died. While it is certainly possible, none of O'Neill's surviving letters show any signs of anti-Semitism whatsoever, and it does not appear in his scrapbooks, known published writing, or speeches and interviews.[6]

O'Neill could be controlling and emotionally dense: he was keenly resentful of "ingratitude." He often used the language of "race" to describe music, as was common in his day. He could be a bully. But he had the deep intellectual curiosity and enthusiasm for experience that militates against bigotry. Early in his Chicago life, before he concentrated on Irish music, O'Neill had learned the Scottish, mouth-inflated bagpipes under the tutelage of a Scots immigrant named William McLean; soon, he told a friend, "I was quite expert in the Scottish Scale and had a fine command of the Lowland pipes, a splendid set of which I still own, but never used for 25 years owing to recurring deaths among friends and family." He added in another letter, "an outspoken Irishman, I was the unopposed choice as Judge of the piping competition of the United Scottish societies at their annual picnics for seven consecutive years." He saved a medal attesting to his position. Late in his life, perhaps under the "intellectual stimulation" of Mercer, he began to see folk music more broadly, more as he had as a young man on the Missouri prairie. It expressed not just a national or ethnic culture but also a shared creative sensibility among ordinary people. *Waifs and Strays of Gaelic Melody* departs from his other work by deliberately broadening the canvas: it treats mostly Scottish music, but also Irish music as it evolved and was modified and altered in the US by "pioneer Paganini[s]."[7]

Some time not long after 1920, O'Neill made a fascinating connection between nationalism and music in one of his scrapbooks when he pasted a clipping about American Jazz and WWI next to an excerpt from Douglas Hyde's essay on the necessity of a de-Anglicized Ireland.

The article on "Jazz on the Battle Line" by Henriette Weber, a Chicago pianist and music critic, praised James Reese Europe's famous

"Harlem Hellfighters" band. The Hellfighters, the segregated African American 369th Infantry regiment formed from New York, served with distinction in WWI. But Lieutenant Europe's regimental band gained the most attention for its mix of military precision with ragtime or jazz. "The way they put jazz on the battle line and pep into their fellow fighters and set France by the ears afterward is one of the most startling stories of the war," Weber wrote. Europe's band, "competing with the greatest bands in the world—the British Grenadiers, the Bande Garde Republicaine and the Royal Italian Band—set a mob of 50,000 people perfectly wild, and could be playing yet had the people had their way." She continued, "Rhythomaniacs the Negroes have been called. Certainly they have an uncanny ability to place the accent where by all the laws of white man's music it should not be placed. And that, if you please, is jazz. There is nothing more contagious than this peculiarly American music which our dark brothers have given us—and which so eloquently expresses our national motto, 'Step lively, please.'" Europe's band, in her view, expressed the nation's distinctive character through distinctive, lively music.[8]

O'Neill, who had several times expressed warm feelings toward African Americans, placed this clipping about the vivifying effects of African American music directly beside Hyde's complaint about the decline of Irish music under English rule. Hyde had written, "In place of the pipers and fiddlers who, even 20 years ago, were, comparatively common, we are now in many places menaced by the German band and the barrel organ. Something should be done to keep the native pipes—and the native airs—amongst us still." O'Neill's decision to place these clippings side by side shows that he understood the connection between music and nationalism, and that he may have seen a commonality between Irish peasants and the people Weber called "our dark brothers," in which the character of a nation emerged from its underclass, its ordinary people.

Earlier in his scrapbook he had pasted an article on "Irish Nationality" in its "true character" and had specifically highlighted a passage describing how "Irish civilization failed after Cromwell and the land was held for a century in darkness. During that period the Irish made all haste to lose their own nationality and assimilate that

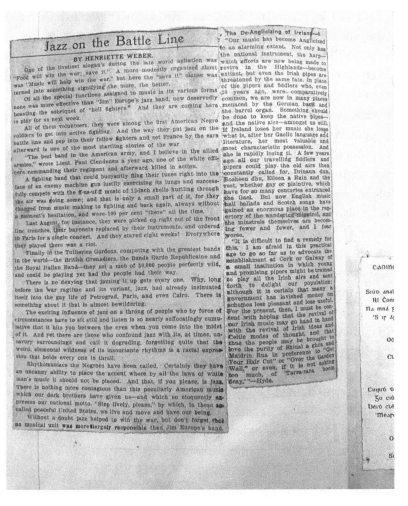

**Figure 35** From O'Neill scrapbooks, from the private collection of Mary Mooney Lesch. A meticulous man, O'Neill clearly saw a connection between these two articles, choosing to paste them side by side. They reflect a relationship between folk culture, popular culture, and nationalism.

of the English." In this dark time, the piece continued, "there arose a sentimental drawing-room craze in Dublin for Irish things. This was exclusively in the Shoneen, or Anglo-Irish class." In "their dim lights and perverted fancies, they invented a brand of de-odorized and disinfected Irishism strictly for polite consumption." "That sham Irishism has been disseminated over the entire world," the article continued, in "harps and shamrocks, round towers, wolf-dogs, green flags, sunbursts and Blarney stones."[9]

O'Neill again insisted on the idea of authentic Ireland distinct from commercial representations, but he also seemingly endorsed the idea that real American music came from America's "peasants," from African Americans, as real Irish music came from ordinary Irish people. Weber, whose article he clipped, wrote enthusiastically and approvingly about ragtime, despite her classical training. "Like it or not, ragtime has come to stay as a rightful heritage of certain phases of the American spirit," she insisted. "It may be noisy, violent, vulgar, but it also is natural and vigorous and shockingly strong." As he grew older, O'Neill grew more open to the appreciation of other forms of music and perhaps to "vulgarity," the mixing of musical genres and forms.[10]

Ireland itself grew increasingly independent of England in the last decades of his life, and he may have felt the task of preserving Irish music could now fall to the Irish themselves. By 1924, Ireland flew its own flag and could work to promote its own national music and, more important, work toward increased autonomy. In 1938 the Dáil Éireann named Douglas Hyde the first president of the newly formed Republic of Ireland.

When Irish musicians and ordinary listeners heard those records from America, they heard music simultaneously the same and different. They heard familiar tunes, presented in a novel context, the context of machine age modernity and professionalized urban performance, inflected by ragtime and jazz. In his collections, O'Neill had drawn a line around "Irish music," but the music of the Sligo fiddlers seemed both authentic and innovative, familiar and hopelessly out of reach, simultaneously diminished and enlarged: diminished because what people played in Sligo in 1930 was possibly not as good, but enlarged because it now represented the intersection of Irish emigrants with the larger world.

The Irish republic had a rocky relationship with traditional music. In 1935 it introduced the Public Dance Halls Act, an attempt to regulate and police "immorality" at pubs, house parties, and crossroads dances. The act, passed with the enthusiastic support of the church, required a license for any gathering with music. It aimed to purge foreign and immoral influences from Irish music, but also to put musical practice under the control of the church/state alliance that then ruled Ireland. The Clare fiddler Junior Crehan recalled it as a scheme to raise money for the church. "So, they barred the country house dance, and the priests was erecting parish halls. All they wanted was to make money—and they got 3d into every shilling tax out of the tickets." Church halls tolerated a sort of hybrid of Irish music and American swing that censorious priest might noddingly approve but Crehan himself detested: "the country house dance was knocked out then, and 'twas fox-trots, and big old bands coming down, and our type—we'd be in a foreign country then. We couldn't put up with it at all, the noise and the microphones, and jazz and so on." Céilí bands, with drums and keys, represented both the influence of American dance bands and an accommodation between tradition and modernity. "Honest to God, I used to nearly cry," Crehan recalled. "Nowhere to go—no one to meet, no Sets in the houses. Nothing left but the hall!" But the previous chapter describes Mike Rafferty, from Galway and of the same generation, who recalled that his Céilí band had *wanted* to play American tunes, but the local officials would not let them. Then, as now, it was exceedingly difficult to balance tradition and modernity: more so if the Church's desire to police the morality of youth entered the mix.[11]

O'Neill followed Irish politics even though he rarely commented on them. In his scrapbook he pasted a clipping of the last words of Padraic Pearse, Joseph Plunkett, and Thomas McDonagh, all of whom died in the cause of the republic during the 1916 Easter Rising, between clippings about Irish festivals, the death of piper Patsy Touhey, the career of U. S. Grant, and accounts of foreign lands. In 1921 he had lamented "revolution and horrors in Ireland" to Henry Mercer, but he continued to write for Irish newspapers, noting in a 1934 article on "Irish Dances and Dance Music" for the *Cork Examiner* that "unaffected by the jazz craze, Irish numbers are regularly on the air every day in the week in the gay U.S.A." O'Neill listened to "the 'Irish Hour' broadcast by the 'Voice of Labor' in Chicago," in which "we are favoured with vocal and instrumental entertainment of a high order." WCFL, the only radio station in the US owned by a labor union, devoted regular time to Irish music. Maurice Lynch, financial secretary of the Chicago Federation of Labor, hosted the program, which ran from 1930 into the 1950s.[12]

O'Neill reminded his Irish readers "that there is an appreciable difference between the rendering of Irish dance tunes, by modern musicians, and the traditional or natural swing of the untutored fiddler, whether hailing from Ireland, the backwoods of Mississippi, or Missouri, the prairies of Illinois, or Indiana, or even the hills of Dixieland." This public insistence, at the very end of his life, that these different genres—especially Dixieland—shared a similar style marked a change in his thinking. He had come to hear the same sense of "swing" in all these styles. He told Irish readers how "Irving Broadus, a pioneer Illinois farmer, who passed his winters on the Gulf Coast, "stole the show" with his fiddling at every entertainment, "although his daughter, a clever pianist and violinist, college trained, was also on the program." Broadus, he added, "never learned to read music." Broadus likely reminded him of the fiddlers he enjoyed as a young man attending weekly barn dances on the prairie in Edina, Missouri.[13]

His praise for the "swing of the untutored fiddler," from wherever he hailed, and his enthusiasm for the playing of Irving Broadus demonstrate his willingness to see commonality. O'Neill could write about "the Irish race" and speculate about the alleged expression of its soul in music, but in the end his experience of the world—as a sailor, as a laborer: as a policemen in Chicago, as a folklorist tracing the genealogy of tunes—left room for a broader understanding of music and musical culture. At the end of his life, he retained his enthusiasm for specifically Irish music but clearly remained open to ways musical cultures influenced one another.

In his last decade O'Neill began disposing of his effects. Selena O'Neill, his final collaborator, tragically suffered from an unknown form of deafness, and by the early 1920s, O'Neill wrote, she could not hold an ordinary conversation and was "deaf as Beethoven." In 1928 O'Neill wrote a letter assigning the printing plates for *Dance Music of Ireland* and the books they worked on together to Selena "in the event of his death."[14]

In 1931 he donated his precious library to the University of Notre Dame. By that time the O'Neills spent much of the year at their winter home in Ocean Springs, Mississippi, a house they called Glengarrif, which they had bought in 1914. "A beautiful spot on the Gulf of Mexico," his granddaughter recalled: "7 1/2 acres—8 room house... There was much fishing crabbing and sailing. . . . There was a 'nickel show' in the small town and my grandfather took us (plus all the kids in tow) every time the picture changed." The community there boasted ties to Chicago: Louis Sullivan had designed one of the local churches. O'Neill fished and enjoyed local music and apparently overcame the blindness that had threatened him ten years earlier.[15]

In late December 1933 he stayed in Chicago and participated in a ceremony marking the thirtieth anniversary of the Iroquois theater fire. It must have meant a great deal to him, revisiting the memory of that awful night, because in 1934 he attended the memorial ceremony again despite the Chicago winter and his advanced age.[16] In early May 1934 Anna died and, after a funeral at St. Thomas the Apostle, joined her son Rogers and her sister Julia in the tomb Francis had built for himself in Chicago's Mount Olivet Cemetery.

In that same year, along with his article for the *Cork Examiner*, O'Neill contributed an address on Irish music to the program of the *Pageant of the Celt*, a grand dramatic history of Celtic culture enacted at Soldier Field during the 1934 Chicago World's Fair. Chicago Irish boosters hired self-invented Irish actor Micheál MacLiammóir to script and produce the huge pageant.[17]

MacLiammóir wrote that "the darkest side of Irish America with its subtle air of conquest, its mania for power and largesse, its furs and jewels and smuggled liquor, its dim airtight background of shamrock, harp and round tower, its wistful patronage to both countries, seemed incarnate in these two men who arrived to ask me to write and Hilton [Edwards] to help produce the *Pageant of the Celt*." The pageant involved "the marshalling of the entire slum-population of the city into various groups of warriors, bards, and druids," wrote

MacLiammóir: "there were Celts everywhere." O'Neill, very much not a man of "furs and jewels and smuggled liquor" but intimately familiar with patronage, power and largesse, contributed a scholarly overview of the history of Irish music from ancient times through the present.

During the summer of 1934, the Harp and Shamrock Orchestra played seven days a week at the fair. "The high point of the band's tenure at the Fair was the appearance one day of the venerable Francis O'Neill. Quite feeble at the age of eighty-five, 'the Chief' presented an autographed copy of *Irish Minstrels and Musicians* to each of the performers." O'Neill wrote a dedication to piper Joe Shannon, "the best left-handed piper since Patsy Touhey," high praise indeed from O'Neill. "Shannon remembers that, at the time, he had no idea of O'Neill's importance or the significance of the occasion."

On January 26, 1936, O'Neill passed away at his home in Hyde Park, aged eighty-seven. "He had been confined to bed since Christmas. Death was attributed to a heart ailment." So ended an eventful and well-lived life. At the time of his death, O'Neill's books were on "special clearance sale" at Lyon and Healey for the price of five cents.[18]

O'Neill had outlived his time, but he had not failed by any means. The Harp and Shamrock Orchestra played the music he loved and played it well, and if musicians now learned tunes from records instead of his books, O'Neill had after all experimented with recording early on and had seen its potential. "Irish Music" and specifically Irish folk music, Irish dance music, persisted as a distinct form in Ireland, the US, England, and Australia especially. It has gone in and out of fashion, reviving with the folk music boom of the 1960s, and then again after the international popularity of Riverdance, and it persists in places with few Irish immigrants like Japan, where Irish bars offer Irish music sessions.[19]

O'Neill had "saved" Irish music less from extinction than from multiculturalism, from merger with other forms. Irish musicians and devotees of Irish music continue to struggle with the problem of purity and authenticity, trying to balance cherished traditions and the value of history against the creative drive to innovate and experiment. Irish music might change, but O'Neill had established a canon of repertoire and performance style that helped define "traditional."

While US newspapers paid relatively little attention to O'Neill's death, obituaries in Ireland celebrated his accomplishments. "A most interesting Gael has passed away in the person of Capt. Francis O'Neill, commonly known as Chief O'Neill," wrote the *Southern Star*, "who has died in the gangster ridden City of Chicago at a venerable age." "An efficient officer, an accomplished Gael, and a recognised authority on Irish music, he lived respected and has died regretted. May God be very good to him." The newspaper ran a longer obituary recounting his career on the first page. "A Great Irishman has passed," declared the *Irish Independent,* under a headline reading "cabin boy becomes chief." "He truly was a credit to the race and typical of its finest qualities."[20]

Irish music historians began taking notice of O'Neill's work in the 1970s, particularly the folklorist Breandán Breathnach, who published a first brief biography of O'Neill in 1977. Nicholas Carolan's 1997 biography *A Harvest Saved* marked the first sustained examination of O'Neill's life and work.[21]

Irish musicians and historians engaged in a major reconsideration of Irish music and its relation to the past in the 1990s, including "The Crossroads Conference," held in Dublin's Temple Bar district in 1996. As one might expect, purists marked one extreme while those advocating for an Irish music that mingled with classical and "world" music marked the other. The most extreme version of the purist position insisted Irish music came from "laws of nature and the law of the land which in this case is the island of Ireland." Flute player Seamus Tansey found it rooted in

> the singing of the birds, the ancient chants of our forefathers, the calls of the wild animals in the lonely countryside, the drone of the bees, the galloping hooves of the wild horses . . . [t]he wind the rain, the flowing rivers that shaped the mind and passion of our ancient forefathers, inspiring them to harness together all those sounds of animal, mineral, bird and insect so as it moulded itself into a melody which is and always will be.

It took some effort of imagination to insist on these rural origins in Dublin in 1996, but it takes even more so if we consider O'Neill's collecting efforts in the rough urban neighborhoods of Chicago, his eager embrace of technology, his use of police administrative procedures and authority, his systematic appropriation of tunes held as personal possessions, and his project of arresting and standardizing the face to face exchange of tunes. One has to ignore the influence of the minstrel show and the history of challenge dancing and jig contests on waterfronts and river towns. It takes considerable blindness to ignore all that and talk about droning bees and mountain streams. Further, if we consider the records that came out of the US in the early twentieth century as industrial objects, mass-produced, the product of the intense and vibrant commercial world of New York, speaking to and influenced by the world of swing dancing and pop music, then what do we make of the arrival of banjos, pianos, and swing guitar to Ireland? Tansey cited "the pipe music of Patsy Touhey" as "music handed down to us by our ancient forefathers." But Touhey, O'Neill's favorite piper, left Ireland at age three and spent his entire adult life performing Irishness on the vaudeville stage. In 1904, in fact, Irish actors at the St. Louis World's Fair refused to share the stage with Touhey because they found his version of Irishness inauthentic and offensive. How does the thirty-six infant months he spent in Ireland "outvote" the fifty years he spent on the American stage?[22]

The answer, of course, is it does not—Touhey played music in dialogue with multiple worlds, the world of his Irish background and community, the world of Irish American in industrial cities, and the world of American popular culture writ large. O'Neill's experiences embodied this dialogue between past and present, the industrial and the traditional. He produced a body of work that made it easier to imagine Irish music sealed off from other influences, self-contained, but even he could not entirely efface the effort that construction took, and he made room, especially at the end of his life, not just for "the ancient chants of our forefathers" but also the "pioneer Paganini's," the vaudeville performers, and even James Reese Europe's band.

Much of the story of the Irish in America could apply to any group of immigrants, working to balance the culture of their birth with the New World. O'Neill established a catalog and scholarly record of Irishness, but he also wanted to imagine Irishness in America as a set of practices, a body of knowledge and muscle memories. You could learn the music and learn the dances, go to competitions and win medals, and internalize the tunes, making it more than just decorative but, at the same time, unlikely to hinder American success. He saw the Irishness of Irish Americans vanishing, eroded by the multiple attractions of American popular culture, and he wanted to find a way to preserve it. He used the techniques of the police because he knew them well.

In 1998 the Cork County Council placed a memorial plaque at the Tralibane Bridge, with the musical score to two of his favorite tunes, the hornpipe "Chief O'Neill's Favorite" and the mournful air "Tralibane Bridge." Two years later, "The Captain Francis O'Neill Memorial Company," organized by local music lovers, commissioned a statue of O'Neill, looking out over the beautiful valley toward his childhood home, holding a flute and about to sound a tune.[23]

A statue closer to O'Neill's character might pose him sitting behind the fiddler, attentively memorizing his tune and poised to write it down without asking permission. O'Neill waxed nostalgic about Tralibane, but at seventeen he could not leave quickly enough. His work, though it concerned and memorialized the music of rural people, was decidedly urban work. It depended on the poverty of colonized Ireland and the flow of emigrants that poverty initiated, but also on his capacity to ignore his own position in the colonial economy in which his family thrived. Only the intense urban concentration of population in Chicago made it possible; his ability to organize and collect music stemmed from the authority of the badge and the administrative technologies of the modern police. He made a vital record of immigrant community but ended up remaking that community in the process.

# Acknowledgments

This book began in collaborations with my colleague Matt Karush. He read many drafts while busily productive with his own work. Deborah Kaplan's wise and judicious edits have made this book vastly more readable. I owe a special debt to Mary Ellen (Eileen) Hawkey, gracious and welcoming host and keen, perceptive, empathic reader. Eileen's sister Anne, herself a historian of immigration, read drafts as well, and together the Finn sisters explained the Irish context to a Yank. Our family is enriched by the relation to the Finns of Saltmill, County Wexford, smart, kind, and interesting people.

Professor Aileen Dillane, in Ireland, let me "give out" about various ideas that steered close to her own. She is one of the few scholars to look at O'Neill in a more broadly critical way and had a pronounced influence on this book. Lucy Salyer shared her own work on Fenians and citizenship and indulged me with conversation. Musician and activist Marta Cook, in Chicago, offered many sharp and perceptive insights into the Irish musical community and its dense and complicated history. Helen O'Shea's accounts of the hierarchy of Irish traditional music dramatically shaped my understanding. Exchanges with Breandán Mac Suibhne and Lillis Ó Laoire greatly illuminated the context of Irish political and cultural economy. Tim Meagher suffered many conversations about this book and corrected many faults: his contributions have been extensive. I plagued the inbox of Charlie McGovern. Terrence Winch and George O'Brien let me join their lunches and tolerated my observations with patient humor. Jennifer O'Riordan explained Irish grammar while Liam Mac Mathúna graciously translated Douglas Hyde's diary passages on O'Neill. Paul DeGrae kindly shared his own excellent research into O'Neill's collecting methods. Luke Gibbons shared parts of his forthcoming work on police surveillance in Joyce's *Ulysses*. Emails with Seamus Kelly and Aileen Saunders, pertaining to their biography of John Ennis, in progress, offered a wider sense of O'Neill's Irish community. Timothy Mennel, the editor of this volume, worked to make the book more focused and concise. The Department of History and Art History at George Mason University provided the funds for a research trip to Ireland. Kerby Miller, the dean of historians of Irish America, generously offered his sharp insights into the final draft.

I must especially thank the gracious and welcoming staff at the Irish Traditional Music Archives; Sadhbh Nic Ionnraic, Maeve Gebruers, Róisín Conlon, and Alan Woods, who warned me about "stray sods" while tramping through Tralibane. Emmet Gill at Na Píobairí Uilleann let me ask him dumb questions at length and offered only smart answers in return. Nicholas Carolan, a gentleman and a scholar, met with me at a very early stage in my research when I had little idea of the full extent of what I didn't know. Mr. Carolan and the staff at ITMA generously shared his research notes for his 1997 biography of O'Neill, *A Harvest Saved,* including many sources impossible to find elsewhere. That book remains essential reading for anyone interested in O'Neill. Melissa Jay continued helping with research in the Henry Chapman Mercer Papers after COVID-19 shut down access. Nick Whitmer and I had many exchanges about O'Neill and his community; his diligently and carefully researched website, *Lives of the Pipers,* is indispensable to anyone interested in Irish music and musicians. Sean Gavin shared his keen insights into the structures and patterns of Irish dance tunes. Thanks to Robert Harris for his delightful blog on West Cork, https://roaringwaterjournal.com/, and for his photo of O'Neill's birthplace.

My cousin Tim O'Malley put me up in Chicago and endured bad flute and whistle playing. Mary Mooney Lesch offered a crucial look at O'Neill's scrapbooks and mementos and generously shared her insights about her great-grandfather. She published, along with Chicago historian Ellen Skerrett, *Chief O'Neill's Sketchy Recollections of an Eventful Life in Chicago* in 2008. It covers his police career primarily and is an extremely valuable source for anyone interested not just in the chief but in Chicago politics. Leslie Martin of the Chicago History Museum helped me navigate its research collections. The kind and perceptive Father Alex Auziayuk shared the history of St. Thomas the Apostle Church and the O'Neills' presence there.

My greatest debt in every sense is to Kathleen Trainor.

# Notes

## Introduction

Number 1640 in *O'Neill's Music of Ireland* (Chicago: Lyon & Healy, 1903), attributed to John Gillan, and number 867 in *O'Neill's The Dance Music of Ireland: 1001 Gems* (Chicago: Lyon & Healy, 1907). The tune appeared in R. M. Levey, *First Collection of the Dance Music of Ireland* (London, 1858). O'Neill included a variant with a third section in his last book, *Waifs and Strays of Gaelic Melody: Comprising Forgotten Favorites, Worthy Variants, and Tunes Not Previously Printed* (Chicago: Lyon & Healy, 1922), 171.

1. W. T. Stead, *If Christ Came to Chicago! A Plea for the Union of All Who Love in the Service of All Who Suffer* (Chicago: Laird & Lee, 1894), 17; Franklin Mathews, "Wide Open Chicago," *Harper's Weekly*, January 22, 1898, 90; Francis O'Neill, *Chief O'Neill's Sketchy Recollections of an Eventful Life in Chicago*, ed. Ellen Skerrett and Mary Lesch (Evanston, IL: Northwestern University Press, 2008), 92.

2. *Chicago Inter Ocean*, June 16, 1901, 46. Newspapers found O'Neill's musical hobby charming and alluded to it fairly often.

3. Lincoln Steffens, *The Shame of the Cities* (New York, 1904), 242–44; O'Neill mentions this in *Sketchy Recollections*, 109–10. The Hoyt King threat also appeared in the *Chicago Tribune*, December 19, 1903, 2. King seems to have something of a moral collapse, and Steffens describes the Municipal Voters League letting him go. He was widely attacked in the *Chicago Inter Ocean* in 1905: see, for example, September 3, 16.

4. Kevin Henry quoted in Sara S. Goek, "'Looking for That Pot of Gold': The Transnational Life of Kevin Henry," *Éire-Ireland* 51, no. 1–2 (2016): 92–117.

5. An extensive literature on Ireland and postcolonialism began in the 1990s. See Colin Graham and Richard Kirkland, *Ireland and Cultural Theory: The Mechanics of Authenticity* (New York: Palgrave Macmillan, 1999). See also Colin

Graham, *Deconstructing Ireland: Identity, Theory, Culture* (Edinburgh: Edinburgh University Press, 2001); Leith Ann Davis, *Music, Postcolonialism, and Gender: The Construction of Irish National Identity, 1724–1874* (Notre Dame, IN: University of Notre Dame Press, 2006); David Lloyd, *Anomalous States: Irish Writing and the Post-colonial Moment* (Durham, NC: Duke University Press, 1993); Peter D. O'Neill and David Lloyd, eds., *The Black and Green Atlantic: Cross-Currents of the African and Irish Diasporas* (New York: Palgrave Macmillan, 2009); Michael G. Malouf, *Transatlantic Solidarities: Irish Nationalism and Caribbean Poetics* (Charlottesville: University of Virginia Press, 2009); Aaron C. Keebaugh, "Irish Music and Home-Rule Politics, 1800–1922" (PhD diss., University of Florida, 2011); Martina Relihan, "A Retrospective and Prospective Look at the 'Happy English Child': The Applicability of Postcolonial Theory to the British Government's Education Policy in Ireland in the Late Nineteenth and Early Twentieth Centuries," *Irish Educational Studies* 24, no. 2–3 (2005): 123–31.

6. Francis O'Neill to Seamus Ó Floinn, October 15, 1918, Nicholas Carolan Collection, Irish Traditional Music Archives, Dublin (hereafter ITMA Carolan).

7. The Irish musician and historian Breandán Breathnach said of O'Neill's 1907 *Dance Music of Ireland*: "it became the bible of the traditional player, so that on hearing the question about a tune, 'is it in the book?' one could be certain it was the *Dance Music* the questioner had in mind." Breathnach argued that O'Neill developed "confidence and self-respect in musicians by making them aware of the history of their music and the value of the heritage which they had in their possession." "It is hard, if not impossible," wrote Nicholas Carolan, "to imagine what Irish traditional music might be like today if Francis O'Neill had not lived." Carolan quote in the introduction to O'Neill, *Sketchy Recollections*, xiii; Nicholas Carolan, *A Harvest Saved: Francis O'Neill and Irish Music in Chicago* (Cork: Ossian, 1997).

8. Quotes from the introduction to Francis O'Neill, *O'Neill's Music of Ireland* (Chicago: Lyon & Healy, 1903).

9. Francis O'Neill to Seamus O'Floinn, October 15, 1918, ITMA Carolan.

10. Francis O'Neill, *Irish Folk Music: A Fascinating Hobby* (Chicago: Regan, 1910), 126.

11. Francis O'Neill, *Irish Minstrels and Musicians: With Numerous Dissertations on Related Subjects* (Chicago: Regan, 1913), 102; O'Neill, *Irish Folk Music*, 87, 98, 123. The mirage analogy comes from Helen O'Shea, *The Making of Irish Traditional Music* (Cork: Cork University Press, 2008), 119: "The well-documented authenticity of the area's music began to recede, like a mirage, as I advanced upon it." O'Shea's book eloquently describes the problems with the idea of authenticity in Irish music.

12. *Chicago Tribune*, August 25, 1901, 38. Thanks to Mary Mooney Lesch, O'Neill's great-granddaughter, for pointing out his methodical nature.

## Chapter One

When affliction beyond the power of pen to describe cast its withering blight on our home, this weird and fascinating air obsessed my waking hours for days un-numbered. To me no other strains in the whole range of wailing dirges so deeply touches the heart or so feelingly voices the language of sadness and despair." Francis O'Neill, *Irish Folk Music: A Fascinating Hobby* (Chicago: Regan, 1910), 77.

1. For an example of how reform efforts typically progressed before, during, and after O'Neill's tenure, see "Chronology of a Comedy," *Chicago Tribune*, March 24, 1904, 1. In this case Sadie Winters, a housekeeper, claimed that Lieutenant Roger Mulcahy had demanded she buy tickets for the policemen's ball, telling her there would be trouble if she did not. After repeated warnings, her employer's home was raided and she was arrested. *Chicago Tribune*, December 12, 1903, 2. To no one's surprise, roughly a month later the police trial board exonerated Mulcahy, claiming that someone had tried "to put up a job on him," that is, to frame him. *Chicago Tribune*, January 12, 1904, 3.

2. "I was music mad": Francis O'Neill to Seamus O'Floinn, October 15, 1918. In the Carolan Collection, Irish Traditional Music Archive, Dublin (hereafter ITMA Carolan). O'Neill's account of the fire appears in Chicago Police Department, *Report of the General Superintendent of Police of the City of Chicago, to the City Council*, 1903, 25–27; and in *Chicago Tribune*, December 31, 1903, 1.

3. *Chicago Tribune*, December 31, 1903, 3. Timothy grass was native to Ireland and grew well there. It was brought to the US in the eighteenth century and naturalized quickly. In the mid-nineteenth century, agricultural experts in Ireland began stressing its value as a hay crop. This is right at the time when O'Neill's older brother John was prospering in the cattle business, just before O'Neill emigrated. See Peter Lawson and Son, *Treatise on the Cultivated Grasses and Other Herbage and Forage Plants* (Edinburgh: P. Lawson Son, 1853), 15–16; William Fetherstonhaugh, *The Handbook, Or Agricultural Catechism for the Small Farmers of Ireland* (Dublin: Farmer's Gazette, 1846), 33–34; William Townsend, *Directions on Practical Agriculture, for the Working Farmers in Ireland* (Dublin: William Curry, 1843), 67. It seems reasonable that O'Neill would have heard it discussed and seen it growing. It is equally possible he was thinking of fields of Timothy growing near Chicago.

4. Francis O'Neill, *Chief O'Neill's Sketchy Recollections of an Eventful Life in Chi-*

*cago*, ed. Ellen Skerrett and Mary Lesch (Evanston, IL: Northwestern University Press, 2008), 3; John Crowley, William I. Smyth, and Mike Murphy, eds., *Atlas of the Great Irish Famine* (Cork: Cork University Press, 2012), 6, 38; Cormac Ó Gráda, *Black 47 and Beyond: The Great Irish Famine* (Princeton, NJ: Princeton University Press, 1999), 200.

5. A standard estimate suggests a male laborer ate up to 14 pounds of potatoes a day. Crowley et al., *Atlas*, 41–43; Ó Gráda, *Black 47*, chap. 1; Christine Kinealy, *A Death-Dealing Famine: The Great Hunger in Ireland* (London: Pluto Press, 1997), 49; Breandán Mac Suibhne, *Subjects Lacking Words? The Gray Zone of the Great Famine* (Hamden, CT: Quinnipiac University Press, 2017).

6. Exact numbers are impossible to determine: the figure of roughly a million deaths between 1847 and 1851 appears often, followed by as many emigrations in the same five-year period. Irish Americans have often wanted to claim a higher ranking in the victim Olympics than their present status in the US suggests. For a skeptical account of the famine's magnitude, one that situates it in a global context, see Liam Kennedy, *Unhappy the Land: The Most Oppressed People Ever, the Irish?* (Sallins, Co. Kildare: Merrion Press, 2016), chap. 1 For a concise and powerful general account of the demoralization of the famine, the way it deranged empathy, see Mac Suibhne, *Subjects Lacking Words?* Exact figures on population loss in Ireland are hard to come by, due to relatively poor recordkeeping. See Kevin Kenny, *The American Irish*, Studies in Modern History (New York: Routledge, 2014); Kerby A. Miller, *Emigrants and Exiles: Ireland and the Irish Exodus to North America* (New York: Oxford University Press, 1985), 280–344; Ó Gráda, *Black 47*, chap. 7; and Crowley et al., *Atlas*.

7. Crowley et al., *Atlas*, 368; Miller, *Emigrants and Exiles*, 284.

8. Sir John Forbes, *Memorandums of a Tour in Ireland* (London: Smith, Elder, 1853), 79.

9. Kevin Hourihan, "Town Growth in West Cork: Bantry 1600–1960," *Journal of the Cork Historical and Archeological Society* 82 (December 1977): 83–97; John East, *Glimpses of Ireland in 1847* (Bath, England: Hamilton, Adams, 1847), 38.

10. Phillip O'Neill, in his seventies when he gave his oral account, was the son of Francis's older brother John. He claimed this mass grave lay "in my grandfather's land in Derrygrenaugh." "Stories of the Famine around Skibbereen," *Dúchas.ie*, accessed May 14, 2021, https://www.duchas.ie/en/cbes/4798759/4795966/5150032. Google maps shows this as "Derryinagh," on the other side of a hill from Tralibane. For accounts of "hungry grass," see https://www.duchas.ie/en/src?q=hungry+grass.

11. On laissez-faire, see Patrick Brantlinger, "The Famine," *Victorian Literature and Culture* 32, no. 1 (2004): 195, 198. Quote about "England's pantry" from Hugh Dorian, Breandán Mac Suibhne, and David Dickson, *The Outer Edge of Ulster:*

*A Memoir of Social Life in Nineteenth-Century Donegal* (Notre Dame, IN: University of Notre Dame Press, 2001). Page 68 reads: "Such is poor Ireland—England's pantry—so that not only the egg laid by the hen must be sent there but also the wild animals, which ... must go to the body already daintily stuffed. The egg the Irish-born peasant must deny himself to meet taxation."

12. Brantlinger, "Famine," 195, 198. An excellent account of the famine as a tool for "reform" of Ireland appears in Christine Kinealy, *This Great Calamity: The Great Irish Famine: 1845–52* (Dublin: Gill & Macmillan, 2006), quote from p. 485.

13. George Petrie, *The Petrie Collection of the Ancient Music of Ireland: Arranged for the Piano-Forte* (Dublin, 1855), 31–32; Ó Gráda, *Black 47*, 222.

14. Francis O'Neill, *Irish Minstrels and Musicians: With Numerous Dissertations on Related Subjects* (Chicago: Regan, 1913), 108, 112.

15. *Griffith's Valuation*, a systematic survey of land ownership and leasing in all of Ireland, was correlated to the Ordnance Survey map, a six-inch-to-the-mile survey of the island conducted mostly in the 1830s. Richard Griffith surveyed County Cork in 1853: the complete survey took more than a decade to finish. Francis's father appears as "John Neill" in *Griffiths Valuation of Tenements, County of Cork*, Barony of West Carbery (west Division), Parish of Caheragh, Townland of Trawlebane, 11, 23. *Griffith's Valuation* is now searchable by name at several sites, including that of the National Library of Ireland, http://www.askaboutireland.ie/griffith-valuation/. The "land war" of the 1870s made it possible for tenants to purchase the land they held.

16. James S. Donnelly Jr., *The Land and the People of Nineteenth-Century Cork: The Rural Economy and the Land Question* (London: Taylor & Francis, 2017), 57, 78; Miller, Emigrants and Exiles, 289; Crowley et al., Atlas, 265–76.

17. Charles Ffrench, *Biographical History of the American Irish in Chicago* (Chicago: American Biographical, 1897), 308. O'Neill referred to this appropriation of wages in his account to Ffrench, and then never again. On resenting the tillage fields, see Francis O'Neill, *Chief O'Neill's Sketchy Recollections of an Eventful Life in Chicago*, ed. Ellen Skerrett and Mary Lesch (Evanston, IL: Northwestern University Press, 2008), 3. On the centrality of cattle, see Conor McCabe, *Sins of the Father: Tracing the Decisions That Shaped the Irish Economy* (Dublin: History Press Ireland, 2011), Kindle ed. loc. 56.

18. Denis McLaughlin, "The Irish Christian Brothers and the National Board of Education: Challenging the Myths," *History of Education* 37, no. 1 (2008): 43–70. See also Michael C. Coleman, "'Eyes Big as Bowls with Fear and Wonder': Children's Responses to the Irish National Schools, 1850–1922," *Proceedings of the Royal Irish Academy: Archaeology, Celtic Studies, History, Linguistics, Literature* 98C, no. 5 (1998): 177, 180, 183; John Coolahan, "Education and Ethnicity," *Paedagogica Historica* 37, no. 1 (2001): 22.

19. Douglas Hyde, *A Literary History of Ireland from Earliest Times to the Present Day* (London: T. F. Unwin, 1906), 635, 636; Coleman, "'Eyes Big as Bowls,'" 177, 180, 183. See also Coolahan, "Education and Ethnicity," 22.

20. *Chicago Tribune*, April 30, 1901, 3. Textbooks included James William M'Gauley, *Lectures on Natural Philosophy* (Dublin: A. Thom & Sons, 1851); *Biographical Sketches of Eminent British Poets* (Dublin: A. Thom & Sons, 1857); and *Fifth Book of Lessons for the Use of Schools* (Edinburgh: William P. Nimmo, 1865). The preceding were all prepared specifically for use in the Irish National Schools and date to the period of O'Neill's attendance. For a general history of the National Schools, see Donald H. Akenson, *The Irish Education Experiment: The National System of Education in the Nineteenth Century*, Studies in Irish History, 2d, vol. 7 (London: Routledge, 2014).

21. O'Neill, *Sketchy Recollections*, 4.

22. O'Neill, *Sketchy Recollections*, 160, 3. The "five foot shelf" phrase refers to the fifty-volume series of the Harvard Classics, marketed after 1910 as "Dr. Eliot's five foot shelf of books." O'Neill's phrase indicates they had a substantial collection, more than fifty volumes, of significant serious books.

23. Paul Huddie, "Irish Society and the Military," in *The Crimean War and Irish Society* (Liverpool: Liverpool University Press, 2015), 120–54.

24. *The Eviction: A Scene from Life in Ireland*, from the celebrated painting by William Henry Powell (New York: J. T. Foley, ©1871). At Prints and Photographs Division, Library of Congress, and online at https://lccn.loc.gov/2004669163.

25. Hugh Dorian, Breandán Mac Suibhne, and David Dickson, *The Outer Edge of Ulster: A Memoir of Social Life in Nineteenth-Century Donegal* (Notre Dame, IN: University of Notre Dame Press, 2001), 191–92. Conor McCabe, in *Sins of the Fathers*, describes "Strong farmer" cattle-raising families like the O'Neills as a "comprador" class, the class that cooperates with colonial authority.

26. Francis O'Neill, *Irish Folk Music: A Fascinating Hobby* (Chicago: Regan, 1910), 142.

27. On Moore and colonialism, see Leith Davis, *Music, Postcolonialism and Gender: The Construction of Irish National Identity, 1724–1874* (Notre Dame, IN: University of Notre Dame Press, 2006). For claims that Moore influenced Stephen Foster, see William H. Williams, *'Twas Only an Irishman's Dream: The Image of Ireland and the Irish in American Popular Song Lyrics, 1800–1920* (Urbana: University of Illinois Press, 1996), 37–38, 45; and Jon W. Finson, *The Voices That Are Gone: Themes in Nineteenth-Century American Popular Song* (New York: Oxford University Press, 1994). On minstrel shows, see Douglas C. Riach, "Blacks and Blackface on the Irish Stage, 1830–60," *Journal of American Studies* 7, no. 3 (1973): 232. By 1846, Irish newspapers had already noticed a distinc-

tion between the more refined stage minstrel shows, free from "the coarseness and vulgarity which has banished nigger dancing and singing from the stage to the taverns and singing houses." This tells us that elements of the American minstrel show had already entered popular culture, at least in the cities, when O'Neill was a boy. See also Margaret Greaves, "Slave Ships and Coffin Ships: Transatlantic Exchanges in Irish-American Blackface Minstrelsy." *Comparative American Studies: An International Journal* 10, no. 1 (2012): 78–94.

28. On the relative cosmopolitanism of County Clare and Ireland in general, see Gearóid Ó hAllmhuráin, *Flowing Tides: History and Memory in an Irish Sound-scape* (New York: Oxford University Press, 2016); and on blackface, 54–55.

29. O'Neill, *Irish Minstrels,* 153, 448; Colm Kerrigan, "Irish Temperance and US Anti-Slavery: Father Mathew and the Abolitionists," *History Workshop,* no. 31 (1991): 105–19; Ó hAllmhuráin, *Flowing Tides,* 59–60, 79; John Borgonovo, "Political Percussions: Cork Brass Bands and the Irish Revolution, 1914–1922," in *Public Performances,* ed. Jack Santino, Studies in the Carnivalesque and Ritualesque (Boulder: University Press of Colorado, 2017), 94; Fintan Lane, "Music and Violence in Working Class Cork: The 'Band Nuisance,' 1879–82," *Saothar (Dublin)* 24 (1999): 17–31; Nicholas Carolan, *A Harvest Saved: Francis O'Neill and Irish Music in Chicago* (Cork: Ossian, 1997), 7.

30. Edward Bunting, *The Ancient Music of Ireland,* 1796, Internet Archive, accessed October 31, 2019, http://archive.org/details/imslp-ancient-music-of-ireland -bunting-edward. For a general history of the collecting of Irish music, see Martin W. Dowling, *Traditional Music and Irish Society: Historical Perspectives* (Burlington, VT: Ashgate, 2014).

31. Leith Davis, "Sequels of Colonialism: Edward Bunting's Ancient Irish Music," *Nineteenth-Century Contexts* 23, no. 1 (2001): 29–57; Bunting, *Ancient Music of Ireland,* 63; Fintan Vallely, "Heads Up! The Traditional Music Revival, Irish National Identity, and Cultural Cringe," *Foilsiú; New York* 2, no. 1 (Spring 2002): 7–18.

32. Arthur Young, *Arthur Young's Tour in Ireland (1776–1779)* (London: George Bell & Sons, 1892), 366; Gearóid Ó Hallmhuráin, "'Amhrán an Ghorta': The Great Famine and Irish Traditional Music," *New Hibernia Review—Iris eireannach nua* 3, no. 1 (1999): 19–44.

33. O'Neill, *Irish Minstrels,* chap. 29; Breandán Breathnach, *Folk Music and Dances of Ireland: A Comprehensive Study Examining the Basic Elements of Irish Folk Music and Dance Traditions* (Cork: Ossian, 1996), 41–42, and chap. 5.

34. O'Neill, *Irish Folk Music,* 272. For an example of an itinerant piper working well into the twentieth century, see Howard Marshall and Ben Taylor, *Out of Darkness: The Blind Piper of Inagh* (Norwich, UK: Cottier Press, 2016), on the life of Garret Barry.

35. O'Neill, *Irish Folk Music*, 13, 14; O'Neill, *Irish Minstrels*, 230.

36. O'Neill, *Irish Minstrels*, 410. O'Neill described Timothy Downing as a "gentleman farmer." *Griffith's Valuation* shows him owning two houses he let to tenants.

37. O'Neill, *Irish Folk Music*, 12. For O'Neill describing his parents as a source, see also Francis O'Neill to A. P. Graves, November 20, 1906, in Carolan Collection, Irish Traditional Music Archives, Dublin.

38. O'Neill, *Irish Minstrels*, 289–90.

39. O'Neill, *Irish Minstrels*, 150, 432.

40. O'Neill, *Irish Folk Music*, 10.

41. O'Neill, *Irish Minstrels*, 23. On the "devotional Revolution," see S. J. Connolly, *Priests and People in Pre-Famine Ireland 1780–1845*, 2nd ed. (Dublin: Four Courts Press, 2001); and Cara Delay, "The Devotional Revolution on the Local Level: Parish Life in Post-Famine Ireland," *U.S. Catholic Historian* 22, no. 3 (2004): 41–60.

42. Helena Wulff, *Dancing at the Crossroads: Memory and Mobility in Ireland* (New York: Berghahn Books, 2007), 10–11; Miller, *Emigrants and Exiles*, 75.

43. O'Neill, *Irish Minstrels*, 426; Sean Williams, *Focus: Irish Traditional Music* (London: Routledge, 2009); Breathnach, *Folk Music and Dances*.

44. Quote from James Kieran Fielding, *The Resurrection of a Nation* (Chicago: Mayer & Miller, 1934), 35. For a general description of Irish traditional music as practiced today, see Williams, *Focus*; and Breathnach, *Folk Music and Dances*.

45. An early attempt to define what's "Irish" about Irish music appears in Annie W. Patterson, "The Characteristic Traits of Irish Music," *Proceedings of the Musical Association* 23, no. 1 (1896): 91–111. Patterson's claims about nonstandard pitch were echoed in Richard Henebry, *A Handbook of Irish Music* (Cork: Cork University Press, 1928); and in Helen Shea, "(Re)Interpreting Fieldwork: Jos Koning in East Clare," *Éire-Ireland (St. Paul)* 54, no. 1 (2019). On the "C supernatural," see Tes Slominski, *Trad Nation: Gender, Sexuality, and Race in Irish Traditional Music* (Middletown, CT: Wesleyan University Press, 2020), 123. On the idea of a different scale in Irish music, see Richard Henebry, *Irish Music: Being an Examination of the Matter of Scales, Modes, and Keys, with Practical Instructions and Examples for Players* (Cork: Ái Cliaí: An Cló-Cumann, 1903). Williams, *Focus*, gives a lively and amusing survey of Irish traditional music and its practice in the past and now. For a fascinating account of efforts to make Irish music non-European, see Aileen Dillane and Matthew Noone, "Irish Music Orientalism," *New Hibernia Review* 20, no. 1 (2016): 121–37.

46. Frederick Douglass, *My Bondage and My Freedom* (New York: Miller, Orton & Mulligan, 1855), 98.

47. Christine Kinealy, *Frederick Douglass and Ireland: In His Own Words*, vol. 2 (London: Routledge, 2018), 79.

48. Kevin Kenny, *The American Irish*, Studies in Modern History (New York: Routledge, 2014), 83–87, 118–19; Crowley et al., *Atlas*, 64–99.

49. O'Neill, *Irish Minstrels*, 23.

50. Matthew Arnold, *On the Study of Celtic Literature* (London, 1867), 100–106.

51. O'Neill, *Sketchy Recollections*, 5. The Cork School of Design had fostered the talent of a young Irish boy slightly older than O'Neill, Thomas Hovendon, who also emigrated to the US, where he became one of the most famous painters of the late nineteenth century. Hovendon's painting of John Brown on the way to the gallows was widely reproduced, and at the 1893 Columbian Exposition, held a few blocks from O'Neill's home, visitors waiting in long lines to weep before Hovendon's *Breaking Home Ties* (1890).

52. O'Neill, *Sketchy Recollections*, 37, 5.

53. The memorial, a tall Celtic cross with ornate Celtic knot-style carvings, is in the Caheragh Old Cemetery on the river Ilen north of Skibbereen. The first name one sees, reading the marker, is "Erected by Captain Daniel Francis O'Neill Chicago, USA."

54. O'Neill, *Sketchy Recollections*, 7.

55. O'Neill *Sketchy Recollections*, 8; Denis McLaughlin, "The Irish Christian Brothers and the National Board of Education: Challenging the Myths," *History of Education* 37, no. 1 (2008): 43–70.

56. "Cabin Boy Becomes Police Chief," *Irish Independent*, January 31, 1936; Letter from Mary Wade, O'Neill's granddaughter, to Nicholas Carolan, October 20, 1997, ITMA Carolan. O'Neill gave a similarly implausible version to the *Chicago Daily Tribune*, April 30, 1901, 3, shortly after his appointment as chief of police in 1901. O'Neill "had letters of introduction" to Bishop Delaney in Cork. The bishop suggested he become one of the Christian Brothers of the Catholic Church or that he should be a teacher in one of the schools of Cork, and gave O'Neill a span of time to make up his mind. Some days later, O'Neill "decided that he would accept the advice of Bishop Delaney and started to his house." According to this account, O'Neill got lost in the streets of Cork, wandering in confusion: "finally he gave up and returned to his lodging-house. The next day the Bishop left the city and the failure to keep that engagement made it necessary for young O'Neill to give up the idea of becoming a monk." In this version, O'Neill expressed ambivalence about a religious life, but once he decides to accept the offer from the Christian Brothers he becomes unable to navigate back to a home he had already visited and apparently unable to ask directions.

57. Patrick O'Brien, *Birth and Adoption: A Book of Prose and Poetry* (The author, 1904). The book is a collection of O'Brien's poetry along with various essays and articles by and about O'Brien. The undated sign sheet for "The Little Shamrock Green" is collected at the Irish Traditional Music Archives in Dub-

lin, online at https://www.itma.ie/digital-library/text/little-shamrock-green/.
Jane Rourke, a twelve-year-old girl, remembered adults singing it in the 1930s
and transcribed it as part of The Schools Collection, Volume 0933, Page 198,
online at https://www.duchas.ie/en/cbes/4758589/4757167.

58. O'Brien, *Birth and Adoption*, 6. On the Fenian invasion, see *New York Times*,
May 26, 1870, 1. This account does not mention O'Brien. Niall Whehlan, *The
Dynamiters: Irish Nationalism and Political Violence in the Wider World, 1867–
1900* (Cambridge: Cambridge University Press, 2012), 127–28; *Baltimore Sun*,
January 12, 1885, 5.

59. O'Brien, *Birth and Adoption*, 7, 51, 174. *The Minneapolis Irish Standard*, in its
obituary on March 1, 1919, called him "one of the greatest exponents of Irish
freedom in this country," a sentiment O'Brien would have hastened to confirm.

60. O'Brien, *Birth and Adoption*, 24–25, 15, 248.

61. Ó Gráda, *Black 47*, 229.

62. O'Neill, *Irish Folk Music*, 11.

63. O'Neill, *Irish Minstrels*, 108; Howard W. Odum, "Folk-Song and Folk-Poetry as
Found in the Secular Songs of the Southern Negroes," *Journal of American Folklore* 24, no. 94 (1911): 351–96; Cecelia Conway, "African American Music in Appalachia: Black Banjo Songsters in Appalachia," *Black Music Research Journal* 23,
no. 1–2 (2003): 149–66; and Barry Lee Pearson's notes accompanying a recording, *Classic African American Songsters: From Smithsonian Folkways* (Washington, DC: Smithsonian Folkways, 2014), https://media.smithsonianfolkways
.org/liner_notes/smithsonian_folkways/SFW40211.pdf.

64. O'Neill, *Sketchy Recollections*, 8. *Anne*, according to the *Kerry Evening Post*, was
a 303 ton vessel captained by P. H. Watson. In February it had arrived in Bally-
cotton Bay, near Cork, "in a very disabled state" thanks to a gale. "Her pumps
had become choked and there were five feet of water in her hold." The cargo,
maize from Odessa, was "much damaged." *Kerry Evening Post*, February 4, 1865.
There is some slight reason to believe O'Neill went back to Ireland for his
father's funeral: Nicholas Carolan suggests this in his biography of O'Neill, *A
Harvest Saved*. One account in the *Chicago Tribune*, April 30, 1901, 3, describes
O'Neill as sailing for the Sandwich Islands from New York, then returning to
Ireland for several months: "a few months there and he decided to return again
to America." No other account of his life mentions this. If it happened, O'Neill
omitted it from his memoir and his surviving letters.

## Chapter Two

"'Big Pat's' tones were clear and full, for his wind was inexhaustible. From
his playing I memorized the double jigs 'Out on the Ocean,' the 'Fisherman's

Widow,' the 'Cliffs of Moher,' and several others." Francis O'Neill, *Irish Folk Music: A Fascinating Hobby* (Chicago: Regan, 1910), 19.

1. "Cabin Boy Becomes Police Chief," *Irish Independent,* January 31, 1936, 9. *Chicago Daily Tribune,* August 25, 1901, made a similar point, claiming that O'Neill's parents "could not make up their minds as to whether their boy would be a pirate or a priest."

2. Francis O'Neill to John G. O'Neill, November 16, 1916, Carolan Collection, Irish Traditional Music Archives, Dublin (hereafter ITMA Carolan); Emily M. Brewer, "Rogue War Hero to Naval Role Model: Robert Southey's Life of Nelson (1813)," *a/b: Auto/Biography Studies* 26, no. 2 (2011): 189; Richard Lovell Edgeworth, *Essays on Professional Education* (London: J. Johnson, 1809), 124. My thanks to my colleague Teresa Michal for these references. Francis O'Neill, *Chief O'Neill's Sketchy Recollections of an Eventful Life in Chicago,* ed. Ellen Skerrett and Mary Lesch (Evanston, IL: Northwestern University Press, 2008), 28.

3. Richard Henry Dana, *Two Years before the Mast: A Personal Narrative* (Boston: Houghton Mifflin, 1911), 44. All quotations here come from the 1911 edition.

4. Jeffrey L. Amestoy, *Slavish Shore: The Odyssey of Richard Henry Dana Jr.* (Cambridge, MA: Harvard University Press, 2015), 66–67.

5. Dana, *Two Years,* 322.

6. Dana, *Two Years,* 125.

7. O'Neill, *Sketchy Recollections,* 8–9; *Jane Duncan* described in *New York Times,* May 15, 1863, 8; September 22, 1863, 8. On the launch of the ship, see "April 14th 1860—SO—Launch of the Brig Jane Duncan from Potts Shipyard, Seaham," accessed November 18, 2019, https://seahampast.co.uk/index.php?option= com_content&view=article&id=130:appril-14th-1860-so-launch-of-the-brig -jane-duncan-from-potts-shipyard-seaham&catid=13:1860&Itemid=4. Some of the material in this chapter matches things he wrote in other places, but O'Neill wrote this memoir in his eighties, and it includes errors of memory. For example, O'Neill said he was by law too old to apprentice in peacetime, yet here he apprenticed to *Jane Duncan.* He gives two mentions of "Fred, the Belgian": O'Neill sees him for the last time, he says, as he boards a ship in Liverpool, but two years later Fred appears as crew mate in a ship to Hawaii. He will misremember several names in minor ways, for example, recalling the surname of Captain Bursley as "Burliegh." These understandable mistakes remind us of the larger difference between memoir and verifiable fact.

8. O'Neill, *Sketchy Recollections,* 12.

9. O'Neill, *Sketchy Recollections,* 15–16.

10. Carmen Tunney and Pat Nugent, "Liverpool and the Great Irish Famine" in *Atlas of the Great Irish Famine*, ed. John Crowley, William I. Smyth, and Mike Murphy (Cork: Cork University Press, 2012), 504–12.

11. O'Neill, *Sketchy Recollections*, 16.

12. Details on the ship's construction in William Armstrong Fairburn, *Merchant Sail* (Center Lovell, ME: Fairburn Marine Educational Foundation, 1945) ,http://hdl.handle.net/2027/mdp.39015004467166. *Emerald Isle* later figured in the deaths of thirty-eight Mormon converts leaving England for the US; see Conway B. Sonne, "Under Sail to Zion," *Ensign*, July 1991, Church of Jesus Christ of Latter-Day Saints, https://www.churchofjesuschrist.org/study/ensign/1991/07/under-sail-to-zion?lang=eng\.

13. O'Neill, *Sketchy Recollections*, 15–16; Glenn A. Knoblock, *The American Clipper Ship, 1845–1920: A Comprehensive History, with a Listing of Builders and Their Ships* (Jefferson, NC: McFarland, 2014), 113–15.

14. Tickets for a ship like *Emerald Isle*, with its three decks, could range from $20 or $30 to five times that amount. Twenty dollars in 1867 might equal about $300 or $400 today. Knoblock, *American Clipper Ship*, 140; O'Neill, *Sketchy Recollections*, 15–16.

15. For Anna Rogers's arrival, see O'Neill, *Sketchy Recollections*, 278n15; Kevin Kenny, *The American Irish*, Studies in Modern History (New York: Routledge, 2014), 106–10; *New York Times*, December 29, 1866, 4. On relative success in western cities, see Kenny, *American Irish*, 142–43; Timothy Meagher, *Inventing Irish America: Generation, Class, and Ethnic Identity in a New England City, 1880–1928* (Notre Dame, IN: University of Notre Dame Press, 2001), 15–16.

16. An 1867 story about the Reed boardinghouse contradicts O'Neill's account. According to the *New York Times*, James Lambert, a lodger at 66 Oliver Street, "had lived with Mr Reed for several weeks, until he could no longer pay his weekly reckoning," at which point Reed turned Lambert out. Lambert stole some clothing and started a fire in revenge. *New York Times*, August 11, 1867, 5. The boardinghouse did not extend Lambert credit. Thanks to Timothy Mennel for finding this and correcting an error in earlier drafts.

17. Dana, *Two Years*, 152–53.

18. Dana, *Two Years*, 335–36; Herman Melville, *White-Jacket* (1850; Heritage Illustrated, 2014), Kindle ed. pp. 48, 88.

19. Dana, *Two Years*, 236, 198.

20. O'Neill, *Sketchy Recollections*, 166.

21. Dana, *Two Years*, 236; Breandán Breathnach, *Folk Music and Dances of Ireland: A Comprehensive Study* (Cork: Ossian, 1996), 53, and chap. 5 *passim*; Catherine Foley, "Perceptions of Irish Step Dance: National, Global, and Local," *Dance Research Journal* 33, no. 1 (2001): 34–45; Marion Casey, "Before Riverdance: A

Brief History of Step Dancing in America" in *Making the Irish American History and Heritage of the Irish in the United States*, ed. J. J. Lee and Marion R. Casey (New York: New York University Press, 2006).

22. Christopher J. Smith, *The Creolization of American Culture: William Sidney Mount and the Roots of Blackface Minstrelsy* (Champaign: University of Illinois Press, 2014). The classic examinations of Irish-black interactions are Noel Ignatiev, *How the Irish Became White* (New York: Routledge, 1995); and David R. Roediger, *The Wages of Whiteness: Race and the Making of the American Working Class* (London: Verso, 1991). For the views of Irish scholars, see the essays in Peter D. O'Neill and David Lloyd, eds., *The Black and Green Atlantic: Cross-Currents of the African and Irish Diasporas* (New York: Palgrave Macmillan, 2009); Peter D. O'Neill, *Famine Irish and the American Racial State* (New York: Routledge, 2017).

23. April Masten, "The Challenge Dance: Black-Irish Exchange in Antebellum America," in *Cultures in Motion*, ed. Daniel T. Rodgers, Bhavani Raman, and Helmut Reimitz (Princeton, NJ: Princeton University Press, 2017), 23.

24. Francis O'Neill, *Irish Minstrels and Musicians: With Numerous Dissertations on Related Subjects* (Chicago: Regan, 1913), 426.

25. Tyler Anbinder, *Five Points: The 19th-Century New York City Neighborhood That Invented Tap Dance, Stole Elections, and Became the World's Most Notorious Slum* (New York: Free Press, 2001), 174. On "Juba," see James W. Cook, "Dancing across the Color Line, I.," *Common-Place* 4, no. 1 (October 2003), https://www.common-place-archives.org/vol-04/no-01/cook/index.shtml.

26. Constance Valis Hill, *Tap Dancing America: A Cultural History* (New York: Oxford University Press, 2014), 3–25; Brian Seibert, *What the Eye Hears: A History of Tap Dancing* (New York: Farrar, Straus and Giroux, 2015), 36–39; Masten, "Challenge Dance," 25–26, 30. It is possible Irish music involved frame drums or tambourines. A 1833 painting by Irish artist Daniel Maclise, *Snap Apple Night*, shows a Halloween party in Blarney, Ireland. Music comes from a piper, a fiddler player, a flute player, and a man holding a large frame drum, which he plays with his hand in the style sometimes used to play the modern Irish bodhran.

27. Smith, *Creolization of American Culture*, 184; Masten, "Challenge Dance," 25.

28. Masten, "Challenge Dance," 59.

29. Lafcadio Hearn, *Children of the Levee* (Lexington: University of Kentucky Press, 1957).

30. Charles Henry Pullen, *Miss Columbia's Public School, Or, Will It Blow Over?* (New York: Francis B. Felt, 1871), 18. The book reprinted a number of Nast's anti-Irish caricatures.

31. Emmeline Charlotte Elizabeth Stuart Wortley, *Travels in the United States, Etc.,*

*During 1849 and 1850* (Paris: Galignani, 1851); Richard Moody, *Ned Harrigan: From Corlears Hook to Herald Square* (Chicago: Nelson-Hall, 1980), 48. Similar "guard" companies marched in Philadelphia: on St. Patrick's Day, 1859, Philadelphia's *Public Ledger* listed Irish guard units including Montgomery Guards, Irish Volunteers, Hibernia Greens, Emmett Guards, Meagher Guards, Shields Guards. See Michael L. Mullan, "Sport, Culture, and Nation Among the Hibernians of Philadelphia: Irish American Civic Engagement and Cultural Nationalism, 1880–1920," *Journal of Urban History* 39, no. 4 (2013): 579–600.

32. Harrigan and Hart played extremely significant roles in the history of Broadway and musical theater generally. Moody, *Ned Harrigan*; Michael Aman, "Edward Harrigan's Realism of Race," *Journal of American Drama and Theatre* 24, no. 1 (2012): 5–30, 83; James H. Dormon, "Ethnic Cultures of the Mind: The Harrigan-Hart Mosaic," *American Studies* 33, no. 2 (1992): 21–40. O'Neill knew the song and late in life asserted it had come from a traditional Irish tune called "Bonaparte Crossing the Alps." "Irish Dances and Dance-Music," *Cork Weekly Examiner*, April 7, 1934.

33. "072.061—McNally's Row of Flats" Levy Music Collection," accessed December 5, 2019, https://levysheetmusic.mse.jhu.edu/collection/072/061. A version of the song was recorded by musician and historian Mick Moloney and can be heard at https://youtu.be/PU6GAMbqRBE

34. *Harper's Weekly*, February 2, 1889, 97–100, reprinted in *The Theatre* (London: Wyman & Sons, 1888), 97. Harrigan insisted that only white men in blackface could perform the Skidmore Guard roles, saying "that they couldn't be natural on stage," and adding that "the minstrel-show black-face Negro has ruined the real Negro for the stage; he tries to exaggerate the white man's impersonation of him." Quotations from Harrigan in Aman, "Edward Harrigan's Realism of Race," 323. The author calls this "the minstrel cycle," in which white people appropriate African American musical forms in parody and then African Americans reappropriate the parody. Michael O'Malley, "Dark Enough as It Is: Eddie Lang and the Minstrel Cycle," *Journal of Social History* 52, no. 2 (2018): 234–59.

35. David Lloyd, *Anomalous States: Irish Writing and the Post-Colonial Moment* (Durham, NC: Duke University Press, 1993); and the essays in O'Neill and Lloyd, *Black and Green Atlantic*.

36. O'Neill, *Sketchy Recollections*, 18.

37. Dan Milner, *The Unstoppable Irish: Songs and Integration of the New York Irish, 1783–1883* (Notre Dame, IN: University of Notre Dame Press, 2019), explores the range of music the Irish in New York sang and which O'Neill ignored. See also William H. Williams, *'Twas Only an Irishman's Dream: The Image of Ireland and the Irish in American Popular Song Lyrics, 1800–1920* (Urbana: University of Illinois Press, 1996), on the role of Irish music on stage.

38. Milner, *Unstoppable Irish*, 198–202.

39. Don Meade, "Kitty O'Neil and Her 'Champion Jig': An Irish Dancer on the New York Stage," *New Hibernia Review / Iris Éireannach Nua* 6, no. 3 (2002): 9–22. Meade revised and updated and posted the updated version at http://blarneystar.com/KittyONeil.pdf. Bill "Bojangles" Robinson danced a sand dance in the 1949 film *Stormy Weather*; the 1951 movie *Yes Sir, Mr. Bones* attempted to re-create old-time minstrels shows by including a dancer in blackface doing a sand jig.

40. Henry Chapman Mercer to Frances O'Neill, August 27, 1920, 3; O'Neill to Mercer, September 6, 1920, 2–3; Mercer to O'Neill, October 1, 1920, 1; O'Neill to Mercer, October 15, 1920, all in Mercer Correspondence, Series 1, folder 71, misc. v291, August-October 1920, Mercer Museum Library, Bucks County Historical Society, Doylestown, PA. As noted earlier, in the nineteenth century the term "jig" might be used to describe any lively dance music. O'Neill thought of the Irish jig in a more formal sense, as a tune in ¾ time.

41. Meade, "Kitty O'Neil," 2.

42. Kathleen O'Neil, "No Irish Need Apply," Brainard and Company, Cleveland, OH 1863, in Levy Music Collection, Johns Hopkins University, http://levysheetmusic.mse.jhu.edu/collection/053/009. For Kathleen as the "Irish Thrush" at the 1893 exposition, see *Buffalo Evening News*, November 3, 1893, 28.

43. *Boston Daily Atlas*, March 24, 1856, 1; and April 7, 1856, 2; "The Hiawatha Mania," *Daily National Intelligencer*, March 29, 1856, 2; "Launch of the Minnehaha," *New York Daily Times*, May 24, 1856, 1; Knoblock, *American Clipper Ship*, 316.

44. O'Neill, *Sketchy Recollections*, 20–21, remembered Bursley's name as "Burleigh": newspapers clearly refer to him as "Bursley." On bringing magazines and books, see ibid., 160.

45. O'Neill, *Sketchy Recollections*, 20–24; and Francis O'Neill to William Halpin, April 8, 1912, in Seán Reid series, Breandán Breathnach Collection, reference BBR-187/1/1, ITMA.

46. O'Neill, *Sketchy Recollections*, 24; Information on Queen Emma from "North American Women's Letters," accessed December 3, 2019, https://nwld-alexanderstreet-com.mutex.gmu.edu/NWLD/bios/A819BIO.html.

47. *Pacific Commercial Advertiser*, October 26, 1867, 2.

48. O'Neill, *Sketchy Recollections*, 24–25. *The Hawaiian Gazette*, July 15, 1868, 3, described the operation on the island, owned by "the American Guano Company," in detail. It reported "ten white persons and one Hawaiian" living on the island. A ship visited five times a year with food and supplies.

49. Full details of the wreck appear in the *Pacific Commercial Advertiser*, January 18, 1868, 3, in a report from Captain Johnson, who wrote regular updates of shipping to and from Baker Island for the Hawaii newspapers. The figurehead may be seen at https://emuseum.history.org/objects/58052/ships-figurehead-minnehaha. The museum writes: "The circumstances by which

the ship's figurehead survived the wreckage and reappeared as follows are unknown: Found in the Virgin Islands (specific location undocumented) by Max Williams (1874–1927), a collector/dealer in prints, ship models, and marine relics; sold to Mr. and Mrs. Elie Nadelman, Riverdale, NY; sold to Edith Gregor Halpert, Downtown Gallery, New York, NY; in 1932, sold to AARFAM's donor, Mrs. John D. Rockefeller, Jr."

50. All quotes above from O'Neill regarding events on *Minnehaha* from *Sketchy Recollections*, 20–27. *The Hawaiian Gazette*, July 15, 1868, 3, says wrecked sailors returned on *Kamehameha V* and the schooner *San Diego. Kamehameha V* visited Baker Island roughly every two months; given that Kamehameha V was at that time king of Hawaii, and O'Neill says the ship was crewed by Hawaiians, it seems safe to assume he sailed on *Kamehameha V*. Hawaiian newspapers mention *Minnehaha* but do not mention a brig named *Zoe*.

51. O'Neill's versions of this story appear in Francis O'Neill, *Irish Minstrels and Musicians: With Numerous Dissertations on Related Subjects* (Chicago: Regan, 1913), 16; and O'Neill, *Sketchy Recollections*, 26–27.

52. John William Troutman, *Kika Kila: How the Hawaiian Steel Guitar Changed the Sound of Modern Music* (Chapel Hill: University of North Carolina Press, 2016), 148; Nathaniel Bright Emerson, *Unwritten Literature of Hawaii: The Sacred Songs of the Hula* (Washington, DC: US Government Printing Office, 1909), 145–46.

53. David A. Chang, *The World and All the Things upon It: Native Hawaiian Geographies of Exploration* (Minneapolis: University of Minnesota Press, 2016), 162–63.

54. O'Neill, *Irish Folk Music*, 16.

55. Henry Chapman Mercer, "On the Track of The Arkansas Traveler," *Century*, n.s., 29 (1896): 707–12. Fifty years later, O'Neill and Mercer corresponded extensively about the song and its origins. "I am including 'the Arkansas Traveler' in my next book," O'Neill wrote to Mercer in 1921, and "welcome all information pertaining to it. Personally I am not much impressed by the emasculated versions of it ordinarily dished out, but in what is considered a fuller setting it is a fairly acceptable reel." O'Neill to Mercer, February 15, 1921, Mercer Correspondence, Series 1, folder 73, misc. 291, January-March 1921, Mercer Museum Library. See also Mercer to O'Neill, February 21, 1921, ibid.. O'Neill compared the song to various tunes in the Irish tradition in *Waifs and Strays of Gaelic Melody; Comprising Forgotten Favorites, Worthy Variants, and Tunes Not Previously Printed* (Chicago: Lyon & Healey, 1922). On the history of the tune, see also Mary D. Hudgins, "Arkansas Traveler: A Multi-Parented Wayfarer," *Arkansas Historical Quarterly* 30, no. 2 (1971): 145–60.

56. For examples of "The Girl I Left Behind Me" as a song played by soldiers and

sailors leaving home, see "Boy," *The Boy's Own Sea Stories; the Adventures of a Sailor, Narrated by Himself* (London: Ward & Lock, 1859), 16; Joseph G. Clark, *Lights and Shadows of Sailor Life: As Exemplified in Fifteen Years' Experience, Including the More Thrilling Events of the U.S. Exploring Expedition, and Reminiscences of an Eventful Life on the "Mountain Wave"* (Boston: B. B. Mussey, 1848), 270; Stephen Bleecker Luce, *Naval Songs: A Collection of Original, Selected, and Traditional Sea Songs* (New York: Wm. A. Pond, 1883), 67.

57. On the guano trade and its relationship to European imperialism, see Gregory T. Cushman, *Guano and the Opening of the Pacific World a Global Ecological History* (Cambridge: Cambridge University Press, 2013).

58. O'Neill, *Sketchy Recollections*, 27.

59. Thomas Carlyle, *Chartism* (London: James Fraser, 1840), 28–29. In the US, Henry David Thoreau saw Irish people in similar terms. See Helen Lojek, "Thoreau's Bog People," *New England Quarterly* 67, no. 2 (1994): 279–97.

60. A Hiberno-Hawaiian, Tom Hennessey, may have been the first person to record Hawaiian steel guitar. See Lorene Ruymar, *The Hawaiian Steel Guitar and Its Great Hawaiian Musicians* (Anaheim Hills, CA: Centerstream, 1996), 27, 88, and Troutman, *Kika Kila*, 74, 269. Hennessey copyrighted at least one song, "Hawaiian Serenade," in 1919. See *Catalog of Copyright Entries* (Washington, DC: US Government Printing Office, 1919), 1298.

61. Masten, "Challenge Dance," 23.

62. Douglas E. Kyle et al., *Historic Spots in California*, 5th ed. (Stanford, CA: Stanford University Press, 2002), 520. Salter ran a post office at Horr's Ranch. US Civil Service Commission, *Official Register of the United States* (Washington, DC: US Government Printing Office, 1868), 345.

63. O'Neill, *Sketchy Recollections*, 28–32.

64. Francis O'Neill to A. P. Graves, November 20, 1906. Also published in the *Journal of the Irish Folk Song Society* 5 (1907): 34; O'Neill, *Irish Minstrels*, 16.

65. O'Neill, *Sketchy Recollections*, 33–36. There appears to be no record of a barque called *Hannah* landing in New York in 1869. O'Neill likely misremembered the name of the ship.

## Chapter Three

Mary Ward and her two daughters, who had been driven to mendicancy as a result of the famine, made our farmhouse their headquarters for a week or so at a time. . . . That explains the source of the writer's acquaintance with 'Rolling on the Ryegrass' and many another tunes either lost or forgotten in this generation." Francis O'Neill, *Irish Folk Music: A Fascinating Hobby* (Chicago: Regan, 1910), 142.

1. How much money was this? Three years later, O'Neill reported working as an unskilled laborer for between $1.25 and $1.75 a day. So by his telling, even an unskilled laborer would make considerably more than this in a single year. We might consider "almost two hundred dollars" less than half a year's wages for an unskilled worker. But sailors did not have to pay rent or buy food while at sea.

2. Cormac Ó Gráda, "Researching the Early History of Savings Banks in New York and in Ireland," UCD Centre for Economic Research Working Papers Series (WP08/24 December 2008), University College Dublin School of Economics, 4; Tyler Anbinder, "Moving beyond 'Rags to Riches': New York's Irish Famine Immigrants and Their Surprising Savings Accounts," *Journal of American History* 9, no. 3 (2012): 741. See also Marion R. Casey, "Emigrant as Historian: Records, Banking, and Irish-American Scholarship," *American Journal of Irish Studies* 10 (2013): 145–63; Records of Philip Neill at Emigrant Savings Bank. *Emigrant Savings Bank Records*, Call number *R-USLHG *ZI-815. Roll 7, account number 33045, New York Public Library, New York, New York, searchable at Ancestry.com. Birth records in Ireland show a Mary O'Neill, born in 1836, Francis's sister. See Nicholas Carolan, *A Harvest Saved: Francis O'Neill and Irish Music in Chicago* (Cork: Ossian, 1997), 5. Francis later mentions a sister "Nancy" living in Chicago, married to Jerry Daly.

3. Timothy J. Meagher, *Inventing Irish America: Generation, Class, and Ethnic Identity in a New England City, 1880–1928* (Notre Dame, IN: University of Notre Dame Press, 2001), 23.

4. Edwin L. Godkin, *Life and Letters of Edwin Lawrence Godkin* (New York: Macmillan, 1907), 182; Kevin Kenny, *The American Irish*, Studies in Modern History (New York: Routledge , 2014), 107–8.

5. On nativist riots in Philadelphia, see Noel Ignatiev, *How the Irish Became White* (New York: Routledge, 1995); and on New York, see Tyler Anbinder, *Five Points: The 19th-Century New York City Neighborhood That Invented Tap Dance, Stole Elections, and Became the World's Most Notorious Slum* (New York: Free Press, 2001); Samuel Finley Breese Morse, *Imminent Dangers to the Free Institutions of the United States: Through Foreign Immigration and the Present State of the Naturalization Laws* (New York: John F. Trow, 1854), n.p.

6. Kerby A. Miller, *Emigrants and Exiles: Ireland and the Irish Exodus to North America* (New York: Oxford University Press, 2010), 4–5.

7. Meagher, *Inventing Irish America*, 33.

8. Francis O'Neill, *Irish Folk Music: A Fascinating Hobby* (Chicago: Regan, 1910), 10, 17.

9. Kennedy quoted in Rebecca Solnit, *A Book of Migrations* (London: Verso, 2011), 75; Miller, *Emigrants and Exiles*, 487. Thanks to Tim Meagher for reminding me of this quote.

10. Francis O'Neill, *Irish Minstrels and Musicians: With Numerous Dissertations on Related Subjects* (Chicago: Regan, 1913), 103.

11. *New York Times*, February 10, 1871, 8

12. David Brundage, *Irish Nationalists in America: The Politics of Exile, 1798–1998* (New York: Oxford University Press, 2016), 102.

13. Rose Irene Novak, "Writing Ireland's Wrongs: Nineteenth-Century Women, Politics, and Violence" (PhD diss., University of Connecticut, 2010), 25; John Rutherford, *The Secret History of the Fenian Conspiracy: Its Origin, Objects, & Ramifications* (London: C. Kegan Paul, 1877), 255–56; Buffalo Historical Society (Buffalo, NY), *Publications of the Buffalo Historical Society* (Buffalo: Bigelow Brothers, 1921), 297–99.

14. David Sim, *A Union Forever: The Irish Question and U.S. Foreign Relations in the Victorian Age*, The United States in the World (Ithaca, NY: Cornell University Press, 2013), 86.

15. *New York Herald*, April 12, 1866; John O'Neil quoted in *Official Report of Gen. John O'Neill, President of the Fenian Brotherhood: On the Attempt to Invade Canada, May 25th, 1870* (New York: John J. Foster, 1870), 3.

16. Accounts of Fenian activities from Sim, *Union Forever*, and from Christopher Klein, *When the Irish Invaded Canada: The Incredible True Story of the Civil War Veterans Who Fought for Ireland's Freedom* (New York: Doubleday, 2019). See also Brundage, *Irish Nationalists*, chap. 4; O'Neill, *Official Report of Gen. John O'Neill*, 4, 58.

17. Mark Twain, *The Choice Humorous Works of Mark Twain* (London: Chatto & Windus, 1880), 528–29.

18. Amy E. Martin, "Fenian Fever: Circum-Atlantic Insurgency and the Modern State," in *The Black and Green Atlantic: Cross-Currents of the African and Irish Diasporas*, ed. Peter D. O'Neill and David Lloyd (New York: Palgrave Macmillan, 2009). Henri le Caron was born Thomas Miller Beach, an Englishman. He met John O'Neill while serving with the Union Army in the Civil War under the name of Le Caron. In 1892 he published a memoir, *Twenty-five Years in the Secret Service* (London: William Heineman, 1892).

19. Sim, *Union Forever*, 89; Meagher, *Inventing Irish America*, 33; John White, *Sketches from America* (London: S. Low, Son, and Marston, 1870), 369.

20. "The Fenian's Comfort Smoking Tobacco," 1858, http://www.loc.gov/pictures/item/2001697794/; "Fenian Collar, Ireland for the Irish," 1866, http://www.loc.gov/pictures/item/96512049/.

21. "The Confidence Woman in the Kitchen Area," *New York Times*, December 17, 1865, 4; David Sim, "Following the Money: Fenian Bonds, Diasporic Nationalism, and Distant Revolutions in the Mid-Nineteenth-Century United States," *Past & Present* 247, no. 1 (May 2020): 77–112; "Counterfeiting of the Bonds of

the Irish Republic," *New York Times*, March 11, 1866, 5; Robert Doan, "Green Gold to the Emerald Shores: Irish Immigration to the United States and Transatlantic Monetary Aid, 1854–1923" (PhD diss., Temple University, 1999), ProQuest 1999.

22. Lucy E. Salyer, *Under the Starry Flag: How a Band of Irish Americans Joined the Fenian Revolt and Sparked a Crisis over Citizenship* (Cambridge, MA: Belknap Press, 2018), 27, 174; Sim, *Union Forever,* chap. 4 *passim*.

23. Boston *Pilot*, April 9, 1864, October 1, 1864. An 1887 history of the county claims McMenomy "had a very pleasing face for a clergyman, and was well suited for such a charge. Notwithstanding that Know-nothingism had been well worked up, he was popular with all classes." *History of Lewis, Clark, Knox, and Scotland Counties, Missouri. From the Earliest Time to the Present* (St. Louis: Goodspeed, 1887).

24. Francis O'Neill, *Chief O'Neill's Sketchy Recollections of an Eventful Life in Chicago,* ed. Ellen Skerrett and Mary Lesch (Evanston, IL: Northwestern University Press, 2008), 38.

25. O'Neill, *Sketchy Recollections,* 39; O'Neill, *Irish Folk Music,* 16. O'Neill taught at a public school, not at the Catholic school run by the Sisters of Loretto. O'Neill visited Broderick again in 1906, on his way back from a trip to Ireland.

26. O'Neill, *Irish Folk Music,* 16–17. Quote about "one third of whom were Irish" from a transcript of letter from Francis O'Neill to A. P. Graves, November 20, 1906, Nicholas Carolan Collection, Irish Traditional Music Archive, Dublin (hereafter ITMA Carolan). Also published *Journal of the Irish Folk Song Society, London*, 1904.

27. O'Neill to Graves, November 20, 1906, ITMA Carolan.

28. Quotes on Ireland from Aileen Dillane, "The Ivory Bridge: Piano Accompaniment on 78 rpm Recorded Sources of Irish Traditional Dance Music America c. 1910–1945" (MA thesis, University of Limerick, 2000), 25; and Harry Bradshaw's booklet accompanying a CD set, *The Music and Life of John McKenna: The Buck from the Mountain,* 2014. See also "John McKenna: Leitrim's Master of the Concert Flute," *Musical Traditions* no. 7 (1987), https://www.mustrad .org.uk/articles/mckenna.htm.

29. Howard W. Marshall, *Play Me Something Quick and Devilish: Old-Time Fiddlers in Missouri* (Columbia: University of Missouri Press, 2012), chap. 7; Howard Wright Marshall, "Irish Echoes in Outstate Missouri," *Missouri Historical Review* 100, no. 4 (2005): 40–53.

30. O'Neill, *Sketchy Recollections,* 39. He remembered the name as *Sunnyside,* but Lesch and Skerrett identified it correctly in their note on page 280.

31. O'Neill, *Sketchy Recollections,* 39–40.

32. The classic study is Hasia R. Diner, *Erin's Daughters in America: Irish Immigrant*

*Women in the Nineteenth Century* (Baltimore: Johns Hopkins University Press, 1983). See also Margaret Lynch-Brennan and Maureen O'Rourke Murphy, *The Irish Bridget: Irish Immigrant Women in Domestic Service in America, 1840–1930* (Syracuse, NY: Syracuse University Press, 2014), 84.

33. *Puck,* May 9, 1883, cover, also at Library of Congress Prints and Photos Division, https://lccn.loc.gov/2012645471.

34. Cartoons from *Puck,* May 9, 1883, 163; January 30, 1884, 352; reprinted in April R. Schultz, "The Black Mammy and the Irish Bridget: Domestic Service and the Representation of Race, 1830–1930," *Éire-Ireland* 48, no. 3 (2013): 176–212. Statistics from Lynch-Brennan and O'Rourke Murphy, *Irish Bridget,* 84; John J. Appel, "From Shanties to Lace Curtains: The Irish Image in Puck, 1876–1910," *Comparative Studies in Society and History* 13, no. 4 (1971): 365–75; M. Alison Kibler, "The Stage Irishwoman (Ethnic Groups)," *Journal of American Ethnic History* 24, no. 3 (2005): 5–30.

35. Francis O'Neill, *The Dance Music of Ireland: 1001 Gems* (Chicago: Lyon & Healy, 1907), 67; Irish Folk Song Society, *Journal of the Irish Folk Song Society,* London 7 (Jan.–June 1909): 36: "Many of the airs are known throughout Ireland, by other names than those given by Capt. O'Neill." For instance, "The Irish Woman," as mentioned in the volume, is known familiarly in Ireland as the "Washerwomen." In his *Irish Folk Music,* p. 140, O'Neill wrote that he was sorry to find "what we believed to be the corrupted name" in earlier tune collections. In 1910 it appeared as "The Irish Washerwoman" in *Popular Selections from O'Neill's Music of Ireland,* and credited to Selena O'Neill, who arranged them for piano.

36. *Chicago Daily Tribune,* April 30, 1901, 3. At some point before 1890, O'Neill did have a sister, "Nancy" Daly, living in Chicago with her husband Jerry. Efforts to place them in Chicago in 1870 are inconclusive.

37. We should note that while O'Neill deplores this low figure, his earnings for nearly three years at sea came to less than $200.

38. Lesch and Skerrett, in their notes to O'Neill, *Sketchy Recollections,* 280, suggest the YMCA.

39. Sam Mitrani, *The Rise of the Chicago Police Department: Class and Conflict* (Urbana: University of Illinois Press, 2013), 84–85.

40. Richard Edwards, *Chicago Census Report and Statistical Review* (Chicago, 1871), 839. Skerrett and Lesch, in their notes to O'Neill, *Sketchy Recollections,* note that O'Neill does not show up in property records until 1880, and that the family moved three times before that to addresses in Bridgeport. In his memoir, O'Neill makes it seem as though the fire led directly to his purchasing a house, but some evidence suggests nearly ten years passed before the O'Neills accumulated enough capital to buy their first home.

41. Francis O'Neill to Seamus Ó Casaide, August 28, 1917, Seamus Ó Casaide Papers, 8116(7), National Library of Ireland; Francis O'Neill to John G. O'Neill, June 16, 1916, ITMA Carolan; "Death of Roger F. O'Neill," *Chicago Citizen*, February 20, 1904; Mary Mooney Lesch, Francis O'Neill's great-granddaughter, personal correspondence with the author, June 18, 2019.

42. O'Neill, *Sketchy Recollections*, 50. Until the mid-twentieth century, by congressional enactment, naturalized citizenship was available only to "free white persons."

43. John B. Jentz and Richard Schneirov, *Chicago in the Age of Capital: Class, Politics, and Democracy During the Civil War and Reconstruction* (Urbana: University of Illinois Press, 2012), 206; Richard C. Lindberg, *Gangland Chicago: Criminality and Lawlessness in the Windy City* (Lanham, MD: Rowman & Littlefield, 2016), 79.

44. Richard Schneirov, *Labor and Urban Politics: Class Conflict and the Origins of Modern Liberalism in Chicago, 1864–97* (Urbana: University of Illinois Press, 1998), 105–8.

45. *Chicago Inter Ocean*, July 25, 1877, 3; *Chicago Tribune*, July 26, 1877, 1; Schneirov, *Labor and Urban Politics*, 109, 111; *Chicago Tribune*, March 7, 1882, 5. See also Sam Mitrani, *The Rise of the Chicago Police Department: Class and Conflict, 1850–1894* (Urbana: University of Illinois Press, 2013), 146.

46. O'Neill, *Sketchy Recollections*, 48–49.

47. Jane Addams, *Democracy and Social Ethics* (New York: Macmillan, 1907), 234, 239.

48. Addams, *Democracy and Social Ethics*; O'Neill, *Sketchy Recollections*, 49; Michael Tracy, *William Tracy (1823–1891): The Life and Times of a Chicago Alderman* (Unknown pub., n.d.), Kindle ed.

49. Mitrani, *Rise of the Chicago Police Department*, 4, 10.

50. "After All, the Best Police School Is Experience, says Ex-Chief O'Neill," *Chicago Daily Tribune*, October 16, 1910, 13; *Chicago Inter Ocean*, May 19, 1901, 43.

51. Mitrani, *Rise of the Chicago Police Department*, 10.

52. *Chicago Tribune*, October 16, 1910, 13.

53. O'Neill relates the story in "After All, the Best Police School," 13; and in O'Neill, *Sketchy Recollections*, 50; contemporary accounts include *Chicago Daily Tribune*, August 18, 1873; *Chicago Times*, August 18, 1873; "Shooting Policemen," *Chicago Tribune*, August 21, 1873, 4. In the first account above, O'Neill suggests that he earned his way onto the force by commandeering a locomotive to chase down a fleeing thief. O'Neill says this event earned him a promotion from probationary status, but newspaper accounts of the shooting refer to him as "Officer O'Neill" and make no mention of probation. An article in the *Tribune* mentioned three other policemen shot that week and claimed "policemen do

not use their pistols enough." O'Neill expressed relief that Bridges, the burglar, did not die needlessly.

54. *Chicago Tribune*, April 23, 1877, 8; *Chicago Inter Ocean*, May 29, 1901, 43.

## Chapter Four

Francis O'Neill, *Irish Folk Music: A Fascinating Hobby* (Chicago: Regan, 1910), 18. "Of the reels memorized from his playing, the 'Flower of the Flock,' 'Jim Moore's Fancy,' and the 'New Policeman' were unpublished and unknown to our people except Mr. Cronin, who had variants of the two last named."

1. Francis O'Neill to A. P. Graves, November 20, 1906, Nicholas Carolan Collection, Irish Traditional Music Archives, Dublin (hereafter ITMA Carolan). O'Neill described Raverty as being from Tyrone; immigration records show Michael Raverty arriving from Tyrone in 1851, age two and a half. The brief story also appears in *Journal of the Irish Folk Song Society* 5 (1907). In 1906 O'Neill said he heard the tune thirty years before.
2. Raverty's career appears briefly in *Chicago Inter Ocean*, August 12, 1875, 3; December 30, 1895, 4; March 6, 1908, 5.
3. O'Neill to Graves, November 20, 1906, ITMA Carolan. "The Mountaineer's March" is a jig, not a march, and appears as number 1030 in O'Neill's collection. It's very similar to a currently popular jig known as "the Kesh."
4. Vanessa Schulman identifies what she calls "the managerial eye" emerging as a visual style in the late nineteenth century, a way of depicting industry corresponding to what a manager needed to "see" in daily work. O'Neill needed to develop a "managerial eye," a different way of seeing. Vanessa Schulman, *Work Sights: The Visual Culture of Industry in Nineteenth-Century America* (Amherst: University of Massachusetts Press, 2015), chap. 5.
5. Francis O'Neill, *Chief O'Neill's Sketchy Recollections of an Eventful Life in Chicago*, ed. Ellen Skerrett and Mary Lesch (Evanston, IL: Northwestern University Press, 2008), 44. This chronology cannot be right because O'Neill did not buy a house until the 1880s, and he sailed on the Great Lakes in 1870.
6. O'Neill, *Sketchy Recollections*, 43–46.
7. Jane Addams, *Democracy and Social Ethics* (New York: Macmillan, 1907), 19–20.
8. Quotations from Louise W Knight, *Citizen: Jane Addams and the Struggle for Democracy* (Chicago: University of Chicago Press, 2006), Kindle ed. loc. 2135, 4610.
9. Addams, *Democracy and Social Ethics*, 30.
10. For an example of self-produced money in reciprocal exchange, see Michael

O'Malley, "Money and the Everyday: Paper Money, Community, and Nationalism in the Antebellum US," in *A Cultural History of Money*, vol. 5, ed. Bill Maurer, Federico Neiburg, and Nigel Dodd (London: Bloomsbury, 2019).

11. O'Neill's story about his house buying omits an interesting fact: the 1880 census shows "Frank O'Neill" living at 2712 Wallace Street with wife Annie O'Neill, daughter Julia O'Neill, age two, and Mary Rodgers, age sixty-three. Clearly Anna's mother had come to live with them. Did she sell the house she owned in Normal, Illinois, and provide her daughter's family with the capital to get started? O'Neill never mentions his mother-in-law or any financial help she might have provided.

12. O'Neill, *Sketchy Recollections*, 46, 281n. Here again we might consider the relative value of the rent O'Neill charged. Fifty cents a week, if the figure is accurate, represents less than half a day's wages for an unskilled worker, or one-tenth of the worker's weekly income. Some record of O'Neill's real estate investment appears in newspapers. The *Chicago Tribune*, September 9, 1892, 10, shows a "Frank O'Neill" securing a building permit for a pair of two-story stores and flats; the *Tribune* April 24, 1906, 7, shows him selling a property he owned in Hyde Park to his son-in-law for $1. According to the *Tribune*, March 30, 1907, 7, O'Neill got a permit for a three-story brick apartment building across the street from his house.

13. *Chicago Evening Post*, February 19, 1896, col. 1, quoted in Knight, *Citizen*, Kindle ed. loc. 7068.

14. O'Neill, *Sketchy Recollections*, 51–52. O'Neill spelled Seavey's first name as "Valorus."

15. Mark Haller's work on Chicago policing describes this tension between professionalized, rationalized administration, and cronyism clearly; see Mark Haller, "Police Reform in Chicago," *American Behavioral Scientist* 13 (1970): 649–66; Mark Haller, "Urban Crime and Criminal Justice: The Chicago Case," *Journal of American History* 57 (1970): 619–35; and Haller, "Organized Crime in Urban Society," *Journal of Social History* 5 (1971): 210–34. *Evening Post* quoted in Charles Fanning, *Finley Peter Dunne and Mr. Dooley: The Chicago Years* (Lexington: University Press of Kentucky, 2015), 59.

16. O'Neill, *Sketchy Recollections*, 55–56.

17. *Chicago Tribune*, June 15, 1890, 13, details the testimony of "repeaters." Quote on "Irish rule" from *America: A Journal for Americans* 4 (1890): 234, 319. Courtroom scene in *Chicago Tribune*, June 21, 1890, 5. Eulogies in *Journal of the Proceedings of the City Council*, February 10, 1892, 1683–87.

18. "He is a magnificent penman," M. L. Ahern, *Political History of Chicago* (Chicago: Donohue & Henneberry, 1886), 221. Anecdote about the mayor's order in O'Neill, *Sketchy Recollections*, 53. The family of Solomon Waixel, a boy who

had been injured by fireworks the prior July, sued the mayor in January 1887. *Chicago Tribune*, January 21, 1887, 8.

19. O'Neill, *Sketchy Recollections*, 71; *Chicago Inter Ocean*, September 26, 1901, 1; *Chicago Tribune*, October 8, 1901; *Chicago Inter Ocean*, October 30, 1901, 12; Chicago Civil Service Commission, *Annual Report—Chicago Civil Service Commission* (Chicago, 1896). O'Neill claimed that Robert Burke, chair of the Cook County Democracy, later rigged a different exam with questions designed to favor his own candidates, showing that the exam alone could not stem the machine's influence. Burke would then go after O'Neill through an ally on the police force, who accused Chief O'Neill of leaking test answers to his favored applicants. The charges did not stick, and O'Neill fired the lieutenant who made them, at the mayor's request.

20. In 1898 one of O'Neill's Irish musical comrades, James Kerwin was "reduced" from sergeant to patrolman because he either failed or did not take the civil service exam. *Chicago Tribune*, March 22, 1898, 12.

21. Finley Peter Dunne, *Observations by Mr. Dooley* (New York: Harper & Brothers, 1906), 100; Finley Peter Dunne, *Mr. Dooley in the Hearts of His Countrymen* (Boston: Small, Maynard, 1914), 36.

22. O'Neill, *Sketchy Recollections*, 58, 84. George Bell Swift served an interim term as mayor after Carter Harrison the elder was assassinated in late October 1893. Swift later served one term as elected mayor from 1895 to 1897, so O'Neill refers to events occurring after the Pullman strike, which took place in July 1893.

23. On O'Neill's reputation, see John Joseph Flinn and John Elbert Wilkie, *History of the Chicago Police: From the Settlement of the Community to the Present Time* (Under the auspices of the Police book fund, 1887), 463–64, which gives a biography of then Sergeant O'Neill and notes "he has never been fined, suspended or reprimanded while connected with the police department." By the time of the brawl, he had distinguished himself in the Pullman strike.

24. O'Neill *Sketchy Recollections*, 85–87. The brawl between Lammers and McCarthy described in *Chicago Tribune*, September 22, 1895. O'Neill's encounter and the subsequent court appearances described in *Chicago Inter Ocean*, February 14, 1896, 8, and February 19, 1896, 8; and in *Chicago Chronicle*, February 13, 1896, 1.

25. Andrew White, "The Government of American Cities," *Forum* 10 (December 1890): 368.

26. *Chicago Inter Ocean*, February 19, 1896, 8; O'Neill, *Sketchy Recollections*, 87.

27. O'Neill, *Sketchy Recollections*, 91; Franklin Mathews, "Wide Open Chicago," *Harper's Weekly*, January 22, 1898, 88; Lloyd Wendt and Herman Kogan, *Lords of the Levee: The Story of Bathhouse John and Hinky Dink* (Chicago: Bobbs-Merrill, 1943), tells the story in colorful and reasonably well-documented form.

28. Mathews, "Wide Open Chicago," 88, 90, 91.

29. W. T. Stead, *If Christ Came to Chicago! A Plea for the Union of All Who Love in the Service of All Who Suffer* (Chicago: Laird & Lee, 1894), 17; O'Neill, *Sketchy Recollections*, 91.

30. We should note again that a police patrolman at that time made $1,000 a year; if we assume a starting salary for a Chicago policeman today as about $50,000, we could consider that Edwards was walking around with the equivalent of $700,000 in cash.

31. O'Neill, *Sketchy Recollections*, 92–93; *Chicago Tribune*, July 29, 1899, 4. A later account in the *Tribune* specifically disputes O'Neill's version of events. See "O'Neill Tells of 'Hounding,'" *Chicago Tribune*, November 6, 1903, 3.

32. The mayor found these stories about the levee district and the national attention they attracted deeply embarrassing. When he appointed O'Neill chief superintendent of police in 1901, he promised a crackdown on crime in the Levee, which crackdown materialized briefly but then evaporated almost as fast, leaving only a few political cartoons in its wake. As both Kipley and Harrison noted, there was no percentage in stopping things people actually wanted. If they wanted to gamble or drink on Sunday, let them do so discreetly. Few people openly defended prostitution, but districts like the Levee concentrated it and kept it contained, and any male buyer foolish enough to enter a brothel with $14,000 in cash deserved plucking.

33. Sam Mitrani, *The Rise of the Chicago Police Department: Class and Conflict, 1850–1894* (Urbana: University of Illinois Press, 2013), 5; Jeffrey S. Adler, *First in Violence, Deepest in Dirt: Homicide in Chicago, 1875–1920* (Cambridge, MA: Harvard University Press, 2006), 1.

34. Paul Avrich, *The Haymarket Tragedy* (Princeton, NJ: Princeton University Press, 1984), 205.

35. *Chicago Tribune*, June 27, 1886, 7. An anonymous police official blamed the riot on Bonfield. *Chicago Tribune*, May 1, 1898; Carl Smith, *Urban Disorder and the Shape of Belief: The Great Chicago Fire, the Haymarket Bomb, and the Model Town of Pullman* (Chicago: University of Chicago Press, 2008), 129.

36. Smith, *Urban Disorder*, 167; "For Fame and Money: How Some Chicago Police Profited by Anarchy," *New York Times*, May 11, 1889, 1. "Schaack knew there were many people in town who were desperately afraid of the anarchists," wrote Frederick Ebersold, chief of police at the time, and "he thought it would be a good thing for him if he could work upon their fears and by continued 'nagging' incite the irresponsible element of his district to some deeds of violence, and after repressing it, come to the front and pose as the capitalist's savior." "Captain Schaack has a lot of gall to talk about trouble-makers," a journalist claimed: "You can bet your life if there was no trouble Schaack would make some. He's a glory hunter and a bastard of the first order!" Quote regarding

Schaack as a bastard from Art Young, *Art Young: His Life and Times* (New York: Sheridan House, 1939), 76. Schaack would be briefly dismissed from the police for concealing evidence in the "Clan Na Gael" murder of Dr. William Cronin, discussed in chapter 5. Friends had him reinstated, but he was removed again for manufacturing evidence in the case of alderman Thomas O'Malley, no relation to the author, accused of murdering a bartender in an effort to secure a box of ballots. *Chicago Tribune*, May 4, 1897; April 28, 1897; Michael J. Schaack, *Anarchy and Anarchists: A History of the Red Terror* (Chicago: F. J. Schulte, 1889). Schaack dismissed by Mayor Cregier: *Chicago Eagle*, May 21, 1898, 4.

37. O'Neill, *Sketchy Recollections*, 112–21.

38. Walter Wyckoff, a Princeton theology graduate who spent several years as an itinerant laborer, wrote about seeking work in Chicago in the early 1890s. He describes finding room and board for $4 a month and making wages of $1.50 a day. Skilled workers might make $15 a week, Wyckoff reported.

39. Richard Ely, "Pullman, a Social Study," *Harper's Monthly Magazine* 70, no. 417 (February 1885): 457, 460, 463, 465–66.

40. US Strike Commission, 1894, *Report on the Chicago Strike of June-July, 1894* (Washington, DC: US Government Printing Office, 1895), 130.

41. Jane Addams, "A Modern King Lear," in *The Jane Addams Reader*, ed. Jean Bethke Elshtain (New York: Basic Books, 2008), 163–76.

42. Frederick Remington, "Chicago under the Mob," *Harper's Weekly*, July 21, 1894, 680–81, had presented the US Army as the heroes of Pullman. Skerrett and Lesch emphasize that O'Neill was very specifically refuting Remington. O'Neill, *Sketchy Recollections*, 283.

43. Quotations from O'Neill's report on Pullman all from O'Neill, *Sketchy Recollections*, 64–84.

44. The time zone borders were not enacted by law but instead generally marked places where railroads already changed their running times. Atlanta in 1883 was on central time but has since moved into the eastern zone. Detroit switched between central and eastern time several times. Michael O'Malley, *Keeping Watch: A History of American Time* (New York: Viking, 1990), chap. 3; and *Chicago Tribune*, November 26, 1883, 3.

45. A. A. Hayes, "The Metropolis of the Prairies," *Harper's New Monthly Magazine*, June-November 1880, 726, 728; William Cronon, *Nature's Metropolis: Chicago and the Great West* (New York: W. W. Norton, 2009), 107, 109, 116, 154; "Report of the Statistician, Department of Agriculture," in *United States Congressional Serial Set* vol. 2212 (Washington, DC: US Government Printing Office, 1884), 461.

46. Addams, *Democracy and Social Ethics*, 23.

47. Mitrani, *Rise of the Chicago Police Department*, 11; Chicago Police Department, *Report of the General Superintendent of Police of the City of Chicago, to the City Council*, 1903, 8; dog pound report 1904, 118. Walter Augustus Wyckoff, *The Workers, an Experiment in Reality: The West* (New York: Charles Scribner's Sons, 1899), chaps. 1–5. Wyckoff, a Princeton theology graduate, spent several years as an itinerant laborer, including in Chicago in the early 1890s. He vividly described being housed at the Harrison Street station and also the police working to develop information about the ethnicity and background of the people who slept at the station.

48. General Superintendent's Report, 9; Annual report of the Municipal Lodging House, in Chicago Police Department, *Report of the General Superintendent*, 1903, 117, 118.

49. *Report of the General Superintendent*, 1904, 57; 1903, 6.

50. *Chicago Tribune*, February 13, 1893, 1; *Chicago Inter Ocean*, August 25, 1903, 6.

51. *Chicago Tribune*, July 5, 1903, 42; Chicago Police Department, *Report of the General Superintendent* , 1903, 77.

52. Captain Evans, in his report to O'Neill for 1904, wrote, "Acting upon your orders, on January 1, 1905, I established the Finger Print System in connection with the Bertillon System." He then gave a detailed explanation of how he had revised the size of fingerprint cards to make them easier to file and handle. The central problem here was organizational: how to store records so they could be easily found and retrieved. On the history of fingerprints, see Simon Cole, *Suspect Identities: A History of Fingerprinting and Criminal Identification* (Cambridge, MA: Harvard University Press, 2002). A classic analysis of photography of administrative surveillance, see Allan Sekula, "The Body and the Archive," *October* 39 (1986): 3–64.

53. O'Neill, *Sketchy Recollections*, 147.

## Chapter Five

"Your sporting Paddy etc. etc. bears no resemblance to a well known reel in Leinster and Munster variously named Rakish Paddy Sporting Pat etc. See No 749." Francis O'Neill to Bernard Bogue, May 28, 1917, ITMA Carolan.

1. Ford quoted in Timothy J. Meagher, *The Columbia Guide to Irish American History* (New York: Columbia University Press, 2005), 255. The author's academic mentor, Lawrence W. Levine, often told a story about how his mother, a Jewish immigrant from Russia, did not want him taking violin lessons from "that Litvak!," a neighboring Jewish immigrant from Lithuania. In antebellum cities, Irish Americans often organized themselves as "Kerryonians" or "Corkonians"

or joined the "Donegal society": that is, they kept a sense of themselves as being from a region while also having a sense of being Irish, in the same way Levine's mother had a sense of being both Jewish and not a Jewish Lithuanian. Life in the US quickly blurred those distinctions. In a similar but more exaggerated way, more recent immigrants from Vietnam, Korea, Mongolia, and China find themselves grouped as "Asians" in the US and actively work to define an Asian American identity that spans different countries of origin.

2. Francis O'Neill, *Irish Folk Music: A Fascinating Hobby* (Chicago: Regan, 1910), 17–18. O'Neill says Moore came to "my home on Poplar Avenue." This must either be a failure of memory or a very temporary home because city directories show O'Neill living on Emerald Avenue in 1875.

3. O'Neill, *Irish Folk Music*, 18.

4. O'Neill, *Irish Folk Music*, 18, 20. By "German flute," O'Neill might have meant the Boehm flute, the familiar silver keyed flute commonly played today, or he might have referred to German-made wooden flutes then commonly available.

5. O'Neill, *Irish Folk Music*, 24–25.

6. "Slavin Contra Wagner," and "The Serenade," in Finley Peter Dunne, *Mr. Dooley in the Hearts of His Countrymen* (London: Grant Richards, 1902), 126, 128, 206–8.

7. O'Neill, *Irish Folk Music*, 211–15. O'Neill details multiple impositions by the powerful on Murphy in his book in these pages and adds another instance of humiliation on page 24.

8. O'Neill, *Irish Folk Music*, 210, 215.

9. O'Neill is typically reticent about his private life, but the evidence that Barney was his brother-in-law is extremely compelling. *Chicago Tribune*, March 22, 1906, refers to Delaney as a relative of former police chief O'Neill. O'Neill, *Irish Folk Music*, 210, refers to Delaney as "my brother in law." See also Nick Whitmer's entry on Delaney at his extremely useful and well-researched site "The Lives of the Pipers," http://livesofthepipers.com/. O'Neill complains about Delaney's ingratitude frequently: the above from O'Neill to William Halpin, December 28, 1911, and O'Neill to Halpin, April 8, 1912, both in Seán Reid series, Breandán Breathnach Collection, reference BBR-187/1/1, Irish Traditional Music Archive (hereafter ITMA Breathnach).

10. On James O'Neill, see Caoimhín Mac Aoidh, *The Scribe: The Life and Works of James O'Neill* (Manorhamilton, Co. Leitrim: Drumlin, 2006). Quote on James from Francis O'Neill to Henry Chapman Mercer, February 15, 1921, Mercer Correspondence, Series 1, folder 73, misc. 291, January-March 1921, Mercer Museum Library, Bucks County Historical Society, Doylestown, PA.

11. Francis O'Neill to John G. O'Neill, June 16, 1916, Nicholas Carolan Collection, Irish Traditional Music Archive, Dublin (hereafter ITMA Carolan). It's not

clear what "Nancy's" name was. Census records show an Anna O'Neill married to Jerry Daly, with a son Joe and another son Phil. O'Neill mentions a nephew Phil Daly. But birth records in Ireland show O'Neill having a sister Mary and a sister Catherine. Emigrant Bank records, mentioned in chapter 2, show Phillip O'Neill living in New York with a sister, Mary.

12. In 1932 the *Tribune* reported on the retirement of Lieutenant Eugene Daly. "He joined the force in 1890 and was appointed lieutenant in 1905 by his uncle, former Chief of Police Francis O'Neill." *Chicago Tribune*, July 31, 1932, 10.

13. Hunt and Bonfield in *New York Times*, August 11, 1907, 4; *Chicago Inter Ocean*, October 8, 1901, 1. O'Neill reception described in *Chicago Citizen*, June 1, 1901, with Kerwin's house described as a mansion with "spacious rooms and parlors." The *Chicago Inter Ocean* commented on Kerwin's retirement and asked how a police patrolman "lives in his handsome house in a part of Wabash avenue where property is not cheap. Moreover, James Kerwin is reputed, on good authority, to be worth $150,000. Truly, he is a fortunate policeman. How did he manage it?" *Chicago Inter Ocean*, April 30, 1905, 12.

14. Francis O'Neill to Henry Chapman Mercer, October 15, 1920, Mercer Correspondence, Series 1, folder 71, misc. 291, August-October 1920, Mercer Museum Library. On Adam Tobin, see Nick Whitmer's *Lives of the Pipers* website, http://livesofthepipers.com/1tobinadam.html.

15. Transcript of Francis O'Neill to Bernard Bogue, May 28, 1917, ITMA Carolan; Francis O'Neill to Seamus O'Floinn, October 15, 1918, ITMA Carolan.

16. "The Freedom Picnic," in Dunne, *Mr Dooley*, 92–93.

17. Mimi Cowan, "Ducking for Cover: Chicago's Irish Nationalists in the Haymarket Era," *Labor* 9, no. 1 (2012): 63–64. The Irish immigrant John Holland built the three-man submarine, christened the Fenian Ram, as a prototype, with money drawn from the Clan Na Gael "skirmishing fund." The Fenian Ram was seaworthy. But it never saw use against the British. A rival faction within the Clan Na Gael stole it away under cover of night, but then realized they had no way to operate it without Holland, who withdrew from the entire project in disgust. Lawrence Goldstone, *Going Deep: John Philip Holland and the Invention of the Attack Submarine* (New York: Pegasus Books, 2017); Paul Collins, "A Ram for the Rebels," *New Scientist* 177, no. 2376 (2003): 44–45. On the Ram in newspapers, see *Chicago Tribune*, July 29, 1881, 2; *New York Times*, August 7, 1881, 1; *Washington Post*, August 1, 1881, 1; *Chicago Tribune*, April 14, 1883, 5. The Fenian Ram resides today in the Paterson Museum in Paterson, NJ. John Holland later designed the first commissioned US Navy submarine.

18. Gillian O'Brien, *Blood Runs Green: The Murder That Transfixed Gilded Age Chicago* (Chicago: University of Chicago Press, 2015), 95, 194.

19. O'Brien, *Blood Runs Green*, 101. Coughlin was eventually acquitted on appeal.

20. Quote from O'Brien. *Blood Runs Green*, 1. On the Clan Na Gael, see O'Brien,

*Blood Runs Green*; and David Brundage, *Irish Nationalists in America: The Politics of Exile, 1798–1998* (New York: Oxford University Press, 2016). On Cronin's funeral, see *Chicago Tribune*, May 27, 1889, 1. See also John T. McEnnis, *The Clan-Na-Gael and the Murder of Dr. Cronin* (Chicago: F. J. Schulte, 1889); and Henry M. Hunt, *The Crime of the Century: Or, The Assassination of Dr. Patrick Henry Cronin* (H. L. & D. H. Kochersperger, 1889).

21. O'Neill is referring to the town of Lake, later incorporated into Chicago. Francis O'Neill, *Chief O'Neill's Sketchy Recollections of an Eventful Life in Chicago*, ed. Ellen Skerrett and Mary Lesch (Evanston, IL: Northwestern University Press, 2008), 64; Richard Schneirov, *Labor and Urban Politics: Class Conflict and the Origins of Modern Liberalism in Chicago, 1864–97* (Urbana: University of Illinois Press, 1998), 104; O'Brien, *Blood Runs Green*, 17.

22. On the Hibernicon, see Michelle Granshaw, "The Hibernicon and Visions of Returning Home: Popular Entertainment in Irish America from the Civil War to World War I" (PhD diss., University of Washington, 2012); and Michelle Granshaw, *Irish on the Move: Performing Mobility in American Variety Theatre* (Des Moines: University of Iowa Press, 2019), chap. 3. Quotes from Granshaw, "Hibernicon," 6, 36, 87–88.

23. *Chicago Tribune*, October 20 1872, 6; Granshaw, "Hibernicon," 154; *Chicago Tribune*, October 26, 1873, 16.

24. Granshaw, "Hibernicon," 54, Alison Landsberg, *Prosthetic Memory: The Transformation of American Remembrance in the Age of Mass Culture* (New York: Columbia University Press, 2004). *New York Clipper* quoted in Granshaw, "Hibernicon," 59.

25. Rebecca Solnit, *A Book of Migrations: Some Passages in Ireland*, rev. ed. (London: Verso, 2011), 20–21.

26. Dale T. Knobel, *Paddy and the Republic: Ethnicity and Nationality in Antebellum America* (Middletown, CT: Wesleyan University Press, 1986), 91.

27. William H. Williams, *'Twas Only an Irishman's Dream: The Image of Ireland and the Irish in American Popular Song Lyrics, 1800–1920* (Urbana: University of Illinois Press, 1996), 85; Nicholas Gebhardt, *Vaudeville Melodies: Popular Musicians and Mass Entertainment in American Culture, 1870–1929* (Chicago: University of Chicago Press, 2017), 78; Granshaw, "Hibernicon," 90.

28. Williams, *'Twas only an Irishman's Dream*, 85. On African American participation in minstrelsy, see Louis Onuorah Chude-Sokei, *The Last Darky: Bert Williams, Black-on-Black Minstrelsy, and the African Diaspora* (Durham, NC: Duke University Press, 2006); David Gilbert, *The Product of Our Souls: Ragtime, Race, and the Manhattan Musical Marketplace* (Chapel Hill: University of North Carolina Press, 2016); Michael O'Malley, "Dark Enough as It Is: Eddie Lang and the Minstrel Cycle," *Journal of Social History* 52, no. 2 (2018): 234–59.

29. M. Alison Kibler, "Paddy, Shylock, and Sambo: Irish, Jewish, and African

American Efforts to Ban Racial Ridicule on Stage and Screen," in *Culture and Belonging in Divided Societies: Contestation and Symbolic Landscapes,* ed. Marc Howard Ross (Philadelphia: University of Pennsylvania Press, 2009), 259–80; M. Alison Kibler, *Censoring Racial Ridicule: Irish, Jewish, and African American Struggles over Race and Representation, 1890–1930* (Chapel Hill: University of North Carolina Press, 2015).

30. On the Irish villages generally, see Jeffrey O'Leary, "Manufacturing Reality: The Display of the Irish at World's Fairs and Exhibitions 1893 to 1965" (PhD diss., Kent State University, 2015), ProQuest 2015; Adrienne Lisbeth Stroik, "The World's Columbian Exposition of 1893: The Production of Fair Performers and Fairgoers" (PhD diss., University of California, Riverside, 2007); Christopher Quinn, "The Irish Villages at the 1893 World's Columbian Exposition Constructing, Consuming and Contesting Ireland at Chicago" (MA thesis, University of Guelph [Canada], 2011); Irish Industries Association, *Guide to the Irish Industrial Village and Blarney Castle* (Chicago: Irish Village Book Store, 1893). On the split between Hart and Aberdeen, see Janice Helland, "Exhibiting Ireland: The Donegal Industrial Fund in London and Chicago," *RACAR: revue d'art canadienne / Canadian Art Review* 29, no. 1/2 (2004): 28–46.

31. *Chicago Tribune,* May 27, 1893, 2.

32. Ishbel, Countess of Aberdeen, "Ireland at the World's Fair," *North American Review* 157 (July 1893): 19–20. Lady Aberdeen wanted to foster Irish cottage manufacture: she early on recognized the value of the American Irish market.

33. "Yanked It Down," *Chicago Citizen,* October 28, 1893; "Hauled Down the Union Jack: Almost a Riot in Lady Aberdeen's Irish Village," *New York Times,* October 22, 1893, 8; "The Aberdeens and the British Flag," *Chicago Citizen,* October 28, 1893, 4.

34. On why the British flag normally did not fly, *Chicago Tribune,* May 29, 1893; claim that the flag removal was a prank, *Chicago Tribune,* October 23, 1893.

35. See, for example, Fintan Cullen, *Ireland on Show: Art, Union, and Nationhood* (New York: Routledge, 2016); Michael Camille, T. J. Edelstein, and David and Alfred Smart Museum of Art, *Imagining an Irish Past: The Celtic Revival, 1840–1940* (Chicago: David and Alfred Smart Museum of Art, 1992); Gregory Castle, *Modernism and the Celtic Revival* (Cambridge: Cambridge University Press, 2001). There is considerable debate about the degree to which Irish culture can be seen as "Celtic" and about what that term might mean. See Barry W. Cunliffe and John T. Koch, eds., *Exploring Celtic Origins: New Ways Forward in Archaeology, Linguistics, and Genetics* (Oxford: Oxbow Books, 2019); Simon James, *The Atlantic Celts: Ancient People or Modern Invention?* (Madison: University of Wisconsin Press, 1999); John Haywood, *The Celts: Bronze Age to New Age* (New York: Pearson Longman, 2004); John Collis, *The Celts: Origins, Myths*

*and Inventions* (Stroud, UK: Tempus, 2003); and Melanie Giles, review of same in *Archaeological Journal* 161, no. 1 (2004): 242–43.

36. Anthropologists now tend to examine linguistic commonalities and shared cultural practices expressed in mobility and trade rather than the idea of a fixed "race." An opening salvo in the study of "tradition" came in E. J. Hobsbawm and T. O. Ranger, *The Invention of Tradition* (Cambridge: Cambridge University Press, 1983). On the uses of folk in the US, see Benjamin Filene, *Romancing the Folk: Public Memory & American Roots Music* (Chapel Hill: University of North Carolina Press, 2000); and Karl Hagstrom Miller, *Segregating Sound: Inventing Folk and Pop Music in the Age of Jim Crow* (Durham, NC: Duke University Press, 2010). For an example of how emigre musicians from Latin America navigated the cultural marketplace in the US and managed the notion of authenticity and tradition, see Matthew B. Karush, *Musicians in Transit: Argentina and the Globalization of Popular Music* (Durham, NC: Duke University Press, 2017). For an example of the vital importance of the idea of "Celtic" to American, Nazis, and the Irish republic, see Mairéad Carew, *The Quest for the Irish Celt: The Harvard Archaeological Mission to Ireland, 1932–1936* (Newbridge, Co. Kildare: Irish Academic Press, 2018), which includes efforts to discover a distinctively Irish Celt and efforts to explain away its failure to appear. The famous "Tara Brooch" offers a good example. This marvelous piece of intricate medieval metalwork was found near a beach north of Dublin: a jeweler with an eye to the Celtic revival market named it the "Tara Brooch," giving it an increased market value via association with legendary Irish high kings for which no evidence exists. Celtic revivalists wanted to make a shared set of similar "Celtic languages" once found across Europe into a racial identity with consistent—and marketable—cultural forms. Philip McEvansoneya, "The Purchase of the 'Tara' Brooch in 1868," *Journal of the History of Collections* 24, no. 1 (2012): 77–88; Niamh Whitfield, "The Finding of the Tara Brooch," *Journal of the Royal Society of Antiquaries of Ireland* 104 (1974): 120–42. For accounts of the Celtic revival at the fair specifically, see Neil Harris, "'Selling National Culture: Ireland at the World's Columbian Exposition,'" in Camille et al., *Imagining an Irish Past*, 82–105; Cullen, *Ireland on Show*, chap. 4.

37. Hyde's essay appears in Charles Gavan Duffy, George Sigerson, and Douglas Hyde, *The Revival of Irish Literature* (London: T. F. Unwin, 1894). On Hyde, see Janet Egleson Dunleavy, *Douglas Hyde: A Maker of Modern Ireland* (Berkeley: University of California Press, 1991); Dominic Daly, *The Young Douglas Hyde: The Dawn of the Irish Revolution and Renaissance, 1874–1893* (Totowa, NJ: Rowman & Littlefield, 1974).

38. On O'Neill and Gaelic League events, see *Irish World and American Industrial Liberator*, July 27, 1901; Sean O'Casey, *Drums Under the Windows* (New York: Macmillan, 1947), 494. O'Casey's semi-fictional autobiography is a fascinating

look at the politics of early twentieth-century Ireland. Written in a mocking and ironic tone—O'Casey had clearly read more than a little Joyce—it nevertheless captures the passion around the subject of Irish nationalism. Socialist O'Casey wanted a secular Celtic republic, speaking Irish and playing Irish sports, open equally to Protestant, Catholic, and nonbeliever. He directs a good deal of anger at the church, which would happily preserve English rule if it could protect its own position.

39. On the particular place of Ireland in discourses of race and nation, see Joe Cleary, "Amongst Empires: A Short History of Ireland and Empire Studies in International Context," *Éire-Ireland* 42, no. 1–2 (2007): 11–57; Colin Graham and Richard Kirkland, *Ireland and Cultural Theory: The Mechanics of Authenticity* (New York: St. Martin's Press, 1999); Colin Graham, *Deconstructing Ireland: Identity, Theory, Culture* (Edinburgh: Edinburgh University Press, 2001).

40. Michael D. Nicholsen, "'File Under Celtic': The Uses and Misuses of a Musical Myth, 1882–1999," *Canadian Journal of Irish Studies* 39, no. 2 (2016): 134–61.

41. Hunt was an ally of "Bathhouse" John Coughlin, Michael Kenna, and the gambler and saloonkeeper James O'Leary, himself associated with the town of Lake. "Inspector Hunt was in charge of the Hyde Park district at the time of the World's Fair of 1893, when he allowed to nestle about the Fair gates a particularly villainous collection of gambling houses, skin games, and worse resorts." *Hampton's Magazine*, January–June 1910, 317.

42. The spelling convention here follows O'Neill's.

43. Francis O'Neill to A. P. Graves, November 20, 1906, ITMA Carolan. On Touhey, see Pat Mitchell, Patrick J. Touhey, and Jackie Small, eds., *The Piping of Patsy Touhey* (Dublin: Na Píobairí Uilleann, 1986), 5; and the excellent and thorough research done by Nick Whitmer and posted online at "The Patrick Touhey Archive," http://www.whitmerpipes.com/touhey_archive.html.

44. Many sets of Taylor pipes exist and are still played. Henry Mercer, the American antiquarian, recognized the artisanal genius of the Taylor brothers and frequently visited their workshop. He avidly sought a set of Taylor pipes for his collections and after William's death tried to acquire his pipe-making tools.

45. Francis O'Neill, *Irish Minstrels and Musicians: With Numerous Dissertations on Related Subjects* (Chicago: Regan, 1913), 313–15. O'Neill got to know both men well. During his six months in Ireland McSweeney often stayed with Sergeant James Early and according to O'Neill might become "almost cordial" or "almost sociable" if drink flowed freely.

46. Mitchell and Small, *Piping of Patsy Touhey*, 1, write that Touhey "took on the best qualities of a nation that was then bursting with vitality"; Jimmy O'Brien Moran, "Capturing Diversity Whilst Creating Canon," in *Ancestral Imprints: Histories of Irish Traditional Music and Dance* (Cork: Cork University Press, 2012), 94–95, claims "Touhey's piping seems to embody what might be called

'the American style' of the period. His playing is flamboyant, showy, and perhaps excessive," and his "rhythm is somewhat mechanical and his playing unsubtle."

47. *Chicago Inter Ocean,* December 10, 1897, 6. The souvenir medal is in the possession of Mary Mooney Lesch, Francis O'Neill's great-granddaughter. The most detailed accounts of the fair appear in the *Chicago Citizen,* which paid extensive attention to the political speeches delivered at the opening. See *Chicago Citizen,* December 4, 1897, 2; December 11, 1897, 1. The organizers had hoped to raise $75,000 toward the construction of a Robert Emmett Memorial Hall. Gross receipts came to more than $20,000, but a month later expenses had reduced the net to $10,500. *Chicago Tribune,* December 19, 1897, 6; January 11, 1898, 4.

48. *Chicago Tribune,* December 7, 1897, 5; December 8, 1897, 6; Caroline R. Malloy, "Irish Villages, Pavilions, Cottages, and Castles at International Exhibitions, 1853–1939" (PhD, University of Wisconsin–Madison, 2013), 80, 104; *Chicago Inter Ocean,* December 19, 1897, 16.

49. *Chicago Tribune,* April 30, 1901, 1; *Chicago Eagle,* June 10, 1905, 2; *Chicago Inter Ocean,* April 30, 1901, 1.

50. *Chicago Record Herald,* May 5, 1901, 16; *Chicago Tribune,* April 30, 1901, 3.

51. *Chicago Inter Ocean,* May 1, 1901, 1, 6. The *Inter Ocean* harped on this theme consistently for the length of O'Neill's three appointments as chief. The editors depicted O'Neill as a good man who unfortunately chose to serve the mayor rather than ideals of justice.

52. "Capt. O'Neill Is Chief," *Chicago Record Herald,* April 30, 1901.

53. *Chicago Tribune,* April 14, 1911, 11; O'Neill's scrapbook thanks to Mary Mooney Lesch; *Chicago Inter Ocean* April 12, 1911, 5. On Irish Mam's and African American Mammy's, see April R. Schultz, "The Black Mammy and the Irish Bridget: Domestic Service and the Representation of Race, 1830–1930," *Éire-Ireland* 48, no. 3 (2013): 176–212.

## Chapter Six

"Although learned in his native Tipperary, Mr. Cronin never heard it named, but to make amends for the deficiency he christened it 'Chief O'Neill's Favorite.'" Francis O'Neill, *Irish Folk Music: A Fascinating Hobby* (Chicago: Regan, 1910), 114

1. Francis O'Neill, *Irish Minstrels and Musicians: With Numerous Dissertations on Related Subjects* (Philadelphia: R. West, 1977), 376–77.

2. Walter Augustus Wyckoff, *The Workers, an Experiment in Reality: The West* (New York: Charles Scribner's Sons, 1899), 91–92; Sam Mitrani, *The Rise of the*

*Chicago Police Department: Class and Conflict, 1850–1894* (Urbana: University of Illinois Press, 2013), 31.

3. "Piano Music," *Chicago Tribune*, June 20, 1901.

4. Francis O'Neill, "Policing a Modern Metropolis," *Saturday Evening Post*, June 6, 1901, 8–9; *Minneapolis Journal*, March 25, 1904, 14.

5. In his defense, O'Neill did add "and where honest and vigilant effort is constantly put forth to discover its outcropping and to punish its appearance" to his argument that gambling should be suppressed to the point where the police don't know about it. But it remains no less absurd for the addition of that clause. It basically says "hide your activities and we will leave you alone," which is pretty much what the second point says. They both amount to "criminals, don't make your activities too obvious."

6. O'Neill, "Policing a Modern Metropolis," 9.

7. Colleran biography in *Illinois Political Directory* (Chicago: W. L. Bodine, 1899), 297. The directory has nothing but praise for the figures it describes.

8. *Chicago Tribune*, August 13, 1901; August 14, 1901; August 16, 1901; September 22, 1901.

9. John Joseph Flinn and John Elbert Wilkie, *History of the Chicago Police: From the Settlement of the Community to the Present Time* (Under the auspices of the Police book fund, 1887), 466; *Illinois Political Directory*, 246; *Chicago Eagle*, August 17, 1901, 1; November 23, 1901, 1. Goldman described her treatment by Captain Herman Schuettler as torture. She was grilled without water for five days, with no attorney, and burned by hot light concentrated in a reflector. Emma Goldman, *Living My Life* (1931; reprint ed. 2011), 299.

10. *Chicago Tribune*, September 27, 1901, 3. On September 8, 1901, 3, the *Tribune* printed a long account of O'Neill questioning anarchists.

11. Goldman, *Living My Life*, 302, 310–11. *Chicago Journal* quoted in Eric Rauchway, *Murdering McKinley: The Making of Theodore Roosevelt's America* (New York: Hill & Wang, 2003), 103–9. On the fight between Burke and Harrison, see also Richard Allen Morton, *Roger C. Sullivan and the Making of the Chicago Democratic Machine, 1881–1908* (Jefferson, NC: McFarland, 2016), 123–30.

12. *Chicago Inter Ocean*, September 26, 1901, 1; *Chicago Eagle*, November 30, 1902, 1, 2. Newspapers were full of accounts of the Colleran case between August and November 1901. A detailed description of the charges appears in *Annual Report of Chicago Civil Service Commission* (Chicago, 1902), 286–91.

13. Francis O'Neill, *Chief O'Neill's Sketchy Recollections of an Eventful Life in Chicago*, ed. Ellen Skerrett and Mary Lesch (Evanston, IL: Northwestern University Press, 2008), 99, 101–2; *Chicago Inter Ocean*, October 8, 1901, 1; November 21, 1901, 1. Colleran's forces had earlier attacked O'Neill by accusing him of helping men cheat on the civil service exam. The charges lacked evidence,

and James Bonfield, who brought them, was fired. See *Chicago Inter Ocean,* October 8, 1901, 1.

14. Richard C. Lindberg, *To Serve and Collect: Chicago Politics and Police Corruption from the Lager Beer Riot to the Summerdale Scandal* (Carbondale: Southern Illinois University Press, 1998), 100. Apparently policemen sometimes "hid the star," scraping their names or numbers from badges, to avoid being identified or so they might lend the badge to a friend. *Chicago Tribune,* November 8, 1901, 3. O'Neill retired as a captain, the highest rank available in the police. He argued that the superintendent, who had authority over all the captains, should have a higher rank. After retirement, he referred to himself as Captain O'Neill rather than as chief.

15. Unidentified newspaper clipping in O'Neill Scrapbook in possession of Mary Mooney Lesch, Chicago. The clipping mentions twelve living ex-police chiefs and names the last as LeRoy Steward, 1909–11. Steward's successor was in office from 1911–13, so the clipping probably dates from 1912.

16. *Chicago Tribune,* April 6, 1905, 5; *Broad Ax,* April 15, 1905, 1. It's likely Mayor Harrison wanted to cultivate some of the votes of African Americans, who were beginning to leave the South in large numbers.

17. Allan H. Spear, *Black Chicago: The Making of a Negro Ghetto, 1890–1920* (Chicago: University of Chicago Press, 1967), 36–41; *Chicago Daily Herald,* May 5, 1905, 3; *Chicago Inter Ocean,* May 26, 1905, 2. Andrew W. Cohen, in *The Racketeer's Progress: Chicago and the Struggle for the Modern American Economy, 1900–1940* (Cambridge: Cambridge University Press, 2004), sees the strike as an example of a premodern craft union working to maintain control.

18. *Broad Ax,* June 17, 1905, 1.

19. *Broad Ax,* June 17, 1905, 1; Spear, *Black Chicago,* 40.

20. *Broad Ax,* August 21, 1915, 1. Julius Taylor's enthusiasm for O'Neill's collections reflected a growing African American interest in cultural nationalism. The Jamaican-born Marcus Garvey had only just founded the United Negro Improvement Association, which advanced an idea of solidarity among children of the African diaspora. Garvey admired Irish nationalism and borrowed from the symbology of Irish nationalism. Garvey declared, in 1919: "The time has come for the negro race to offer up its martyrs upon the altar of liberty even as the Irish has given a long list." Bruce Nelson, *Irish Nationalists and the Making of the Irish Race* (Princeton, NJ: Princeton University Press, 2012), details the influence of Irish nationalism on Garvey and on other African American intellectuals, in chapter 7. See also Michael G. Malouf, *Transatlantic Solidarities: Irish Nationalism and Caribbean Poetics* (Charlottesville: University of Virginia Press, 2009).

21. *Chicago Tribune,* November 6, 1903, 3.

22. Chicago Police Department, *Report of the General Superintendent of Police of the City of Chicago, to the City Council*, 1903, 10. Mark H. Haller, "Historical Roots of Police Behavior: Chicago, 1890–1925," *Law & Society Review* 10, no. 2 (1976): 319, argues sweat box interrogations were commonplace. "Indeed, standard interrogation in important cases, and many less important cases, was to place a suspect in the 'sweat box,' as it was called, for hours or days, until he broke down under continuous questioning. Newspapers often reported such events without comment." The use of torture is described in detail in Elizabeth Dale, *Robert Nixon and Police Torture in Chicago, 1871–1971* (DeKalb: Northern Illinois Press, 2016), and on O'Neill specifically, in her blog at https://patternpractice.org/2016/06/10/the-stomach-pump-continued/.

23. O'Neill, *Sketchy Recollections*, 128–35.

24. "Southwestern Chicago" referred to the town of Lake, later incorporated into the city. The town formed part of the Stockyards district, run by an odd coalition of Father Maurice Dorney, "Gambler" Jim O'Leary, and Police Inspector Nicholas Hunt. O'Neill would tangle with Hunt again shortly.

25. *Chicago Tribune*, October 8, 1902.

26. O'Neill, *Sketchy Recollections*, 128–35.

27. *Chicago Tribune*, March 24, 1904, 1.

28. O'Neill, *Sketchy Recollections*, 138–40; *Chicago Inter Ocean*, February 21, 1901, 1; *Chicago Record Herald*, February 21, 1902, 1; *Chicago Morning American*, February 21, 1901, 1; *Chicago Tribune*, February 21, 1901, 1.

29. *Chicago Tribune*, February 21, 1902, 1; *Chicago Inter Ocean*, February 22, 1902, 1; *Chicago Morning American*, February 21, 1902, 1.

30. *Chicago Eagle*, March 1, 1902, 2; *Chicago Inter Ocean*, February 21, 1901, 1.

31. *Chicago Tribune*, February 22, 1902, 2.

32. Tom Munnelly, "Junior Crehan of Bonavilla," *Béaloideas* 66 (1998): 78–79; Henry Glassie, *Passing the Time in Ballymenone*, reprint ed. (Bloomington: Indiana University Press, 1995), 100, 104; Paul Wells and Mike Casey, "An Interview with Mike Rafferty," *A Guide to the Irish Flute*, July 2002, http://www.irishfluteguide.info/mike-rafferty-interview-1/.

33. Munnelly, "Junior Crehan," 82. The usage of "have" becomes doubly interesting in light of Irish history—a history of people dispossessed of their land and watching their language fade from use year by year; people who had little and who found what little they had subject to seizure and loss. Further, the Irish language has no verb "to have." An Irish speaker, asking whether you have a cat, will literally say, "is a cat at you?" If you respond in Irish, you will say "a cat is at me." Likewise, a house and car are at you; a song is at you. Jennifer O'Riordan, Assistant Director of Irish Studies, Catholic University of America, to the author March 8, 2019.

34. Francis O'Neill, *Irish Folk Music: A Fascinating Hobby* (Chicago: Regan, 1910), 217–18.

35. O'Neill, *Irish Folk Music*, 66, 51.

36. Francis O'Neill to A. P. Graves, November 20, 1906, Nicholas Carolan Collection, Irish Traditional Music Archive, Dublin (hereafter ITMA Carolan). O'Neill told variants on this story multiple times. In some instances, Gillan follows the fluter through the streets and then pays him for the tune. In others, Gillan buys the tune from Kennedy, who got it from the fluter.

37. O'Neill, *Irish Folk Music*, 217, 96–97.

38. "Blacksmith Who Is Musical Prodigy," *Chicago Tribune*, July 28, 1901, 44.

39. O'Neill, *Irish Folk Music*, 40–41; Francis O'Neill to A. P. Graves, November 20, 1906, ITMA Carolan. We can add to the social and emotional complications the fact that O'Neill's only surviving son, Rogers O'Neill, was almost exactly the same age and also played the fiddle. West, an orphan, was offered a job as a blacksmith's helper. Rogers, born into a prosperous family, was bound for college. What would the two of them have felt about the relationship? Would a seventeen-year-old orphan boy of great musical talent have found this relationship nurturing or stifling? Francis O'Neill himself, recall, had run off to sea at seventeen, thwarting the ambitions of his elders.

40. O'Neill, *Irish Folk Music*, 41–42.

41. Newspaper accounts from the 1930 mention a "George West" playing the fiddle in Los Angeles, Spokane, and the Napa Valley; it is hard to know whether this is the same George West. *Los Angeles Times*, July 28, 1938; *Spokane Chronicle*, September 29, 1939; *Napa Journal*, September 21, 1938, 5.

42. *Chicago Tribune*, March 2, 1902, 53.

43. In *Irish Folk Music*, 54, O'Neill wrote that the idea of a committee proved too cumbersome and also "the more modest, but by no means the less skillful, gradually subsided, not caring to be engaged in continuous debate, until one opinionated and domineering member had it all to himself. One meeting demonstrated plainly that our scheme of consultation was a failure, and the "inquest committee," as it came to be facetiously called, convened but once. The two O'Neills were obliged to exercise their own best judgment in continuing the work undertaken."

44. *Chicago Tribune*, March 2, 1902, 53; *Chicago Inter Ocean*, June 5, 1901, 5.

45. O'Neill, *Irish Folk Music*, 37; O'Neill, *Sketchy Recollections*, 154.

46. *Chicago Tribune*, March 2, 1902, 53; Francis O'Neill to Henry Chapman Mercer, October 15, 1920, Mercer Correspondence, Series 1, folder 71, misc. 291, August-October 1920, Mercer Museum Library, Bucks County Historical Society, Doylestown, PA; Francis O'Neill to Bernard Bogue, May 28, 2017, ITMA Carolan.

47. Aileen Dillane, "Sound Tracts, Songlines, and Soft Repertoires: Irish Music Performance and the City of Chicago" (PhD diss., University of Chicago, 2009), 51; and "Irish Traditional Music Dissemination at the End of the Long Nineteenth Century: Francis O'Neill's *Music of Ireland* (1903) and the City of Chicago," in *Knowledge Dissemination in the Long Nineteenth Century: European and Transatlantic Perspectives*, ed. Marina Dossena and Stefano Rosso (Cambridge: Cambridge Scholars, 2016), 79. Dillane is one of the few scholars to situate O'Neill's work in the context of industrial Chicago and to see it as a product of life in that city rather than simply as a product of ethnic cultural continuity. See also the perceptive take of Michael D. Nicholsen, "Identity, Nationalism, and Irish Traditional Music in Chicago, 1867–1900," *New Hibernia Review / Iris Éireannach Nua* 13, no. 4 (2009): 111–26; and "'File Under Celtic': The Uses and Misuses of a Musical Myth, 1882–1999," *Canadian Journal of Irish Studies* 39, no. 2 (2016): 134–61.

48. Patrick Sky's introduction to the reprint of the 1883 edition, William Bradbury Ryan, Patrick Sky, and Elias Howe, eds., *Ryan's Mammoth Collection: 1050 Reels and Jigs: Hornpipes, Clogs, Walk-Arounds, Essences, Strathspeys, Highland Flings and Contra Dances, with Figures: And How to Play Them* (Pacific, MO: Mel Bay, 1995), includes a solid account of the background and origins of the collection.

49. Paul F. Wells, "Elias Howe, William Bradbury Ryan, and Irish Music in Nineteenth-Century Boston," *Journal of the Society for American Music; Cambridge* 4, no. 4 (2010): 403; Henry Chapman Mercer to Francis O'Neill, October 1, 1920, Mercer Correspondence, Series 1, folder 71, misc. 291, August-October 1920, Mercer Museum Library, Bucks County Historical Society, Doylestown, PA; Patrick Sky, "Elias Howe and William Bradbury Ryan," *Ryan's Mammoth Collection*, 14; Caoimhín Mac Aoidh, "William Ryan's Mammoth Task," *Irish Music* 2, no. 10 (1997): 50; Mac Aoidh, *The Scribe: The Life and Works of James O'Neill* (Manorhamilton, Co. Leitrim: Drumlin, 2006), 69; Sally K. Sommers Smith, "An Eventful Life Remembered: Recent Considerations of the Contributions and Legacy of Francis O'Neill," *Journal of the Society for American Music* 4, no. 4 (2010): 430.

50. Paul De Grae, "Captain O'Neill and the Americans," in *Ancestral Imprints: Histories of Irish Traditional Music and Dance* (Cork: Cork University Press, 2012), discusses O'Neill's use of *Ryan's* extensively. See also O'Neill referencing *Ryans* in O'Neill to Henry Chapman Mercer, September 6, 1920, Mercer Correspondence, Series 1, folder 71, misc. 291, August-October 1920, Mercer Museum Library, Bucks County Historical Society, Doylestown, PA.

51. Chicago Police Department, *Report of the General Superintendent of Police of the City of Chicago, to the City Council*, 1903, 25–27; *Chicago Tribune*, December 31, 1903, 1, 3. On Timothy grass, see chap. 1, note 4.

52. Francis O'Neill to John G. O'Neill, June 16, 1916, ITMA Carolan; Francis O'Neill to Seamus O Casaide, August 28, 1917, Seamus Ó Casaide Papers, 8116(7), National Library of Ireland.

53. *Chicago Inter Ocean*, April 13, 1904, 3.

54. Alexander R. Piper, *Report of an Investigation of the Discipline and Administration of the Police Department of the City of Chicago* (Chicago, 1904), 5, 10–11, 13–14.

55. *Chicago Tribune*, March 20, 1904, 3; July 5, 1904, 7.

56. O'Neill, *Sketchy Recollections*, 155.

57. *Chicago Eagle*, July 1, 1905, 1, contains a long series of insinuations about Hunt and his relationship to gambling magnate James O'Leary; see also *Chicago Tribune*, July 4, 1905, 4.

58. Mahoney's charges, along with a picture of O'Neill, appear in the *Chicago Inter Ocean*, August 29, 1906, 3, and on the front page of the *Chicago Tribune*, same date. O'Neill's testimony described in the *Tribune* on September 22, 1906, 5. The entire affair is summarized in Charles Edward Russell, "Chaos and Bomb Throwing in Chicago," *Hampton's Magazine* 24 (March 1910): 316–17; and in Richard C. Lindberg, *To Serve and Collect: Chicago Politics and Police Corruption from the Lager Beer Riot to the Summerdale Scandal* (Carbondale: Southern Illinois University Press, 1998), 74–75.

59. A series of articles on the protective association appears in the *Chicago Tribune*, January 15, 1902, 3; January 20 1902, 3; January 25 1902, 12; July 14, 1905, 1; July 15, 1905, 14; *Rock Island Argus*, January 17, 1902, 1.

## Chapter Seven

"'The King of the Pipers' created a sensation when first introduced by Mr. Cronin. None among his audience had heard [it] before." Francis O'Neill, *Irish Folk Music: A Fascinating Hobby* (Chicago: Regan, 1910), 88.

1. *Chicago Tribune*, July 25, 1905, 2; Mary Wade to Nicholas Carolan, October 20, 1997, Nicholas Carolan Collection, Irish Traditional Music Archives, Dublin (hereafter ITMA Carolan). O'Neill promenading with dog Mickey from unidentified newspaper clipping ca. 1912 in O'Neill scrapbooks, in possession of Mary Mooney Lesch. Historic maps of the Palos area show a number of properties owned by a "Pat Shea" and then "J. Shea," presumably his son Jack, himself a police captain. Many Irish names dot the map in that area, suggesting O'Neill bought land among his fellow Irish Americans. Based on the names on historic maps and O'Neill's description of the property as "watered," it seems likely O'Neill's farm was in an area directly south of the town of Willow

Springs and now part of a large nature preserve, possibly White Oak Woods. Max Rondonell, Snyder's real estate map of Cook, Du Page, and part of Will Counties, Illinois (Chicago: William L. Mitchell, 1898), https://www.loc.gov/item/2013593089/; L. M. Snyder & Co., Snyder's real estate map of Cook County, Illinois: indexed (Chicago: L. M. Snyder, 1886), https://www.loc.gov/item/2013593088/; F. M. Snyder, Snyder's real estate map of Cook and Dupage Counties, Illinois (Chicago, Illinois: F. M. Snyder, 1890), https://www.loc.gov/item/2013593076/.

2. Francis O'Neill, *Chief O'Neill's Sketchy Recollections of an Eventful Life in Chicago*, ed. Ellen Skerrett and Mary Lesch (Evanston, IL: Northwestern University Press, 2008), 120, quotes a letter to O'Neill from a George Thorndyke, in which Thorndyke claimed enemies of O'Neill had enlisted his help in a scheme to lure the chief to a place that would compromise his reputation. O'Neill excised the enemy's name, leaving only H——T K——G. An account in the *Tribune* makes it clear that the man was lawyer Hoyt King. *Chicago Tribune*, December 19, 1903, 2. It should come as no surprise that O'Neill declared himself completely innocent.

3. Aileen Dillane, "Sound Tracts, Songlines, and Soft Repertoires: Irish Music Performance and the City of Chicago" (PhD diss., University of Chicago, 2009), ProQuest 2009, 78.

4. Francis O'Neill, *O'Neill's Music of Ireland* (Chicago: Lyon & Healy, 1903).

5. *Irish Standard*, March 8, 1902, 1; *Citizen* quoted in Francis O'Neill, *Irish Folk Music: A Fascinating Hobby* (Chicago: Regan, 1910), 361.

6. *Ulster Journal of Archaeology* (Ulster Archaeological Society, 1904); Australian Patrick O'Leary, Francis O'Neill, *The Dance Music of Ireland: 1001 Gems* (Chicago: Lyon & Healy, 1907), 2; *Chicago Tribune*, May 6, 1903, 16.

7. Accounts of the address appeared in many Irish newspapers. See "Fielding Harangue," *Irish Examiner (Cork)*, November 23, 1903, 5; "Harangue," *Dublin Evening Herald*, Monday, November 23, 1903, 4, November 23, 1903; "An Extraordinary Harangue," *Kilkenny People*, December 28, 1903, 2; "Fielding Harangue," *Fermanagh Herald*, November 28, 1903, 3.

8. *Gael (an Gaodhal)*, v. 23 review April 1904, 150; article on Piper report May, 1904, 171; and O'Neill's response May 1904, 196.

9. O'Neill, *Irish Folk Music*, 56; Nicholas Carolan, *A Harvest Saved: Francis O'Neill and Irish Music in Chicago* (Cork: Ossian, 1997), 45–46.

10. On the Gaelic League and Hyde, see Janet Egleson Dunleavy, *Douglas Hyde: A Maker of Modern Ireland* (Berkeley: University of California Press, 1991); Úna Ní Bhroiméil, *Building Irish Identity in America, 1870–1915: The Gaelic Revival* (Dublin: Four Courts, 2003); and Úna Ní Bhroiméil, "The Creation of an Irish Culture in the United States: The Gaelic Movement, 1870–1915," *New Hibernia Review / Iris Éireannach Nua* 5, no. 3 (2001): 87–100.

11. Dunleavey, *Douglas Hyde*, 267, 263.

12. *Chicago Tribune*, January 8, 1906, 4.

13. O'Neill, *Irish Folk Music*, 222–25.

14. Hyde's diaries are in the National Library of Ireland. Translation from Hyde's diaries by Liam Mac Mathúna, personal correspondence with the author, May 10, 2019. See Liam Mac Mathúna, Niall Comer, Brian Ó Conchubhair, Máire Nic an Bhaird, and Cuan Ó Seireadáin, eds., *Douglas Hyde: My American Journey* (Dublin: University College Dublin Press, 2020).

15. Francis O'Neill to Seamus Ó Casaide, March 23, 2011, National Library of Ireland MS8116 (5). On the typewriter—which was probably *not* the only Gaelic font typewriter in the world—see *Chicago Tribune*, December 17, 1894, 9. On sermons delivered in Irish, see *Chicago Tribune*, March 18, 1894, 4, and March 18, 1903, 5. On O'Carroll, see *The National Cyclopedia of American Biography* (New York: J. T. White, 1897), 251.

16. Ní Bhroiméil, "Creation of an Irish Culture," 99.

17. O'Neill, *Sketchy Recollections*, 156–58; *Skibbereen Eagle*, July 28, 1906, 2.

18. O'Neill, *Irish Folk Music*, 288, 58. O'Neill completely missed a legendary musician from Clare, Garret Barry, the blind piper. For an account of the life of the itinerant Barry, see Howard Marshall and Ben Taylor, *Out of Darkness: The Blind Piper of Inagh* (Norfolk, UK: Cottier Press, 2016).

19. Tupper quoted in Roxanne M. O'Connell, "The Golden Age of Irish Music: The Cultural Impact of 78 RPM Recordings in Ireland and Irish America 1900–1960" (PhD diss., Salve Regina University, 2010), 72.

20. O'Neill, *Irish Folk Music*, 95. On Touhey's mail order recordings, see the links at Nick Whitmer's Patsy Touhey archives, http://www.whitmerpipes.com/touhey_1900–04.html; and for an example, see *Irish World* (New York), February 8, 1902, 7. Not all the recordings survived. The O'Neill cylinder recordings can be heard at the Dunn Family Collection at https://archives.irishfest.com/dunn-family-collection/Music.htm and at http://epu.ucc.ie/henebry/. Two recordings of O'Neill playing tin whistle with Cronin and Tom Kiley on mandolin exist. Of poor quality and uncertain provenance, the recordings announce the names of the players: the voice is almost certainly O'Neill's. His whistle is only occasionally audible. The recordings of "The Boys of Bluehill" and "the Fermoy Lasses," are posted at *thebeatcop.com*. Thanks to Emmett Gill of Na Píobairí Uilleann in Dublin for sharing copies.

21. Francis O'Neill to Bernard Bogue, May 28, 2017, ITMA Carolan; Francis O'Neill to Henry Chapman Mercer, October 15, 1920, Mercer Correspondence, Series 1, folder 71, misc. 291, August-October 1920, Mercer Museum Library, Bucks County Historical Society, Doylestown, PA.

22. Solo playing was the norm but not a rule: in *Irish Minstrels and Musicians*, 394, O'Neill describes Cronin playing with Tom Kiley on mandolin. But he also

refers to the mandolin as "the Connemara fiddle," which suggest strictly single note playing.

23. O'Neill, *Irish Folk Music*, 87. Francis O'Neill, *Irish Minstrels and Musicians: With Numerous Dissertations on Related Subjects* (Chicago: Regan, 1913), 394, places Cronin at the Deering Harvester Works.

24. Sale to Mooney in *Chicago Tribune*, April 24, 1906, 7; O'Neill to Mercer, October 15, 1920, Mercer Correspondence, Series 1, folder 71, misc. 291, August-October 1920, Mercer Museum Library.

25. On the life of James O'Neill, see Caoimhín Mac Aoidh, *The Scribe: The Life and Works of James O'Neill*, (Manorhamilton, Co. Leitrim: Drumlin, 2006); *Chicago Tribune*, April 24, 1906, 7; O'Neill to Mercer, February 15, 1921, Mercer Correspondence, Series 1, folder 73, misc. 291, January-March 1921, Mercer Museum Library. James O'Neill did appear as the editor on a book issued in 1908, *O'Neill's Irish Music: 250 Choice Selections Arranged for Piano and Violin*. On Cronin, see O'Neill, *Irish Minstrels and Musicians*, 394. "Temperament and professional jealousy brought it all to an abrupt end without apparent cause." At least not apparent to O'Neill.

26. Francis O'Neill to Bernard Bogue, May 28, 1917, ITMA Carolan; Francis O'Neill to William Halpin, November 15, 1911, and December 28, 1911, both in Seán Reid series, Breandán Breathnach Collection, reference BBR-187/1/1, Irish Traditional Music Archive (hereafter ITMA Breathnach). By 1920, Delaney was suffering the effects of tertiary syphilis, and Francis wrote a letter to Captain James Mooney, his son-in-law, asking "will you please write to the Police Officials at Havana, Cuba and try to dig Barney up. He may have gotten drunk after getting out of the hospital or may have been slugged or thrown into the Bay or other hiding place." O'Neill to Jim Mooney, October 20, 1919, https://digitalchicagohistory.org/items/show/1719, and in possession of Mary Mooney Lesch, Mooney's granddaughter. Delaney died at the Illinois Hospital for the Insane in 1923. By this point, Delaney was O'Neill's former brother-in-law since Julia Delaney, Anna's sister, had died in 1915.

27. *Chicago Inter Ocean*, Newspapers.Com, February 15, 1911, 7.

28. O'Neill's dedications to Selena all copied in ITMA Carolan. "Modern fancy" quote from O'Neill to William Halpin, April 8, 1912, ITMA Breathnach.

29. *Kerry News*, July 22, 1912, 6; *Kerry Sentinel*, July 3, 1912, 3; Francis O'Neill to Seamus Ó Casaide, July 22, 1912, National Library of Ireland MS8116 (5).

30. *Chicago Citizen*, May 3, 1912, 8; Francis O'Neill to John O'Neill, November 16, 1916, ITMA Carolan.

31. *Chicago Tribune*, July 20, 1913, B6.

32. *Chicago Daily Tribune*, July 29, 1912, 5.

33. *Chicago Tribune*, July 20, 1913, B6; "Gaelic Feis Monster Success," *Chicago Citi-*

*zen*, August 9, 1913. On divisions over the use of the space, see Francis O'Neill to Seamus O'Floinn, October 15, 1918, ITMA Carolan. The Feis was revived in 1930.

34. O'Neill to O'Floinn, October 15, 1918; O'Neill to Halpin, December 28, 1911.

35. O'Neill to Halpin, January 27, 1914, ITMA Breathnach. O'Neill is likely referring to Robert Stewart Castlereagh, *Memoirs and Correspondence of Viscount Castlereagh, Second Marquess of Londonderry*, vol. 3, *Military and Diplomatic* (London: H. Colburn, 1850), 80–86.

36. O'Neill to Halpin, December 30, 1913, ITMA Breathnach; O'Neill to O'Floinn, ITMA Carolan; O'Neill to Mercer, March 6, 1921, Mercer Correspondence, Series 1, folder 73, misc. 291, January–March 1921, Mercer Museum Library, Bucks County Historical Society, Doylestown, PA.

37. "The Parish That Came Back," *Ecclesiastical Review* 61 (July 1919): 25–37; Candace Scheidt, *St Thomas the Apostle Catholic Church: Celebrating 150 Years* (Chicago: St. Thomas the Apostle Church, 2019); Sarah Caring Bond, *The Art and Architecture of St. Thomas the Apostle Church: A Guided Tour* (Chicago: St. Thomas the Apostle Church, 2018).

38. For an assessment of the value of the books by an expert in the field, see Carolan, *Harvest Saved*, 46–52.

39. John Ennis, "Feis Ceoil," *Chicago Citizen*, March 2, 1901; James Kieran Fielding, *The Resurrection of a Nation* (Chicago: Mayer & Miller, 1934), 19, 29. The latter book collects a number of Father Fielding's essays and speeches. "Sassenach" is a derogatory term for "English."

40. O'Neill to Halpin, December 28, 191, ITMA Breathnach. In 1911 a consumer could hear music on Edison cylinders, which came to market first, or on the flat 78 rpm disks invented by Emile Berliner. O'Neill had a cylinder machine but no disk player.

41. Scott Spencer, "Wheels of the World: How Recordings of Irish Traditional Music Bridged the Gap Between Homeland and Diaspora," *Journal of the Society for American Music* 4 (November 2010): 442.

42. On the impact of recordings generally, see Scott Spencer, "Wheels of the World" and Spencer, "Transatlantic Migrations of Irish Music in the Early Recording Age," in *The Irish in the Atlantic World*, ed. David T. Gleeson (Columbia: University of South Carolina Press, 2010), 53–75.

43. "Michael Coleman, The Irish Kriesler, Is Dead," *Irish American Advocate*, January 20, 1945; "Michael Coleman His Music," *NY Irish American Advocate*, November 17, 1973, 5; Michael Kelly, "The Musical Mcloughlin Clan," *An Piobaire*, April 2017, 20–21; *Irish Advocate*, September 28, 1918, 2; *Irish American Advocate*, June 29, 1918. In Patrick Mullin's 1993 documentary *From Shore to Shore*, Coleman's daughter describes his dancing and recalls her memory of

him dancing and playing on the stage in Chicago, and also being a featured performer in stage in Philadelphia in the 1920s. Helen O'Shea situates Coleman in an international context in *The Making of Irish Traditional Music* (Cork: Cork University Press 2008), 26–29. The best account of Coleman's life is Harry Bradshaw's extensive booklet accompanying a two-cd set, *Michael Coleman* (Dublin: Gael-Linn/Viva Voce, 1992).

44. Fintan Vallely, *The Companion to Irish Traditional Music* (New York: New York University Press, 1999), 388; Hilary Bracefield, "Gramophone or Radio: Transatlantic Effects in the Development of Traditional Music in Ireland," *Irish Journal of American Studies* 13/14 (2004): 115–21; Gearóid Ó hAllmhuráin, *Flowing Tides: History and Memory in an Irish Soundscape* (New York: Oxford University Press, 2016), 85.

45. Scott Spencer, "'Wheels of the World': How Recordings of Irish Traditional Music Bridged the Gap Between Homeland and Diaspora," *Journal of the Society for American Music*, September 27, 2010, 445.

46. On the influence of piano, see the excellent MA thesis of Aileen Dillane, "The Ivory Bridge: Piano Accompaniment on 78 rpm Recorded Sources of Irish Traditional Dance Music America c. 1910–1945" (MA thesis, University of Limerick, 2000); quote from Bracefield, "Gramophone or Radio."

47. Nuala O'Connor, *Bringing It All Back Home: The Influence of Irish Music at Home and Overseas* (Dublin: Merlin, 2001), 61.

48. Ó hAllmhuráin, *Flowing Tides*, 115–16.

49. Mick Moloney, "Irish Ethnic Recording and the Irish-American Imagination," in *Studies in American Folklife* (Washington, DC: American Folklife Center, Library of Congress, 1982), 92; Tom Munnelly, "Junior Crehan of Bonavilla," *Béaloideas* 66 (1998): 79; Sally K. Sommers Smith, "Landscape and Memory in Irish Traditional Music," *New Hibernia Review / Iris Éireannach Nua* 2, no. 1 (1998): 132–44.

50. *Irish American Advocate*, November 17, 1973; Harry Bradshaw, *Michael Coleman* (Dublin: Gael-Linn/Viva Voce, 1992), 22, 24. Chicago musician Malachy Towey knew Coleman's brother Jimmy in Ireland and recalls that another brother, Eoghan, resented the focus on music and "kicked him out" of the family home. Neighbors esteemed his music very highly, so much so that they gifted a plot of land and a house to Jimmy. See https://www.youtube.com/watch?v=i16LyHZxgmg. Thanks to Marta Cook for this reference.

51. Francis O'Neill, *Irish Minstrels and Musicians: With Numerous Dissertations on Related Subjects* (Philadelphia: R. West, 1977), 313–15.

52. For example, see O'Neill, *Irish Folk Music*, 18–19, 36, 60, 102, 121, 157, 275, 291–92; O'Neill, *Irish Minstrels and Musicians*, 244, 312, 368, 377, 395, 400, 406–8; Francis O'Neill, *Waifs and Strays of Gaelic Melody; Comprising Forgotten Favorites,*

*Worthy Variants, and Tunes Not Previously Printed* (Chicago: Lyon & Healey, 1922), 134.

53. A considerable amount of mystification surrounds the idea of "swing," and the presence or absence of "swing" often serves as a policing tool to dismiss the playing of people outside a tradition or as a criteria of authenticity, as we see O'Neill using it. The sense of swing lends itself to digital quantification and analysis: in a Digital Audio Workstation, you can apply "swing" to a tune and the software will impart a recognizable if not pleasant sense of "swing." See, for example, Vincent Rosinach and Caroline Traub, "Measuring Swing in Irish Traditional Fiddle Music" (International Conference on Music Perception and Cognition, Bologna, Italy, August 22–26, 2006), https://www.researchgate.net/publication/229037657_Measuring_swing_in_irish_traditional_fiddle_music.

54. Daniel Cassidy has tried to claim, somewhat persuasively, that the word "jazz" comes not from Africa but from the Irish word "teas," meaning "heat, passion or excitement" or "teasaí," meaning "passionate, exciting, or hot." Depending on region, an Irish speaker might pronounce "teas" as "jass," "chass," or "t'ass." Daniel Cassidy, *How the Irish Invented Slang: The Secret Language of the Crossroads* (Petrolia, CA: CounterPunch, 2007). The biggest problem with this argument comes from the fact that in the early twentieth century, most Irish immigrants did not speak Irish; neither did most people in Ireland. Certainly a word used to describe a specific feeling might persist, but modern Irish people will commonly interject the nonword "hup!" to encourage or acknowledge musical excitement, not the word "teas."

55. These recordings appear in the website accompanying this volume, *thebeatcop .com*.

56. O'Neill *Waifs and Strays*, 134; O'Neill, *Dance Music of Ireland*, intro.; Mick Moloney, "Irish American Popular Music," in *Making the Irish American: History and Heritage of the Irish in the United States*, ed. J. J. Lee and Marion R. Casey (New York: New York University Press, 2006), 383. On Emmett, see Howard L. Sacks, *Way up North in Dixie: A Black Family's Claim to the Confederate Anthem* (Washington, DC: Smithsonian Institution Press, 1993). Sacks's argument is plausible but unproven. Emmett did scour the countryside for material to use in minstrel shows, drawing on African American sources. He wrote down one tune from the Snowden family he called "Genuine Negro Jig." You can hear the tune played by the Carolina Chocolate Drops as "Snowden's Jig" at https://youtu.be/N3gcCAXm-ek.

57. O'Neill, *Waifs and Strays*, 134; O'Neill, *Irish Minstrels*, 480.

58. English origin for the tune documented in Stephen Winick, "Turkey in the Straw," Folklife Today," last modified May 15, 2014, http://blogs.loc.gov/folklife/2014/05/turkey-in-the-straw/.

59. Richard K. Spottswood, *Ethnic Music on Records: A Discography of Ethnic Recordings Produced in the United States, 1893–1942*, vol. 5, *Middle East, Far East, Scandinavian, English Language, American Indian, International* (Urbana: University of Illinois Press, 1990), 2823. Morrison called it "the wreck of the 99," but it's the same as "the Wreck of the Old 97" recorded a decade earlier by Vernon Dalhart.

60. Dillane, "Ivory Bridge," 29, 55; Bracefield, "Gramophone or Radio," 119; Paul Wells and Mike Casey, "An Interview with Mike Rafferty," A Guide to the Irish Flute, July 2002, http://www.irishfluteguide.info/mike-rafferty-interview-1/.

## Epilogue

"To Bob Spence, a fellow boarder, in 1870, I am indebted for our setting of 'Happy to Meet and Sorry to Part,' a grand and spirited double jig not found in any previous Irish collections, although printed in one American volume of miscellaneous dance music. Spence was a devoted student, and while he patiently sawed away on his fiddle, a receptive memory enabled me to learn his tune and retain it." Francis O'Neill, *Irish Folk Music: A Fascinating Hobby* (Chicago: Regan, 1910), 101.

1. Mercer's life and work are well described in Cleota Reed, *Henry Chapman Mercer and the Moravian Pottery and Tile Works* (Philadelphia: University of Pennsylvania Press, 1996). The museum, tile works, and Fonthill are well documented online.

2. Henry Chapman Mercer to Francis O'Neill, October 1, 1920, Mercer Correspondence, Series 1, folder 71, misc. 291, August-October 1920, Mercer Museum Library, Bucks County Historical Society, Doylestown, PA.

3. Henry Chapman Mercer to Francis O'Neill, August 27, 1920, and O'Neill to Mercer, October 15, 1920, both in Mercer Correspondence, Series 1, folder 71, misc. 291, August-October 1920, Mercer Museum Library. O'Neill, with characteristic blunt insensitivity, told Mercer that the tune he loved was "not Irish."

4. Francis O'Neill, *Waifs and Strays of Gaelic Melody: Comprising Forgotten Favorites, Worthy Variants, and Tunes Not Previously Printed* (Chicago: Lyon & Healy, 1922), 9.

5. As of this writing, the project website has not been announced. The project is described at this link: https://www.itma.ie/latest/news/oneill-dedication-pages.

6. The dedication says only "To the renowned Henry Ford, with Compliments of the Author." For background, see Neil Baldwin, *Henry Ford and the Jews* (New York: PublicAffairs, 2002). For examples of Chicago newspapers cover-

ing Ford's anti-Semitism, see *Chicago Tribune*, January 31, 1921, 13; May 19, 1924, 12; January 8, 1925, 3.

7. Francis O'Neill to Seamus Ó Casaide, August 28, 1917, and August 28, 1917, in Seamus Ó Casaide Papers, 8116(7), and June 7, 1917, National Library of Ireland MS8116 (7).

8. Undated clipping, ca. 1919–20, probably from the *Chicago Record Examiner*, in O'Neill scrapbooks in possession of Mary Mooney Lesch, Chicago. Weber was an active pianist and music critic, and O'Neill might have read her pieces regularly in the *Record Examiner*, where she served as music critic.

9. O'Neill scrapbook, 140–43.

10. Henriette Weber, *Putting Young America in Tune: How to Teach the Child Appreciation of Music* (Chicago: F. J. Drake, 1920), 153.

11. Tom Munnelly, "Junior Crehan of Bonavilla," *Béaloideas* 66 (1998): 71; Paul Wells and Mike Casey, "An Interview with Mike Rafferty, Part 2: Learning to Play," A Guide to the Irish Flute, July 2002, http://www.irishfluteguide.info/mike-rafferty-interview-3/.

12. O'Neill to Mercer, March 6, 1921, Mercer Correspondence, Series 1, folder 73, misc. 291, January-March 1921, Mercer Museum Library; Francis O'Neill, "Irish Dances and Dance-Music," *Cork Weekly Examiner*, April 7, 1934; Nathan Godfried, *WCFL, Chicago's Voice of Labor, 1926–78* (Urbana: University of Illinois Press, 1997). O'Neill says the "Irish Hour" was every day of the week, but other accounts suggest it was Sundays only.

13. *Cork Weekly Examiner*, April 7, 1934.

14. O'Neill to Mercer, October 15, 1920, and February 15, 1921, Mercer Correspondence, Series 1, folder 71, misc. 291, August–October 1920, and folder 73, misc. 291, January–March 1921, Mercer Museum Library, Bucks County Historical Society. Selena O'Neill made a few recordings of Irish music in 1928. In 1940 she reprinted an edition of *Dance Music of Ireland* from the original plates. She worked during WWII at the Pullman factory making material for the war. See Nicholas Carolan, *A Harvest Saved: Francis O'Neill and Irish Music in Chicago* (Cork: Ossian, 1997), 48–49.

15. Mary Wade to Nicholas Carolan, October 20, 1997, Nicholas Carolan Collection, Irish Traditional Music Archive, Dublin.

16. *Chicago Tribune*, December 31, 1933, 8; *Chicago Tribune*, December 31, 1934, 8.

17. Francis O'Neill, "Irish Music," in *The Pageant of the Celt* (Chicago: Pageant of the Celt Committee, 1934), copy in Irish Traditional Music Archives, Dublin.

18. Micheál MacLiammóir, *All for Hecuba: An Irish Theatrical Autobiography* (London: Methuen, 1946). MacLiammóir was born Alfred Willmore in England. As a young man, he reinvented himself as Irish and lived more or less openly as a gay man in Dublin, one of the most socially conservative places in Europe

in the 1940s and 1950s. Lawrence Ervin McCullough, "Irish Music in Chicago: An Ethnomusicological Study" (PhD diss., University of Pittsburgh, 1978); *Chicago Tribune*, December 31, 1933.

19. For example, *The Session*, a website devoted to Irish music, allows users to enter an address and find Irish music sessions. In December 2020, a search disclosed four active sessions in Argentina, three in Moscow, and more than a dozen in Japan. See https://thesession.org/sessions.

20. *Chicago Tribune*, January 29, 1936; *Southern Star*, February 8, 1936; "Cabin Boy Becomes Police Chief," *Irish Independent*, January 31, 1936; "From the Hill Tops (on the Life and Death of Capt. Francis O'Neill of Chicago)," *Catholic Bulletin* 26 (March 1936): 203–4.

21. Breandán Breathnach, "Francis O'Neill, Collector of Irish Music," *Dal gCais* 3 (1977): 111–19, and *Folk Music and Dances of Ireland: A Comprehensive Study Examining the Basic Elements of Irish Folk Music and Dance Traditions* (Cork: Ossian, 1996); Nicholas Carolan, *A Harvest Saved: Francis O'Neill and Irish Music in Chicago* (Cork: Ossian, 1997).

22. Nick Whitmer, "Trouble in the Irish Village," *An Píobaire*, July 2015, 26–28. Actors from the Abbey Theater in Dublin, hired to perform at the 1904 St. Louis World's Fair, "condemned the 'anti-Irish tone' of Touhey's act, and a later account says their indignation was provoked because Touhey 'sang a song which was a vile caricature on the Irish race.' They also objected to his costume and some of the jokes he told. The next day or the day thereafter, . . . [at] least [ten] actors and musicians sent a written letter of protest to the management of the Irish Village."

23. The general location itself is lovely and appropriate, but the statue sits on an island of rock in a parking lot. Nearby a memorial wall has been added commemorating donors to the annual Chief O'Neill music festival. A concrete pad in front of the wall allows dancing, but the wall and the statue don't match and don't speak to each other, aesthetically. The chief deserves the services of a landscape architect.

# Index

*Page numbers in italics refer to illustrations.*